AVID

READER

PRESS

THE
Poets&Writers
COMPLETE GUIDE TO
BEING A WRITER

EVERYTHING YOU NEED TO KNOW ABOUT
CRAFT, INSPIRATION, AGENTS, EDITORS, PUBLISHING AND THE BUSINESS OF BUILDING A SUSTAINABLE WRITING CAREER

WITHDRAWN

KEVIN LARIMER AND MARY GANNON

AVID READER PRESS

NEW YORK   LONDON   TORONTO   SYDNEY   NEW DELHI

AVID READER PRESS
An Imprint of Simon & Schuster, Inc.
1230 Avenue of the Americas
New York, NY 10020

First Avid Reader Press hardcover edition April 2020

For information about special discounts for bulk purchases, please contact
Simon & Schuster Special Sales at 1-866-506-1949 or business@simonandschuster.com.

The Simon & Schuster Speakers Bureau can bring authors to your live event.
For more information or to book an event, contact the Simon & Schuster Speakers Bureau
at 1-866-248-3049 or visit our website at www.simonspeakers.com.

Interior design by Ruth Lee-Mui

Manufactured in the United States of America

1   3   5   7   9   10   8   6   4   2

Library of Congress Cataloging-in-Publication Data is available.

ISBN 978-1-9821-2307-9
ISBN 978-1-9821-2308-6 (ebook)

in memory of our friend and colleague Jim Andrews

and for every writer who believes in the
transformative power of the written word
and the importance of sharing it with others

Special thanks to Michael Bourne for his significant contributions to the chapters about the business of publishing, to Debra Englander for her insights on self-publishing, and to Bonnie Chau for her inspiring writing prompts.

Contents

I

II

III

IV

I

The Freedom and the Power

Being a writer—or, to put it another way, telling stories, which is what we're really talking about when we talk about writing, whether it's poetry, fiction, nonfiction, or some combination thereof—is not a hobby. That might be how your big-shot uncle thinks of it, or your cousin who works in corporate finance, or anyone who is decidedly *not* a writer. We develop words, language, expressions of thought and feeling as tools with which to tell stories, and these stories help us make sense of ourselves and the world around us. We recognize the power of thinking deeply about our stories, what they mean and how to tell them, and then we record them in the best, most powerful way we know: We write them. As Coleridge said about poetry, putting "the best words in the best order." And that act has the power to change the world.

There is no higher art form, in its intrinsic beauty and complexity, its capacity for delivering truth, its illumination of emotion and feeling, and its potential for personal transformation. Writing is bigger than borders, it's bigger than governments, it's bigger than the biggest corporation in the Dow Jones Industrial Average. Through writing we are able to get closer to what it means to be human than through any other activity—and if that sounds bold, consider what science and religion and philosophy would be without stories. The stories we write—the poems, the novels, the essays— they define us.

"The universe is made of stories, not of atoms."
—MURIEL RUKEYSER

We all have a different story to tell, of course. Talk to anyone, anywhere, for long enough and you'll hear it eventually. And maybe that's your project as a writer, telling someone else's story. Or maybe it's telling your own. Or maybe it's making up the stories of people who don't even exist except as characters in a story of your creation, summoned out of the ether by the sheer force of your imagination. No matter how seemingly mundane or traumatic, no matter how far-fetched or fantastical, each and every one of our stories, fact or fiction or poetry, is connected through human experience, and it is our self-appointed job as writers to make those connections through empathy and understanding, imagination and emotion. So, the fiction writer in Houston who writes at night after her shift at the twenty-four-hour diner and the grad student sleeping on his friend's couch in Portland, Oregon, and the poet who tends bar in Austin after caring for her mother who is suffering from dementia and the tattoo artist in Toronto and the grandmother in Cleveland and the adjunct professor in Boise who drives a rusted-out Toyota Celica can read one another's stories and recognize something of themselves. And by reading these stories they can understand themselves—and the shared world in which we live—a little better. "Writing remains the best route we know toward clarity of thought and feeling," writes Pulitzer Prize–winning nonfiction writer Tracy Kidder and writer/editor Richard Todd in *Good Prose: The Art of Nonfiction*. Amen.

Toni Morrison was acutely aware of the writer's unique ability to make sense of the great suffering inherent in the human experience. "Certain kinds of trauma visited on peoples are so deep, so cruel, that unlike money, unlike vengeance, even unlike justice, or rights, or the goodwill of others, only writers can translate such trauma and turn sorrow into meaning, sharpening the moral imagination," the Nobel laureate said upon accepting the 2008 PEN/Borders Literary Service Award in New York City.

Carolyn Roy-Bornstein turned to writing after her seventeen-year-old son was hit by a drunk driver while walking his girlfriend home from a study date. Carolyn's son sustained a traumatic brain injury; his girlfriend was killed. In the months and years that followed, journaling became a way to document her son's recovery and process her parallel trauma. It was also a way for her to exert power over something none of us can ever control—the past. "Ultimately, revisiting the pain through writing . . . helped those wounds to heal," she writes. For her, and for countless writers like her, writing is a redemptive act that can provide, if not a way to change the past, at least a way to understand it better and regain some semblance of control. Although the subject matter that drives us to write may be dark, the act of writing is ultimately an illuminating and positively radiant act—a way of applying order to disorder, reclaiming what was lost or taken away. In Roy-Bornstein's case, her early writing led to the publication nine years later of a memoir, *Crash: A Mother, a Son, and the Journey from Grief to Gratitude*.

For Kaveh Akbar, author of the poetry collection *Calling a Wolf a Wolf*, writing poetry became a life raft once he became sober after years of alcoholism and drug use. "I had no idea what to do with myself, what to do with my physical body or my time. I had no relationship to any kind of living that wasn't predicated on the pursuit of narcotic experience," says Akbar, who teaches at Purdue University and in the low-residency MFA program at Randolph College. "In a very real way, sobriety sublimated one set of addictions (narcotic) into another (poetic). The obsessiveness, the compulsivity, is exactly the same. All I ever want to do today is write poems, read poems, talk about poems. But this new obsession is much more fun (and much easier on my physiological, psychological, and spiritual self)."

Poet Robin Coste Lewis, whose debut collection, *Voyage of the Sable Venus and Other Poems*, won a National Book Award, has a story of turning to poetry that has much in common with the stories of Roy-Bornstein and Akbar. In 2000 Lewis fell through a hole in the floor of a San Francisco restaurant and suffered injuries that left her unable to read or write more than a sentence a day. Even with such dramatic physical and neurological constraints, Lewis pushed on, focusing her imagination and honing her poetic craft, every day over many months, to write just one line of poetry. "Poetry was the means by which I learned to reenter the world," Lewis says. "What compelled me to write was the desire to continue living an engaged life. Poetry allowed me to reenter my work, but from a different door."

To live an engaged life. Whether moved by a traumatic event or a more ordinary occurrence in our lives—maybe just a creative impulse that has no identifiable trigger—as creative people we want to dig just a little deeper, think a little harder about the world and our place in it, or simply celebrate life by investigating it a little further. The act of writing allows us to do this. Or maybe, like poet Jonathan Fink, whose debut collection, *The Crossing*, was published by the Detroit-based small press Dzanc Books, we are simply in love with the feeling of writing. "What poetry offers," Fink says, "is the visceral engagement with language that welcomes attention to imagery, tone, rhythm, narrative, metaphor, politics, ethics, humor, myth, and justice, among many other things. Like a painter who simply likes the smell of paint or a potter who likes the feel of clay, the pleasure of embarking on a writing project, for me, always resides in the tactile pleasures of language."

Even someone as successful as Salman Rushdie, who has published nearly twenty books, most famously the novel *The Satanic Verses*, takes a rather workmanlike approach to his craft and those tactile pleasures of language. "I've always had this view that you wake up every day with a little nugget of creative juice for the day and you can either use it or you waste it," he told fellow author Porochista Khakpour. "My view is, therefore, you write first. Get up, get out of bed, get to your desk, and work. . . . Do the work first; otherwise it doesn't get done. I've always thought of the novelist as a long-distance runner; that's the marathon. . . . It's long-form, you have to chip away at it, let the mark posts go by and trust that one day the finish line will come. You can't even think about the finish line when you start."

We all start writing—and continue writing—for different but equally important reasons. This book is intended, first and foremost, to serve, assist, recognize, validate, and celebrate that remarkable fact. Writing is also, most of the time, a solitary activity: an act of intellectual and emotional faith typically undertaken apart from the bustling crowds, removed from the noise of the day. It is work that is done in the still-dark, as you try to squeeze a few minutes of writing from your morning—before the busy workday begins, or classes start, or the chores take over, or the kids wake up—before the machine of everyday life starts to whir into motion. Or after it's wound down, when the rest of the world is asleep. Or, for some, it's work that is done right smack in the maw of the machine—in the middle of the great chaos of the city, or the clamor of workaday life. You write. Whether you write poems, stories, essays, articles, memoirs, novellas, or novels—no matter the genre—you write. *You* are a writer, and that is a remarkable, miraculous, life-fulfilling, soul-sustaining thing. It's a way of life, but it can also be a means to building a rewarding career.

In the following chapters we will look at the writer's journey from inspiration to publication and beyond. One of our goals in this book is to offer professional perspectives on the entire ecosystem of writing and publishing, that ever-changing network of teachers, tech leaders, agents, editors, publicists, small-press publishers, designers, literary arts administrators, contest coordinators, reviewers, critics, booksellers, and so many others. As a writer, you stand in the center of this incredibly engaging and engaged community of passionate people working in literary agencies, publishing houses, writing programs, nonprofit organizations, bookstores, and publications large and small. And as a writer, your focus is often on sitting down to write and making the words flow. And that's how it should be. But if you really want to make the most out of your life as a writer—if you're in it for the long haul—it's imperative that you also learn as much as you can about this ecosystem and your place as a writer within it.

The two of us have been offering guidance to those on this journey for a combined twenty-five years; over the last fifteen we've served as some combination of editor, editor in chief, and editorial director of *Poets & Writers Magazine*. The magazine is published by Poets & Writers, the nation's largest nonprofit organization serving poets and writers of literary prose. Since its inception fifty years ago, Poets & Writers has had one mission: to serve writers.

That Poets & Writers is a nonprofit organization means we've been able to dedicate ourselves to serving writers without having to worry about the bottom line the way commercial publications do. We've never focused on publishing fluff or offering unrealistic promises but instead have focused simply on what writers need to know to further their careers and inspire their writing lives. We aren't in the business of selling get-rich-quick schemes. We aren't believers in the Six Simple Steps to Success approach to the writer's life. While there are commonsense ways to think about what you want to get out of your career, we've always approached writing as a lifelong pursuit. But we've also always believed that the art of writing is not antithetical to the business of publishing. Both represent enormously important, interconnected yet distinct pieces of the same creative ecosystem.

A lot has changed both in the writing community and the publishing industry over the last five decades, of course, and our role has been to stay abreast of these changes and report them to our readers, as well as to celebrate the diverse range of literary writers practicing the art form around the world. We've also seen it as our mission to provide readers with information about opportunities that will enable and empower them to share their work with the widest possible audience.

One segment of our coverage that has seen extraordinary growth over the past few decades is writing contests. From its very first issues *Poets & Writers Magazine* has been the most trustworthy source of information about writing contests, grants, awards, writing conferences, and residencies on the market. The Grants & Awards section has expanded from the early days of featuring a couple dozen listings in each issue to more than a hundred in each issue today. In 2019 alone, we shared details about 595 contests offering over $5.6 million to writers.

The past few decades have also seen a proliferation of MFA programs, and while we've never believed that pursuing a degree in creative writing is essential to becoming a writer, it is a path many writers choose to follow. As a result, *Poets & Writers Magazine* has dedicated an annual special section to exploring the pros and cons of this form of higher education, providing extensive coverage of those programs that offer funding, again using practical information that is most beneficial to writers as our lodestar. We see it as our responsibility to not only share information but also to help writers contextualize and weigh that information so they can make the best choices for their writing and their careers.

We've also witnessed a seismic shift in book publishing, which was, not all that long ago, a cottage industry—a collection of independent, family-run businesses dedicated to championing the work of the writers they published for many years, often for the duration of their careers. By the early 1960s the landscape of trade publishing in the United States started to change as a variety of houses merged and large corporations began to acquire the bigger publishers. For example, Random House acquired Alfred A. Knopf in 1960 and Pantheon Books in 1961. Four years later, in 1965, the American electronics company RCA Corporation bought Random House along with its newly acquired imprints. (This was, of course, well before Random House was acquired by the German media conglomerate Bertelsmann AG.)

Shortly thereafter, around the time Poets & Writers was founded, the first big chain bookstores, Barnes & Noble and Waldenbooks, began to open retail outlets in shopping malls across the country. Then, in the 1980s, those same retail companies began to open superstores, driving many independent booksellers out of business. Publishers began to rely heavily on bestsellers that guaranteed big profits, and additional waves of mergers and acquisitions swept through the industry.

John B. Thompson, in his exhaustively researched and excellent book *Merchants of Culture: The Publishing Business in the Twenty-First Century*, surveys the transformation. "By the 1990s the shape of the industry had changed dramatically," he writes. "In a field where there had once been dozens of independent publishing houses, each reflecting the idiosyncratic tastes and styles of their owners and editors, there were now five or six large corporations, each operating as an umbrella organization for numerous imprints, many of which still bore the names of previously independent houses, which were now part of a larger organization, operating with varying degrees of autonomy depending on the strategies and policies of the corporate owners." With the latest big merger, in which the Bertelsmann-owned Random House merged with Penguin Group, owned by the British company Pearson, in 2013, approximately sixty percent of English-language books are published by five companies: Penguin Random House, Hachette, HarperCollins, Simon & Schuster, and Macmillan. The rise of online retailer Amazon has of course changed the ecosystem of publishing even further.

As all of this was happening, advances in technology opened up opportunities for everyone—desktop publishing tools became available to anyone with a decent computer and an internet connection. Hundreds of small presses, some large but many of them tiny, run by individuals or small groups of people, in kitchens and spare rooms in the homes of the editors, were formed. Similarly, the number of literary magazines, both print and online, has grown over the past fifty years. Access to publishing platforms has also led to the booming industry of self-publishing, which has flooded the market with an even wider range of books.

Learning how to navigate this changed landscape has become crucial for writers, and Poets & Writers has been there to help them at every turn. Along with the magazine's regular coverage of the publishing industry, in 2008 we launched our popular Agents & Editors series, which aims to demystify the publishing business and provide writers with an inside look at how publishing professionals think and make decisions. In 2001 we introduced our annual issue on independent publishing. Nine years later we introduced Agent Advice, a regular column that invites questions from writers and offers answers from literary agents who are themselves looking for new talent. And in 2014, in response to the growing availability and popularity of self-publishing platforms like Lulu and Kindle Direct Publishing, we launched the Savvy Self-Publisher column, which offers the stories and strategies of authors who have taken on the responsibilities of publishers and contrasts them with the advice and analysis of literary agents, freelance editors, indie publicists, and marketing experts. Our coverage has also tracked the rise, the leveling off, and the decline in e-book sales as well as the tremendous growth of audiobook sales over the last couple of decades.

From the start, we've been committed to showcasing a range of writers in the pages of *Poets & Writers Magazine*, always striving to provide balanced coverage of poets, fiction writers, and creative nonfiction writers from across the country, reflecting a vibrant diversity of ages, genders, ethnicities, academic backgrounds, and publishing experience. But when it became obvious that debut authors in particular weren't benefiting from the limited efforts of the shrinking publicity departments at commercial publishers (and often nonexistent publicity departments at smaller presses), in 2001 we launched an annual special section on debut fiction writers. In 2005 we published our first annual roundup of debut poets, in 2016 we added an annual look at debut authors over the age of fifty, and a year later we launched an annual roundup of debut creative nonfiction.

As we've navigated the always expanding and contracting business of publishing and the changing ways in which writers and readers connect with one another, we've always returned to the core question: What kinds of information do writers need in order to archieve their goals?

The Poets & Writers Complete Guide to Being a Writer is designed to answer this question. Its chapters represent one version of chronological order, moving from inspiration to craft to education to first steps in publishing to book deals to publicity and promotion. Along the way we share short essays by George Saunders, Christina Baker Kline, Ocean Vuong, and others, all of whom have experienced the challenges and rewards of each step, and sprinkled throughout are words of wisdom, inspiring gems, and pieces of smart advice—glimpses inside the minds of brilliant writers and behind the doors of agents and editors at some of the most successful publishing companies in the world. We asked authors Cheryl Strayed, Natalie Diaz, and Anthony Doerr, among others, to recommend books for further reading. And we've also put together a series of action items designed to keep you moving forward, as well as sidebars that call out more information and additional resources.

We've also included a section of short chapters that look at the world of writing through the lens of some big-picture themes—time, money, happiness, family, respect, and the law—with the intention not of offering definitive answers to some of life's biggest questions but rather of provoking deeper thinking about how you want to move through the world as a writer and tackle the real-life challenges you'll inevitably encounter along the way.

But you don't need to follow this chronology to use our book effectively—after all, writers rarely ever follow such a straight line. This book is intended for writers of all levels of experience, so you can dip into chapters depending on where you are in your career. Just starting out? We suggest reading from the beginning. Have you had some luck publishing your work in literary magazines, and you're looking to approach an agent? By all means skip ahead to chapter 16. Then read the chapters on working with your editor and publicist, or peruse the section about promoting your work yourself. No matter your level of experience, this book has inspiration and guidance for you.

Just as you must decide for yourself what you want out of your writing practice, you must decide for yourself whether you want to make your work public, and if you do, just how involved you want to be in that process. We believe that if you're going to publish your work, you should do it right, and what is right depends on what you want out of it. Set goals, establish your expectations, and make decisions based on them. To make good decisions, you need information, you need to understand the big picture and then focus on the details that are important to you and that will affect you and your work. All these choices are yours, and our aim is to provide you with the information you need to make smart decisions. And once you do, to succeed.

A successful writer is an informed writer. So let's get started.

ONE

Getting Started

How do you envision your ideal life as a writer? What does success look like to you? What drives you and your art? These may seem like obvious questions, but obvious questions are usually the most important kind to ask yourself. After all, they form the bedrock beneath everything you try to build on top of them. And despite what you might assume, the answers to these questions are far from universal.

"What success really looks like to each of us is actually radically different from person to person," Lauren Cerand, an independent publicist whose clients have included poets Chris Abani and Eileen Myles and fiction writers Tayari Jones and Daniel Handler, told poet Tess Taylor. "I always ask writers, 'What do you want that you don't have?' And I ask my writers to name not only, say, prizes, but also the principles behind the recognition they want. There's an idea that everyone wants to be successful in the same way, but that's not true. You might be a food writer who wants to change the way we talk about how we eat, or a poet whose dream is to have your poems on the subway."

ACTION ITEM 1

Write a mission statement for yourself as a writer. What is it you're trying to do with your writing? Is it to express and/or work through feelings for your own benefit? Document history for yourself or family or friends? Create art for the widest possible audience? Become famous? These are all valid answers—there are no wrong answers—just be honest with yourself about what you hope to achieve.

We can't stress enough the importance of establishing goals as a writer and doing the research so you can make smart decisions that will help you achieve those goals. Writing is a lifelong endeavor, and one that doesn't end when you finish a poem, story, essay, or longer writing project. There is no finish line. But that doesn't mean there aren't mile markers that ought to be acknowledged along the way. So when we talk about goals we aren't only referring to things like Get a Story Published in a Literary Magazine, Land an Agent, Publish a Book, or Win the Pulitzer Prize, we're also talking about things like Write Five Hundred Words Today, Outline the Third Chapter of My Novel This Weekend, and Identify Five Journals to Which I Can Submit My Essay.

ACTION ITEM 2

Start writing a list of goals, beginning with short-term objectives such as daily word-count targets and submission plans, gradually working your way to long-term goals for what you want out of your career.

It can be useful to consider your goals as a creative writer grouped into one of five general categories: Educational Goals, Writing Goals, Publishing Goals, Financial Goals, and Higher Goals. Each of these categories may contain short- and long-term objectives. Let's briefly consider each one and how they can help you determine what you're trying to accomplish and, more important, how you can achieve and even exceed your goals.

Educational Goals

The education of a writer is never finished, and like the practice of writing itself, there are endless ways to achieve it. Most writers will tell you that living a full life is the best education a writer can get. "You don't need writing classes or seminars any more than you need this or any other book on writing," writes Stephen King in his book *On Writing: A Memoir of the Craft*, which was an instant bestseller when it was published in 2000. (Apparently the millions of readers who have bought King's book respectfully disagree with his assessment.) "Faulkner learned his trade while working in the Oxford, Mississippi, post office," King continues. "Other writers have learned the basics while serving in the Navy, working in steel mills, or doing time in

America's finer crossbar hotels. I learned the most valuable (and commercial) part of my life's work while washing motel sheets and restaurant tablecloths at the New Franklin Laundry in Bangor."

For those who have the resources to pursue a more formal education, the master of fine arts (MFA) degree has become the academic standard for creative writers in this country. Since the Iowa Writers' Workshop at the University of Iowa in Iowa City was established in 1936, hundreds of MFA programs have been launched and now exist in every state in the country. These programs offer a concentrated period of time for aspiring writers to hone their skills under the guidance of established writers, to learn about the literary canon, and to develop a writing practice among other like-minded students. The MFA experience can also provide a network of lifelong readers of your work, among other benefits to support your writing life for years to come. It is also considered a terminal degree, meaning that an MFA grad is qualified to teach at the college level. However, these programs require a significant investment of both time—usually taking two to three years to complete—and money. While some programs offer a range of financial support, not all do, and tuition can be expensive.

ACTION ITEM 3

Under each item in your list of goals, jot down specific tasks required to achieve those goals. If your goal is to be accepted into an MFA program, for example, your tasks will include researching programs, narrowing your search down to five to ten schools, contacting current or former students at those schools through the program administrator to talk to them about their experience, gathering the required application materials, and applying by the deadline.

Low-residency MFA programs allow writers to earn a degree on a more flexible schedule, which is ideal for those whose personal or professional obligations prevent them from enrolling in a full-time program. Most low-residency programs take two years to complete—students usually attend one- to two-week residencies on campus twice a year and most of the coursework is completed independently in consultation with a faculty adviser. These programs tend to be more affordable but not to offer as many financial-aid options as full-residency programs.

If you don't have the inclination, or the lifestyle or resources, to pursue an MFA—it's worth noting that the likes of Emily Dickinson and William Faulkner never received an MFA, not to mention contemporary authors such as Colson Whitehead, Viet Thanh Nguyen, Jennifer Egan, Laila Lalami, Chuck Palahniuk, Min Jin Lee, Jonathan Lethem, Dave Eggers, Monique Truong, Nicholson Baker, Jonathan Franzen, and Jonathan Safran Foer—there are plenty of other opportunities to enrich your literary education. Many colleges and universities offer undergraduate classes in creative writing. Local writing centers such as Grub Street in Boston, the Loft Literary Center in Minneapolis, the Center for Fiction in New York City, Beyond Baroque Literary Arts Center in Los Angeles, and Literary Arts in Portland, Oregon, to name a few, offer workshops, lectures, and master classes throughout the year. There are also over 150 writers conferences that offer a mix of intensive writing classes, readings by established writers, face time with publishing professionals, and networking opportunities, often in inspiring settings—everywhere from the rugged coast of Washington State to Campobello Island in New Brunswick, Canada, just off the coast of Maine.

ACTION ITEM 4

Visit the databases in the Find Your Community section of pw.org. They provide comprehensive information about MFA programs, literary conferences, and writing centers, searchable by location. Each entry includes a full description, including application fee and faculty. Make a list of those that are in your area and/or appeal to your sensibilities and find out as much about them as possible—including how and when to apply or visit.

If what you really need is one or several trusted readers of your writing to offer feedback, you can try plugging into or establishing a writing group. These can be in-person meetings once a month at your local coffee shop or weekly critiques through e-mail.

And if you only have the time and inclination for reading—and there's certainly nothing wrong with that because, as we know, you can't be a good writer without first being a good reader—put together a reading list that is tailored to your interests and commit to a schedule of serious reading. (See Terrance Hayes's Five Healthy Reading Habits for Living a Life in Poetry, which can be applied to any genre, on page 18.) Just to get you started thinking about some of the books about writing that you might potentially add to your to-be-read pile, here's a list of select classics:

- Eudora Welty's *One Writer's Beginnings*
- Charles Baxter's *Burning Down the House: Essays on Fiction*
- Stephen King's *On Writing: A Memoir of the Craft*
- Annie Dillard's *The Writing Life*
- John Gardner's *The Art of Fiction: Notes on Craft for Young Writers*
- Natalie Goldberg's *Writing Down the Bones: Freeing the Writer Within*
- Jane Hirshfield's *Nine Gates: Entering the Mind of Poetry*
- Charles Johnson's *The Way of the Writer: Reflections on the Art and Craft of Storytelling*
- Anne Lamott's *Bird by Bird: Some Instructions on Writing and Life*
- Betsy Lerner's *The Forest for the Trees: An Editor's Advice to Writers*
- Ursula K. Le Guin's *Steering the Craft: A 21st-Century Guide to Sailing the Sea of Story*
- Audre Lorde's *Sister Outsider: Essays and Speeches*
- Muriel Rukeyser's *The Life of Poetry*
- Richard Russo's *The Destiny Thief: Essays on Writing, Writers and Life*
- Toni Morrison's *The Source of Self-Regard: Selected Essays, Speeches, and Meditations*

Many more titles appear in our list of 140 Books for Every Serious Writer's Bookshelf and the Sources section at the back of this book. Some of the passages on craft in chapter 4 come from these books as well.

"You should write because you love the shape of stories and sentences and the creation of different words on a page. Writing comes from reading, and reading is the finest teacher of how to write."

—ANNIE PROULX

TERRANCE HAYES RECOMMENDS

Five Healthy Reading Habits for Living a Life in Poetry

First, a simple suggestion for reading habits: Read casually, you will not be tested. Skim everything once, stopping as you please. Read again for what you missed after skimming.

DAILY HABIT: Read your own notebooks as well as the notes you've taken on your phone, on the fly, on your flesh. . . . Write everything that moves you in these places. Reread regularly with scrutiny, listening for music. I will sometimes toy with a note of nonsense or syntax for months before it becomes a sentence.

WEEKLY HABIT: Read someone else's poetry. Read the poems of friends. Encourage your friends to write poems. Read poems in print and online journals once a week. Subscribe to a couple of literary journals. I don't have a writing pal but I teach workshops, treating the poems there as I do the poems of my peers. I read anticipating a conversation with the poet.

MONTHLY HABIT: Read at least one new book of poems a month. I rely heavily on debut collections to maintain my poetry-reading diet. There are dozens and dozens of first-book contests. Support them to feed yourself.

SIX-MONTH HABIT: Read two to three poetry books you've read before. This can include anthologies and classics as well as debut books you want to reread. I am often returning to *Actual Air* by David Berman, *Song* by Brigit Pegeen Kelly, *Mercurochrome* by Wanda Coleman, and *The Essential Etheridge Knight*, as well as old editions of *The Best American Poetry*.

YEARLY HABIT: Read three to four books of prose a year—more when you can or please. I'm typically revisiting something by Roberto Bolaño or Toni Morrison or Vladimir Nabokov while trying to keep up with National Book Award winners and finalists. I always read poetry, but when I'm unable to finish novels, I don't quite feel like I'm reading sufficiently.

TERRANCE HAYES *is the author of six poetry collections, including* American Sonnets for My Past and Future Assassin, *which was a finalist for the 2018 National Book Critics Circle Award in Poetry, the 2018 National Book Award in Poetry, the 2018*

T. S. Eliot Prize for Poetry, and the 2018 Kingsley Tufts Poetry Award. His essay collection, To Float in the Space Between: A Life and Work in Conversation with the Life and Work of Etheridge Knight, *won the Poetry Foundation's 2019 Pegasus Award for Poetry Criticism and was a finalist for the 2018 National Book Critics Circle Award in Criticism. Hayes is a professor of English at New York University.*

Writing Goals

So often writers hold up as their models of success a shelf of successfully published books—novels and memoirs, short story and poetry collections—and that makes perfect sense. Those are examples of the art form at its highest level. The work behind that spine is a piece of art that was pushed and revised and polished until it was "finished," however the author defined that word. And certainly there are goals to be found in reading great books. Striving for the stunning beauty, moral clarity, and artistic vision of Toni Morrison, the violent lyricism of Cormac McCarthy, or the urgent music of Joy Harjo will launch a thousand writing careers, but the work begins with a single word and then another word, strung along to form a sentence or a line and repeated in a paragraph or a stanza, page after page after page.

> *"Get it down. Take chances.*
> *It may be bad, but it's the only way you*
> *can do anything really good."*
> —WILLIAM FAULKNER

Reading about and comparing the daily word-count goals of famous writers is a little like studying the stats on the back of baseball cards. We'll trade Ernest Hemingway (500 words/day) for your Anne Rice (3,000 words/day) and we'll throw in Nicholas Sparks (2,000 words/day). The fact is, everyone develops their own writing routine, their own writing process, and their own writing speed. Too often we hear the same advice as if it's a universal ideal or even a practical possibility for those of us whose list of obligations is longer than our list of publication credits: Plant your butt in the chair and write, write, write, no matter what. The reality for most of us is different, so we go with advice that's slightly more measured. Live your life, don't neglect your responsibilities, but when you have an hour to write, avoid distraction and write. That's really what writing goals are all about. It's not a sprint; it's a marathon.

One key to achieving your writing goals is putting in place a routine that works for you. Joyce Carol Oates, surely one of the most prolific American authors—since her first book, the 1963 story collection *By the North Gate*, she's published more than fifty novels, as well as a number of plays and novellas, and many volumes of short stories, poetry, and nonfiction— has an enviable schedule for her writing life. In his fascinating book *Daily Rituals: How Artists Work*, Mason Currey describes how the career author writes from eight or eight thirty in the morning until one in the afternoon, then again from four until around seven, when she breaks for dinner. "I write and write and write, and rewrite, and even if I retain only a single page from a full day's work, it is a single page, and these pages add up," Oates says. Even though Gertrude Stein wrote for just a fraction of the time Oates devotes to her writing each day, Stein had a similar feeling about her output. In *Everybody's Autobiography* she asserted, "If you write a half hour a day it makes a lot of writing year by year. To be sure all day and every day you are waiting around to write that half hour a day."

ACTION ITEM 5

Develop a daily, weekly, and monthly schedule for yourself that covers not only the time you devote to activities like writing your poems or researching your novel but also things like preparing your story for submission to a writing contest, or reaching out to reading series coordinators to inquire about opportunities to appear at an event, or applying to next spring's writers residencies.

Ernest Hemingway, who would wake up early in the morning—at first light, usually around five thirty or six—developed a routine designed to sustain momentum as a creative motivator. In a 1958 "The Art of Fiction" interview in the *Paris Review*, Hemingway explained:

> When I am working on a book or a story I write every morning as soon
> after first light as possible. There is no one to disturb you and it is cool or

cold and you come to your work and warm as you write. You read what you have written and, as you always stop when you know what is going to happen next, you go on from there. You write until you come to a place where you still have your juice and know what will happen next and you stop and try to live through until the next day when you hit it again. You have started at six in the morning, say, and may go on until noon or be through before that. When you stop you are as empty, and at the same time never empty but filling, as when you have made love to someone you love. Nothing can hurt you, nothing can happen, nothing means anything until the next day when you do it again. It is the wait until that next day that is hard to get through.

Henry Miller echoed Hemingway's sentiment: "I don't believe in draining the reservoir," he said. "I believe in getting up from the typewriter, away from it, while I still have something to say."

For most of us, of course, a regular job eats into our writing time and can dictate our daily routine, but even that restriction can yield benefits. "I find that having a job is one of the best things in the world that could happen to me," said Wallace Stevens, who started working at the Hartford Accident and Indemnity Company when he was thirty-six years old. "It introduces discipline and regularity into one's life." Stevens would wake up early, around 6 a.m., and read for two hours before work. It was during the long walks to and from work, and occasionally at lunch, that he would compose his poems.

Maya Angelou would write in hotel rooms, which she would go to when her husband went off to work each morning. She didn't seek out a particularly nice hotel room, but rather, as she described it, "a tiny, mean room with just a bed, and sometimes, if I can find it, a face basin. I keep a dictionary, a Bible, a deck of cards and a bottle of sherry in the room. I try to get there around 7, and I work until 2 in the afternoon. If the work is going badly, I stay until 12:30. If it's going well, I'll stay as long as it's going well. It's lonely, and it's marvelous."

Stephen King would likely appreciate Angelou's routine. "Like your bedroom, your writing room should be private, a place to go to dream," he writes in *On Writing*. "Your schedule—in at about the same time every day, out when your thousand words are on paper or disk—exists in order to habituate yourself, to make yourself ready to dream just as you make yourself ready to sleep by going to bed at roughly the same time each night and following the same ritual as you go."

National Novel Writing Month (NaNoWriMo) is an increasingly popular initiative that motivates writers to get the words flowing through an annual challenge to write a fifty-thousand-word novel during the month of November. Grant Faulkner, the executive director of National Novel Writing Month, is, like many of us, a busy person—with household chores, parenting duties, and professional obligations all demanding significant time away from his writing. Before he became involved in NaNoWriMo, Faulkner found himself trapped not only by those real-life challenges but also by limitations of his own devising. "My approach formed itself around what I'll call 'ponderous preciousness.' I'd conceive of an idea for a story and then burrow into it deliberately. I'd write methodically, ploddingly, letting thoughts percolate, then marinate—refining and refining—sometimes over the course of years. It was as if I held a very tiny chisel and carefully maneuvered it again and again through the practically microscopic contours of my story world," he writes. "A story, a novel, or even one of my pieces of flash fiction had to be as finely aged as a good bottle of wine in order for all of the nuanced tannins and rich aromas to fully develop. My writing moved slowly from one sentence, one paragraph, to the next, and I often looped back again and again, driven by the idea that I needed to achieve a certain perfection before I could move forward."

> *"I am not a great writer, but I am a great reviser."*
> —MARY KARR

Sound familiar? For Grant Faulkner, the answer to his "ponderous preciousness" was found in letting go of the goal of writing perfectly, finding a way to open the floodgates and ride the flow of words. For him, the answer was found in National Novel Writing Month and the premise it is built upon. Those fifty thousand words written during the month of November might not be gold, of course, but then you have a substantial amount of material to sift through for that shiny nugget.

Poet, critic, and essayist Craig Morgan Teicher doesn't write a novel in November, but he does agree with the idea that freeing the mind of unrealistic goals of perfection is conducive to creative thinking and production. "Writing is a habit like anything else, and it comes with certain reflexes, one of which is self-censorship, which can prevent you from getting your words down, from generating your material," writes Teicher. "The ego wants to be the best at everything, but in my experience at least, the best writing comes much less frequently than the desire to write. Like athletes, we need to keep our writing muscles in shape. If we can allow ourselves to write badly, to keep our pens moving, the chances are high that they'll be moving when our great writing is ready to come out."

A body in motion stays in motion, to cite physicist Isaac Newton. Writing consistently assures that your project continues to move forward and keeps it top of mind, so that each time you return to it it's easier to jump back in. And you won't have to spend as much time trying to remember where you were or what you were writing about.

As Pulitzer Prize–winning author Annie Dillard notes in her classic guide *The Writing Life*:

> The page, the page, that eternal blankness, the blankness of eternity which you cover slowly, affirming time's scrawl as a right and your daring as necessity; the page, which you cover woodenly, ruining it, but asserting your freedom and power to act, acknowledging that you ruin everything you touch but touching it nevertheless, because acting is better than being here in mere opacity; the page, which you cover slowly with the crabbed thread of your gut; the page in the purity of its possibilities; the page of your death, against which you pit such flawed excellences as you can muster with all your life's strength: that page will teach you to write.

So pick a writing goal—whether it's one hundred words a day or five thousand words every two weeks—and stick with it. Wake up early, stay up late, steal an hour from your day and write. This requires discipline, clearly, but once you stick with it long enough you'll fall into a routine, which will lead to a rhythm that can sustain you through any difficulty. "I know that to sustain these true moments of insight," said Henry Miller, "one has to be highly disciplined, lead a disciplined life." There are little things you can do to help establish routine. Set up a home office where you can do your work—because you're a writer and, yes, this is your work—or, if you don't have an extra room in your house or apartment, clear some space in the pantry or a corner of your bedroom or living room. Or find a quiet coffee shop that serves your favorite chai latte. Or maybe the bus or train ride to work in the morning is when you can get those words down; if so, make sure you have your favorite notebook and that perfect pen or pencil—the tools of your trade. We'll explore this idea of creating a writing space in the next chapter, but the point here is that we need to be proactive about creating an environment that will allow us to succeed, a consistent scenario that will feed the habit of writing. Once you're in the habit, that regular writing goal will become easier to hit. Remember, the purpose of this goal isn't perfection; that comes later, during revision.

Publishing Goals

Setting the goal of getting your work published can be tricky. If you're talking about the traditional process of sending your work to a magazine or online journal or writing contest or publishing house (either by yourself or with the help of an agent) the outcome is determined—and goal reached—by an almost purely subjective decision. Still, getting published remains the most obvious and widely coveted indicator of success as a writer (more about just how accurate this is later) and setting it as a goal is beneficial in more ways than just getting your work read widely. Another way of looking at publishing goals is to think of them as submission goals, which is an activity you have complete control over. By approaching a piece of writing with an eye toward submitting it for publication, you are applying a schedule to the work—whether it's a set of external deadlines (contests have deadlines; literary magazines and some smaller presses have specific open reading periods) or more arbitrary but no less specific time targets, both of which can be excellent motivators. If it's January and you know that Four Way Books has an open reading period in June, then you can break up the next five months into achievable writing goals that will allow you to meet your publishing or submission goals.

An aspect of submitting your work that can too often be seen as a negative component of publishing goals is, of course, rejection. No one is submitting work with the goal of getting rejected, but there is much to be gained from this—let's face it, inevitable—result. Receiving a rejection letter or e-mail means that someone—maybe it was an agent, an editor, an editorial assistant, or simply an unpaid intern—has read your work and found it lacking in some regard. Okay, fine, that sucks. But now you have two options:

ACTION ITEM 6

Set up a Google calendar or a simple spreadsheet of deadlines and publishing targets. Fill out all the places—agents, presses, contests, magazines, and so on—where you'd like to submit your work.

First, you can absorb the rejection as an inevitable and necessary part of the writer's life (which it most certainly is) and realize that the person who decided your work wasn't right is just a human being—a person who has bad days and momentary lapses of judgment, who may have gotten a parking ticket that morning or who was up late the previous night with a new baby, who is most likely overworked, and whose opinion counts for exactly one perspective in the world. That editor or agent or assistant is often called a gatekeeper, but the truth is that person holds the keys to one castle, not the entire kingdom. You've been told "no" by one person in the world. Treat that rejection as such.

> *"I love my rejection slips. They show me I try."*
> —SYLVIA PLATH

Second, you can use this feedback to your advantage. A reader who more than likely does not know you and doesn't give a hoot about your feelings has just told you something about your work. Hopefully they took the time to write a rejection letter; look for any details about why they didn't find your work suitable. But even if they didn't offer constructive criticism, take this opportunity to read your work again with fresh eyes and, if necessary, revise. And then get it right back out there.

"I discovered that rejections are not altogether a bad thing. They teach a writer to rely on his own judgment and to say in his heart of hearts, 'To hell with you.'"
—SAUL BELLOW

So, one way to stay focused on your writing practice is to create project-based goals and structure your writing deadlines around submission requirements. Tailor this strategy to where you are in the arc of your writing life. Are you just beginning and aiming for your first publication? Have you had your work published in literary magazines before and would like to see your work published in a specific literary magazine? Or would you like to see it published in a number of venues to expand the audience for your writing?

If, for example, you're a short story writer and aim to publish a story in a literary magazine, make a list of the top five magazines where you'd like to see your story appear. Research their submission guidelines and determine the earliest date for submission. Then, working backward from that date, create a work plan for finishing your story a week before that deadline. (Trust us: All writers need padded deadlines.) How many words will you need to write a week to finish a strong draft well before the deadline? How many weeks will you need for revision? Will you want to share your final draft with a trusted reader before sending it out? (The answer to that last one is yes.)

Do you have a book-length project that you want published? Do you want literary representation? If so, research literary agents' submission guidelines and develop a goal around that. Or perhaps your publishing goals are tied to the potential for monetary return, which leads us to the following set of considerations.

Financial Goals

The riches of a writing life are impossible to quantify, but your hard work and dedication may not always pay off in cold hard cash. We all know the rags-to-riches cases—how J. K. Rowling went from living in relative poverty to becoming the world's first billionaire author following the success of her books about the boy wizard—but we don't hear as much about the midlist author who stitches together a living with teaching gigs and freelance writing assignments.

In 2018 the Authors Guild, an organization whose mission is to support working writers, conducted a survey of over five thousand published book authors. The survey found that in 2017 the median income for full-time authors—folks whose days are devoted solely to writing and writing-related activities such as speaking engagements, freelance journalism, and ghostwriting—was $20,300. (For comparison, the federal poverty line for a household of three during that same year was $20,420.) The median income for all published authors—including part-time and full-time, as well as traditionally published, self-published, or some combination thereof—for all writing-related activities was only $6,080.

These are grim figures, no doubt about it, but you likely didn't need the Authors Guild to tell you that writing is not a lucrative career path for the vast majority of those who choose it. However, it's important to be clear about what kind of writing we're talking about here. Creative writing tends to pay less, especially when one is just starting out. More than a few poets we know consider payment sort of beside the point. The goal for many is to simply share the work. But let's be clear: Writers *should* be paid for their work, period. And there are other kinds of writing—freelance writing, journalism, technical writing, and so on—that are clearly driven by market forces, and payment is based on a simple equation of supply and demand.

MONEY MATTERS

LITERARY MAGAZINES: Fees vary, but the majority of literary journals, either online or in print, pay little to nothing for the rights to your work, offering instead the honor of having your work published and perhaps a few free contributor copies of the print magazine in which your work appears. Some larger magazines, including *One Story*, *SLICE*, the *Iowa Review*, and *Virginia Quarterly Review*, pay anywhere from $100 to $500, depending on the genre.

SMALL PRESSES: Independent and nonprofit presses are publishing some of the most exciting, dynamic literature in the world these days, but they tend to pay less than commercial houses and the smaller ones don't always offer advances against royalties (see below). Many of these presses, which range from micropresses consisting of one or two people doing everything from editing to production and distribution, to larger houses like Graywolf Press, whose titles are often in contention for the big literary prizes each year, accept unagented submissions.

WRITING CONTESTS: The Grants & Awards section of *Poets & Writers Magazine* includes information about upcoming deadlines for contests open to poets, fiction writers, and creative nonfiction writers, as well as news of recent winners. Each year this section lists around six hundred contests—sponsored by magazines, presses, nonprofit organizations, colleges and universities, and government agencies—offering millions in prize money. But here's the rub: The majority of these contests (nearly eighty percent at last count) charge an entry fee, usually around $20.

SELF-PUBLISHING: The phenomenal success stories of self-published writers such as E. L. James and Amanda Hocking can make anyone with a great idea and the writing chops to match giddy with excitement over their chances at cashing in as an indie author. Anything is possible, and as a self-published author you are in control of every step of the process, but just remember that you need to put down the money for the self-publishing service first—not to mention the fees for any editing, proofreading, interior design, cover design, marketing, and publicity—before any money from sales starts rolling in.

LITERARY AGENTS: No legitimate literary agent charges money to read your work. Agents get paid only if they sell your book or idea, for which they typically take fifteen percent of your earnings.

BOOK ADVANCES: A book advance is, as the term suggests, an advance payment against royalties an author earns from sales of a book and thus represents an up-front bet the publishing house is making on a book's future success. Contract terms vary enormously, but authors typically receive advance payments in three installments: the first when they sign the contract, the second when the manuscript has been accepted by the publisher, and the third upon publication of the book. (In some cases, especially if an advance is larger, publishers will include a fourth installment, to be paid when the book comes out in paperback.)

Michael Bourne has written extensively about the current market for freelance writing. "Today, with the blogosphere adding new digital-native publications daily and venerable print publications like the *New Yorker* and the *Paris Review* running their own content-hungry websites, an enterprising freelancer needs no more than a good idea and a serviceable prose style to get that first byline," he writes. "But because there are so many websites competing for readers—and because much of the ad revenue that used to go to news outlets has migrated to online platforms like Facebook and Google—it is hard for a writer breaking in to turn a pleasurable sideline into a paying profession. Still, a dedicated freelancer, especially one willing to combine occasional bylined features with a steady diet of marketing and technical copy, can make writing pay."

This leads us to a basic question that every writer is wise to consider sooner rather than later: Are you comfortable with looking at your writing practice as a set of business decisions? Do you want to make decisions about your art based on money? Some writers are more comfortable with this notion than others. Maybe you have a novel in you that needs to come out and no Hollywood trends are going to sway you from your course. Or maybe you're more calculating than that; you read *Publishers Weekly* and you subscribe to the Publishers Lunch newsletter to identify the most lucrative book deals.

It needn't be an all-or-nothing proposition, of course. Perhaps you make money through freelance assignments, or through textbook writing, while writing your novel without the market in mind. Or perhaps you write po-etry at night and work at a literary nonprofit during the day, or teach college students during the school year and write your memoir during the summer.

The reality of book publishing is that unless you're one of the relatively few who publishes a book with a commercial publisher that has the re-sources to offer a significant advance and the marketing power behind it to promote your book so that it connects with a substantial audience, thereby resulting in substantial book sales, odds are you won't make a living wage by writing books alone.

ACTION ITEM 7

Get a better sense of your financial requirements and goals by filling out the Valuing Your Time worksheet found in chapter 8.

Having said that, you don't have to be a starving artist, either. There are plenty of ways to augment your art with income from work in the literary field. We'll be getting into this in more detail in chapter 23, but many cre-ative writers who are up to the challenge of stitching together assignments and hustling in order to estab-lish relationships with editors pay the bills freelance writing and editing. The rise of MFA programs has created a demand for professors to teach the thousands of budding writers who enter these programs each year as well as administra-tors to run the programs (not enough demand to account for the thousands who graduate each year, but more on this in chapter 6). Some writers serve the literary field as staffers at the many literary nonprofits around the coun-try, and others support themselves by working at the small presses, liter-ary magazines, and commercial houses that comprise the robust publishing industry.

The point is: Making a living as a writer can take many forms. If you're honest with yourself about your expectations, do the required research, and investigate your opportunities, you can take great pride in living a literary life and supporting yourself in a field that is dedicated to creative expression and the support of literature in its many forms.

Higher Goals

Now that we've briefly considered our goals as they relate to education, writing, publishing, and money, it's time to pause to think about the big picture. One of the foundational principles of this book—and one of the assumptions we've always held—is that writing is a lifelong pursuit. We should treat it with the gravitas that a way of life demands. So, let's consider the important goal we may have for our writing—not money and fame, even though that may be important to you, but rather the message, if any, you hope to send with your writing.

Why are you embarking on this journey to begin with? Perhaps you don't even know, and that's okay. For some writers it can feel as if writing chose them, rather than the other way around. But now that you're a writer—and you *are* a writer—it's important to think about what you want. Do you have a creative vision you're trying to bring to light? A character whose story needs to be told? "I just need to tell a story. It's an obsession," writes Isabel Allende in *Why We Write: 20 Acclaimed Authors on How and Why They Do What They Do*. "Each story is a seed inside of me that starts to grow and grow, like a tumor, and I have to deal with it sooner or later." Or is simply engaging in the writing process the point? "Especially when I'm writing a first draft, I feel as if I've been transported out of myself," writes Jennifer Egan in the same collection. Is writing, for you, a method of personal—even spiritual—transformation? Do you use it to access parts of yourself that regular, everyday life doesn't touch? Do you have a political or social truth you're trying to articulate? If so, which genre will be most effective in delivering that message? What do you want to show the world? "I write entirely to find out what I'm thinking, what I'm looking at, what I see and what it means," Joan Didion wrote in the *New York Times Magazine* in 1976. "In many ways writing is the act of saying *I*, of imposing oneself upon other people, of saying *listen to me, see it my way, change your mind.*" Who are your ideal readers and how would you expand that group? Is engaging with a specific community—or the writing community in general—important to you? How do you want to positively affect that community?

There are so many different opportunities for writers, so many different routes to achieve your goals. The first step is to identify those goals, and the second is to figure out how you want to achieve them. Part of that is being proactive and living a deliberate life as a writer. This concept goes back to none other than Henry David Thoreau.

> *"I went to the woods because I wished to live deliberately, to front only the essential facts of life, and see if I could not learn what it had to teach, and not, when I came to die, discover that I had not lived."*
>
> —HENRY DAVID THOREAU

What does it mean to live deliberately as a writer? It means to stop, often, and ask yourself, *Is this what I want for myself and my writing?* As writers we can sometimes feel pressure to achieve certain benchmarks by a certain age, to have our work appear in specific venues someone has designated as hot right now, or to join the chorus of voices on social media. Maybe that's exactly what you want to do as a writer; maybe not.

ACTION ITEM 8

Take thirty minutes to jot down some thoughts on your definition of *success*. Can it be measured in book sales or the size of your advance? Or is it something harder to quantify?

"I think this is where the real attraction [of being a writer] lies," Zadie Smith once said. "Not in the freedom to express oneself, but in the freedom not to. To me writing is precisely my escape from the partial, subjective reality in which I live."

What an empowering position: As a writer, you have the ability to express yourself however you'd like—and in the manner, and time, that makes the most sense for you and your work.

To live and write deliberately is to make your own decisions, to achieve your own goals, and to dream your own dreams. And to give yourself time to figure out what those things are for you, what they mean to you. For every success story in which an author made one series of decisions, there are countless other success stories featuring entirely different decisions.

There is no road map. We're going to show you some topographical features of the landscape, point out the contours of the hills and valleys, provide some examples of how other authors have found their way through, but you draw your *own* road map.

Live your own life, and always write.

GEORGE SAUNDERS ON MOTIVATION

When we start out on the artistic path our motivations are . . . multiple. We want to be known, we want to make money, we want—well, mostly we want some form of power. We want "a thing" that is ours. But also, we want to pay tribute: to the beauty of the world, to the artists who have moved us. For my part, I had a long-standing feeling of inadequacy that was at odds with the affection I felt for other people and for the world, and somehow felt that if only I could *do* something (something remarkable, something lovely)—or *be* somebody (somebody famous and/or beloved for his work), that feeling of inadequacy would go away—I would, through accomplishment, earn a place in the world.

And so it begins.

One key to a happy, lifelong artistic practice is to be aware of, and always working with, this multiplicity of motivation. Some of my students seem to distrust and want to disavow the "urge to power" motivation, seeing it as cheap or wrong somehow. The "pay tribute to beauty" motivation seems more wholesome. It's more in keeping with their artistic self-image.

But my feeling is this: To do the kind of all-in, super-intense work we want to do, we have to learn to be skillful curators of that unruly group of motivations lurking there behind our writing minds—not disavowing a single one of them, and especially not a powerful, reliable, energy-giving one. I find that, even within a given writing day (even within a few writing moments), these motivations are constantly flickering on and off—each stepping forward momentarily for their moment in the sun, then receding.

Another way to say this: We might start out (a career, or a day) feeling a strong desire to kick some ass—to write something that will sell, that will (finally!) get the world's attention. I say, Great. We should bless that motivation, if that's what gets us going. Then we start. Soon, we'll find that our training kicks in and another motivation takes over. In my case, it has something to do with assessing the way the words look on the page. I feel strong preferences for *this* wording over *that* and get real pleasure from making those changes and from the resulting feeling of increased order/ decreased entropy, and the way the fictive world is being brought into increasingly sharper focus. At this point, where has the urge to kick ass gone? Still there, but transformed, I'd say. "Urge to power" has converted to "urge to make beauty" or "urge to do good work." It has acquired some legs and is now busy doing its thing. Is that holy or unholy? Always feels holy to me, and natural—like, if you looked up and a Frisbee was coming for your head and you could catch it, you *would*. It's a small form of celebration, to do the natural thing, the thing that makes the world incrementally better. You read a sentence, see a possible improvement, make it.

The process of completing a work of fiction (for me, anyway) goes something like this: *1) Ah crap, I have no ideas, I'm washed-up; 2) Oh, this might be one; 3) Ah, this is one but I hope I don't screw it up; 4) I'm not! I'm not screwing it up! Now if I can only find an ending; 5) I did! 6) Will someone publish it, and will anyone like it? 7) They did publish it, and it was somewhat liked! and 8) Ah crap, I have no ideas, I'm washed-up.* And there I am again, back at the beginning, no more confident than before.

After we've been through this process a few hundred times, we may find ourselves asking, "Jeez, when can I rest? When will I become such a master that there'll be no anxiety in the process?" The answer is: never. Someone who writes with no anxiety is likely a hack. ("Being a good artist" means "I never get to go on autopilot in my work.") Or we might ask, "Okay, then where is the real, reliable, trustworthy *pleasure* in this process?" For me, the answer is: In that "Frisbee moment," that moment when, lost in the work, we spontaneously make an improvement. In that moment, we are actually a different version of ourselves; we're literally in a different state of mind, and it's one I prefer. I feel I'm my best self: not ruminating, but imagining; not constructing, but reacting.

The rest of it, the publication (or not), the success (or not), is beyond our control and, ultimately, not trustworthy, since these things are not necessarily reliable indicators of anything.

So, now: Those new, good changes under our belt, we might get a little surge of a victory feeling. ("This is getting so cool! Surely someone will take it! And someone should make a movie of it!") Is that good or bad? Neither. It just *is*. It's natural and completely understandable. The question is: What are we going to *do* with that little surge of victory feeling, a.k.a. "energy"? Bless it or curse it? Smile at/with it, or be ashamed of it and shun it? What we'd want to do, I think, is *use* it—plow it back into the work. (If you were running a mile for time and flashed on a happy memory of an old friend and that gave you a burst of energy, would you "take" it? Of course you would, to the extent that the race was important to you.)

Above, I asked, "Where is the real, reliable, trustworthy pleasure located in the writing process?" Another decent answer is: In all of it. We have to learn to enjoy the whole stinking deal—even the parts that are, really and truly, torture. We have to try to feel something like, "Ah, I feel like crap because I can't find an ending—that's *part of it*. It really is. There will never come a time when I get to the ending without feeling like crap first. There will never come a time when, devoid of ideas, I won't feel like a faker." So, in the same way that there will never come a day without hunger, we might want to get into an intelligent relationship with this process—instead of feeling like a loser because we "suffer from" hunger, we'd say, "Well, that's part of being a *person*." So the torment of the aspiration/accomplishment cycle (the very real torment, if we care about excellence in our work) is part of being an *artist*. It just is.

This all sounds both holy and tidy, and I can assure you I am still fame-minded and still trying to write my way out of my feeling of not being good enough to live in such a beautiful world. But it's helpful sometimes, for me, to remember where the real bliss is in writing, and that the best motivation is that holy, unknowing, open state of mind I get to go into for a few precious minutes a day.

GEORGE SAUNDERS *is the author of nine books, including the novel* Lincoln in the Bardo, *winner of the 2017 Man Booker Prize, and the story collections* Pastoralia *and* Tenth of December, *which was a finalist for the National Book Award. He has received fellowships from the Lannan Foundation, the American Academy of Arts and Letters, and the Guggenheim Foundation. In 2006 he was awarded a MacArthur Fellowship. In 2013 he was awarded the PEN/Malamud Award for Excellence in Short Fiction and was included in* Time's *list of the one hundred most influential people in the world. He teaches in the creative writing program at Syracuse University.*

TWO

Inspiration

Writers don't need a guide to inspiration—it seems to us that the very act of guiding is antithetical to that of wondrous discovery—but thinking about where ideas come from and how to put yourself in a position of creativity can help you start that new project, or return to writing after some time away from the page.

First, some assumptions: Inspiration is not divine intervention. Calliope, Euterpe, and Erato look mighty fine glazed on a Grecian urn, but they won't do us much good when we're sitting in a Starbucks trying to ignore the muffled basslines flowing through the earbuds of fellow coffee drinkers. Inspiration isn't a light bulb that suddenly glows above our heads, or a lightning strike that leaves our hair smoking and a fully formed idea seared into our minds. Have you ever seen a flash or a spark as you're writing? Ever yelled *"Eureka!"*? Neither have we. These are romanticized images of inspiration that we've all picked up from ancient and popular culture, from Renaissance and neoclassical art and Greek mythology to cartoons and Hollywood movies. It can be fun to think about such a mysterious phenomenon in these ways, but demystifying inspiration may help us understand it better and put ourselves in a position to experience it more often.

There is no prescription for inspiration, but there are countless songs, movies, books, plays, activities, depravations, exercises, prompts, and attitudes that other writers—other *inspired* writers—report as having worked for them. We've asked the question "What inspires you?" of a great many authors over the years. "I listen to the Rolling Stones of the early 1970s play a live version of 'Jumpin' Jack Flash,'" says *New Yorker* staff writer and author Adam Gopnik. "I return to *Bird by Bird* by Anne Lamott like the literary scripture it is," says poet and novelist Hala Alyan. On the other hand, novelist Eimear McBride says, "I never read when I get stuck. It doesn't leave enough room to let the devil slip in." Instead, she turns to other art forms for answers to any problems she's having with her work. "Often music helps, but increasingly I'm interested in photography and the work of the German photographer Wolfgang Tillmans, particularly."

"When I run out of words, I find it helpful to run out the door," says novelist Idra Novey. "Even if I have only fifteen minutes and it's February and freezing, I find physically moving quickly gets my mind going again." Vendela Vida warns, "Don't spend too much time alone."

And on and on it goes, a chorus of voices extolling the virtues of a remarkable variety of inspiring activities, from reading the gleeful nihilism of Romanian philosopher Emil M. Cioran to watching Tim Burton's 1994 biopic *Ed Wood*, from engaging in some good old-fashioned eavesdropping to enjoying a long soak in the bathtub. The one thing that all these recommendations have in common is the way the activities, media, or art forms make the writers feel: inspired, ready to create, excited about their craft. But what's really happening when we feel that? And is it the same for everyone?

In his book *On Writing*, Stephen King debunks the notion that there is a well of creativity into which all a writer needs to do is dip a hand and scoop out a new idea. "There is no Idea Dump, no Story Central, no Island of the Buried Bestsellers; good story ideas seem to come quite literally from

ACTION ITEM 9

Visit pw.org/writers_recommend and browse the hundreds of movies, music, books, plays, activities, and philosophies that have inspired fellow writers. Jot down a list of those that sound the most interesting to you and try them out. Write down what inspires you most and see if you can recognize any patterns or similarities among them that could lead you on the path to discovering more.

nowhere, sailing at you right out of the empty sky: two previously unrelated ideas come together and make something new under the sun," he writes. "Your job isn't to find these ideas but to recognize them when they show up." One way to put yourself in a position to recognize them is to simply remain open to the possibility. Keep an open mind, expose yourself to new ideas. In her lecture after receiving the 2007 Nobel Prize for Literature, Doris Lessing said: "Writers are often asked, 'How do you write? With a word processor? An electric typewriter? A quill? Longhand?' But the essential question is, 'Have you found a space, that empty space, which should surround you when you write?' Into that space, which is like a form of listening, of attention, will come the words, the words your characters will speak, ideas—inspiration." Lessing wasn't talking about space as some kind of room, or a writing studio, but rather a state of mind in which we are receptive to ideas when, as King put it, "they show up."

But not all ideas are new, and not all ideas, on their own, are enough to incite an innovative project. So not only should we try to remain open to new ideas when they occur to us but we should also keep the neural pathways of our brains open for connections between new and old ideas to establish themselves. In his fascinating book *Where Good Ideas Come From: The Natural History of Innovation*, best-selling author Steven Johnson writes, "We have a natural tendency to romanticize breakthrough innovations, imagining momentous ideas transcending their surroundings, a gifted mind somehow seeing over the detritus of old ideas and ossified tradition. But ideas are bricolage; they're built out of that detritus. We take the ideas we've inherited or that we've stumbled across, and we jigger them together into some new shape."

A big part of being a writer—of being any kind of creative person—is a proclivity for intense observation. We watch, we listen, we engage all our senses in an attempt to understand the world. "How sense-luscious the world is," writes Diane Ackerman in her book *A Natural History of the Senses*. We note how the sun feels as it evaporates water droplets on our skin, or how the music from a passing car seems to warp and bend, like a ribbon streaming from the window, fluttering in the breeze. Our job as writers is to record our own observations and take note of the observations of others when those passages of novels, plays, poems, essays—any art form—speak to us.

"The air is full of tunes, I just reach up and pick one."
—URSULA K. LE GUIN

In his book, Johnson cites scientist Stuart Kauffman, who coined the term "the adjacent possible" to explain all the possible combinations of atomic elements that were achievable in the primordial soup resulting in life on our planet. Johnson uses this notion to explain how innovation and creative change are possible:

> What the adjacent possible tells us is that at any moment the world is capable of extraordinary change, but only *certain* changes can happen.
>
> The strange and beautiful truth about the adjacent possible is that its boundaries grow as you explore those boundaries. Each new combination ushers new combinations into the adjacent possible. Think of it as a house that magically expands with each door you open. You begin in a room with four doors, each leading to a new room that you haven't visited yet. Those four rooms are the adjacent possible. But once you open one of those doors and stroll into that room, three new doors appear, each leading to a brand-new room that you couldn't have reached from your original starting point. Keep opening new doors and eventually you'll have built a palace.

So how do we explore those boundaries—and thereby extend and expand the boundaries of the adjacent possible? How do we keep ourselves open to new ideas while retaining the possibility for connections to old ideas, or half-formed ideas?

One simple approach is to read those books or watch those movies or listen to that music—participate in or experience some of the media and art forms your fellow writers recommend, or whatever touches *you* deeply. By doing so you are opening up whatever part of you registers emotion or intellectual stimulation, and this exposure invites open thinking where new connections can be made. But that sounds a little bit like waiting for lightning to strike, albeit while holding a steel rod in one hand. Perhaps there's a way for us to be more proactive, more deliberate in making those connections.

"A good idea is a *network*," writes Johnson. "A specific constellation of neurons—thousands of them—fire in sync with each other for the first time in your brain, and an idea pops into your consciousness. A new idea is a network of cells exploring the adjacent possible of connections that they can make in your mind." He adds: "An idea is not a single thing. It is more like a swarm." The challenge for us is to create the conditions under which that swarm can occur.

Like Johnson suggests, we recommend keeping some version of a commonplace book. The concept of the commonplace book dates back to fifteenth-century Europe, but it became a recognized practice about two hundred years later, when folks such as John Locke, Francis Bacon, and John Milton kept regular collections of sayings and personal observations in bound notebooks. Ralph Waldo Emerson, Henry David Thoreau, Margaret Bayard Smith, Samuel Taylor Coleridge, Thomas Hardy, Mark Twain, Virginia Woolf, and W. H. Auden kept the tradition going with their own commonplace books, and countless contemporary authors keep their own versions today.

It's a simple practice, and you likely do a version of it already, but being intentional, perhaps developing a routine around it, can yield surprising results. First, as you read books, magazine articles, newspaper reports—*anything* you read—underline passages that strike you, that resonate with something you've been thinking about, or that echo something else you've read. Don't be shy: Use a highlighter, a pen, a pencil, a marker. If you're reading on a screen, add a bookmark, highlight the text (most digital editions and e-readers make it easy to mark your place). Write notes in the margins—accumulate marginalia. Don't just write down facts but also realizations, epiphanies, obsessions, hunches, wisdom! After you've finished reading that book or magazine or newspaper, transfer the underlined passages, along with your marginalia, into a notebook, a journal, a scrap-book, or even onto a stack of index cards. The point here isn't necessarily to do the work of connecting the thoughts and ideas as you write them down but rather to collect new and old ideas and observations in one place. To gather the swarm. And it needn't simply be what you read—take a note or two after you finish watching a movie, or after you see a play, or while walking down the street, or when doing chores. Remember Wallace Stevens and his walks to and from work and during lunch? He'd often pause to scribble down a note or a line of poetry on a piece of paper for later. Emily Dickinson used to jot down lines on envelopes. Keep some paper and a pen or pencil in your pocket or in your purse or in your jacket at all times. Even when you're not actively writing you're still a writer—remember that—and you never know when something will occur to you that will make its way into a future project. That observation about the bird you saw on your walk this morning may remind you of the shot in the Fellini movie you watched last night, and the passage from the novel you read last year—the one by Richard Powers about the trees. Maybe *that's* what we're talking about when we talk about inspiration. Maybe it's that connection—the joining of two disparate images or ideas that result in something entirely new. Or maybe it's something even simpler: the answer to a problem, or a question we hadn't thought to ask, or a single word that leaps out on the page, the one that fills the empty space inside and makes you feel less alone.

Don't worry about the connections while you're keeping your commonplace book. Just record it all, collect it all, and period-ically read it all through and be mindful of patterns, trends, connections. See what happens. "Each rereading of the commonplace book becomes a new kind of revelation," Steven Johnson writes. "You see the evolutionary paths of all your past hunches: the ones that turned out to be red herrings; the ones that

ACTION ITEM 10

Find a blank notebook, or just clip together some printer paper, or repurpose an old photo box, and start your own commonplace book. Don't worry about sounding smart or writing perfect sentences. Just record passages, snippets of conversation, images, scenes—anything you observe or digest throughout your day. You never know what connections you'll discover.

turned out to be too obvious to write; even the ones that turned into entire books. But each encounter holds the promise that some long-forgotten
hunch will connect in a new way with some emerging obsession."

Mihaly Csikszentmihalyi, the psychologist who coined the term "flow,"
a phenomenon of optimal experience that can result in losing track of time
or feeling outside of yourself (likely what Jennifer Egan is referring to when
she reports that when she writes fiction she forgets who she is, slipping into
"utter absorption mode"), outlines five traditional steps of creativity. In his
book *Creativity: The Psychology of Discovery and Invention*, Csikszentmihalyi lists Preparation, Incubation, Insight, Evaluation, and Elaboration
as the fundamental phases of the creative process. It's the second phase,
Incubation, "during which ideas churn around below the threshold of consciousness," that results in the connections we've been discussing. "It is during this time," he writes, "that unusual connections are likely to be made.
When we intend to solve a problem consciously, we process information
in a linear, logical fashion. But when ideas call to each other on their own,
without our leading them down a straight and narrow path, unexpected
combinations may come into being." Consider your commonplace book an
incubator. It's where you're keeping warm what Johnson calls "detritus" and
Diane Ackerman might call "vibrant morsels" so that they might percolate
and mingle.

Of course, our ability to remain receptive to new ideas and open to connections among old or half-formed ideas requires an attention span that is
under constant attack in our almost complete transition to a digital culture.
It's a move that Maryanne Wolf, in her book *Reader, Come Home: The Reading Brain in the Digital World*, points out is changing us "in ways we never
realized would be the unintended collateral consequences of the greatest
explosion of creativity, invention, and discovery in our history." On the one
hand, we have at our fingertips the equivalent of Jorge Luis Borges's Library
of Babel; on the other, it is becoming increasingly difficult, if not impossible, to shut out the noise of status updates, hot takes, news crawlers, meme
loops, streaming video, and a constant, 24/7, never-ending torrent of opinion and information.

For some writers this isn't a problem; it's a preference. "I recommend overstimulation," writes Morgan Parker, author of the young adult novel *Who Put This Song On?* and the poetry collections *Magical Negro, There Are More Beautiful Things Than Beyoncé,* and *Other People's Comfort Keeps Me Up at Night.* "If it's too quiet, I find it's hard to hear my voice. When I write, I overwhelm myself: The TV's on in the background playing a movie or a reality show, I'm listening to music, I'm texting five friends, the window's open, and I'm eavesdropping on the conversations and arguments on my . . . street below, the coffee table is stacked with books—art books, poetry collections, essays. Because I don't know what stimulus will jump-start a poem, which voice or atmosphere will turn me on, I douse myself in all of them at once."

And some writers easily negotiate the frenetic pace of the digital world with the contemplative demands of the writing life. You see them tweeting sometimes funny and other times really meaningful, even profound declarations, all hours of the day or night—and somehow they are able to shift gears and write and publish books. For these writers the internet, social media, doesn't count as distraction, it's communication, community, and creativity all rolled into one. Everyone manages these things differently.

Others of us must be more intentional about shutting out the noise. Never before has the phrase "carve out some time" felt so accurate. This is where establishing a writing routine comes back into play. Consider finding a private place to write, without a lot of distractions. Maybe it's a windowless room. In an interview with Powell's, the stalwart independent bookstore in Portland, Oregon, novelist and story writer Benjamin Percy, whose craft book, *Thrill Me: Essays on Fiction,* was published by Graywolf Press in 2016, described his writing space: "I work in the basement," he said. "There's a closet that the previous owner used as a dark room for his photography, and I use that space as my nightmare factory; the walls are taped and tacked with newspaper articles and story blueprints and lists of ideas I want to write." The only distractions are of his own choosing (his nightmare factory, by the way, sounds a lot like a big commonplace book). If you're prone to online distraction, consider turning off your Wi-Fi, or using one of a growing number of anti-distraction software applications that have been developed to combat this very problem.

EIGHT APPS TO HELP YOU FOCUS WHILE WRITING

FOCUSWRITER (gottcode.org/focuswriter) is "a simple, distraction-free writing environment. It utilizes a hide-away interface that you access by moving your mouse to the edges of the screen, allowing the program to have a familiar look and feel to it while still getting out of the way so that you can immerse yourself in your work."

FREEDOM (freedom.to) allows you to block distracting websites and apps and offers the ability to "plan out sessions that recur daily or weekly."

HOCUS FOCUS (hocusfoc.us) "automatically hides application windows that have been inactive for a certain period of time, leaving only the applications you're using visible."

LEECHBLOCK (www.proginosko.com/leechblock) is "a web browser extension designed to block those time-wasting sites that can suck the life out of your working day."

RESCUETIME (www.rescuetime.com) tracks how you spend your time on your devices. "Everything you do is automatically categorized so you can quickly see the time you spend on specific apps, websites, and projects and gauge your daily productivity."

SELFCONTROL (selfcontrolapp.com) lets you "block your own access to distracting websites, your mail servers, or anything else on the internet. Just set a period of time to block for, add sites to your blacklist, and click 'Start.' Until that timer expires, you will be unable to access those sites—even if you restart your computer or delete the application."

STAYFOCUSD (chrome.google.com/webstore/category/extensions) is "a productivity extension for Google Chrome that helps you stay focused on work by restricting the amount of time you can spend on time-wasting websites. Once your allotted time has been used up, the sites you have blocked will be inaccessible for the rest of the day."

WRITEROOM (www.hogbaysoftware.com/products/writeroom) is "a full-screen
writing environment. Unlike the cluttered word processors you're used to, Write-
Room lets you focus on writing."

This is exactly what freelance writer Frank Bures did a decade ago when
the cacophony became too great. "Obviously, this problem was caused by
technology," Bures writes. "So maybe it was in technology that I could find
a solution." On his computer he installed SelfControl ("Not the respectable,
old-fashioned, internal kind, but rather an elegant application named for
precisely the thing that I lacked") and essentially shut off the internet for a
predetermined period of time. "I just set a timer, hit start, then listen as the
cacophony falls away and a silent space opens into which I can hear words,
thoughts, ideas emerge. Alone in there, I feel something start to grow that
hasn't for a long time: inspiration."

FRANK BURES ON DISTRACTION

Being a writer requires many things: hard work, tenacity, vision, luck, a love of
reading, and so on. But none of those matter unless you have the thing we all
crave most: time. The struggle for time is a war on distraction. Which is to say, a
war on the infinite shiny objects that live on the internet and our phones. Writing
has always been a balance between input and output—consumption of things
others have written and production of the things we want to write. Today we are
in an endless battle for the most valuable real estate in the world: the space in
our heads. The companies that want to occupy it invest billions to get in there
and stay as long as possible. But as Annie Dillard once observed, "How we spend
our days is, of course, how we spend our lives." So if you want to have been a
writer when you die, you have to spend your days—or a good portion of them—
writing.

For me this means two things. First, I block the internet from my computer
for two to six hours every day, via, ironically, an app. This is not always convenient,

and I need to plan ahead. It can also be problematic if you have a day job. But whenever I hit that button, I feel a wave of relief.

Second, I've never owned a smartphone. This isn't always easy, either, but it's also not as hard as you'd think. It's just a matter of valuing my time—my life—and the things I want to do with it. I work best with a wall between myself and the world so I can give every story my full attention to report, imagine, reimagine, and immerse.

CHERYL STRAYED RECOMMENDS

Five Books to Read When You Need to Be Brave on the Page

CITIZEN: AN AMERICAN LYRIC by Claudia Rankine
Innovative in form and deeply intelligent in content, this potent book should be required reading for every citizen.

BECAUSE THEY WANTED TO: STORIES by Mary Gaitskill
Near-perfect stories about desire, longing, cruelty, and compassion by a master of the form.

CRAZY BRAVE: A MEMOIR by Joy Harjo
A gorgeous book by a powerfully wise writer about resilience, love, loss, forgiveness, and finding your voice.

HEAVY: AN AMERICAN MEMOIR by Kiese Laymon
An intensely honest memoir that is so wrenching and real in places that I literally gasped while reading it.

THE CHRONOLOGY OF WATER: A MEMOIR by Lidia Yuknavitch
Raw, visceral, sad, and beautiful—nobody writes with such wildly blunt truth about the body like Lidia Yuknavitch.

CHERYL STRAYED *is the author of the #1* New York Times *best-selling memoir* Wild, *the* New York Times *bestsellers* Tiny Beautiful Things *and* Brave Enough, *and the novel* Torch. Wild *was chosen by Oprah Winfrey as her first selection for Oprah's Book Club 2.0. Strayed's books have been translated into nearly forty languages around the world and have been adapted for both the screen and the stage. She lives in Portland, Oregon.*

THREE

Writing Prompts

Feel it? Poised on the precipice of your next great writing project, you are open to creativity, alive to the possibilities of language. You're a note away from a symphony of ideas—your mind a tuning fork before the overture slices the incredible silence. It feels good, doesn't it? But sometimes that first note won't come. And the silence, well, it can feel a little uncomfortable. You stand teetering on the edge of an idea—the promise, the potential all around you—and there you remain, unmoved. Maybe you need a little nudge, a push, a direction to fall in before you take flight.

Or maybe you just need an exercise—something to get you started, to get the blood flowing, the synapses firing. This is where writing prompts can be extremely useful. The following is a selection of thirty-six prompts that will help you start thinking about your next project or perhaps offer new ways of thinking about an existing project that you've been stuck on. The prompts are grouped by genre—a dozen each for poetry, fiction, and nonfiction—but all of them contain fascinations and inspirations that can stimulate thinking about any form of writing. Resist thinking of them as instructions that need to be followed to the letter but rather as suggestions that you can experiment with, expand on, revise, distort, or use in any way that works for you. Many are inspired by our own reading and our obser- vations of the books, photographs, films, music, and other art forms that influence us, so consider this a reminder to take notes as you think about and digest your own experiences in your writing life.

Poetry

Walk with Me

"It's my lunch hour, so I go / for a walk among the hum-colored / cabs," writes Frank O'Hara in his poem "A Step Away from Them." So often we miss out on the potential for inspiration from our daily routines, passing muses on morning commutes, lunch breaks, or evening strolls. Read O'Hara's poem and then go out into your neighborhood with no set destination, carrying a notepad. Observe and write down everything and everyone you see. Invent background narratives, involve your senses, and record sounds and overheard phrases. At home, write a poem that starts with the time of day ("It's eight in the morning," or "It's my lunch hour," or "It's midnight") and take the reader through the streets with you.

Help Yourself

Struggling to stay motivated? In 2018, researchers at the University of Chicago Booth School of Business found that people having trouble achieving their goals can benefit from the very act of giving advice to others. This week, try offering some advice to someone in a poem. Write a list of suggestions for handling a challenge, perhaps something you know very little about to add some levity. It can be specific, like what to do when your car breaks down on the side of the highway during a thunderstorm, or something more general, like how to resolve an argument. Using an idea from your list, write a humorous poem addressed to someone who may or may not appreciate your guidance.

Be Kind

"There's only one rule that I know of, babies—God damn it, you've got to be kind." Take to heart Kurt Vonnegut's words from his 1965 novel, *God*

Bless You, Mr. Rosewater, or Pearls Before Swine, and spread some kindness through your poetry. Pick someone you admire and write a poem to this person about all the things you want to say to them, no matter how personal or embarrassing. Try to avoid focusing on physical appearance or material possessions, and instead celebrate the personality traits or the fond memories you've shared. Consider sharing your poem with this person, or at least say some of the lovely things you've written to them. Kind words have such power; they can lift your spirits, boost your self-esteem, and even change your life—and your poem.

Into the Sea

In her fourth poetry collection, *Oceanic*, Aimee Nezhukumatathil explores themes of love, discovery, family, motherhood, and home, often through a lens of connectedness with the natural world, focusing on the wonders of the ocean and the shapes, movements, and behaviors of flora and fauna. In "Penguin Valentine," a penguin waits for his partner, and the poem's speaker asks, "During those days of no sun, does he / remember the particular bend / of his mate's neck, that hint of yellow / near her ears?" Look to the flora and fauna in your local neighborhood, at the park or the beach, or on a vacation or a trip, for inspiration. Write a love poem that uses animal or plant behavior as a lesson about how we interact as humans. How might tendencies or characteristics of nature resonate with your own relationships?

Shape-Shifting

Manipulating the shape of a poem on the page has a long history, from George Herbert's seventeenth-century religious verse "Easter Wings," which was printed sideways, its outlines resembling angel wings, to the "concrete poetry" of the 1950s in which the outline of poems depict recognizable shapes. More recently, Montana Ray's gun-shaped poems in *(guns & butter)*, published by Argos Books in 2015, explore themes of race, motherhood, and gun violence, and Myriam Gurba uses a shaped poem in her 2017 book, *Mean*, to probe acts and cycles of assault on and abuse of women's bodies. Write a series of concrete poems, perhaps first jotting down a list of resonant images, subjects, or motifs that already recur frequently in your work. How can you subvert or complicate the reader's initial response to the shape of the poem? How does your word choice shift when you're confined to predetermined shapes and line breaks?

Motion Capture

While scientists might describe the motion of snakes as rectilinear, Emily Dickinson's "A Narrow Fellow in the Grass" refers to the snake as "a Whip Lash / Unbraiding in the Sun." This week, read scientific descriptions or browse through video clips of your favorite animal's movements. Then write a poem that employs unusual word choice, unexpected imagery, or mimics in some way the physical motion of an animal. Perhaps the manipulation of rhythm, sound, spacing, or repetition will help highlight the movement you capture in your poem.

Corn Sweat

Heat dome, corn sweat, and *thundersnow.* Meteorologists and weather reports often coin new words and phrases for the purposes of both explaining and entertaining. Learn some new weather-related terminology, or create your own phrases that explain existing and made-up weather phenomena. Select one of these terms as the title of a poem, and allow it to guide your imagination as you write your lines. Do you end up with a poem that is somehow connected to meteorology, or does the title lead you in a completely different direction?

Mothers and Fathers

"Children begin by loving their parents; as they grow older they judge them; sometimes they forgive them," writes Oscar Wilde in *The Picture of Dorian Gray.* Drawing on your own experiences with parents, guardians, or mother and father figures—or your own history as a parent—compile a short list of specific memories and observations divided into three categories: love, judgment, and forgiveness. Would you agree with Wilde that children's love for and judgment of parents are inevitable, but forgiveness of them may be less so? How might you see forgiveness as a more conscious component of a parent-child relationship? Write a three-part poem that explores the many nuances of a parent-child relationship as it evolves with age.

Word Aversion

A 2016 study by Paul Thibodeau, a professor of psychology at Oberlin College, examined the phenomenon of "word aversion"—the extremely visceral distaste that some people have in response to certain words, such as *moist*, *luggage*, and *phlegm*. Write down a list of five words you find particularly repulsive, words that might not otherwise have any definitively negative connotations. Use these words in a poem and explore how word choice can propel you toward certain subject matter. Do you find yourself pulled to other repellant images and memories, or pushed to offset those words with more pleasing evocations?

Pandora's Box

In the story of Pandora's box in Greek mythology, Pandora, the first female created by the gods, opens the lid of a container, thereby allowing all the evils stored inside to escape into the world. In contemporary colloquial usage, to "open a Pandora's box" refers to an action that seems small or harmless but ultimately proves to have disastrous consequences. Write a poem that starts with a seemingly innocent action, which then unexpectedly unleashes a dramatic chain of events.

A New Color

Visual artists who have been productive over long stretches of time often create works with shared characteristics such as similar color palettes, giving expression to these artists going through certain "periods" in their art. For example, Paul Cézanne and Henri Matisse both had dark periods, Pablo Picasso had his Blue and Rose periods, and Victor Vasarely had a black-and-white period. Consider embarking on a new period in your own work. Write a series of short poems inspired by your observations of the different colors, moods, and scenery around you that signal a new season. To begin a green period, for example, what might be your key points of inspiration, in terms of imagery and vocabulary?

Line of Inquiry

Several years ago New York Public Library staff discovered a box filled with file cards of written questions submitted to librarians from the 1940s to 1980s, many of which have been collected in the book *Peculiar Questions and Practical Answers: A Little Book of Whimsy and Wisdom from the Files of the New York Public Library*. Some of the questions include: "What does it mean when you're being chased by an elephant?" "Can you give me the name of a book that dramatizes bedbugs?" and "What time does a bluebird sing?" Write a poem inspired by one of these curiously strange questions. Does your poem provide a practical answer, or avoid one altogether, leading instead to more imaginative questions?

Fiction

Fairy-tale Redux

Authors such as Karen Russell, Kelly Link, and Carmen Maria Machado have drawn inspiration for their stories from well-known fairy-tale tropes and styles, and other writers have adapted classic fairy tales for their own use, like Anne Sexton's 1971 collection, *Transformations*, and Helen Oyeyemi's 2014 novel, *Boy, Snow, Bird*. *My Mother She Killed Me, My Father He Ate Me*, a 2010 anthology of fairy tale–inspired writing edited by Kate Bernheimer, includes stories such as Joy Williams's "Baba Iaga and the Pelican Child" and Kevin Brockmeier's "A Day in the Life of Half of Rumpelstiltskin." Write your own interpretation of a fairy tale, imagining well-known characters in the present or future, and incorporating relevant issues of contemporary society revolving around class, poverty, crime, race, war, or gender. How might you incorporate new technology, politics, or communication habits while maintaining the emotions, relationships, mood, and themes at the core of the tale's plot?

Not the Same Old Story

In 2015 Adrienne LaFrance reported in the *Atlantic* that researchers using computer systems to analyze the emotional trajectories of protagonists in nearly two thousand works of English-language fiction found that there are just six basic storytelling arcs: "1. Rags to Riches (rise), 2. Riches to Rags (fall), 3. Man in a Hole (fall then rise), 4. Icarus (rise then fall), 5. Cinderella (rise then fall then rise), 6. Oedipus (fall then rise then fall)." Think of a story that you often tell in your own life, perhaps a childhood memory that involves school friends or a family occasion, or an adventurous incident that happened on a trip or vacation. Does it seem to align with one of these basic plotlines? Write a short fiction piece that maps the major elements of your story onto a different, unexpected arc.

Fish Out of Water

A black bear wanders into a backyard in Florida and tries lounging in a hammock. A sloth is found stranded on a highway in Ecuador, clinging to a guardrail for dear life, and is rescued by transportation officials. A rabbit gets catapulted up onto a roof during a windy storm in Northern Ireland and is saved by firefighters. Write a scene in which a character—human or animal—finds themselves in a situation where they are a fish out of water. Do they explore the new and foreign environment surrounding them, or are they in need of rescue?

Stream of Consciousness

ACTION ITEM 11

Sign up for The Time Is Now newsletter by visiting pw.org /writing-prompts-exercises. You can also browse the archive of hundreds of writing prompts for poets, fiction writers, and creative nonfiction writers.

Though in many ways the act of writing can be considered an exercise in control—over everything from plot arc to characters to the weather in your setting—what happens when you take a more passive position and relinquish control, allowing a story to emerge from your unconscious mind? Many scientists, spiritualists, and artists have reported on "automatic writing," in which a person steers clear of putting any conscious intention behind the words that are put down. Try your hand by first writing about what comes to mind immediately: perhaps the changing colors and textures of autumn leaves outside, or everyday details about upcoming holidays and visiting family. Try not to pause or edit yourself. Gradually let your mind progress into an associative stream of consciousness. Take a look at what you've written and, using your favorite elements, write a short story with a seasonal theme, allowing it to be nonsensical, absurd, or surreal.

On the Menu

"I wanted to write a story and fit it all on a menu and call it 'Myself as a Menu,'" writes Lynne Tillman about a story she wrote for *Wallpaper* magazine in 1975. "This way I would have a structure and humorously author 'a self' as an assortment of so-called 'choices,' while representing a text as arbitrary, like a menu of disparate dishes and tastes." Write a story inspired by this menu form, perhaps using a real restaurant menu as a template or launchpad. Create a persona by choosing certain "courses" or "sides" to further elaborate on your character's personality.

Fashion Statement

Coco Chanel famously said, "Fashion has to do with the ideas, the way we live, what is happening." This week, focus on the way one of your characters gets dressed: Do they throw on the first thing they see, or will it take hours for them to get ready? Is a typical outfit an accurate representation of their personality, or more of a disguise? Write a scene describing your character's clothing in detail, and what is revealed about their demeanor through their attire.

Re-creating Fear

"Can we really mold a narrative around something that defies narrative itself? How can we re-create an experience that eludes the conscious mind?" In "This Is Your Brain on Fear," an article published in *Poets & Writers Magazine*, J. T. Bushnell asks these questions as he explores the relationship between narrative storytelling and the often fragmentary, uncertain nature of memory and observation when people experience trauma. Write a scene of high stress, fear, or trauma for a first-person narrator that makes use of "selective description of external details." Resist the temptation to fill in the blanks or describe the passage of time in a linear way. Explore the way the human brain processes events and incorporate your findings into your story-telling.

Deus Ex Machina

In modern storytelling a deus ex machina is a plot device in which a dramatic and oftentimes contrived occurrence suddenly saves the day or solves a seemingly impossible problem. This week, write a short story using this device in the form of a character, object, or newfound ability. How will you manipulate the pacing to create the most effective sense of surprise? Consider the tone of the story, perhaps incorporating tragedy and comedy, as you lead up to the unexpected turn of events.

Picture a Story

Take some time to discover the work of a well-known photographer. Whether you visit an exhibition at a museum or peruse the internet, look for photographs that capture your imagination. Examine a photograph closely and write the story you see in the frame. Rely heavily on descriptive language and offer details of the composition through your writing. What did the photographer keep in focus?

Digging Deep

Strong characters are key elements in any well-constructed story. You may have clearly illustrated their history, occupation, likes, and dislikes, but to make them truly compelling you must have a basic understanding of these characters' psyches. Choose a story you've written and make a list of the characters you don't really know yet. Next to each name, jot down notes about what that character's aspirations and motivations are. How do these characters see the world? Who are the people they look up to, want to impress, or model themselves after? Where do these characters want to be in the next five years—or the next fifty? Will they reach their dreams, or are they destined to get sidetracked? Let this information serve as a reference when you are deciding how a character should react in a situation, or how the plot should progress.

Reclaimed by Nature

In her photography series titled "Home," Gohar Dashti explores the interiors of houses in her native Iran that have been abandoned and reclaimed by nature. The images create an ambiguous effect; an old bedroom overrun with wildflowers is lovely in one sense, but also hints at a darker history. What happened in these houses and why did the people who once lived in them leave? This week, imagine what it would look, sound, and smell like, and how it would feel to have your childhood home overtaken by nature. Try using this eerie space as the setting for a short story.

Jumping to Conclusions

Have you ever, out of impatience or curiosity, turned to the last page of a novel you were in the middle of reading in order to relieve your anxiety about the ending? This week, if you are staring at a blank page or screen unsure of where to begin, soothe yourself by fast-forwarding to the final page of the story. Write a stand-alone conclusion without halting to examine plausibility or the actions that could have gotten your characters to this place. Perhaps this exercise will lead you to write an origin for the story and flesh out your characters and the setting.

Nonfiction

Lunch Hour Footnotes

"At almost one o'clock I entered the lobby of the building where I worked and turned toward the escalators, carrying a black Penguin paperback and a small white CVS bag, its receipt stapled over the top." The entirety of Nicholson Baker's debut novel, *The Mezzanine*, takes place during a ride up an office escalator during a lunch break. Baker inserts extensive footnotes about ordinary phenomena such as shoelaces, milk cartons, perforated paper, plastic straws, paper towel dispensers, and the contents of his lunch into the story. Write a personal essay that uses footnotes to delve into the details of an hour in your daily routine. Incorporate minutiae about your physical movements and observations of mundane objects to express the significance of your everyday experience.

Open House

"I saw the book as another kind of house. How did I want the reader to pass through it? What room would they enter first, and how should that room feel?" writes Sarah M. Broom about the structure of her National Book Award–winning debut memoir, *The Yellow House.* Write a memoiristic piece, or revisit one already in progress, and work on constructing it like a house that the reader must pass through. Plan out the entry and exit points, and organize different sections or vignettes to be experienced as rooms visited one after another.

Rewind

In 2019 quantum physicists succeeded in un-aging a single, simulated particle, essentially moving it backward through time for one-millionth of a second. The feat required so much manipulation and was considered so impossible for nature to replicate that scientists presented it as reinforcement of the irreversibility of time. But what if the reversal of a single moment in time was possible? Write a personal essay that reflects on one moment in your life that you would do over, if you could. What actually happened, and what do you perceive as the long-term consequences if things changed?

Reshaping the Past

In *The Art of Memoir* Mary Karr writes that "from the second you choose one event over another, you're shaping the past's meaning." Think of a significant event from your past that you've written about before. Make a list of three other events or changes that were occurring in your life around that time. Write an essay about one of these "secondary" events, focusing on deriving personal or emotional meaning from this seemingly less impactful event.

Street Name

Look to the name of your street for inspiration. Or, if you prefer, choose the name of a previous street you lived on, or a particularly fascinating street name in your city or town. Is the street designated for a famous person, a defining local feature, or a natural landmark? Are there Dutch, Spanish, or Native American roots to the name? Write an essay about the street's origin, and how the name might be fitting or outdated. Reflect on the ways you connect with where you live, and how your own history intertwines with the street names that surround you.

Tableaux Vivants

The Pageant of the Masters is a tableaux vivants—or "living pictures"—event held every summer at Laguna Beach's Festival of Arts in Southern California. The long-running tradition features hundreds of costumed volunteers who stand still for ninety-second intervals, posing in elaborate re-creations of masterpieces of art. Write an essay describing the artwork—classical or contemporary—you would choose to "live" in. What would your role and pose be? Who would be your supporting cast of posers? What narration and music would accompany your tableau vivant?

Self-Defense

In times of conflict we often experience an instinct for self-preservation. In July 2017 a truck transporting thousands of hagfish in Oregon was involved in a collision that resulted in the eel-like creatures spilling out and releasing massive amounts of slimy mucus onto the highway and cars. In their natural deep-sea habitat, their slime-spewing is a defense mechanism, clogging the gills of attacking predators. Think of a time when you've responded in a stressful situation with a defense mechanism of your own. Write an essay about the encounter, exploring your emotional responses and aspects of your personal history that may have contributed to your instinctive reaction.

A Different Tongue

In a *New York Times* review of three books by British-born artist and author Leonora Carrington, Parul Sehgal described Carrington's habit of writing in rudimentary Spanish or French as an example of exophony, the practice of writing in a language that is not the writer's native tongue. Sehgal also referenced Samuel Beckett, who after adopting French stated in a letter: "More and more my own language appears to me like a veil that must be torn apart in order to get at the things (or the Nothingness) behind it." Write a short essay about a particularly resonant memory. Then try rewriting the same memory either in another language, even if you only have a basic knowledge of it, or in a style of English that has been "torn apart" and defamiliarized. Do you find this practice freeing or limiting? Which elements of the memory and your storytelling are drastically altered, and what remains consistent throughout both versions?

On Beauty

"You can always tell prettiness from beauty. Beauty arises from contradiction, even when it's under the surface. Any report of experience will be contradictory. And part of the reportage is to include those contradictions," said Chris Kraus in a conversation with Leslie Jamison for *Interview* magazine. Write a personal essay exploring the idea that an underlying contradiction is intrinsic to the value of beauty. What are some images, scenes, or emotions in your life or art that you've found to be beautiful, and what contradictions might lie within them? How can you effectively integrate contradictions into your own reportage to explore true beauty?

Elegant Things

In *The Pillow Book of Sei Shōnagon*, translated and edited by Ivan Morris, the eleventh-century Japanese poet and courtier created a series of lists based on her daily life. Her topics included Hateful Things ("A carriage passes by with a nasty, creaking noise"); Elegant Things ("A pretty child eating strawberries"); Things That Have Lost Their Power ("A large tree that has been blown down in a gale and lies on its side with its roots in the air"); and

Things That Should Be Large ("Men's eyes"), among others. The list form allowed her to celebrate, or denigrate, details that may have otherwise gone unnoticed. Take ten minutes to invent and populate a list of your own—the more specific, the better. Make more lists each day if the spirit strikes you.

Nuts for Nutella

A supermarket chain in France held a promotion that slashed prices of Nutella, the popular hazelnut and chocolate spread, by seventy percent, causing shoppers in some stores to stampede as they scrambled to snatch up the bargain. Think of one of your favorite foods, perhaps a gourmet item that you treat yourself to only occasionally but wish you could have every day. Write a lyric essay about this item, integrating your personal history and specific memories with references to researched tidbits or fun facts about the food.

Missed Connections

The "missed connections" section of the classified advertisements website Craigslist has long been a virtual bulletin board to share a memory ("I smiled at you on the train and you smiled back") in hopes that someone will reply. Write a personal essay recalling a situation in which you may have missed an opportunity to connect with someone, whether a romantic or professional prospect, or a potentially significant person who may have slipped through your fingers. Explore ideas of fate and chance, persistence, lost opportunities, and assertiveness. How have your approaches to meeting new people evolved over time? Are there any missed connections from your past that might be picked up again now, years later?

OCEAN VUONG ON BECOMING A POET

I n the fall of 2008 I stepped off the Metro-North train from New Haven and walked up the platform into the growing, gentle roar of Grand Central Station—its warm, ambient glow of high-ceilinged grandiosity opening over hundreds of tourists and commuters. I had just turned nineteen and, with exactly $764 in cash (money saved from working on a tobacco farm in rural Connecticut) and a backpack jammed full of (terrible) handwritten poems, I began my life in New York City. Like most young writers before me, I came to the city hoping to hone my writing chops and join the exciting and innovative conversations taking place. But more practically, I came to the city to go to school. My single mother, being an immigrant from Vietnam and living in a housing project in Hartford, Connecticut, couldn't afford to pay for my education—let alone support my ambiguous desire to become a writer. Luckily, I received a scholarship from Pace University, which was enough for me to pack my bags and head to the big city.

Other than a couple of distant acquaintances (friends of relatives) in the city, I knew no one. My small list of couch-surfing connections soon dried up and I found myself on the streets for over two weeks, sleeping and writing in Penn Station. Eventually, through a friend's recommendation, I ended up living with Grazina, an eighty-four-year-old Lithuanian widow who spent most of her days watching *The Price Is Right* in a two-story town house in Bushwick, Brooklyn. Grazina suffered from frontal lobe dementia and, in exchange for caring for her, I was given a tiny upstairs bedroom in her home—where I stayed until my graduation in May 2012.

•　　•　　•

I had no idea what the literary community in New York would look like—in fact, I had no idea such communities even existed. Growing up in a predominantly black and Hispanic neighborhood where there was strong pride in the blue-collar work ethic, reading and writing were a sign of pretension and often frowned upon—even considered a betrayal. Most of my friends' fathers were incarcerated, my own father among them. Our strongest and most convenient role models were hypermasculine hip-hop artists, basketball stars, or worse—drug dealers. Reading was for the weak, the passive: the conformist to middle-class power structures. I remember skipping lunch every day to read in the back of the library, a worn copy of Steinbeck's *Grapes of Wrath* in my lap, my forehead pressed down against the Formica desk. If anyone saw me, I could just say I was sleeping.

My only representatives of the literati were dead. From the biographies of early heroes like Lorca, Rimbaud, Whitman, Ginsberg, Plath, and Nguyen Chi Thien, who wrote most of his poems in a communist concentration camp, I expected the literary life to be exactly how I was living it after arriving in Grand Central: spontaneous, nomadic, financially impoverished, and utterly alone. I had never heard of a "writing workshop" and couldn't even fathom the idea of an MFA.

I sought out readings whenever I could, hoping to at least meet other poets. But because this was before Facebook (at least for me) and other popular social media outlets, my only resource was a now-defunct online calendar of random New York City poetry readings. Sometimes I would show up at a dingy bar on the Lower East Side or a local library in Queens and sit for hours, waiting for poets who would never appear. Some readings led me to strange yet charming places, like an underground church on the outskirts of Park Slope lit with a single fluorescent light bulb over a round table of exactly four poets—all in their sixties. There was also the living room of someone's fourth-floor walk-up sprawling with half a dozen cats, one of which would shriek whenever someone dropped a piece of paper, or the Bengali take-out restaurant the size of a U-Haul van where poets took turns shouting over a gurgling soda machine, much to the bewilderment of the servers behind the counter.

One of the most memorable venues, however, was St. Veronica's on Christopher Street. On a wintery February afternoon, I stood in front of the church gate, checking the address scrawled on my palm. The gate was cracked open. Taped to the red door was a piece of paper that read, in black marker: POETRY DOWNSTAIRS, followed by an arrow pointing toward a side staircase that led to the basement. I walked into a hallway that also doubled as the church's storage space: Columns of stacked chairs and tables lined the walls, music and microphone stands huddled in the corners, boxes and boxes of plain wooden crosses. At the end of the hall was a single lit room emitting the distinct sound of laughter. I entered what appeared to be an old classroom filled with roughly twenty people. Leaning over a plastic podium whose corners were smooth and shiny from overuse, a man donning a wooden leg, giant sunglasses that nearly hid his forehead, and an Elvis-like wig, recited a poem about the woes of his ex-wife—to everyone's delight. I settled into my seat.

The readers did not publish any books, win awards, hold teaching positions—or even degrees. In fact, I soon discovered that most of them were chronically homeless, some scraping by with odd jobs and little government assistance. Like Cecil, who, after being released from psychiatric care at Bellevue Hospital, took to the streets after his family rejected his decision to identify himself as a queer man. I watched as Cecil leapt from his seat and clapped his hands when the host, Joshua, read his name from the list. He stood behind the podium, where he belted an emotional rendition of "Jesus Loves Me," his head tilting back until he was looking directly at the ceiling, his arms raised as he urged us to sing with him. *Yes*, we sang, *Jesus loves me—this I know, for the Bible tells me so. . . .* He ended his session with an original poem dedicated to his hero, Langston Hughes.

There was also Marianne, a sixty-two-year-old grandmother of four who had been living on the streets for nearly a decade. At nineteen, I never imagined a woman who spends most of her days roaming the city collecting other people's refuse would stand up, take off her purple knitted hat, and recite impeccable Shakespearean sonnets by heart, her index finger twirling out the iambic stresses. Then there was George, a retired private school teacher who would greet me every week by holding out a paper bag full of old books and saying, "Just some sustenance for the soul!" This was how I encountered Crane, Lowell, Bishop, Stevens, Dickinson, Pound, H.D., Auden, and Milton. I would gratefully accept the books and ask a few questions about last week's reading, to which George would offer a private lesson, followed quickly by a short verbal examination—to which he often answered himself over my clumsy stammering.

Strangely, I never found myself concerned with the quality of the poems being read. It seemed that merely the *possibility* of poetry was enough. It wasn't even what was said that mattered, per se—but that there was a space, despite being literally buried under the earth, under the house of God, where these folks could have a voice. And I realized that I, too, longed to be heard. Like most of these people, I had been regularly and unconditionally marginalized by the system in which I lived, that to speak *and* be heard was to carve myself out of thin air and into visibility, into existence. We were there because we had been exiled, one way or another, by a larger, more dominant community. One could imagine my delight when Joshua, who had been running the series for over ten years, asked me to "feature" (read for five minutes longer than everyone else). I remember leaving the church absolutely ecstatic: Exiled or not, I thought to myself, I had my very first featured reading in one of the greatest cities in the world. One day I showed up and there was a note on the gate. The readings were canceled—for good. No explanation. I don't know what happened to that reading series, but one thing was certain: It was not until those kind folks in that basement introduced me as such did I have the chutzpah to call myself a poet.

•   •   •

With nowhere else to go, I returned to the refuge of books. Besides, caring for Grazina was basically a full-time job—on top of being a full-time student. From making sure she took every one of her pills from the daily twelve-pill cocktail, to quieting the occasional dementia attack, to convincing her once again that her long-dead mother was really not coming to dinner that night and making twenty stuffed cabbages would not be necessary (after which we would sometimes end up with twenty stuffed cabbages anyway). Most of my evenings were spent sitting next to Grazina with a book in my lap as she watched *The Office*—which she firmly believed to be the nightly news (maybe it was all the suits they wear).

Luckily, Grazina's late husband had been an avid collector of books. The basement walls were lined with shelves stacked three books deep, most of which were pulp fiction ranging from the 1950s to the early '80s. One afternoon, as I was sifting through old paperbacks, I spotted a back wall covered with a large black cotton bedsheet. I worked through the dust, one arm over my mouth, and peeled back the fabric. As dust billowed through the beam of my flashlight, I saw the hidden books. Rows and rows of Western literature's most timeless classics: Homer, Baldwin, Tolstoy, Morrison, Flaubert, Turgenev, Faulkner, Nabokov, Salinger, Atwood, O'Connor, and on and on. There was also the entire collected works of Steinbeck and Hemingway in hardback. Most of the books were paperbacks from the 1950s, cheaply made and printed for vast distribution. But that didn't change what was written inside them.

My mouth agape, my heartbeat rising, dust in my lungs, I dove into the books. The years had glued the covers together and, as I attempted to dislodge them from the shelves, some books came out attached in twos, even threes. Others were eaten almost entirely by rats. I lifted a trio of Camus's books and peered into a golf-ball-sized hole burrowing right through three existentialist masterpieces—cover to cover. Luckily, there were often duplicates of the books and I managed to salvage both *The Stranger* and *The Rebel*.

Since I had no TV and no internet connection, the "secret" library became my new pleasure. I would finish a book, return it, and grab another from the shelf, making my way through centuries of groundbreaking literature, spending hours and hours after school lost in dust, mildew, and exquisite language. Nights, I would lie on the floor in my room, often holding vigil over Grazina's volatile dementia attacks, deep in the pages of *War and Peace* ringed with mold and falling apart in my hands. I would turn a page and it would break off, debris falling on my chest and neck. The book was literally disintegrating as I read it. When I finished, there was only the worn back cover between my fingers.

I placed the cover down. The book had vanished from the world only to enter me, leaving no trace. Alone, an unwilling hermit of condition, I thrived by allowing language to fall apart inside of me. In other words, I was becoming a poet.

OCEAN VUONG *is the author of the novel* On Earth We're Briefly Gorgeous *(Penguin, 2019), an instant* New York Times *bestseller, and the critically acclaimed poetry collection* Night Sky with Exit Wounds *(Copper Canyon Press, 2016), a* New York Times *Top 10 Book of 2016, winner of the T. S. Eliot Prize, the Whiting Award, the Thom Gunn Award, and the Forward Prize for Best First Collection. In 2019 he was awarded a MacArthur Fellowship. Selected by* Foreign Policy *in 2016 as a Leading Global Thinker alongside Hillary Rodham Clinton, Ban Ki-Moon, and Angela Merkel, Vuong was also named by BuzzFeed Books às one of "32 Essential Asian American Writers." Born in Saigon, Vietnam, he lives in Northampton, Massachusetts, where he serves as an assistant professor in the MFA program at the University of Massachusetts in Amherst.*

FOUR

One Hundred Notes on Craft

A writer learns the craft of writing by reading, reading, reading and listening, listening, listening—absorbing as many of the lessons from past and present masters of the form as possible—and then living, living, living while writing, writing, writing one's own way through the endlessly mysterious and forking paths of discovery and creativity.

"Creative people love to claim they know what *works*, but in reality all they know is what *worked*. Fortunes are lost and hearts broken in that shift of tense," writes Richard Russo in his book *The Destiny Thief: Essays on Writing, Writers and Life*.

So how do you know what worked? You read, a lot.

"Fiction isn't machinery, it's alchemy. Anybody who claims to shed complete light on the mechanisms by which fiction operates is peddling snake oil," writes Peter Orner in *Am I Alone Here? Notes on Living to Read and Reading to Live*. "A piece of fiction can have all the so-called essential elements, setting, character, plot, tension, conflict, and still be so dead on the page that no amount of resuscitation would ever do any good."

So how do you transform your writing into art using such subtle and elusive alchemy? Not only do you read, a lot, you write even more. Write every chance you get.

We aren't peddling snake oil here, as Orner warns, nor are we claiming we know what *works*, as Russo cautions. But we are trying to provide as many sparks and starting points for writing as possible. The following is a collection of notes from authors whose voices have resonated with us in our own winding journey through craft. We present them here with hopes that they might provide a spark that will catch fire and spread through your writing life.

1

"Sometimes craft isn't advice or technique, but simply a suggestion—a way of thinking, a method of approach," writes Dan Beachy-Quick, author of *Wonderful Investigations: Essays, Meditations, Tales.*

2

"I think all writing and all art is a spiritual act. I always talk about writing from a perspective of being spiritual. I don't mean it in connection with any religion, but I mean spiritual in the sense of being really present and alive in the moment," says Sandra Cisneros, whose novel *The House on Mango Street* has sold over six million copies and has been translated into more than twenty languages.

3

"I always start with questions that I can't answer," said Barbara Kingsolver, author of *The Poisonwood Bible*, in a conversation with Richard Powers in the summer of 2018. "Otherwise you get bored halfway through if you already know the answers. If you're asking what seem to be unanswerable questions, then you have to keep showing up."

4

"I've always been restless," said Richard Powers, author of the Pulitzer Prize–winning novel *The Overstory*, in that same conversation with Barbara Kingsolver, which took place in her backyard in Virginia on a hot day in late August. "Every book has seemed to run its course and present new questions that take me to some new place and make me want to commit for another three or four years to some new place, to become knowledgeable about some new domain."

5

"When you're writing, you're trying to find out something which you don't know," said novelist, playwright, activist, and literary icon James Baldwin, thirty-four years before Richard Powers and Barbara Kingsolver met. "The whole language of writing for me is finding out what you don't want to know, what you don't want to find out. But something forces you to anyway."

6

ACTION ITEM 12

Start keeping a dream journal. Keep it near your bed, with a pencil or pen handy, so that you can record your dream immediately upon waking.

Adrienne Rich, whose last book of poems was titled *Telephone Ringing in the Labyrinth*, said, "Poems are like dreams: in them you put what you don't know you know."

7

"I think any poem, and any writer, is always breaking open the questions beneath the poem, or the writing," says Claudia Rankine, author of *Citizen: An American Lyric*. "You're always trying to figure out: what gives me the right to say x or y? What does that mean? When I say this, what does it mean? How does it mean might be even more important than what does it mean. And so I think that circling questions is really what writing is. That constant investigating of any statement, any word, any question mark, any punctuation . . . you know, all of those things. That's writing."

8

"It's more important to give yourself permission to put words down on a page than it is to labor long and hard over making a poem 'perfect' by fiddling with it endlessly," writes Gregory Orr, whose twelfth poetry collection is titled *The Last Love Poem I Will Ever Write*. "It's more important for a beginning poet to explore subject matter and different ways of using language than it is to complete any given poem."

9

"I usually start with character, rather than a concept or an idea. If I do want to deal with an idea, I must create a character, in order to work from there, from that angle," said the poet Ai, who won a National Book Award for *Vice: New and Selected Poems*.

10

"In great fiction the main element of importance is the fusion of character and event, their interplay, the way the latter reveals the former, and the way the former leads inevitably to the latter," writes Charles Johnson, author of the novel *Middle Passage*. "One must also see how event transforms character even as it is produced by character."

11

"The better you know the characters, the more you'll see things from their point of view," writes Anne Lamott in *Bird by Bird: Some Instructions on Writing and Life*. "You need to trust that you've got it in you to listen to people, watch them, and notice what they wear and how they move, to capture a sense of how they speak. You want to avoid at all costs drawing your characters on those that already exist in other works of fiction. You must learn about people from people, not from what you read. Your reading should *confirm* what you've observed in the world."

12

"The action of the character should be unpredictable before it has been shown, inevitable when it has been shown," wrote Elizabeth Bowen, author of ten novels and more than eighty stories.

13

"Elderly people are not always craggy, wrinkled, stooped over, forgetful, or wise. Teenagers are not necessarily rebellious, querulous, or pimple-faced.

Babies aren't always angelic, or even cute. Drunks don't always slur their words," writes memoirist and novelist Dani Shapiro. "Characters aren't types. When creating a character, it's essential to avoid the predictable. Just as in language we must beware of clichés. When it comes to character, we are looking for what is true, what is not always so, what makes a character unique, nuanced, indelible."

14

"I have been told, both in approval and in accusation, that I seem to love all my characters," wrote novelist and short story master Eudora Welty in Jackson, Mississippi, in 1980. "What I do in writing of any character is to try to enter into the mind, heart, and skin of a human being who is not myself. Whether this happens to be a man or a woman, old or young, with skin black or white, the primary challenge lies in making the jump itself. It is the act of a writer's imagination that I set most high."

15

"Listen to people talking and copy down the choicer bits of what you hear. Copy phrases, sentences. In this way, you will learn how people really speak. We don't speak very coherently or neatly. We are often very brief in our exchanges. We often communicate in sentence fragments—that is, when we're not being overly long, stumbly and messy, as we grope to express what we mean. Your dialogue should reflect how we speak, though it will always be notched up a degree or two in order to be more intense, more colorful, and more dramatic. But above all, dialogue should not consist entirely of neat, complete sentences." This is Lydia Davis, whose stories "make us more acutely aware of life on and off the page," wrote Peter Orner in the *New York Times Book Review*.

ACTION ITEM 13

Do exactly as Lydia Davis suggests: Go ahead, eavesdrop in the name of art.

16

This is author, art collector, and expat extraordinaire Gertrude Stein, sixty-five years earlier: "One of the things that is a very interesting thing to know is how you are feeling inside you to the words that are coming out to be outside of you."

17

"No character should utter much above a dozen words at a breath—unless the writer can justify to himself a longer flood of speech by the specialty of the occasion," wrote the very Victorian novelist Anthony Trollope.

18

"Dialogue is not what your characters say to each other; it's what they do to each other," said Danielle Evans, author of the story collection *Before You Suffocate Your Own Fool Self*, in a workshop in the MFA program at the University of Wisconsin in Madison, as recalled by one of her students, fiction writer Dantiel W. Moniz.

19

"The line of dialogue belongs to the character; the verb is the writer sticking his nose in. But 'said' is far less intrusive than grumbled, gasped, cautioned, lied. I once noticed Mary McCarthy ending a line of dialogue with 'she asseverated,' and had to stop reading to get the dictionary," said Elmore Leonard, whose stories were adapted into the films *3:10 to Yuma* and *The Tall T* as well as the FX series *Justified*.

20

In a nearly four-hundred-page book devoted to the power of verbs, Constance Hale writes, "Variety doesn't always lead to vivacity. Many common verbs (*is, does, has, goes*) are so generic and imprecise as to be yawners. But the verbs at the other end of the spectrum—long, uncommon, and unwieldy—spoil sentences just as much, if not more. The worst are pompous, highfalutin, and abstract. Some have been cobbled from Latin and Greek by writers wanting to seem erudite. Be wary of verbs like *bequeath, commence, conjoin, interrogate*, and *remunerate*—it's as though you took the synonyms *give, start, join, grill*, and *pay* and dressed them up in uncomfortable tuxedos."

21

"I learned from reading Jamaica Kincaid that simple words could be torpedoes," writes Veronica Chambers, author of the memoir *Mama's Girl*.

22

"One of the things I think I might have done in my life is just to try to speak for those who have not yet spoken, to try to tell the stories that have not yet been told. Maybe that's what a poet does. Maybe what a poet does is to try to keep alive the whole story of what it means to be human, to try to tell the truth." This is Lucille Clifton, who in 1988 became the first author to have two books—*Good Woman: Poems and a Memoir: 1969–1980* and *Next: New Poems*—named finalists for the same year's Pulitzer Prize. (William Meredith won for *Partial Accounts: New and Selected Poems*.)

23

Toni Morrison's first novel, *The Bluest Eye*, was published in 1970. She was thirty-nine years old. "I wrote the first book because I wanted to read it," she said. "I thought that kind of book, with that subject—those most vulnerable, most undescribed, not taken seriously little black girls—had never existed seriously in literature. No one had ever written about them except as props. Since I couldn't find a book that did that, I thought, 'Well, I'll write it and then I'll read it.' It was really the reading impulse that got me into the writing thing."

24

"Poetry is a political act because it involves telling the truth," said June Jordan, who wrote about civil rights, women's rights, and sexual freedom in more than two dozen books of poems, essays, libretti, and work for children.

25

"A lot is being said today about the influence that the myths and images of women have on all of us who are products of culture," wrote Adrienne Rich, whose poetry collection *Diving into the Wreck* won a National Book Award in 1974. "I think it has been a peculiar confusion to the girl or woman who tries to write because she is peculiarly susceptible to language. She goes to poetry or fiction looking for *her* way of being in the world, since she too has been putting words and images together; she is looking eagerly for guides, maps, possibilities; and over and over in the words 'masculine persuasive force' of literature she comes up against something that negates everything she is about: she meets the image of Woman in books written by men."

26

"The poem is compelled into existence by the very thing that prohibits its speech." —Dawn Lundy Martin, author of *Good Stock Strange Blood*.

27

"For women, then, poetry is not a luxury. It is a vital necessity of our existence," wrote Audre Lorde in an essay collected in *Sister Outsider*. "It forms the quality of the light within which we predicate our hopes and dreams toward survival and change, first made into language, then into idea, then into more tangible action. Poetry is the way we help give name to the nameless so it can be thought. The farthest external horizons of our hopes and fears are cobbled by our poems, carved from the rock experiences of our daily lives."

28

"So long as artists exist, making what they please and think they ought to make, even if it is not terribly good, even if it appeals to only a handful of people, they remind the Management of something managers need to be reminded of, namely, that the managed are people with faces, not anonymous numbers," wrote W. H. Auden, whose first book, *Poems*, was published in 1930, when he was twenty-three.

29

"The first lie of fiction is that the author gives some order to the chaos of life: chronological order, or whatever order the author chooses. As a writer, you select some part of a whole. You decide that those things are important and the rest is not. And you write about those things from your perspective. Life is not that way. Everything happens simultaneously, in a chaotic way, and you don't make choices. You are not the boss; life is the boss. So when you accept as a writer that fiction is lying, then you become free. You can do anything. Then you start walking in circles. The larger the circle, the more truth you can get. The wider the horizon—the more you walk, the more you linger over everything—the better chance you have of finding particles of truth." —Isabel Allende, who won worldwide acclaim in 1982 with the publication of her first novel, *The House of the Spirits*, which began as a letter to her dying grandfather.

30

"We live entirely, especially if we are writers, by the imposition of a narrative line upon disparate images, by the 'ideas' with which we have learned to freeze the shifting phantasmagoria which is our actual experience," writes Joan Didion in *The White Album*, seven sentences after the iconic and oft-quoted "We tell ourselves stories in order to live."

31

"The truth is always something that is told, not something that is known. If there were no speaking or writing, there would be no truth about anything. There would only be what is," wrote Susan Sontag in *The Benefactor*, an experimental novel published in 1963, when she was thirty years old.

32

"The immersion memoirist is interested primarily in understanding the Self, that tricky and elusive notion, and not so small a task," writes Robin Hemley, author of *Turning Life into Fiction*. "As Emerson wrote, 'To believe your own thought, to believe what is true for you in your private heart is true for all men—that is genius. Speak your latent conviction, and it shall be the universal sense' ("Self-Reliance"). To write honestly about the Self more often takes courage and generosity than egoism."

33

"I know many think that writing sort of 'clears the air.' It doesn't do that at all," said poet, singer, memoirist, and civil rights activist Maya Angelou onstage at the YMHA in Manhattan in 1990. "If you are going to write autobiography, don't expect that it will clear anything up. It makes it more clear to you, but it doesn't alleviate anything. You simply know it better, you have names for the people."

34

"A memoir is experience alchemized into art," writes William Giraldi, author of the memoir *The Hero's Body*.

35

After receiving the 2017 Ivan Sandrof Lifetime Achievement Award from the National Book Critics Circle, John McPhee, who was a finalist for the Pulitzer Prize in General Nonfiction four times (winning once, for *Annals of the Former World*), said in a speech:

> Creative nonfiction is a term that is currently having its day. When I was in college, anyone who put those two words together would have been looked upon as a comedian or a fool. Today, Creative Nonfiction is the name of the college course I teach. Same college. Required to give the course a title, I named it for a quarterly edited and published at the University of Pittsburgh. The title asks an obvious question: What is creative about nonfiction? It takes a whole semester to try to answer that, but here are a few points: The creativity lies in what you choose to write about, how you go about doing it, the arrangement through which you present things, the skill and the touch with which you describe people and succeed in developing them as characters, the rhythms of your prose, the integrity of the composition, the anatomy of the piece (does it get up and walk around on its own?), the extent to which you see and tell the story that exists in your material, and so forth. Creative nonfiction is not making something up but making the most of what you have.

36

"The successful personal essay is always an experiment in form, finds its own best structure, never quite exactly like any other," writes fiction writer and essayist Bill Roorbach, who edited *Contemporary Creative Nonfiction: The Art of Truth.*

37

"To me, the way a story is told is almost more important than the story itself. I think I might be incapable of telling a story in chronological order," says Arundhati Roy, whose debut novel, *The God of Small Things*, was translated into forty-two languages, sold eight million copies, and won the Man Booker Prize. "For me, a story is like the map of a great city or, at the very least, a large building. You can't explore it by driving down the main street or entering from the front door and exiting through the back. You have to live in it, wander through the by-lanes, take blind alleys, and have a smoke with the people who live there, look into the rooms from the outside in. That's the fun of it!"

38

"*Anna Karenina* is more than eight hundred pages long. So why does it feel shorter than many three-hundred-page books?" writes Christina Baker Kline, author of the novel *Orphan Train.* "Tolstoy often ends a chapter in a moment of suspense—a door opens, a provocative question is asked, a contentious group sits down to dinner, characters who've been circling each other finally begin to talk—which propels the reader forward into the next chapter."

39

"As novelists, we should ask or imply a question at the beginning of the story, and then we should delay the answer," writes Lee Child, author of the Jack Reacher novel series.

40

Ursula K. Le Guin was the author of twenty-one novels, eleven volumes of short stories, four collections of essays, twelve children's books, six volumes of poetry, and four works of translation. Before her death in 2018, she won six Nebulas, seven Hugos, and SFWA's Grand Master, along with the PEN/Malamud and many other awards, including the 2014 National Book Foundation Medal for Distinguished Contribution to American Letters. Her work contained whole galaxies, but her take on the writer's craft was simple: "The chief duty of a narrative sentence is to lead to the next sentence—to keep the story going."

41

"*Qua* story, it can only have one merit: that of making the audience want to know what happens next," wrote E. M. Forster, author of *A Room with a View*, *Howards End*, and *A Passage to India*. "And conversely it can only have one fault: that of making the audience not want to know what happens next."

42

"When you repeat a word, phrase, or other element of language or narrative, make sure it is worth repeating," writes Roy Peter Clark, author of a number of books on writing, including *The Art of X-Ray Reading*. "Make sure that each repetition advances the story in some way. Ineffective repetition slows down a narrative. Effective repetition helps it gain traction. Each reappearance of a character or repetition of a phrase can add meaning, suspense, mystery, or energy to a story." Ineffective repetition slows down a narrative. See?

43

"Details are everything," said James Salter, author of *A Sport and a Pastime*, in a lecture on "The Art of Fiction" at the University of Virginia only months before he died at the age of ninety.

44

"I write as I walk because I want to get somewhere and I write as straight as I can, just as I walk as straight as I can, because that is the best way to get there." —H. G. Wells, whose *The War of the Worlds*, published in 1898, was adapted for radio and famously read by Orson Welles forty years later.

45

"You write the story, but a narrator, a persona, tells it," says John Dufresne, author of the novel *Louisiana Power & Light*. "Your choice of narrator is a question of POV. Who is speaking and how? Through whose consciousness is the story understood? This is how both the reader and the writer come to understand the story."

46

"Whoever tells the story controls the world." —Laila Lalami, author of four novels, including *The Other Americans*, a finalist for the 2019 National Book Award in Fiction.

47

"A story is told in the first person when one of its characters relates the story's action and events," writes Janet Burroway, whose *Writing Fiction: A Guide to Narrative Craft* is currently in its tenth edition. "This character may be the protagonist, the *I* telling *my* story, in which case that character is a *central narrator*; or the character may be telling a story about someone else, in which case he or she is a *peripheral narrator*."

48

"There is the option of using second-person narration, which includes the reader as an actor in the fiction," writes novelist Walter Mosley in *Elements of Fiction*. "This device works primarily by using the pronouns associated with *you*."

49

"Third person, in which the author is telling the story, can be subdivided again according to the degree of knowledge the author assumes," adds Burroway, who then goes on to elucidate *omniscient*, *limited omniscient*, and finally *objective*, in which "you restrict your knowledge to the external facts that might be observed by a human witness: to the senses of sight, sound, smell, taste and touch." (Interestingly, she writes in second person to explain the types of third-person narration.)

50

"The house of fiction has many windows, but only two or three doors," writes James Wood, author of *The Broken Estate: Essays on Literature and Belief*. "I can tell a story in the third person or in the first person, and perhaps in the second person singular, or in the first person plural, though successful examples of these latter two are rare, indeed. And that is it. Anything else probably will not much resemble narration; it may be closer to poetry, or prose-poetry."

51

"Most of us who write poems rather than prose have very high formal appetites. Lineation affords quite evident and audible opportunities for making pattern. . . . But it's useful to remember that other sorts of pattern are also there for us to use— rhythms inherent to the language we write in, the source of its muscle and sinew and music, its clarity and its resonance and its power," writes poet Ellen Bryant Voigt, whose collection *Messenger* was a finalist for the Pulitzer Prize.

ACTION ITEM 14

Jot down passages from your favorite craft books. And try writing your own observations about craft. What have you realized about the art of writing along the way?

52

"The first pleasures of meter are physical and intimately connected to bodily experience—to the heartbeat and the pulse, to breathing, walking, running, dancing, working, lovemaking. The meter of a poem can slow us down or speed us up; it can focus our attention; it can hypnotize us," writes poet and critic Edward Hirsch, whose book *How to Read a Poem: And Fall in Love with Poetry* was a national bestseller. "Imagine you have gone down to the ocean in the early morning. You stand in the water and feel the waves breaking against the shore. You watch them coming in and going out. You feel the push and pull, the ebb and flow, of the tide. The waves repeat each other, but no two waves are exactly the same. Think of those waves as the flow of words washing across the lines and sentences of a poem. To measure the rhythmic pattern of those waves is to establish its meter."

53

"Writing for me is no different than playing basketball, it's my body moving among and pushing up against and being moved by other bodies of language and the energy of language," says poet Natalie Diaz, the author of *Postcolonial Love Poem* and a former professional basketball player.

54

"In music, a certain beat is set up and you find yourself patting your foot. These are the same rituals in poetry. That's the reason for the devices in poetry—rhyme and rhythm. They set up a oneness. If anyone is patting their feet at the same time, a ritual is being played out," said Etheridge Knight, whose debut volume, *Poems from Prison*, was published in 1968. "Basically, I see the poet as singing in a sense that his sounds are put together in harmony or in a structure which differs from just plain talking. I see poets basically as singers, as preachers, as prophets."

55

"Good writing has a musical quality to it, a mathematical quality, a balance and a rhythm," Laura Hillenbrand, the author of the bestseller *Seabiscuit*, says. "You can feel that much better when it's read aloud."

56

"A novel, like all written things, is a piece of music, the language demanding you make a sound as you read it. Writing one, then, is like remembering a song you've never heard before." That is the third entry in "100 Things About Writing a Novel" by Alexander Chee, from *How to Write an Autobiographical Novel*.

57

Eudora Welty on ending a story: "It's really part of plotting to know the exact moment you're through. I go by my ear, and this may trick me. When I read, I hear what's on the page. I don't know whose voice it is, but some voice is reading to me, and when I write my own stories, I hear it too. I have a visual mind, and I see everything I write, but I have to hear the words when they're put down."

58

A. Van Jordan, whose poetry collections include *Rise*, *M-A-C-N-O-L-I-A*, *Quantum Lyrics*, and *The Cineaste*: "The image is what comes to mind first. Trying to correlate that image with an emotion is the rest of the process."

59

"The poet's mind is in fact a receptacle for seizing and storing up numberless feelings, phrases, images, which remain there until all the particles which can unite to form a new compound are present together," wrote T. S. Eliot in "Tradition and the Individual Talent," which was originally published in 1919 in *The Egoist* and collected one year later in the poet's first book of criticism, *The Sacred Wood*.

60

"Poetry is the spontaneous overflow of powerful feelings: it takes its origin from emotion recollected in tranquility," said William Wordsworth, who, with the help of Samuel Taylor Coleridge, launched the Romantic Age in English literature, more than a century before Eliot.

61

"If emotion is strong enough, the words are unambiguous," Marianne Moore, whose *Collected Poems* won both a Pulitzer Prize and a National Book Award, told Donald Hall in 1961.

62

Denise Levertov, who with Muriel Rukeyser and several other poets established Writers and Artists Protest Against the War in Vietnam in the 1960s, said this about organic form in poetry: "A manifestation of form sense is the sense the poet's ear has of some rhythmic norm peculiar to a particular poem, from which the individual lines depart and to which they return. . . . This sense of the beat or pulse underlying the whole I think of as the horizon note of the poem. It interacts with the nuances or forces of feeling which determine emphasis on one word or another, and decides to great extent what belongs to a given line. It relates the needs of that feeling-force which dominates the cadence to the needs of the surrounding parts and so to the whole. . . . Form is never more than a *revelation* of content."

63

"In March 1876, forty-seven years before Denise Levertov was born, French novelist Gustave Flaubert wrote this in a letter to fellow author George Sand: "The form and the matter are two subtleties, two entities, neither of which can exist without the other."

64

"One of the purposes of counterpoint is to create tension," writes Stephen Dobyns, author of more than a dozen volumes of poetry. "When a line is broken at a piece of punctuation or a natural pause, that break creates a rest. When a line is broken between pauses or pieces of punctuation, that creates tension."

65

"Poetry is the voice of what can't be spoken, the mode of truth-telling when meaning needs to rise above or skim below everyday language in shapes not discernible by the ordinary mind. It trumps the rhetoric of politicians," says U.S. poet laureate Joy Harjo, a member of the Muscogee Creek Nation. "Poetry is prophetic by nature and not bound by time."

66

"The word 'stanza' in Italian means room," former U.S. poet laureate Mark Strand and poet Eavan Boland write. "In a simple, practical way, the stanza in poetry has that figurative purpose. It is as self-contained as any chamber or room. And yet to be in it is to have the consciousness at all times that it also leads somewhere."

67

"You have to have achieved something inside. You can't make a poem out of something that's not there. And it won't be there unless you want it to be there," said Jack Gilbert, whose *Collected Poems* was published in 2012, the same year he died.

68

In a lecture titled "The Lives of the Poems" that he delivered in Spokane in January 2014 (and again in New York in May 2014 and again in Tucson that September, each time using different poems to illustrate his points and thereby fundamentally changing the nature of the lecture), poet, translator, and Wave Books editor Joshua Beckman said: "and I want for a moment you to think of the poem as a temporary accumulation of resonances— and the poem in time the way music is in time—basically there when it is happening and not when it is not—not like a painting, which feels as if it's making the same damn face whether the Louvre is open or closed—but like music—and the text is a score and the poem is that thing that happens when you animate it—"

69

"'How it feels to be oneself' has a great deal to do with the experience of time," writes poet Mark Doty, author of *What Is the Grass: Walt Whitman in My Life*. "It's oddly difficult to describe what subjective time feels like. The clock on the wall simply ticks, persisting in its steady progression, while those in the body and psyche call for a great variety of verbs to describe less readily chartable motions. The time of interiority pools, constricts, tumbles, and speeds. We live in a felt narrative progression, through which experience is transformed into memory. And memory edits its records of the past like a brilliant *auteur*—cutting, juxtaposing, creating a pace determined by the direction and emotion of a story."

70

"Experience itself cannot be seen as a point in time, a fact," wrote Muriel Rukeyser, who developed new forms of documentary poetics in long poems such as *The Book of the Dead*, about the Hawks Nest Tunnel disaster in 1931 in Gauley Bridge, West Virginia. "The experience with which we deal, in speaking of art and human growth, is not only the event, but the event *and the entire past of the individual*. There is a series in any event, and the definition of the event is the last unit of the series. You read the poem: the poem you now have, the poem that exists in your imagination, is the poem and all the past to which you refer it."

71

"It is common for people to regret or even renounce their earlier lives," writes poet Christian Wiman, author of *My Bright Abyss: Meditation of a Modern Believer*. "It is common for poets to use language like 'I had to forget everything I ever learned to make way for new work' or 'You must learn all the rules so that you can break them.' This is, paradoxically, cliched thinking, a symptom of our fragmented existences rather than a useful ingenuousness or regenerative naïveté. Art—including our own, perhaps especially our own—should help us integrate existence rather than mark it off."

72

"Writing is always secondary," writes poet Nikki Giovanni, who was nominated for a Grammy Award for her poetry album, *The Nikki Giovanni Poetry Collection*. "And you cannot write in a vacuum. And so the writing is always the second thing that happens. First you conceptualize it. Or you experience it. But experience is no excuse. I mean nothing is worse than somebody saying, well this is what actually happened. Nobody cares what actually happened. What you're trying to get the student to bring out is what does this mean? What is the larger context here? And the writing is always going to be secondary to the life. And that's what's hard to get over because people think that writing is the product. But it's not. It's the by-product. The product is the life."

73

"For some poets, poetry derives from a place," wrote Donald Hall, whose last book was *A Carnival of Losses: Notes Nearing Ninety*. "Poem after poem reaches back and touches this place, and rehearses experiences connected with the place: Wordsworth's 'Nature'; the Welsh farms of Dylan Thomas; T. S. Eliot's St. Louis and Dry Salvages; Wallace Stevens's Florida; Walt Whitman and Paumanok; architectural Italy for Ezra Pound; Gloucester for Charles Olson. . . . But I am not thinking only of poetry which is geographic or descriptive. I am thinking of places which to the poets embody or recall a spiritual state." After moving from Michigan to his family's farmhouse at Eagle Pond Farm in Wilmot, New Hampshire, in 1975, Hall also wrote, "For me, it was coming home, and it was coming home to the place of language."

74

"I don't think I have much of an imagination at all, at least not in the traditional sense of making stuff up or feeling compelled by things that aren't there," writes Maggie Nelson. "In my mind, I don't hear characters talking; I see book shapes; I hear tonal juxtapositions; I hear music shepherded around the page; I imagine what kind of sentence or shape could or should house a particular idea."

75

"Something fascinating about sentences," writes Jane Alison in *Meander, Spiral, Explode: Design and Pattern in Narrative*, "is that when I'm in the thrall of one, I'm held in its temporal and spatial orbit; it begins and ends when it must, holding and directing me until ready to let me go. I move slowly through tricky syntax; luxurious language makes me linger; or I warily await a final word that will snap the whole into sense."

76

"When I'm writing, I nearly always begin with setting; characters come later, and I wouldn't be able to imagine them if I didn't have a sense of where they lived, or in some cases, how far from home they had traveled," says Karen Russell, whose debut story collection was *St. Lucy's Home for Girls Raised by Wolves*. "I was just on a wonderful panel with Luis Alberto Urrea and Emily Fridlund and we discussed the fictional and real landscapes to which we keep returning: swamps, forests, borders. Luis said, 'There's place, the physical location. And then there are the stories you tell about that place.' I'm so interested in how the sight lines, soundscapes, flora and fauna of our childhoods shape us—how those earliest encounters with the land become part of our private, interior vocabularies of dream and thought. And I love novels and stories where geography shapes plot and gives rise to character. I think the question 'What's possible or impossible for this human personality in this landscape?' is a good starting place for fiction."

77

"Good fiction always begins with story and progresses to theme; it almost never begins with theme and progresses to story," writes Stephen King, whose first novel, *Carrie*, was published in 1974, paving the way for over fifty subsequent books of horror, supernatural fiction, and suspense.

78

"Place is not just what your feet are crossing to get to somewhere," writes Dorothy Allison, author of the novel *Bastard Out of Carolina*. "Place is feeling, and feeling is something a character expresses."

79

"The more emotionally charged a situation, the more emotional restraint one must use in writing, and then the result will be emotionally powerful. There is no need for laying it on thick," Russian playwright and short story master Anton Chekhov wrote in a letter to fellow author Lydia Avilova in Moscow on March 1, 1893.

80

"You want to write a sentence as clean as a bone," said James Baldwin. He also said, "Write. Find a way to keep alive and write."

81

"If it was really sudden, you wouldn't have needed to write the word 'sudden.'" —poet Jericho Brown, author of *The Tradition*, overheard by fellow poet Julian Randall, at the Watering Hole in Columbia, South Carolina.

82

"Opacity is fear," wrote the poet Max Ritvo to his teacher, Sarah Ruhl, in February 2013, while undergoing treatment for the cancer he fought for over three more years, until his death on August 23, 2016. He was twenty-five years old.

83

"There is a tradition of poetry that's about the limitations of language and how there is something else there that is trying to express itself beyond what is on the page," says poet Cathy Park Hong, author of *Minor Feelings: An Asian American Reckoning*. "The way the poem expresses the incommunicable is through the music."

84

"Plots are interesting, characters are fascinating, scenery can be totally enveloping, but the real art is the deep structure, the way that information is revealed and withheld so that the reader gets to find out things appropriately, or in a time frame that makes it an intimate experience," said Toni Morrison.

85

"The autobiographical 'I' has always been controversial. By claiming an 'I' as fully autobiographical, the poet gives up a landscape of invention and imagination," says Tina Chang, poet laureate of Brooklyn, New York. "I have freedom to work with material when I release the autobiographical 'I.'"

86

"A great danger, or at least a great temptation, for many writers is to become too autobiographical in their approach to their fiction. A little autobiography and a lot of imagination are best," said Raymond Carver in 1983, two years after the publication of his story collection *What We Talk About When We Talk About Love.*

87

"Writers are natural murderers," writes Lynn Freed, author of *The Last Laugh.* "Their murderousness is a form of sociopathy, fueled by resentment, scorn, glee, and deep affection. Before they can even begin writing, they must kill off parents, siblings, lovers, mentors, friends—anyone, in short, whose opinion might matter. If these people are left alive and allowed to take up residence in the front row of the audience, the writer will never be able to get the fiction right. More than this, she will never want to get it right. What she must do, if the fiction is to take breath, is to defictionalise the life, to disentangle it from the myths and fictions that we all create in order to control what we cannot alter. And then to work down, down, down, to the morally anaerobic heart of the matter within."

88

"If you have in one scene a kid getting his hand cut off," says George Saunders, author of *Lincoln in the Bardo*, "I think in some funny way you're more willing to accept a sentimental scene. I don't know if you're more willing to accept it, but maybe the juxtaposition of those two things is more interesting. As a writer I'm really aware of my defects and how much I have to find other things to substitute, so humor helps. It's got its own inherent energy so if you can sustain funniness you almost always have to sustain something else. Pure funny you see sometimes in humor columnists who are just funny, but in fiction, to keep funny going you almost always dredge something else up."

89

"What isn't said is as important as what is said," writes Colson Whitehead, author of *The Underground Railroad.*

90

In *The Hidden Machinery: Essays on Writing*, Margot Livesey offers six rules governing romances in fiction:

1. The lovers are often unlikely in some obvious way.
2. They meet early and are then separated—either physically or emotionally—for most of the narrative.
3. There must be significant obstacles—dragons or demons—to be overcome.
4. Changes of setting, even from drawing room to street, are vital for revealing the characters and moving the narrative forward.
5. Many minor characters will assist the lovers in their journey.
6. A subplot, or two, is required to keep the lovers apart, to allow time to pass, to act as a foil to the main plot and to entertain the reader.

91

In a letter to French novelist and playwright Honoré de Balzac dated October 30, 1840, Marie-Henri Beyle, better known by his pen name, Stendhal, wrote, "I see but one rule: to be clear. If I am not clear, all my world crumbles to nothing."

92

"There are no rules," writes Colum McCann, author of *Let the Great World Spin*. "Or if there are any rules, they are only there to be broken. Embrace these contradictions. You must be prepared to hold two or more opposing ideas in the palms of your hands at the exact same time."

93

"First, entertain," said novelist Tom Wolfe, the father of New Journalism, presumably wearing his signature white suit, in 2004.

94

"The first draft of anything is shit," said Nobel laureate Ernest Hemingway.

95

"I used to consider editing something you did once a story was completed," writes Benjamin Percy, author of *Thrill Me: Essays on Fiction*. "I now begin each day by reading what I have already written. If it's a short story, I mean from the first line forward. If it's a novel, I mean from the start of the chapter I'm working on. I sometimes spend hours editing before I shift to an imaginative mode and begin to punch out new material. So I'm essentially in a constant state of revision, and by the time I finish the story, I might have edited it two dozen times, turning it over and over in my hands, sanding it until it's free of slivers."

96

"The fastest way to revise a piece of work is to send it, late at night, to someone whose opinion you fear. Then rewrite it, praying you'll finish in time to send a new version by morning," writes Sarah Manguso in *300 Arguments*.

97

"Finally, put it aside. Put it out of your head at least a week. You want it to set up like jello. And when you pick it back up, ask yourself, What haven't I said? How might someone else involved have seen it differently?" writes Mary Karr, author of the best-selling memoirs *The Liars' Club*, *Cherry*, and *Lit*, in *The Art of Memoir*.

98

"If the writer understands that stories are first and foremost stories, and that the best stories set off a vivid and continuous dream, he can hardly help becoming interested in technique, since it is mainly bad technique that breaks the continuousness and checks the growth of the fictional dream. He quickly discovers that when he unfairly manipulates his fiction—pushing the characters around by making them do things they wouldn't do if they were free of him; or laying on the symbolism (so that the strength of the fiction is diminished, too much of its energy going into mere intellect); or breaking in on the action to preach . . . ; or pumping up his style so that it becomes more visible than even the most interesting of his characters—the writer, by these clumsy moves, impairs his fiction. To notice such faults is to begin to correct them," wrote John Gardner in *On Becoming a Novelist*.

99

"The moment that you feel that, just possibly, you're walking down the street naked, exposing too much of your heart and your mind and what exists on the inside, showing too much of yourself. That's the moment you may be starting to get it right," said author Neil Gaiman in his commencement address at Philadelphia's University of the Arts in 2012. It was later renamed his "Make Good Art" speech.

100

"To become great at anything," writes Eric Gorges, host of the PBS series *A Craftsman's Legacy*, "you have to persist past the point where you even know what you're doing. It's stepping onto a bridge that you haven't built yet."

YIYUN LI RECOMMENDS

Five Books to Remind You Why You're a Writer

MOBY-DICK; OR, THE WHALE by Herman Melville
I love this book and read it once a year. In almost every chapter I can discover and rediscover something—a phrase, a sentence, a passage, a thought—that reminds me that much of my own writing is also preparing me to reread this novel.

A REGION NOT HOME: REFLECTIONS FROM EXILE by James Alan McPherson
Essays in this book remind me that a hero can be as much of a cliché as a villain, and a mind that interrogates itself with the same intensity as it interrogates an unfriendly word is a truly free mind.

SURPRISED BY JOY: THE SHAPE OF MY EARLY LIFE by C. S. Lewis
A book that reminds me that writing, in the end, is about real joy.

THE COLLECTED STORIES by William Trevor
These stories, as Trevor said in an interview, were written "out of bafflement." The same bafflement reminds me that the world is always unknown and there are always stories for me to write.

THE COMPLETE ESSAYS by Michel de Montaigne
This is another book to which I keep returning, to have a conversation with a mind that is long gone.

YIYUN LI *is the author of five works of fiction*—Where Reasons End, Kinder Than Solitude, A Thousand Years of Good Prayers, The Vagrants, *and* Gold Boy, Emerald Girl—*and the memoir* Dear Friend, From My Life I Write to You in Your Life. *A native of Beijing and a graduate of the Iowa Writers' Workshop, she is the recipient of many awards, including a PEN/Hemingway Award and a MacArthur Foundation fellowship, and was named by the* New Yorker *as one of the "20 Under 40" fiction writers to watch. She teaches at Princeton University.*

FIVE

Finding Community

Whether it's found in crowded rooms or e-mail folders, Twitter threads or Facebook group chats, community is as deeply necessary to a writer as reading. It is a source of assistance, understanding, and camaraderie. It is an exchange of ideas, a wellspring of inspiration, and sometimes, quite literally, a lifeline. But community is also give-and-take; it's collaborative, mutual, organic. This idea of *community*—and the notion of being a *good literary citizen* within that community—is tossed around so often that we can lose track of exactly what we mean when we use those words. So let's take a moment.

For most of us, two opposing forces are exerting pressure within our minds as writers. Not quite seismic in strength, they nevertheless result in a paradox that each of us must resolve in our own way. We can all agree that in order to write, one must work, at least the majority of the time, in relative solitude. Editing, revising, and publishing are collaborative, no doubt, and even some kinds of writing (such as the exquisite corpse, in which a poem or story is collectively assembled) are accomplished with others, but for the most part it's you, and you alone, using the tools of your trade: your intellect and your emotions, your eyes and your fingers. You might be writing by candlelight in a remote cabin somewhere in the Adirondacks, or behind the closed door of your pantry turned office in the middle of the night, or on the couch while the baby takes her afternoon nap. Even if you're writing in a crowded Starbucks, finishing the fourth tercet of your villanelle while the barista yells out the name of the person whose Triple Venti Half Sweet Non-Fat Caramel Macchiato is ready, you're still acquiescing to the seclusion your writing requires, albeit in a very modern setting: At its core, this is between you and the words on the page or the screen, no one else, at least in the first stages of drafting a piece of writing. And of course there is something very, very exciting about that: You are the author of that world.

Writing is a solitary act, but as writers, as creative people, we also crave feedback, we want company (as long as it comes at the right time), we want validation, and we want to feel like we're not alone in our compulsions. It is our very solitude that fuels our desire for solidarity, for community. At some point in your life, you first felt the excitement—mixed with the relief—of realizing that you were talking to someone who understands a little something about your life as a writer, with all of its demands, routines, superstitions, eccentricities, confusions, and wonders. Isn't that a tremendous feeling? Maybe not as great as the realization or confirmation that you've just written a truly great poem, or the thrill of typing the final period of your novel, but still worth chasing.

In this chapter we will discuss this need for exchange with open-minded creative people and how you can find it by exploring a number of traditional and nontraditional avenues, but first, it's helpful to attempt a deeper understanding of why community is important to us.

One could say that by virtue of being a writer you are automatically a member of the community of writers in this country. But this loose affiliation, awesome in a Six Degrees of Kevin Bacon sort of way, is pretty limited. If you've ever felt like a stranger walking the aisles of a huge bookfair—like the annual one organized by the Association of Writers & Writing Programs, held in a different city each year and typically attended by more than ten thousand people—you know that it can be exciting, but perhaps not as personally rewarding as we need it to be. (Are we the only ones who feel a little anxious walking into a massive crowd of people who comprise our "community" at its most general level?) Still, it is important to recognize our community on that scale for two reasons. It affirms our commitment to writing *(See, I'm not crazy, look at all these other fools blindly pursuing a dream that rarely pays dividends!)* and it shows us the size and strength of the infrastructure that exists to support writers: how many resources, activities, and energies are devoted to writing and the various industries that have grown up to celebrate, support, and capitalize on it.

Just by virtue of being a published author one can join the Authors Guild, "a professional organization dedicated to supporting and protecting the writing life for all working and aspiring authors." There is certainly a degree of validation—perhaps a sense that you've "arrived," not to mention benefits such as contract reviews and legal advice—that comes from being a card-carrying member of such an organization; the Authors Guild represents community in a broad sense of the term. As does a subscription to a trade magazine or literary journal. It feels like you're participating in—and caring about and supporting—a shared project of literary expression. It would be difficult to overestimate the power and importance of such a feeling. If you're surrounded by family members who don't read books for personal enjoyment, or who don't value "clarity of thought and feeling," as Tracy Kidder and Richard Todd put it, you know how important it is to get that magazine in the mail every two months, or to visit the website that's devoted to the work of writers just like you, who hold it as one of life's principal values.

But these days, when so much of our "social activity" is accomplished by tapping a heart or a thumbs-up icon (which is not to say that plenty of writers aren't able to cultivate meaningful followings on social media, where real expressions of emotion, reasoned opinions, and constructive criticism are possible, if not common), writers are more hungry than ever for in-person interactions and a sense of community that is marked by an actual conversation or collaboration and is punctuated by a handshake or even—come on, let's admit it, we all need one once in a while—a hug.

Whether it's a huge industry event or a more intimate gathering of friendly writers, community is a feeling that you are among your people. Maybe it's a group of literary essayists who grew up in the same relatively underserved area of Oklahoma talking about the geography of memory, or it's fiction writers in Alaska who want to address the issue of climate change through their work, or it's essayists who gather to discuss markets for their writing, or poets who meet to talk about prison writing and the language of incarceration. Or it's an open mic held in the back room of a hotel bar every other Tuesday evening. Or a writing group that shares work online every week and meets in person every month for a submission party. From community you can get a sense of belonging, but you can also clarify your sense of self. You can get motivation from community, accountability, support. You can feel recognized, and you can feel a part of something larger than yourself.

Community is also an important part of the creative process because it stimulates us and our thinking, sometimes pushing us further and deeper into our projects. In his book *Where Good Ideas Come From: The Natural History of Innovation*, Steven Johnson explains how everything that happens in your brain is, technically speaking, a network, and that good ideas have signature patterns in the networks that make them. "To make your mind more innovative, you have to place it inside environments that share that same network signature: networks of ideas or people that mimic the neural networks of a mind exploring the boundaries of the adjacent possible. Certain environments enhance the brain's natural capacity to make new links of association."

ACTION ITEM 15

Jot down some notes about what you, as a writer, crave from others when you're alone. Do you wish you had someone to talk to about a plan for a writing project? Do you wish you had someone who could offer a critique? Someone to hold you accountable to your writing goals? Or maybe someone to discuss new markets for your work? If you have a good idea what you're looking for, you're more likely to find it.

We would argue that a healthy, stimulating community is the perfect example of an environment that promotes creative thinking. Like an organic, flesh-and-blood version of the commonplace book, which we discussed in chapter 2, a community allows for connections among writers and their ideas and observations. To say nothing of the emotional support, educational exploration, and camaraderie that community can provide.

For some writers, that feeling of validation, of support and community, can fill a void created by generations of marginalization, by institutional racism and the failure of social, political, and literary institutions to acknowledge and extend their missions and services to underserved communities. In recent decades there have been a number of literary organizations that have been formed with the express goal or mission of providing support and a sense of community for specific, historically underrepresented groups of writers such as African American poets (Cave Canem), Asian American writers (Kundiman and the Asian American Writers' Workshop), Latinx writers (CantoMundo), Arab American writers (Radius of Arab American Writers, or RAWI), queer writers (Lambda Literary Foundation), and disabled writers (Zoeglossia). These organizations and many more like them—see the list of 15 National Organizations Serving Writers and Writing at the back of this book—host readings and organize retreats, sponsor literary prizes, maintain websites that offer valuable information, and/or offer other literary activities that can be life-changing.

Poet and attorney Reginald Dwayne Betts saw the retreat sponsored by Cave Canem, a nonprofit organization founded in 1996 "to remedy the under-representation and isolation of African American poets in the literary landscape," as a kind of home. "Cave Canem opened up the space to think about who I was, and for me that meant it gave me permission to chase the thing that might make me weep. And what is writing, if not this?" he writes. The retreats organized by Kundiman, a nonprofit founded in 2004 to provide "a safe yet rigorous space where Asian American poets can explore, through art, the unique challenges that face the new and ever changing diaspora," fostered a similar feeling of belonging in Duy Doan, winner of the Yale Series of Younger Poets prize for *We Play a Game*. "I would never be able to overemphasize the positive impact that the Kundiman retreats have had on me—writing, musing, connecting with other Asian–Pacific Islander American writers, being taken in by a richly talented and generous community," he writes.

The point is, community means different things to different people, but for everyone it's a vital source of some key ingredients of the writing life. It's easy enough to say that writing is all about placing yourself in a chair and grinding it out, you and the words, applying pressure to the rock until diamonds appear in the dust. Solitary seduction, suffering, and success. And it *is* that—until it isn't. Then there is a need to share, commiserate, question, discover, inspire, and be inspired with others. When you find the right people, it's a beautiful, necessary miracle: Your world opens up, the universe expands, and guess what? You're no longer alone.

Let's take a quick look at a few of the different kinds of traditional venues where writers can find, form, and develop community. We'll be exploring academic communities in the next chapter, so for now let's consider literary festivals, writers conferences, trade shows, writers retreats, writing groups, and readings and reading series. Not all writers have the means or ability to attend all these events, but we hope you can, among these many options, find a few that make sense for you.

Literary Festivals

It's tricky to attempt a definition of a literary festival without considerable overlap with the definition of a writers conference. They are often used interchangeably, but in general a literary festival is a one- or two-day event that is open to the public, offering readings and panel discussions and sometimes a bookfair with booths featuring the wares of local presses, literary magazines, nonprofit organizations, and writing groups. Often organized in conjunction with the city or town in which they are held, literary festivals are celebrations of literary culture on a local level.

Some of the most popular ones include the Brooklyn Book Festival, New York City's largest free literary festival, launched in 2006 and attended by approximately 40,000 people; the Library of Congress National Book Festival, which was launched in 2001 by then First Lady Laura Bush and then Librarian

ACTION ITEM 16

Search the Conferences and Residencies database at pw.org for information about more than a hundred writers conferences and festivals held in just about every state in the country. Save those that look most appealing to your My P&W page for easy reference.

of Congress James H. Billington and held in the nation's capital each summer; the Miami Book Fair, founded by Miami Dade College and community partners in 1984, featuring a street fair with hundreds of publishers and booksellers exhibiting and selling books; and the Los Angeles Times Festival of Books, founded in 1996 and attended by 150,000 people annually.

Typically attended by readers as well as writers, literary festivals are an inspiring mix of the literary set and the general public, a celebration of books and the people who write them. Perhaps the best part? They're usually free.

TWENTY-FIVE OF THE BEST BOOK FESTIVALS IN THE UNITED STATES

AJC DECATUR BOOK FESTIVAL in Georgia (www.decaturbookfestival.com)

ALABAMA BOOK FESTIVAL in Montgomery (www.alabamabookfestival.org)

BALTIMORE BOOK FESTIVAL (brilliantbaltimore.com/baltimore-book-festival)

BELIEVER FESTIVAL in Las Vegas (believerfestival.org)

BOSTON BOOK FESTIVAL (www.bostonbookfest.org)

BRATTLEBORO LITERARY FESTIVAL in Vermont (brattleboroliteraryfestival.org)

BROOKLYN BOOK FESTIVAL (www.brooklynbookfestival.org)

DODGE POETRY FESTIVAL in Newark, New Jersey (www.dodgepoetry.org)

FALL FOR THE BOOK in Fairfax, Virginia (fallforthebook.org)

FORT COLLINS BOOK FESTIVAL in Colorado (www.focobookfest.org)

IOWA CITY BOOK FESTIVAL (www.iowacitybookfestival.org)

LITQUAKE in San Francisco (www.litquake.org)

LOS ANGELES TIMES FESTIVAL OF BOOKS (events.latimes.com/festivalofbooks)

MIAMI BOOK FAIR INTERNATIONAL (www.miamibookfair.com)

NATIONAL BOOK FESTIVAL in Washington, D.C. (www.loc.gov/bookfest)

PORTLAND BOOK FESTIVAL in Oregon (literary-arts.org/what-we-do/pdxbookfest)

SAN ANTONIO BOOK FESTIVAL (festival.saplf.org)

SAVANNAH BOOK FESTIVAL (www.savannahbookfestival.org)

SIX BRIDGES BOOK FESTIVAL in Little Rock, Arkansas (cals.org/six-bridges book-festival)

TEXAS BOOK FESTIVAL in Austin (www.texasbookfestival.org)

TUCSON FESTIVAL OF BOOKS (tucsonfestivalofbooks.org)

TWIN CITIES BOOK FESTIVAL (twincitiesbookfestival.com)

VIRGINIA FESTIVAL OF THE BOOK in Charlottesville (www.vabook.org)

WEST VIRGINIA BOOK FESTIVAL in Charleston (wvbookfestival.org)

WISCONSIN BOOK FESTIVAL in Madison (www.wisconsinbookfestival.org)

Writers Conferences

Just like a literary festival, a writers conference often features readings and panel discussions, but typically in a more focused format and intended for writers who want to learn from successful authors about elements of craft and the art of writing. Conferences also frequently offer lectures, craft classes, and workshops with established writers as well as meetings with agents and editors and sessions devoted to specific topics of importance to writers. Most conferences cost money to attend, and registration fees vary widely. Founded in 1926, the annual Bread Loaf Writers' Conference in Ripton, Vermont, holds intensive workshops for emerging poets and prose writers with faculty who also give lectures and craft talks. To apply, writers must submit a manuscript with a $20 application fee, and those who are accepted pay tuition (in 2019 the fee was $3,525, which included lodging and meals), though financial aid is available. Others, like the Atlanta Writers Conference, which provides sessions with agents and editors and is held annually at the Westin Atlanta Airport Hotel, offer registration on a first-come, first-served basis, and writers can choose from an à la carte menu of sessions, each of which cost between $50 and $170. Some conferences are rather exclusive, like Bread Loaf, while others, like the annual conference and bookfair organized by the Association of Writers & Writing Programs (AWP) and held in a different host city each year (and sponsored by a university writing program in that city), are more like industry gatherings, where seemingly everyone (but don't fall for that: it's *not* everyone) who has a connection to literature, including writers, book editors, magazine editors, literary agents, publicists, and teachers, is in attendance.

Writers conferences are usually held over multiple days, with discounted rates sometimes offered at designated hotels, and writers are given frequent opportunities for social activities—communal meals, drinks at the bar, off-site readings at local establishments, and even organized tours of the city's attractions. Accessibility information for writers with disabilities should be easy to find on the event website, but some sponsoring organizations have a ways to go with making this information readily available, so if you are a writer with a disability, contact the conference organizer to make sure the event is accessible and that they will work with anyone who requires assistance.

FOURTEEN CONFERENCES AND RETREATS FOR UNDERREPRESENTED VOICES

There are more conferences and workshops devoted to poets and writers from historically underrepresented communities today than ever before. From the now-historic Macondo Writers Workshop, founded in 1995 by writer Sandra Cisneros, to newer ventures such as the Pink Door Writing Retreat, these programs offer members of specific communities the opportunity to collaborate, celebrate, network, and study with accomplished and supportive literary mentors. Most of these conferences charge tuition, though many offer financial aid. Visit the websites for more information, including dates, registration details, and associated costs.

BINDERCON: Biannual two-day professional development conference for women and gender-nonconforming poets and writers at the University of California in Los Angeles in April and Cooper Union in New York City in October. www.bindercon.com

CANTOMUNDO RETREAT: Three-day retreat for Latinx poets at the University of Arizona Poetry Center in Tucson in June.
www.cantomundo.org

CAVE CANEM RETREAT: Weeklong retreat for African American poets at the University of Pittsburgh in Greensburg, Pennsylvania, in June.
www.cavecanempoets.org/retreat

HURSTON/WRIGHT FOUNDATION SUMMER WRITERS WEEK: Weeklong guided retreat for black fiction and nonfiction writers in Washington, D.C. in August.
www.hurstonwright.org/writers-week

JACK JONES RETREAT: Two-week retreat for emerging women poets, fiction writers, and nonfiction writers of color in autumn at the Immaculate Heart of Mary Retreat Center in Santa Fe, New Mexico.
www.jackjonesliteraryarts.com/the-retreat

KIMBILIO FICTION RETREAT: Weeklong retreat for African American fiction writers at Southern Methodist University in Taos, New Mexico, in July.
www.kimbiliofiction.com

KUNDIMAN RETREAT: Five-day retreat for Asian American poets and writers at Fordham University in New York City in June.
www.kundiman.org/retreat

LAMBDA LITERARY WRITERS RETREAT FOR EMERGING LGBTQ VOICES: Weeklong workshop for LGBTQ poets and writers at Otis College of Art and Design in Los Angeles in August.
www.lambdaliterary.org/writers-retreat

MACONDO WRITERS WORKSHOP: Four-day workshop for poets and writers belonging to any historically marginalized group in San Antonio in July.
www.macondowriters.com

PINK DOOR WRITING RETREAT: Five-day retreat for women and gender-nonconforming poets and writers of color in Rochester, New York, in July.
www.pinkdoorretreat.com

THE RAWI CONFERENCE: Three-day conference featuring readings, panels, workshops, and roundtables every other year that emphasizes Arab American voices and inclusivity.
www.arabamericanwriters.org

RETURNING THE GIFT INDIGENOUS STORYTELLING AND LITERARY FESTIVAL: Four-day conference for indigenous poets and writers, as well as academics, tribal dignitaries, community members, and youth, at the University of Oklahoma in Norman in July.
www.rtglitfest.com

SULA'S ROOM RESIDENCY: Weekend-long funded residency for New York–based women poets and writers of color in Hudson, New York, in November and December.
www.sulasroom.org

VOICES OF OUR NATION ARTS FOUNDATION (VONA) VOICES WORKSHOP: Weeklong workshop for poets and writers of color at the University of Pennsylvania in Philadelphia in June.
www.vonacommunity.org

Trade Shows

Typically huge events where big business and writers intermingle, trade shows are where industry insiders gather to discover new books and authors as well as learn about advances in technology, publishing trends, and new distribution channels. Unlike conferences and bookfairs or festivals, the big trade shows are not gatherings for writers (unless they've been invited by their publishers to attend). It's not the kind of event where writers should just show up and start pitching their work to agents on the show floor. The publishing professionals who attend these events are typically scheduled down to the minute with meetings, and the last thing they want to do is listen to a stranger pitch a book. There are events where that is acceptable and even encouraged, but the typical trade show is not one of them.

The biggest trade show of them all, attracting more than a quarter million people from all over the world, is the Frankfurt Book Fair, or Frankfurter Buchmesse, held over five days in mid-October. At the 2018 event, Juergen Boos, the fair's director, said, "As the most international event of its kind, Frankfurter Buchmesse is the ideal place to discuss topics affecting the global community." It is also considered the most important bookfair for international rights deals—U.S. publishers pick up the rights to books published in other countries; foreign publishers make deals for rights to books published in the U.S.—so big publishers spend a lot of resources to launch books in Frankfurt in order to negotiate these international sales. Also in attendance are agents, technology companies, booksellers, librarians, film producers, translators—anyone and just about everyone with a horse in the race.

The biggest trade show in the United States is BookExpo America, or BEA as it is known to people in the business. Held every May in a large city, typically New York, although it has been held in Los Angeles, Chicago, and Washington, D.C., as well, BEA attracts over eight thousand booksellers, agents, editors, publishers, and writers—much the same kind of crowd as the one in Frankfurt but with less of an emphasis on foreign rights deals. One of the most exciting aspects of BEA is the Editors' Buzz Panels, for which a selection of forthcoming titles in three categories (adult fiction, young adult, and middle grade) are chosen by a committee of booksellers, librarians, and other professionals. These highly anticipated books are expected to be especially resonant with readers. The books are presented and discussed in front of a big crowd of publishing's finest, including many media representatives and book critics, so you can imagine how influential an Editors' Buzz selection can be. Some recent titles on the adult Buzz panel include *We Are Not Ourselves* by Matthew Thomas, *Station Eleven* by Emily St. John Mandel, *Room* by Emma Donoghue, *The Art of Fielding* by Chad Harbach, and *Brain on Fire* by Susannah Cahalan. If you recognize these titles, you're not alone. They were all huge books, due in no small part to the attention they were paid at BEA.

Other trade shows include the London Book Fair, the Guadalajara International Book Fair, and the Beijing International Book Fair. While only relatively few writers get to attend these events, they nevertheless offer a powerful sense of community for people involved in the many connected sectors of the publishing industry.

Writers Retreats

Writers retreats, or writers colonies or residencies, may seem like a funny topic to explore in a chapter about community, since the most obvious appeal of retreats is time alone, dedicated to your project, but they're not just about time to work. As Alexander Chee writes, "They are also full of smart, talented people, and your conversations are often momentous." Countless lifelong friendships and meaningful connections have been made at writers retreats, and the shared experience often results in its own sense of community.

But before we get into the hundreds of writers retreats, or writers residencies, available in just about every state in the country, let's acknowledge that one need not necessarily spend the money and energy often required to attend a traditional writers retreat. As we discussed in chapter 1, it's crucial to have an everyday writing routine and a writing space that is yours and yours alone. It's where you go to work. It's the kitchen table where you sit for the two hours you steal from the morning, or the corner table at the diner where you spend the last thirty minutes of your long day, to get the real work of being a writer done. But sometimes you need something more, a little more devoted time, a change of scenery, a stretch of days when your only responsibility is to yourself and your writing project. Maybe you take a day or two off work and make it a long weekend, or you devote your spring break from classes to focus on your writing. One can be just as productive at home, or at a DIY retreat, as at one of the alluring oases promised at a place like the MacDowell Colony or the Vermont Studio Center.

SIX IDEAS FOR DIY WRITERS RETREATS

DO A HOUSING SWAP: Swap houses or apartments with a friend or family member for a weekend (or longer, if you can manage). It doesn't have to be a cabin in the woods; sometimes simply a new environment can be enough to get the gears turning.

GET A ROOM: Whether it's a Motel 6 a few miles away or a beachside resort in November, hotel rooms and bed-and-breakfasts can be an affordable short-term escape, especially if you book in advance and during the off-season.

GO TO THE LIBRARY: If your city or town has a public library, it can be a great place to camp out for long hours over the course of a few days. Bars and cafés may also work but tend to get loud, require you to buy something, and often discourage laptop loitering.

WRITE OUTSIDE: If you have a quiet park in your city or town, it might be a great space to write if the weather's nice. If you live in the country, take a hike to your favorite secluded spot. Pack a picnic and make a day of it.

GO CAMPING: If you have a car and like to camp, hit the road for a weekend, pack a tent, and stay at campsites (which typically charge a fee of only a few dollars) at night. Bring a notebook or laptop and write at each stop.

RIDE THE TRAIN: Book a round-trip train ticket for a destination several hours away. Write as you ride, then get off at the end of the line. Have lunch and take a stroll around town, then get back on the train and write your way home. (A bonus for those who like to partake in a libation at the end of the day while they write: the bar car.)

Still, our lives can get so filled up with chores and obligations that it can be difficult to focus on one's writing unless drastic measures are taken. Even if you are all alone in your own home—your kids are at a sleepover, or your partner has a work event until late, or your roommate is on a business trip— the funniest things happen: That squeaky hinge or the leaky faucet can start to feel like a priority. Never is our kitchen counter cleaner than when we have a free afternoon to write. There's always a load of laundry to do, or a letter to write, or a bill to pay. Or your mother to call. And even if you find yourself with another scrap of time that you've carved out of your busy schedule, the headspace required to get substantial work done on a writing project may only open up during vistas of time and freedom. Sometimes you need to mix it up and bust out of your usual routine.

ACTION ITEM 17

Search the writers retreats listed in the Conferences and Residencies database at pw.org. Filter by location and determine which would be easiest for you to get to, then make notes about application fees and deadlines.

Some retreats allow writers to stay and work in exotic locales such as the Dora Maar House in Ménerbes, France (Brown Foundation Fellows Program); a traditional Portuguese house in the historic town of Messejana, Portugal (Buinho Creative Hub Residencies Program); and a private estate in the Cetona foothills of Tuscany, Italy (Lemon Tree House Residency); while others offer writers time and seclusion in slightly more familiar but still dreamy destinations such as The Mount, Edith Wharton's former home in Lenox, Massachusetts (Edith Wharton Writer-in-Residence Program); a Victorian farm in Reisterstown, Maryland (Good Contrivance Farm Writer's Retreat); and a cattle ranch in the Lower Piney Creek Valley in Wyoming (Jentel Artist Residency Program).

Writers retreats typically offer attendees a degree of solitude—a quiet place where one can focus on the writing—along with meals, sometimes shared in a communal setting, and perhaps a reading or a craft talk by fellow guests, who are sometimes also visual artists or playwrights or creative folks working in other mediums. At some retreats there is a natural environment to explore, a little nature to replenish one's soul, and at others the experience is more about four walls and a desk, zero additional distractions. "Imagine six hand-hewn cottages nestled into the most mossy, peaceful woods, with a view of Mount Rainier on clear days and llamas grazing out front," writes Dani Shapiro about Hedgebrook, one of the only retreats for women, located on Whidbey Island, about thirty-five miles northwest of Seattle. "Imagine one cup, one plate, one glass. A stained glass window. A loft bed covered with a quilt that could have been made by your grandma. Each morning, after you light the wood stove: precious, cosseted solitude. And as the sun goes down, a delicious dinner lovingly prepared for the small group of women writers . . . who sit around the farmhouse table in literary camaraderie."

So how do you know if you're ready for a writers retreat? Any writer at any stage could take advantage of the time and space, no doubt, so it's not really a matter of whether you qualify (though some retreats require manuscripts or project descriptions as part of the application process). More important is having a goal or intentions clearly established in your mind.

Time at a retreat can be spent reading and recording observations in your commonplace book—amassing the raw material that will inspire your next book—or outlining your essay, or starting your novel, finishing your novel, or writing your proposal to send to agents. There is no wrong way to spend your time at a writers retreat, but there are

ACTION ITEM 18

Before you go to a writers retreat, sit down and write a clear list of goals you hope to accomplish while you're there. Be realistic. Set daily goals, a weekly goal, and, if you're so lucky, monthly goals. What will you need to meet these goals, besides the gift of time you are about to enjoy?

more or less gratifying ways, and it's all about having a clear plan. Set a goal—set daily goals—and try to establish a new routine at the retreat so that you can meet those goals. But also, be kind to yourself.

Don't beat yourself up if you don't hit that word count on your first day. Try hard, but if instead you find yourself in the middle of the woods and you discover that for the first time in a long while you're actually able to take a deep breath, your lungs filling with air so clean and cool you can almost taste it, and your mind feels open to the world in a way that feels strangely reminiscent of childhood, then you've accomplished something. It might not be words on the page, yet, but you're doing something truly important. As a writer, that kind of thing can be just as important as nailing that flashback with your protagonist and her recently deceased aunt on page ninety-four of your manuscript.

TWELVE RESIDENCIES ABROAD

Long-term residencies abroad offer both ample time for writing and the opportunity to approach your work in a new cultural context, with the fresh eyes and sense of possibility that travel brings. The following residencies, all between a month and a year in length, offer poets and writers the chance to explore the world, forge cross-cultural conversations, and devote valuable time and space to their works in progress. Most of these residencies are fully funded; some offer additional stipends and allowances for food and travel expenses. Visit the websites for more information, including required application materials and any associated costs.

360 XOCHI QUETZAL ARTIST AND WRITERS RESIDENCY: One- to four-month residency in Chapala, Jalisco, Mexico.
www.360xochiquetzal.com

ARQUETOPIA FOUNDATION ARTIST AND WRITERS RESIDENCY: Three- to eight-week residency in Oaxaca, Mexico, during spring or summer.
www.arquetopia.org

BALTIC WRITING RESIDENCY: Three- to four-week residency in London, Stockholm, and Brora, Scotland, including stipend, offered year-round.
www.balticresidency.com

BANFF CENTRE FOR ARTS AND CREATIVITY WRITING STUDIO: Monthlong residency in Alberta, Canada, in the spring.
www.banffcentre.ca/literary-arts

BERLIN PRIZE RESIDENCY FROM THE AMERICAN ACADEMY IN BERLIN: Residential fellowship in Berlin for one to two semesters of the academic year, including stipend and travel expenses.
www.americanacademy.de/apply

BOGLIASCO FOUNDATION RESIDENTIAL FELLOWSHIP: Monthlong residency in Bogliasco, Italy, during fall or spring.
www.bfny.org

BOUBOUKI WRITERS RESIDENCY: Two- to six-week residency in Mesana, Cyprus, beginning in November or February.
www.toboumbouki.wordpress.com

BRIDGE GUARD ART RESIDENCY: Residency of flexible length in Centre Štúrovo, Slovakia, including stipend, offered year-round. Resident is expected to observe and log operations of the historic Maria Valeria Bridge.
www.transartists.org/air/bridgeguard

EST-NORD-EST WRITERS RESIDENCY: Eight-week residency in Quebec, Canada, in spring, summer, or fall, including stipend.
www.estnordest.org/residency

M LITERARY RESIDENCY: Six- to eight-week residency in Shanghai or Beijing during summer or fall.
m-restaurantgroup.com/all-things-literary/

TAIPEI ARTIST VILLAGE ARTIST-IN-RESIDENCE: Eight- to twelve-week residency for an artist in any discipline, including literary art, in Taipei, Taiwan. www.artistvillage.org

VILLA STRÄULI ARTIST-IN-RESIDENCY PROGRAM: Three-month residency in Winterthur, Switzerland, offered three times annually, including stipend. www.villastraeuli.ch/en/general-information

With so many retreats available in so many different locations, how do you decide which one is right for you? There are many factors that go into the decision, of course, but one place to start is determining how much money you're willing to spend. While some retreats do not have an application fee, others require anywhere from $20 to $50 just to consider you. Next, you should look at whether the retreat is fully funded. Some, such as Djerassi Resident Artists Program and the Headlands Center for the Arts, are free to those accepted through a competitive application process, while others charge tuition and/or fees for lodging and meals. A four-week residency at the Vermont Studio Center costs more than $4,000, for example, though fellowships are available. But if you consider how much it would cost to go on vacation or travel for an entire month, suddenly $4,000 doesn't sound so steep.

Other questions to ask yourself:

How long do you want to be away? Typical writers retreats vary from a week to six weeks and even longer. Sometimes a week is as long as you can muster, and that's fine, but just be prepared for an adjustment period at the beginning, when you may not be as productive as you would like. Think about your last weeklong vacation and how it felt like you were just starting to feel fully relaxed about five days in.

How much structured time do you want at the retreat? Some writers prefer to set their own daily schedule, while others like to have meals at a certain set time, and a few activities planned for them.

How alone do you want to be? This gets at the paradox we discussed at the beginning of this chapter. For one writer, uninterrupted days and nights of focusing on nothing but the machinations of the mind sounds like heaven; for another, it sounds like a horror movie starring Jack Nicholson. Read a description of the retreat carefully—and call the administrator, or e-mail another writer who has been there—to make sure it's right for you.

Is this a space that is accessible for you, and will a coordinator work with you to ensure that all necessary accessibility accommodations are offered?

No matter which retreat you choose—a traditional residency that you've applied for or a DIY retreat you've created for yourself or with friends—get the most out of it by having a plan with clear and achievable goals, and think about how you want to spend the gift of time.

ELEMENTS OF A WRITERS RETREAT APPLICATION

A WORK PLAN OR PROJECT DESCRIPTION: Not always required but still useful to have on hand, if only for your own reference, a work plan is a course of action that you would put in place if you were to attend the residency or retreat—a description of the project you will make significant strides toward completing while there. "The real purpose of a work plan might be to simply prove that you have one," Grant Faulkner writes. "Show that you're planning to get some serious writing done."

A LETTER OF RECOMMENDATION: Some residencies require this but certainly not all of them, and it isn't typically meant to show the quality of your work but rather your work ethic and your creativity. Ask someone who knows you well to vouch for you and to point out to the application committee that you are a serious writer who can put the time at a retreat to good use. Consider teachers, obviously, but also other directors of retreats and organizers of conferences you have attended.

A RÉSUMÉ: Tailor your résumé to include not only your work history but also any literary experience, your publication history, and any awards you've received for your writing. Put serious thought into how you portray your academic and/or professional accomplishments.

A MANUSCRIPT OR WORK SAMPLE: Likely the most important element of your application, obviously this should consist of your best work. It need not be published (unless the application guidelines specify otherwise) but should demonstrate your talent and skill. Show it to teachers or peers for feedback before sending it with your application. You may also want to consider including samples related to your work plan or project description. If you state that you need the time and space to finish your novel, consider sharing the first chapter or chapters to prove how important this residency will be. Read the application instructions very carefully and put together a manuscript that is exactly what they are requesting.

Writing Groups

For writers who aren't interested in a writing program, or whose days at a college or university are behind them, or who find retreats and conferences inaccessible or not financially feasible, writing groups can be a powerful way to gain a sense of community and keep one's writing in the forefront. Writing groups differ from writing workshops in that they tend to be smaller, more intimate, and more casual. They often consist of a handful of friends and acquaintances who meet regularly in someone's living room or at a café to discuss general issues relating to writing and publishing, hold one another accountable for producing new work, help one another out with contacts and ideas, and read and critique one another's work. Some writing groups are formed online, with participants never actually meeting one another in person and sharing work via e-mail or Google Docs.

The appeal of a writing group is clear—these are people you can turn to for a manuscript critique, professional advice, inspiration, and emotional support; a pat on the back or a kick in the pants—but because of how important the group can be to your writing practice, it's extremely important to find the right members. With the wrong chemistry, a writing group can be ineffectual at best and harmful at worst. This is why writing groups are sometimes formed by students who established a connection in a community writing class, or alumni of a writing program, or writers who know one another through some shared experience. But not everyone has had those experiences.

Novelist Hannah Gersen says one of the reasons her small group—just three women who met in a Manhattan novel-writing class at the 92nd Street Y led by Joseph Caldwell—has been together for more than ten years now is that they don't know one another socially outside the group, they love one another's writing (but are not shy about offering constructive criticism), they meet at a neutral place such as a coffee shop, and they've held themselves to a professional standard, as one would at a business function. "One reason it has been helpful for me to treat our writing group as a professional obligation is that I don't feel as guilty telling my husband he has to come home early from work, or a friend or family member that, sorry, I can't help out, not tonight, because I have an important meeting to attend," she writes. Another important feature of her group is that the members are women who share a commitment to writing and who take one another's work seriously. "I see it as an extension of Virginia Woolf's famous dictum that a woman needs a room of her own in order to write. Our writing group is a room of our own creation, a place we meet to nourish and challenge one another's imaginations."

Readings

If you want to feel the pulse of any local literary community, go to a reading and listen to the writers read their work. It might be at a bookstore or a university, a café or a bar. Wherever it is, you're sure to find people like you who are passionate about writing and supporting writers. Part of being in a community of writers is supporting your fellow authors, and sometimes that means showing up on a Wednesday night when an essayist is reading from her work in progress. Not only can it be an enriching and informative experience to listen to a fellow author read her work, but it's also a big part of being a good literary citizen. There might even be an open mic in the back room of a local restaurant where you can sign up and read from your own work. Authors with books under contract with commercial and large independent publishers sometimes get the benefit of in-house publicists or even speaking agents who are working to schedule readings for them, but the vast majority of writers need to do this for themselves.

So how do you find out where the readings are happening and, more to the point, what opportunities are out there to read your own work in front of an audience? Often there are online listings of local events, of course—try your local library or newspaper, or the nearest literary arts center, or the Poets & Writers Literary Events Calendar. Or—and this gets back to the fundamental importance of being a part of a writing community—talk to your peers. The more writers you know, especially those who live nearby, the more information you can access by simply consulting them.

ACTION ITEM 19

Jump on the Literary Events Calendar at pw.org or download the mobile app Poets & Writers Local and find a reading that's happening near you tonight.

If you want to give your own reading, the first thing to do is join the audience at another writer's reading. Then repeat—many, many times. Just as you can't be a good writer without being a good reader, you can't give a good reading until you've attended many—dozens, hundreds—yourself.

"An oral version of what writers do on the page, a reading has no predetermined outcome. In the sacred space of the public event, writers can try things out: a new idea, a way of seeing around what's in front of us."
—JOHN FREEMAN

Once you've identified a reading series that you'd like to be a part of, do a little research and identify the reading series coordinator and find out whether that person is open to queries. Then contact those bookstores, libraries, universities, bars, restaurants, cafés, community centers, and other venues that host readings. If you can, send the event coordinator a free copy of your book before you call or e-mail. Then it really just comes down to kindly asking if you can schedule a reading, maybe even a book signing. Just remember that the coordinator is likely fielding a lot of queries, and juggling an immensely complicated schedule, and that often the coordinator isn't even paid to do this work, so approach with kindness, courtesy, and patience.

In the end, finding community is about what you can offer others even more than what others can offer you. Writers who approach a community situation thinking only about what they can get out of it will likely be disappointed. Folks who are in a warm, healthy community can spot that kind of attitude a mile away. You get what you give. And supporting others—whether it's by sharing information and advice or offering feedback and a compassionate ear—is just as important as being supported. We are all writers—and one thing we've noticed time and again is that there are no trade secrets. Writers help one another. Flowing through this entire enterprise there is a sense of camaraderie: We teach and help our own. Go to the back of any well-published book, including the one you're holding now, and you'll see just how much community matters. The acknowledgments pages are filled with the names of those who offered a helping hand. It's not just the agent, the editor, and the publicist who are often acknowledged; it's the members of the writing group, or the trusted reader who spent nights poring over a manuscript and offering notes—not for payment, not for glory, but rather because we're part of a community.

ACTION ITEM 20

Browse the Reading Venues database at pw.org to find contact information for venues that are open to queries from writers who would like to read there.

CHRISTINA BAKER KLINE
ON ENCOURAGEMENT

I am often asked when I first knew I wanted to be a writer. A better question, I think, is why do most people stop? Most of us are born with the desire to create. Children draw and paint freely, dance and sing with abandon, invent tales and poems. Making up stories is viewed as an activity we eventually outgrow, like building sandcastles at the beach or skipping rope at recess.

When I was in the fifth grade, my teacher, Mrs. Carey, gave the class a creative writing assignment. She collected the stories on a Friday, and on Monday she went up and down the rows of the classroom handing them back. When she got to my desk, she leaned down and whispered, "I enjoyed your story so much that when I was at home this weekend, I read it out loud to my husband, and he liked it, too."

I was stunned. Home? Husband? I'd never considered that Mrs. Carey had either. Most important, she enjoyed my story.

And she read it out loud to someone.

And he liked it, too.

Mrs. Carey's measured response—she did not, after all, say she "loved" the story—was all the encouragement I needed to keep living in the land of make-believe, writing stories that no one read and inventing characters as real to me as my siblings and friends—sometimes more so. I became addicted to the feeling of being in two places at once: in the supposed real world and in the fantasy world inside my head. It felt like a superpower.

Over the next decade I continued to find encouragement in the flimsiest of places, straining to hear the yeses, no matter how faint, and tuning out the nos. I became addicted to the buzz of invention, the way that in my imagination I could turn the elements of my ordinary life into something meaningful, even if only to me. I loved that on the page I could surprise myself.

Some years ago, I was writer in residence at a university in New York City. One evening, after hosting a reading with a visiting novelist, I commuted back to my suburban town with a journalism professor. When I asked what she thought of the event, she said, "I have to confess, I don't get 'fiction.' I don't understand why anyone likes reading it, much less writing it. I mean, come on—it's silly, don't you think? Sitting in a room all day making stuff up?'"

This hit me like a thunderbolt.

I used to feel sorry for people who don't live with a constellation of characters inside their heads, who don't sit upright in the middle of the night with clarity about how to solve a problem in an alternate world that doesn't actually exist. The professor's observation made me realize that, to many people, the idea of writing (and even reading!) fiction is kind of weird.

Most adults do not actually want to sit in a room all day making stuff up.

Writing fiction can be lonely, terrifying, and soul-scraping. Sometimes I can't figure out how to navigate a simple sentence, much less craft an entire book out of thin air. I find it nearly impossible to translate the vision in my head into a living, breathing world on the page. I usually feel as if I am failing. But I am my most authentic self when I'm working on a novel. Wrestling with questions about the meaning of life and the potential for grace in a mad and brutal world, I feel close to the bone. I hum with purpose.

Ultimately, to me, it's not just about making up stories. It's about creating narratives that reflect our lives back to us and give us some measure of meaning. Through the granular specifics of story, we access larger truths about aspects of the human condition that often seem unfathomable: love and friendship, war and death. Inhabiting another universe, as a writer and as a reader, helps me make sense of this one.

CHRISTINA BAKER KLINE *is the* New York Times *best-selling author of eight novels:* Tin Ticket, A Piece of the World, Orphan Train, Orphan Train Girl, The Way

Life Should Be, Sweet Water, Bird in Hand, *and* Desire Lines. *Her novels have received the New England Prize for Fiction and the Maine Literary Award, among others, and have been chosen by hundreds of communities and universities as "One Book, One Read" selections. They have been published in more than forty countries.*

SIX

A Writer's Education

What do writers need to know, and how can they go about learning it?

Obviously, writers need to know how to write. But can such a thing really be taught? Certainly the rules, principles, and techniques—the mechanics of grammar, the elements of form and craft—can be learned, honed, improved (and then those same rules can be purposely broken, those same principles challenged). But what about imagination, empathy, emotion, humor? What about structure and style? And substance! After all, you can be the best writer in the world, but if you don't have anything to say . . . who's going to want to read it? How much does being a good writer depend on talent or aptitude? Is it a gift, or the hard-earned result of learning and labor?

It seems clear that such things as grammar and syntax can be taught. We know that from our most basic classes in elementary school. The more complex lessons of how to use that grammar, syntax, and a hundred other tools of the writer's trade can also be learned, but mostly through the doing, through the years-long practice and failure (no great thing can be accomplished without failure) that comes from revision and rejection and perhaps a fair amount of struggle.

No one can teach you how to be a *great* writer. The real lesson is in the doing.

INTERVIEWER: *Do you really think creative writing can be taught?*

KURT VONNEGUT: *About the same way golf can be taught. A pro can point out obvious flaws in your swing.*

As for the prerequisite of God-given talent? There are only two things a writer truly must possess: a love of words and a need or drive for human expression. Without those two things, forget it. "I don't believe writers can be made, either by circumstances or by self-will," writes Stephen King in *On Writing.* "The equipment comes with the original package. Yet it is by no means unusual equipment; I believe large numbers of people have at least some talent as writers and storytellers, and that those talents can be strengthened and sharpened."

ACTION ITEM 21

Compile a reading list of books composed of titles gleaned from old course syllabi, suggestions from friends and family, discussions on social media, the *New York Times* bestseller lists, Goodreads, and so on. Better yet, pick a small press from the database at pw.org and choose a recently published title. Expand your comfort zone. Take risks. Be a risky reader.

So where can writers turn to learn the teachable stuff? There are a number of possible answers, but only one is absolutely essential. Luckily it's also the easiest: reading. (And mark that down as the third essential thing a writer needs: a love of reading.) We're not talking about reading only books like the one you're holding—although certainly that is one of our chief aims in these pages: to help you become a better-informed and inspired writer—but rather reading widely. Read the classics. Read books that were published before you were born. Read books you've never heard of before. Read books by both living and dead writers. Read books in translation. Read books by writers who have been incarcerated. Read books published by small presses that are new to you. Read books in genres you have no intention of writing in. Read newspapers and magazines. Read literary journals. Go to the library or the nearest independent bookstore and ask for suggestions, scour book reviews, consider the short lists and nominations for major prizes, get recommendations from friends— and then just read. Follow your bliss. Compile a reading list if it helps.

Without reading, there is no writing. It is the most important ingredient in the writing life.

MFA Programs

Which brings us to MFA programs, those incubators of literary talent that are so common these days. Let's get this out of the way at the outset: You don't need a master of fine arts (MFA) degree—or an MA or PhD, for that matter—to be a successful writer. Period. Talk to any agent or editor, in New York City or elsewhere, and they'll all say the same thing. If given a choice between a mediocre manuscript from a writer with an MFA and a remarkable one from a writer who never even went to college, they will always choose the best writing. "If I mentally scan my own client list, yes, there are a few MFA graduates, but overwhelmingly that degree is absent," says agent Molly Friedrich, whose clients include Melissa Bank, Gish Jen, Valerie Martin, Terry McMillan, Esmeralda Santiago, Jane Smiley, and Elizabeth Strout. "Give me a flawed, imperfect, but original voice and I'll flip out because that's always what matters the most." Friedrich goes on to echo King's point about writers being born with the necessary equipment: "I'm convinced you're born with an original voice," she says. "It isn't something you can necessarily cultivate thousands of dollars later."

So why would you want to attend an MFA program? We've thought about this question for the better part of three decades. We've heard answers from writers, professors, and program directors alike. Perhaps you have a manuscript you want to develop and expand, with an eye toward publication. Perhaps you've finished a four-year undergraduate degree and you want more time to write and hone your craft. Or perhaps you want to pursue a career in teaching and need that terminal degree (an MFA qualifies you to teach at the most basic college level). Or you see the MFA

ACTION ITEM 22

Make a list of all the reasons you might want to attend a writing program. Try a pros/cons list. Then do the real work of figuring out the financial impact of the decision. We've heard from a lot of people who have attended MFA programs and not one of them has said it's worth going into massive debt over.

as the bridge to a PhD. All of these are valid reasons to attend a writing program.

The reason that has made the most common sense to us over the years—the one that carries with it the lowest possibility of disappointment, the one that doesn't rely on outside factors beyond one's control—is the desire to step into an environment in which you can devote yourself to your writing for an extended period of time. While an MFA program won't necessarily make you a better writer, it will give you an opportunity to spend more time concentrating on writing and learning about your craft than you'd likely be able to pull off if you weren't in an MFA program.

Think about that for a bit.

Like it or not, the world we live in is designed to take time away from your writing, dull your focus, diminish your concentration, fill your days with anything, everything *but* the time to sit down and stare at a screen or a piece of paper and find the words to describe what it's like to be alive. Most of us have an entire world of information—and more hours of streaming entertainment than hours left in our lives—at our fingertips. And most of us have to work at least forty hours a week in order to keep the lights on. And then there's everything else: kids, family, meals, cleaning, dog-walking, doctor's appointments, car repairs, house maintenance, and on and on.

So do not underestimate the opportunity to take a few items off that list of things that are *not* writing to which your time is allotted—or to take advantage of a time in your life when that list is mercifully shorter. Cameron Finch says the program at Vermont College of Fine Arts in Montpelier, where she received her degree in 2019, gave her two years to focus on writing, but that any MFA program only gives a writer as much as that writer puts into it. "I fully believe that it is our duty as artists to seek out inspiration," she says. "The classroom is only the seed for conversations and discovery. I chose to look at this program not only as a place to learn, but as a place to make connections, to have time to write and read, to go to events, to be fully immersed in the community, to suck the marrow out of my limited time on this campus."

Another great reason to attend an MFA program is to meet and establish relationships with people for whom writing is just as important as it is for you. This is no small perk. The older you get and the more set in your ways and routines, the fewer opportunities there are to meet other people and really get to know them and explore the ways in which you're similar and different. If nothing else, an MFA program is a nearly perfectly designed venue in which to learn from your peers. Raquel Gutiérrez, who received her MFA in poetry and fiction from the University of Arizona in Tucson in 2019, says the greatest benefit of the program was having faculty and peers encourage her to mine her life's experiences for her work. "I didn't have to compartmentalize my identities there to feel like a writer to be taken seriously," she says. "My differences—or rather the fact that I wasn't straight and white and male—were treated as my strengths."

You've no doubt heard about or read arguments about MFA writing—the idea that such programs cultivate a sanitized, watered-down version of literature that has not nearly enough to do with what it feels like to live a life and way too much to do with what it feels like to live or study behind the proverbial gates of our country's educational institutions. There is a certain voice that can be manufactured around workshop tables, say the MFA critics—the implication being that it is an inherently unoriginal voice. It's writing by committee. "There is perhaps a certain polished, hyper-crafted writing that occasionally emerges from these MFA programs, at least from the mediocre ones," acknowledges Molly Friedrich.

This is no doubt true, but at the same time this gives the MFA model an awful lot of credit for the development of one's writing style. Chad Harbach, author of the best-selling novel *The Art of Fielding* and editor of *MFA vs NYC: The Two Cultures of American Fiction*, takes it a step further when he writes, "MFA programs themselves are so lax and laissez-faire as to have a shockingly small impact on students' work." We wouldn't go quite that far. It depends on the program. "MFA programs are generally split into two categories: academic and studio programs," says Gionni Ponce, who received her MFA in fiction from Indiana University in 2019. "Studio programs often have less strict requirements for the classes you take and may not require you to sign up for literature courses. Academic programs will often require you to take graduate-level courses in literature, which often require fifteen-to twenty-page academic essays."

And just as in the "outside world" there are many things that can influence a writer's work while he or she is enrolled in an MFA program, the leanings of a workshop leader are just one of them. Of greater import, perhaps, is the influence of peers. During the two or three years of a typical full-residency MFA program, social time and creative time necessarily overlap, so that a casual lunch with your new friends can and often does turn into a debate about craft or a reading or writing group session. In relationships formed and developed in a writing program—relationships that can last a lifetime—writing is always a topic of conversation. You can meet some of the best close readers of your life in an MFA program. That point is worth pausing over. Let's say you have a job, maybe it's even a creatively fulfilling one. And you have plenty of friends. You meet for dinner once a week or month, or you stay in touch through social media. That's great, but knowing someone who understands your art—who shares your sensibilities—and who is willing to read it with a critical eye is one of the most valuable relationships you'll ever have. Again, real life does not provide such opportunities very often. It's practically baked into any MFA program.

SIX AUTHORS ON WHETHER TO PURSUE AN MFA

"Getting my MFA was the best decision of my adult life. . . . I wanted to be able to teach at the college level, I knew what I wanted to work on, and I had some money saved to pay for part of it. But I think it depends what a writer is looking for in their creative life (structure, guidance, encouragement, time), the package offered by the school, and their long-term career goals. If you have the resources to devote two or three years to the world of language and ideas, I found it a powerful and blissful experience." —**Sarah McColl** is the author of the memoir *Joy Enough* (Liveright, 2019). She holds an MFA from Sarah Lawrence.

"I have an MFA, and I'm very grateful to have it because it 'certified' me to teach at the college level, as I've done for many years. But when my students ask me that same question, I pause and consider the individual. If it's something they feel they absolutely have to do, and I can see that it feels necessary to them, then I tell them to go for it. If they see it as a way to spend two years focusing on their writing and it won't put them into massive debt, then I say go for it. If they think it will secure some sort of future path as a writer and/or writing professor, though, that's a longer discussion. It's hard to get published, and teaching jobs are scarce even if you publish well. I don't think an MFA is necessary, but at the same time it can be a good way to connect with other writers, get regular feedback, and grow as a writer. You can also do that out in the real world, though, through community workshops and just plain old life experience." —**Laura Sims** is the author of a novel, *Looker* (Scribner, 2019), and four books of poetry, including *Staying Alive* (Ugly Duckling Presse, 2016). She has an MFA from the University of Washington and teaches at New York University.

"If you can get into a funded program, yes—it is better pay, hours, and easier than working retail. If you can afford to pay for an MFA, it seems you have access to most resources the MFA provides and your money would be better spent elsewhere. . . . It seems to me not worth going into debt over." —**Jos Charles** is the author of the poetry collection *feeld*, winner of the National Poetry Series, published by Milkweed Editions in 2018, and a finalist for the 2019 Pulitzer Prize. She received her MFA from the University of Arizona.

"I don't see it as a one-size-fits-all situation—I think sure, why not, if it's fully funded and you feel like you're getting something out of it. Otherwise, no. The key is to protect your own writing and trust your gut as far as what you want and need." —**Catherine Chung** is the author of the novels *Forgotten Country* and *The Tenth Muse*. She received her MFA from Cornell University.

"I knew exactly what I planned to do while I was there, I just needed time and space to work, and some guidance and encouragement from a community I could trust. I was also older—in my thirties—when I did it. So although I had lots of growing to do as a writer, I'd already found my voice, knew what I was going to work on, and I'd lived a little. I think all of those factors contributed to why it was such a successful experience for me. It might not be the right thing for someone else and I don't believe that you need it to write." —**Mona Awad** is the author of the novel *Bunny* and the linked story collection *13 Ways of Looking at a Fat Girl.* She received her MFA from Brown University.

"Not unless it is fully funded. I cannot in good conscience recommend that any-one without a trust fund or wealthy no-strings-attached parents/patrons go into debt for a degree in the arts. Read every single interview in the *Paris Review* instead; you will learn there are as many different ways to write a book as there are writers. Read widely across genres and write terrible drafts of things you are ashamed of. But if an MFA program is fully funded, then definitely go. Being a professional student is the most fun job I've ever had." —**Domenica Ruta** is the author of the novel *Last Day* and the memoir *With or Without You.* She re-ceived her MFA from the Michener Center for Writers at the University of Texas in Austin.

Full- Versus Low-Residency MFA Programs

Broadly speaking, there are two different kinds of MFA programs: full residency and low residency. A full-residency program requires a commitment of two to three years in a specific place; typically students who are enrolled in such a program live on or near campus. And while the hours students spend in the classroom vary—it could be as low as five or six hours a week—it is meant to be an immersive experience that brings with it all the benefits and resources of typical grad school campus life. A low-residency program, on the other hand, is designed to offer the same kind of training during several one- or two-week residencies a year on a campus. The rest of the time students live their lives back home, work their jobs, take classes and workshops remotely, and write in between the pressures of the world like everyone else. This is a clear benefit for those writers who don't want to quit their jobs or who have children to raise, or any of a hundred other reasons why a writer wouldn't want to necessarily bring their current routine to a screeching halt for two or three years.

TWENTY-ONE QUESTIONS TO ASK

Everyone has advice for those considering an MFA in creative writing, including us (a program should offer funding; no one should have to go into debt to receive the degree). But advice is rarely universal, and the decision to pursue a graduate degree is one that requires individualized attention. One writer's expectations for an MFA program might be radically different from those of another. So rather than spout platitudes about this uniquely personal decision, we'd like to offer some simple questions that prospective grad students might want to consider, starting with perhaps the most important one. There are no wrong answers, but taking the time to explore your motivations, preferences, goals, and priorities can be a helpful first step in deciding what the right path is for you.

1. Why do you want an MFA?
2. Does the program offer funding—and if so, how much?
3. Are there on-campus jobs, work-study opportunities, or travel and research stipends available that could offset tuition and living costs?
4. Are you willing to carry some debt after you graduate?
5. Do you want to move somewhere for at least two years (full residency), or do you want to stay put and attend brief residencies (low residency)?
6. Do you want to live on the coast, in the mountains, or somewhere in between?
7. Do you want to work with a small group of peers or a larger cohort filled with a multitude of voices?
8. Is the program centered on workshops, or is it more academically rigorous?
9. Does the faculty reflect a diverse community?
10. How about recent alumni—do they reflect a diverse community? What are they doing now?

11. Do you know any writers who have attended the program and would be willing to share their opinions?

12. Do you know the work of the faculty?

13. What have you heard about the teaching styles of the faculty?

14. Will there be any faculty members on sabbatical during your residency?

15. Do you want to teach while in an MFA program? If so, does the program require teaching or are there elective teaching opportunities available? Or do you want your writing to be your only focus?

16. Do you want to work on the staff of a literary journal, small press, or university press while pursuing your MFA? And if so, does the program offer such opportunities?

17. Does the MFA program have a regular reading series or other extracurricular programs?

18. What have you heard about the program on social media, at writing conferences and events, or out in the world?

19. Can you visit the campus and/or talk to a few current students and faculty?

20. Does the program allow you to take classes or workshops in other genres?

21. What are the application requirements, e.g., GRE scores, personal statement, writing sample?

HOW TO CHOOSE: With well over two hundred MFA programs in the United States, choosing which ones to research, much less apply to, can be a daunting prospect. One good place to start is the MFA Programs database at pw.org. Once you have chosen which programs you want to investigate further, you can take the time to familiarize yourself with each one and determine whether it's a good match for you. Most databases and useful lists of programs provide the basic specs as well as some application information to help you stay on schedule, but many of the most important and unquantifiable aspects of a program—curriculum, precise funding structure, and so on—require more research. Much of this information should be accessible on each program's website, but some are better than others when it comes to offering comprehensive information about the application process and funding.

Many writers are understandably searching for "the best" program. And yes, there are some that have a long-standing reputation for excellence, such as the Iowa Writers' Workshop, the University of Michigan in Ann Arbor, the University of California in Irvine, the University of Virginia in Charlottesville, and New York University. All great programs. But they may not be the best for *you*. It really comes down to whether or not a program is a good match for *your* priorities and preferences.

ACTION ITEM 23

Search the MFA Programs database at pw.org for information about more than two hundred MFA programs; filter by genre, residency requirements, application deadlines, and more.

We recommend you pay particular attention to a program's funding: At last count, more than sixty full-residency programs in the United States offer full tuition support to all students for the duration of the program. Ninety-three others reported that they offer partial funding, which can range from just a handful of small scholarships to full assistantships or fellowships for eighty-five percent of students. As always, the impact of funding must be contextualized against the cost of tuition: One program's tuition might be so high that even if you are offered a partial tuition waiver, it might cost less to attend a program that offers you no funding. Many programs list estimated tuition on their websites; if not, current tuition rates are usually available on the website of the host university or college.

Do some financial planning. Funding might not be your top priority, but it should be part of your planning. Make sure you'll have enough money to live on, at least somewhat comfortably, while you're a student. If a program doesn't offer full funding, look into jobs on campus, work-study opportunities, travel and research stipends, and other monetary resources the program might offer. And, not least, understand the long-term costs of student loans—and interest rates.

Size matters. What's more important to you: an intimate environment with a small group of peers whose work (and personalities and social proclivities) you'll get to know closely, or a larger cohort and workshop environment where you'll get to know and work with many writers (and perhaps have slightly more anonymity)?

Read books by the faculty. Don't pick a program just because you recognize the names of the faculty. Know their work, too. You'll want to find at least one faculty member whose writing style, sensibilities, and aesthetics resonate with your own. Once you've narrowed down your top programs, contact an administrator to ensure the teachers you aspire to work with will be teaching and not on sabbatical during your residency. Also, ask the administrator for the contact information of students in the program who are willing to share their experiences. Contact them to ask if that amazing author is also a generous teacher.

Decide if you want to teach. A teaching assistantship is the most common means of funding for students in a full-residency MFA program. As part of the deal, the university typically grants a tuition waiver and pays a modest stipend. In exchange, the graduate student must teach one or two sections of an undergraduate course, usually freshman composition. If you decide to go this route, be sure to understand what your course load and time commitment will be. (In a semester system, a 1-1 course load means teaching one class in the fall and one in the spring; 1-2 means teaching one class in the fall and two in the spring; and so on.) Don't forget about the time you'll spend outside the classroom reading, grading, and prepping. And there's also office hours. Think hard about how well you can balance the responsibility to your students with the responsibility to your own writing.

Location is important. If you choose to attend a full-residency program, you'll probably be spending the next two or three years in a new place. Would you prefer to live in a big city or a small town? Somewhere warm or cold? Near the coast or in the mountains? What kind of environment will foster your writing discipline? And what resources—socially, culturally, environmentally, gastronomically, or otherwise—might you need to thrive?

Review your residency options. Maybe you're committed to where you live or your current job, but you could manage spending a week or two a year to attend a residency. Depending on your career or family situation, you may want to consider a low-residency program.

Explore the curriculum. Is the program focused on the workshop model? Does it offer courses in craft, theory, or literature? What about genre fiction, or cross-genre study? You may have a traditional or more experimental focus in your work—make sure the program you choose accommodates your interests. Indiana University MFA grad Gionni Ponce says some of the students there were unaware of the difference between a studio program and a more rigorous academic program before they arrived and warns prospective students to distinguish between the two models. Determine what kind of program you want, and be sure to apply to the right kind.

Consider extracurriculars. Do you want to work on the staff of a literary magazine? Are you interested in leading workshops in prisons or community centers? Does the program have a regular reading series? What about student groups, campus organizations, or volunteer opportunities? Think about what will help make your time in the program more dynamic and fulfilling, and make sure those opportunities are offered.

Talk to current and former students. Do some research and ask students as well as alumni about their experiences in the programs you're considering. Ask your friends and followers on social media and try to connect with poets and writers who are in those programs. Ask them about the faculty, the local community, the social scene, the rental market—anything and everything that matters to you.

Visit the campus. If your dream program is nearby, drop in for a visit. If it's across the country, perhaps wait until you've been accepted, then consider visiting and sitting in on a workshop before deciding to attend. Take a stroll around campus. Visit the library, gym, or graduate student center to get a feel for the environment. Set up meetings with faculty and administrators. If you can, go out to a reading or have drinks with current students. Ask questions, and don't be shy. You'll get to know a lot more about a program and a school—including its community, politics, diversity, and atmosphere—this way than you ever could from a website.

EIGHT ELEMENTS OF UNIQUE MFA PROGRAMS

When the first graduate creative writing program was established in 1936—the renowned Iowa Writers' Workshop—the formula was straightforward: small, focused workshops and literature seminars in poetry and fiction. Eighty-four years later, more than two hundred full- and low-residency MFA programs populate the literary landscape and offer a diverse array of opportunities, genres, and pedagogical approaches. Schools now afford students the chance to try on the many hats of a writer—researcher, editor, teacher, activist, curator—and to study in environments increasingly tailored to their aesthetic concerns and interests. The following are unique elements that help a handful of MFA programs stand out in a crowded field.

SOCIAL JUSTICE: The low-residency program at Antioch University in Los Angeles focuses on social justice and on developing the social consciousness of its students along with the craft of their writing. Under the core faculty's guidance, students are required to design and complete a field study in their local community, whether it be volunteering once a week to help teach creative writing to pregnant teens and teenage parents, teaching writing to incarcerated individuals, or managing and writing a publicity campaign for jazz musicians displaced after Hurricane Katrina. In New York City, the full-residency program at the Pratt Institute encourages students to probe the cultural and political dimensions of writing. Pratt's curriculum includes seminars that cover topics such as writing and social practice, ecology and poetics, queer rhetoric and writing, and feminist writing traditions. Furthermore, second-year students conduct a yearlong fieldwork residency with a community organization; the program maintains an alliance of local groups willing to work with students, including a circus and theater troupe, a farm alliance, and a feminist collective.

GENRE BENDING: Not all programs stick to strict genre distinctions, but instead encourage—or even require—students to blur the lines. The full-residency program at Brown University in Providence, Rhode Island, is one such example, with both a cross-disciplinary track and a digital language-arts track in addition to its more traditional fare of poetry and fiction. Cross-disciplinary students pair writing with music, visual art, or performance art, while digital language-arts students draw on modern technologies such as computer graphics, animation, electronic music, sound art, and virtual environments. With an illustrious origin as the brain-child of poets Allen Ginsberg and Anne Waldman, the Jack Kerouac School of Disembodied Poetics at Naropa University in Boulder, Colorado, continues to push against convention with an open-genre curriculum and its championing of radical, experimental work. With both a low- and full-residency track, the program requires students to take interdisciplinary seminars and classes in poetics, urging students to investigate, as Naropa faculty member Bhanu Kapil describes it, "the borderland spaces of genre."

MULTIGENRE DEGREES: While the majority of programs grant degrees in one of two or three genres, Pittsburgh's Chatham University—which runs both a full- and low-residency program—offers a dual-genre degree, as well as additional concentrations in travel writing, nature writing, food writing, and literary publishing. Students who concentrate in travel writing enroll in a program- subsidized field seminar; recent seminars have been held in Vietnam, Iceland, Turkey, Ecuador, Brazil, and Costa Rica. At Western Washington University's full-residency program in Bellingham, all students are required to study at least two genres. A majority of the core faculty specializes in both a single genre and in hybrid forms—their combined publication record runs the gamut from lyrical short fiction to prose poems to collaborative short fiction.

COMMUNITY FOCUS: While open to writers of all backgrounds, the low- residency program at the Institute of American Indian Arts in Santa Fe, New Mexico, is dedicated to advancing Native American arts and culture. More than seventy-five percent of the faculty members are Native American or First Nations authors, including Tommy Orange and Sherwin Bitsui. In consultation with faculty mentors, students compile individual reading lists where at least twenty-five percent of the books must be by indigenous North American writers. Situated on the Mexico-U.S. border, the University of Texas in El Paso is shaking things up with the first fully bilingual MFA in the United States. All coursework is conducted in both English and Spanish: class discussions, workshop critiques, and writing move fluidly between the two languages. While not all students enter the full-residency program bilingual, the program reports that many emerge fluent in both languages.

EDITORIAL TRAINING: At most MFA programs, students can sharpen their editorial chops by working on the staff of a literary journal—but at the University of Baltimore's full-residency program, students receive a more extended apprenticeship in the art of publishing. Students not only write a thesis, but they also design, print, and produce the thesis as a finished book. Courses are offered in design and type, book arts, and print and digital publishing. At the University of North Carolina in Wilmington, students in the full-residency program can intern, study, and work at the university's twenty-year-old Publishing Laboratory. At the Pub Lab, housed in its own building and furnished with publishing equipment, students learn the ropes of publishing a book or literary journal from start to finish. Students also learn both the business management and marketing sides of publishing.

INTERNATIONAL EMPHASIS: Students at the full-residency program at the University of Nevada in Las Vegas spend at least one semester abroad in a non-English-speaking country, either on independent study or enrolled at a university. The program adheres to the belief that great writing extends beyond self-expression and instead comes from a larger understanding of the world. Students also have the option of completing their MFA while serving in the Peace Corps.

ENVIRONMENTAL FOCUS: The full-residency program at Iowa State University in Ames adopts a more environmental perspective on the MFA, sending its students out—sometimes literally—into the field. As part of the program's thesis requirement, all students complete at least ninety hours of fieldwork with an organization devoted to the environment. In the past, students have traveled as far as Spain to research medicinal plants and Zimbabwe to collect data about farmworkers. To complete their degree, students also take several environmental courses.

TRANSLATION DEGREES: A select few programs offer full degrees in translation, including the fifty-four-year-old full-residency program at the University of Arkansas in Fayetteville, where students emerge with experience in both poetry and fiction translation; the full-residency program at Queens College in New York City, which also offers an advanced certificate in English-language teaching and hosts the Trends in Translation event series; and the international low-residency program at the Vermont College of Fine Arts in Montpelier. The full-residency program at the University of Texas Rio Grande Valley in Edinburg offers a degree in translation between Spanish and English, and the low-residency program at Fairleigh Dickinson University in Madison, New Jersey, also confers a translation degree.

What You Need to Apply to MFA Programs

Every MFA program has its own set of requirements to apply, so it's important to do your research and find out exactly what your school of choice needs from you. Most MFA programs require that you have already completed a bachelor's degree (BA), and some require a grade point average of 3.0 or higher. The following is a list of things you'll likely need to provide with your application:

Application Form: The length and level of detail of the form will vary depending on the program, but most require standard biographical information. Just remember to carefully read the instructions and make sure that your information contains no errors.

Application Fee: It is the rare program that doesn't charge an application fee, but there are a few (the University of Arkansas in Fayetteville, for example); most charge anywhere from $30 (Florida State University in Tallahassee) to $110 (Columbia University in New York City).

College Transcripts: Your official transcripts are considered confidential information and can be requested in person, through the mail, or online through the college or university you attended. Some graduate programs request that these transcripts be delivered directly by the institution.

GRE Test Results: The GRE, or Graduate Record Examination, is a multiple-choice test meant to evaluate your verbal reasoning, quantitative reasoning, and analytical writing. The GRE is required by some graduate schools, and includes its own registration fee of a couple hundred dollars.

Letters of Recommendation: Many programs require three letters of recommendation sent directly to the program. Think long and hard about who you want to ask for this important document. It should be someone who knows your writing well, who has worked with you during the course of your undergraduate studies, perhaps, and who genuinely respects and appreciates your work and who can speak to your work ethic and your level of commitment to your writing. Give these people plenty of time to write the letter—remember that you may not be the only one asking them to do this—and always follow up with a sincere thank-you.

Cover Letter: Read the instructions in the application materials, as some programs require a brief cover letter outlining your work experience and objectives while others require a longer letter about your academic experience.

Résumé or Curriculum Vitae: The same applies here: Read the instructions. This document may be comparable to the résumé you would send to a potential employer or it may need to be tailored toward academic achievements.

Personal Statement: Also called an artistic statement or an application essay, generally speaking it is a document that simply tells the admissions board who you are, how you view your writing, and what you'd want out of a writing program. Requirements vary: It could be anywhere from a couple hundred words to a thousand or more. Think carefully about how you want to portray yourself and your work. "In their artistic statements, many applicants comment on the time they need to write," says Manuel

Muñoz, the director of the creative writing program at the University of Arizona in Tucson. "That is certainly valuable, but our best writers have been the ones who can articulate how they are ready to transform and grow once they get here, rather than stick rigidly to their initial understandings. Can you take measure of all the resources available and find which will inspire a spirit of imagination and collaboration? Does a program provide a supportive atmosphere for you to experiment and try new things?" Finding a way to convey a deeper understanding of a given program—one that is genuine to your feelings about yourself and your writing—will help you stand out from the rest.

Writing Sample: Every part of the application process is important—leaving any part out will get you rejected faster than you can say *MFA*—but the writing sample is the meat of the matter. As with every other part of the application, read the requirements carefully, then choose your selections just as carefully. No spelling errors, formatted perfectly, you know the drill. This is the greatest hits collection. Include your very best work, but also take time to consider work that shows your potential. Maybe don't include all sonnets about animals—unless that's exactly what you've been writing for the past decade. Readers of this material want to see not only accomplished work but the promise of more. Get feedback from others, including teachers of your undergraduate classes. Show friends and colleagues. Then put your best work forward.

ACTION ITEM 24

Whether you're planning to apply to an MFA program or not, take the time to write a personal statement. Explore what writing means to you and what you are driving at in your art. For inspiration, read Ada Limón's Writer's Notebook on page 414.

Who Is Reading Your Application?

Once you have chosen the programs to which you'd like to apply, gathered and prepared all the parts of your application, and submitted those materials by the deadline, what happens next? Who, exactly, is reviewing those materials? Generally speaking, once they've been processed, applications end up with an admissions board made up of program faculty. For a larger program, in which there could be forty, fifty, or more incoming students across all genres, there are typically a number of boards, one for each genre, comprised of faculty in that genre. For smaller programs, all creative writing faculty may evaluate the applications.

"Files are generally all electronic now so we review them on our own and then meet to discuss our rankings," says poet Ruth Ellen Kocher, a professor and associate dean for arts and humanities at the University of Colorado in Boulder. "We begin by looking for candidates we've all included in our top five to ten. We then move to candidates two or three of us have, and so on." At Boulder, Kocher says, there are often a few spots available so that a member of the admissions board can make a case for a candidate who wasn't chosen by the other members.

One thing to keep in mind is that good candidates can still be rejected. "Occasionally, not often, there will be a great candidate who, for reasons of style and project, just isn't a fit for the program, which means we cannot imagine who the person would be able to work with to receive the kind of mentorship necessary," Kocher says. "For example, we had a writer who was a formalist apply many years ago. There was obvious talent but this program leans toward experimental." All the more reason, then, to put in the research to find the right fit.

ADVICE FROM MFA GRADUATES

"Give yourself time to find the right opportunity; it may take a few years. Cast a wide net when applying; it may take extra money. It may feel like others are getting the best options on their first try, but the reality is that getting a great offer requires first investing in yourself. It cost me roughly $650 to sign up for a workshop to get a better portfolio, about $300 for my first round of applications, about $1,300 for my second round of applications (including the GRE), which racks up to about $2,250. That's no small sum of money, but investing in myself over the course of two or three years allowed me to study reading and writing and teaching

for three years for free. If you're able to spare extra money, (smartly) invest in your own work. If you don't have that money now (which I didn't when I first decided to do this), give yourself time to get there—both in your finances and your writing."
—**Gionni Ponce**, 2019 MFA in Fiction from Indiana University in Bloomington

"Focus on your writing sample above all else. And if you don't get in the first time, keep writing and writing. I just graduated, twenty years after I first applied to an MFA. I hope that's more inspiring than depressing to MFA hopefuls." —**Mary Pauline Lowry**, 2019 MFA in Fiction from Boise State University in Idaho

"Do your research! Join MFA groups online and don't be afraid to ask about past experiences. Don't be afraid to speak up either if you feel your work is being erased or ignored." —**Threa Almontaser**, 2019 MFA in Poetry from North Carolina State University in Raleigh

"1) Just do it. You are smart enough. Your voice has value. You belong in that classroom. 2) Read. Read as if your life depends on it. Read your genre. Read outside your genre. Read it all. . . . You can't know where to go if you don't know where we are and where we've already been. 3) The workshop is hard but necessary. Don't let it scare you. 4) Be bold enough to ask for what you want from your program and humble enough to know when it is appropriate to do so. I didn't know it then, but most programs have a procedure in place for important requests or complaints about the syllabi, staff, or overall community. Don't be afraid to be the change. 5) Research where the working writers of your genre are teaching. If they've published in the last three to five years, they are probably still obsessed with the process and willing to talk about it with you. 6) Make sure the teaching staff is balanced in critical theory and approach to content, as well as in representation. 7) Send your best work. Edit. Let someone else read it. Edit again. Remember that your readers are probably receiving hundreds of applications and you have to do your best to stand out in the best way in the shortest amount of time. Save the slow burn for the workshop—after you've been accepted. 8) Follow the directions. Nothing will get you denied quicker than going over the requested page totals or neglecting to include important info. 9) Contact other people currently in the program to see what they think. A lot of people are more than willing to share their experiences. 10) Do your research. You can easily find out what students who were in the program are now doing professionally. It will give you a good idea about what to expect, network-wise. . . ." —**Faylita Hicks**, 2018 MFA in Poetry from Sierra Nevada College in Incline Village, Nevada

"First and foremost, plan ahead. Ask at least a month ahead of time for letters of recommendation from professional contacts who can speak to your writing skills, your passion for the literary community, your work ethic, and your dedication to your work. Talk to alums of the program if you can. While no two students are exactly the same, a good review makes all the difference, and a bad review can raise some red flags. Definitely apply for fellowships and scholarships." —**Cameron Finch**, 2019 MFA in Writing & Publishing from Vermont College of Fine Arts in Montpelier

"Above all else: Don't go into debt for a writing MFA. Don't get caught up in the prestige of any institution, the shiny faculty—until you know that what they're offering is enough that you won't have to stress (as much) about making rent or getting a side-hustle. Make sure you can eat and live, or else the benefit of the time won't be as effective. I'm not saying you're going to be living lavishly with full funding, you're still a grad student, but the MFA is meant to be a kind of bubble, insulation between you and the real world while you're still finding your voice and learning how to do what you do better. Take care of yourself during the application process, find your support group, and if you're a part of Facebook Draft or Grad Café [a database of over half a million graduate admissions results and discussion forum], maybe take a little break during notification season. What's yours is already yours, so breathe." —**Dantiel W. Moniz**, 2019 MFA in Fiction from the University of Wisconsin in Madison

"Be exhaustive in your research not only in faculty and students but also of campus resources for your work. Apply not just with a vision of attending a program, apply with an eye toward a whole life you will be inhabiting." —**Julian Randall**, 2019 MFA in Poetry from the University of Mississippi in Oxford

"There is no one-size-fits-all. What's best for another writer may not be best for you. Trust your heart, do your homework and give more than you expect to get back in your work and for your community." —**Rowena Alegria**, 2018 MFA in Fiction from the Institute of American Indian Arts

"Don't apply unless you're truly prepared to put in the work. Be ready to constantly walk the line between questioning your skill and being confident in your art." —**Jonathan Wlodarski**, 2018 MFA in Fiction from Northeast Ohio MFA

"It's going to shake your faith. Cultivate an unshakeable sense of self before saying yes to upending your life and taking on an MFA experience." —**Raquel Gutiérrez**, 2019 MFA in Poetry and Nonfiction from the University of Arizona in Tucson

MA and PhD Programs

The MFA is not the only advanced writing degree available. There are a number of colleges and universities that offer a master of arts, or MA, in creative writing—or an MA degree in English with a creative writing emphasis. While not a terminal degree, an MA is similar to an MFA in many ways. Like many MFA programs, the typical MA program is two years, during which students take workshops and lecture classes while cultivating valuable teaching experience—often leading freshmen through composition courses—and other professional experience, including the chance to work for the university's literary journal or university press and participate in conferences, literary festivals, and so on. And while an MFA program is by far the more popular choice, this preference can actually work to your benefit if you aim to attend an MA program: Fewer applicants means less competition for available slots. And, if you are interested in one day pursuing your PhD, an MA program may be preferable to an MFA because some of the literature seminars and theory courses can be applied to PhD course requirements.

A PhD program is typically longer than an MA or MFA program—twice as long in most cases, from four to six years—and therefore requires more of a time commitment. Students can also expect to focus more on literary theory and research in a PhD program, though the workshop is still present in most programs. A PhD program culminates in a creative dissertation: a book-length manuscript that is likely more polished and closer to being ready for submitting to publishers than the collection of stories or poems or novel-in-progress that most MA and MFA students are able to complete by graduation day. And while job placement is no guarantee for any writing program, a PhD student can reasonably expect to qualify for teaching jobs beyond the adjunct positions pursued by many MFA grads.

Carefully consider what you want out of an academic program—for your writing and your education, of course, but also for your future. What kinds of jobs are you looking at further down the road? Don't assume that an MFA is the right choice. There are other options.

Nonacademic Writing Programs

For writers uninterested or unable to pursue a degree at a college or university, there are a growing number of independent writing workshops, including Grub Street in Boston; Gotham Writers' Workshop and Sackett Street Writers' Workshop, both in New York City; the Loft Literary Center in Minneapolis; the Lighthouse Writers Workshop in Denver; the Richard Hugo House in Seattle; Writing Workshops Los Angeles; the Madison Writers' Studio in Wisconsin; and many others in most highly populated cities in the country. While many of the older private workshops, created by well-known nonprofit organizations such as the Loft and Hugo House, offer courses online or in classrooms on the premises, other, newer writing workshops sometimes meet in teachers' homes. Classes are small, often no more than eight students per workshop, and tuition is low, typically ranging from

$400 to $500 for an eight-week class. Instructors tend to be younger, MFA-educated writers with one or two published books or an impressive record of publication in literary magazines. While no degree is conferred, the value of meeting with others and discussing a work in progress at an independent workshop can be every bit as gratifying as meeting at an MFA program.

In response to the traditional workshop model wherein students are able to focus on only a story or a chapter or two of a book during any given semester, some writing centers have also designed courses offering intensive instruction and feedback for writers working on a long project, such as a novel. One of the most notable examples of this kind of book-length workshop is Grub Street's Novel Incubator program, for which students sign up for a year of weekly workshops, consultations with the instructor, and a final manuscript review from an established author.

Online Programs

If you aren't interested in a traditional program, whether it's accredited or not, there are a number of options that don't necessarily require you to leave the comfort of your own home. Colleges and universities such as Harvard, Lindenwood University, Wilkes University, the University of Texas in El Paso, and National University offer online MFA programs. Similar to low-residency programs, online programs utilize discussion boards, videos, and other tools to deliver the same kind of classes. Some, like the program at Harvard, require brief residencies once a year, while others, like the one at the University of New Orleans, offer optional monthlong residencies. In UNO's case, the residencies take place each June or July in either Cork, Ireland, or at Brunnenburg Castle in South Tyrol, Italy.

Parting Thoughts

No matter how you approach your education as a writer, keep in mind that there is no right or wrong way to learn. And there are no guarantees one way or another. A poet can spend thousands of dollars and years of their

life in an MFA program and come out with a published book and an excellent job—or directionless and more confused than ever about their art and
its place in the current culture. Conversely, a writer who has never stepped
foot in a classroom can end up writing next year's *New York Times* bestseller.
If there are specific things you want to achieve in your career, be deliberate about identifying exactly what those things are and what is required to
achieve them. Then make your decisions based on the time, resources, and
opportunities available to you.

Although it's not always possible (after all, there are bills to pay and
mouths to feed—even if it's just your own), a good way to think about your
education as a writer is to keep your writing at the forefront. Learn as much
as you can, read as much as you can, and push your writing as far as it can
go. If going to school is going to help you do that, then consider applying
to some programs. If not, then don't. The point is to enrich your mind, to
develop or enhance your talent. While there are some career opportunities
that can open up in the right situation—again, no guarantees—the decision
to attend a program of any kind should be based on how it will help you
grow as a writer, a reader, and a person.

NATALIE DIAZ RECOMMENDS

Five Books to Read When Constellating Indigeneity and Our Individual and Collective Relationships to Bodies of Land, Language, Water, and Flesh

EL RÍO by Dolores Dorantes
"We were power, or we / were once. *The water / isn't an attribute of your / circumstances. Crossing over / isn't an attribute of your / circumstances.* We were, / or we were once, the stone / head jutting out from the / water."

OSSUARIES by Dionne Brand
"if we could return through this war, any war, / as if it were we who needed redemption, / instead of this big world, our ossuary."

THE BLACK SHOALS: OFFSHORE FORMATIONS OF BLACK AND NATIVE STUDIES
by Tiffany Lethabo King
"The erotic becomes a source of power and information that is crucial for decolonial resistance. . . . I situate and discuss the erotic as a site of Black and Indigenous gathering (shoaling) or coming together."

THE DESERT by Brandon Shimoda
"From afar incarceration looks like internment / It is always day / No Japanese Americans exist."

IN THE PRESENCE OF ABSENCE by Mahmoud Darwish, translated by Sinan Antoon
"Do not regret a war that ripened you just as August ripens pomegranates on the slopes of stolen mountains. For there is no other hell waiting for you. What once was yours is now against you."

NATALIE DIAZ *was born and raised in the Fort Mojave Indian Village in Needles, California, on the banks of the Colorado River. She is Mojave and an enrolled member of the Gila River Indian tribe. Her first poetry collection,* When My Brother Was an Aztec, *was published by Copper Canyon Press, and her second book,* Postcolonial

Love Poem, *was published by Graywolf Press in March 2020. She is a 2018 MacArthur Fellow, as well as a Lannan Literary Fellow and a Native Arts Council Foundation Artist Fellow. She was awarded the Princeton Holmes National Poetry Prize and a Hodder Fellowship. She is a member of the Board of Trustees for the United States Artists, where she is an alumna of the Ford Fellowship. Diaz is the Maxine and Jonathan Marshall Chair in Modern and Contemporary Poetry at Arizona State University.*

II

SEVEN

Writing and Time

A book is made from a tree. It is an assemblage of flat, flexible parts (still called "leaves") imprinted with dark pigmented squiggles. One glance at it and you hear the voice of another person, perhaps someone dead for thousands of years. Across the millennia, the author is speaking, clearly and silently, inside your head, directly to you. Writing is perhaps the greatest of human inventions, binding together people, citizens of distant epochs, who never knew one another. Books break the shackles of time—proof that humans can work magic.

—CARL SAGAN

In the hierarchy of worries that writers carry around with them, *time*—or, more specifically, the lack thereof—ranks right up there with money as a problem in continual need of solving. As with so many elements of the writer's life, there isn't one formula for time management that works for everyone. Some writers need great swaths of uninterrupted time in which to lose themselves in a writing project. Others work best when they're stealing minutes away from a commute to write a line of poetry or pulling out a small notebook to record an observation when they're standing in line at the grocery store—and then transferring the day's lines to the screen after the kids go down for the night. And others thrive using some combination of the two.

"I write where I can, when I can," says Catherine Chung, author of the novels *The Tenth Muse* and *Forgotten Country*. "I've written in bathtubs of hotel rooms so as not to wake my companions, I've written on napkins in restaurants, I've written on my phone on the train, sitting under a tree or on a rock, and on my own arm in a pinch. I've walked down streets repeating lines to myself when I've been caught without a pen or my phone. I've also written on my laptop or in a notebook at cafés and in libraries or in bed or at my dining table. As to how often I write, it depends on childcare, what I'm working on, on deadlines, on life!"

And that's really the crux of the matter, isn't it? Life—all the stuff that isn't writing—does have a way of demanding more and more of one's time. But there is a way of perceiving this struggle with time as a positive force in the creative process. "You're fighting against the constraints of time, life, business—and you're never going to win. You're not meant to. That's frustrating, but it's also beautiful," writes Eric Gorges, owner of Voodoo Choppers in Detroit, in his book *A Craftsman's Legacy: Why Working with Our Hands Gives Us Meaning*. "The struggle keeps you growing. It gives us all a little kick, an extra engine. That's something we can all use to become our best selves. That's why I keep up the fight."

Every writer must prioritize and schedule time in a way that makes the most sense to them. But assuming you're fulfilling your obligations—to yourself and to those who depend on you—give yourself permission to insist on time for your art. For some of us, this isn't quite as hard as it sounds. Instead of looking at your phone on your half-hour commute, pull out your notebook or laptop—and voilà, an hour of writing time every weekday. Or, instead of turning the television on every Saturday night, devote that time to writing. But it can get tricky when your friends or your partner or your family doesn't understand or, worst case, respect the role of writing in your life. Strike a balance and give yourself permission to turn down that invitation to hang out or go to the movies. Your writing is important; prioritize it accordingly.

Learning to Say No

Of course, sometimes writing-related obligations can eat up one's writing time. As your writing life continues to grow, so can the list of demands on your time. As you benefit from the support of others, others will look to you for support. This is a tricky one, because as we've discussed in earlier chapters, it's important to be a good literary citizen and play a positive role in your community. But it's equally important to learn to say no. Throughout our careers, we've been on the asking side of the table countless times. The very nature of our jobs has required us to send requests to so many authors—to interview a fellow author, to be interviewed for a certain article, to write a paragraph about this writers retreat or that writing contest, to write an essay or compile a reading list for this very book, or to appear at an event. Generally speaking, writers say yes a little over half the time. Sometimes they simply can't, but other times it's clear they are protecting their time. And while it's disappointing when writers decline our requests and invitations, we always, without question, understand and respect the decision. It's okay to say no; the writing comes first. As Cheryl Strayed writes in her book *Brave Enough*, "No is golden. No is the power the good witch yields."

How Long It Takes to Write a Book

Widely considered one of the pioneers of creative nonfiction, John McPhee is a true master of the form. A staff writer at the *New Yorker* since 1965, he has written over thirty books, including *Encounters With the Archdruid* and *The Curve of Binding Energy*, both of which were nominated for National Book Awards in the category of Science, and *Annals of the Former World*, for which he won the Pulitzer Prize in 1999. In 2018 he accepted the Ivan Sandrof Lifetime Achievement Award from the National Book Critics Circle. In his acceptance speech, he addressed the question of how much time it takes to complete a writing project:

ACTION ITEM 25

Create a weekly schedule that takes into account your job and/or your classes, your commute, your meals, your recreation time, the time you spend planning and caring for others, the time you go to sleep on an average night—everything but your writing time. Be as exacting as possible. Now look at the schedule and highlight any unaccounted blocks of time. Might that be time spent writing?

William Shawn, the *New Yorker*'s editor for some forty years, understood the disjunct kinship of creative work—every kind of creative work—and time. The most concise summation of it I've ever encountered was his response to a question I asked him just before we closed my first *New Yorker* profile and he sent it off to press. It was about Bill Bradley in college basketball, and after all those one-on-one sessions with Mr. Shawn discussing back-door plays and the role of the left-handed comma in the architectonics of the game—while the *New Yorker* magazine hurtled toward its deadlines—I finally said in wonderment, "How can you afford to use so much time and go into so many things in such detail with just one writer when this whole enterprise is yours to keep together?" He said, "It takes as long as it takes."

As a writing teacher, I have repeated that statement to two generations of students. If they are writers, they will never forget it.

Indeed, if you are approaching a writing project such as a novel or a poetry or essay collection with the question "How long is this going to take?" then you might want to consider doing something else with your time. That question works well when you're staring at a freelance writing or editing assignment and you have bills to pay next month, but not so well with a book of imagination. As William Shawn said, it's going to take as long as it takes, and trying to rein it in before you even get started is one surefire way to doom the creative process (and limit the thrill of discovery). But editors do give deadlines, and all of us are programmed at a very early age to expect and adapt to schedules.

To give you a sense of how long it can take to complete a book, here's how a few authors with recent books answered the question.

"Nine years, more or less." —**Julie Orringer**, author of the novel *The Flight Portfolio*

"When I found out I was pregnant, I began pounding the keys of my laptop every day for a couple of hours to force out an ugly first draft before

I became a single mother. In the first six months of my son's life I wrote nothing. After that I worked a little at a time whenever I could, meaning whenever I could afford childcare. So, the short answer is five years, but not continuously." —**Domenica Ruta**, author of the novel *Last Day*

"All of my twenties and the early part of my thirties." —**Xuan Juliana Wang**, author of the story collection *Home Remedies*

"*Dissolve* took about seven years to complete. Most of those seven years I spent revising the poem. It was a challenge to harmonize all its layers and dimensions." —**Sherwin Bitsui**, author of the poetry collection *Dissolve*

"It took eight years. This is a little embarrassing to admit because it's not like the book is a thousand pages long. At one point during the writing of it a friend who works in finance asked how long it would physically take to type a book if you knew all the words already, and the answer in my case, given how fast I type, was one week. And yet it still took eight years." —**Keith Gessen**, author of the novel *A Terrible Country*

"The poems in *Library of Small Catastrophes* were written over a three-to-four-year span. However, I would venture to assert that the book has taken a lifetime to write in terms of the necessity to live, experience, read, and hone my craft over time. While I don't hope to glorify suffering in the service of artistic practice, I do think it is important to celebrate living, awareness, observation, and the act of being present in the world. Many of the poems in this book are based on experiences that I have witnessed or been a part of, and I had to live them and be present within them to translate them into poems." —**Alison C. Rollins**, author of the poetry collection *Library of Small Catastrophes*

"Five years. I started writing the poems in *Brute* in 2012. About three years into it, I had a book-length manuscript, but it felt incomplete to me. I wound up cutting or revising more than half of it, and then I spent another

two years rethinking, rewriting, and rearranging it before I fully understood what shape it should take. In that time, I changed so much as a person that the manuscript began to feel closed off to me. Trying to write back
into it was like being in conversation with a ghost of myself—a voice that
draped itself in my clothes and spoke about my experiences, but from the
point of view of someone who was a few steps removed from me. I found
that in order to keep working on the book, I had to write my way back into
it in a way that honored the time and distance that separated the new self
from the ghost. As a result, there are a lot of poems in the book in which
I address my younger self and try to reassemble her memories with the
wisdom of recovery." —**Emily Skaja**, author of the poetry collection *Brute*

"About six years, though in my defense I had a full-time job (as a jour-
nalist) that whole time. Mostly I wrote on weekends." —**Juliet Lapidos**,
author of the novel *Talent*

"The stories in this collection took twelve years—stories accrue over time.
I don't sit down to write a collection of stories. I have ideas for them that
can take years to form and there is a compression to storytelling, the sense
that the story is already in progress by the time the reader comes to it—
which means that I, like, know what it's all about before diving in. And
there's also an editorial/curating process—we build the collection—so
once I have six to eight stories I like, I start to think about the balance
of voices within the stories, about narrative threads, ideas that appear in
multiple stories—and sometimes we put a few stories aside and I write one
or two more." —**A. M. Homes**, author of the story collection *Days of Awe*

Lest you think contemporary writers have a harder time wrestling with
time than their counterparts, say, 170 years ago, consider the following,
from a letter Herman Melville sent to Nathaniel Hawthorne in 1851:

In a week or so, I go to New York, to bury myself in a third-story room,
and work and slave on my "Whale" while it is driving through the press.

That is the only way I can finish it now,—I am so pulled hither and thither by circumstances. The calm, the coolness, the silent grass-growing mood in which a man *ought* always to compose,—that, I fear, can seldom be mine. Dollars damn me; and the malicious Devil is forever grinning in upon me, holding the door ajar.

How Long It Takes to Publish a Book

The short answer is: It depends. It depends on how long it takes you to develop and hone your proposal. It depends on how long it takes to find an agent and/or editor. It depends on how long it takes your agent to sell your book. It depends on your publisher and how far out they've scheduled their lists. At Alice James Books, a small poetry press in Farmington, Maine, editorial director Carey Salerno says they're scheduled for the next three years. "Most independent publishers of poetry right now are running at about two years." At Akashic Books, too, editorial director Ibrahim Ahmad says the indie press is scheduled three years out. "We're at an interesting point now where we have so many projects in the pipeline that we're being more selective than ever. Our commitments will bring us into 2022, so we're really just looking at the cream of the crop and those things that we know if we were to say no to them would keep us up at night."

At larger publishing houses that employ more people and are able to publish more books per season, such as W. W. Norton and the Hachette imprint Little, Brown, the typical time between signing a contract and publishing the book is a year and a half—and that's if the manuscript is in good shape, adds Little, Brown senior editor Ben George. That may seem like a protracted timetable, but keep in mind there are scheduling considerations (the publisher may want to release the book in a specific season, taking into account any time pegs for the book, such as an anniversary or an election, while juggling many other titles on any given list) and multiple steps of the publication process, such as editing, copyediting, proofreading, cover and interior design, and prepublication promotion and publicity, that shouldn't be rushed. (Most of the big houses try to get galleys, otherwise known as advance reading copies, or ARCs, out to potential reviewers and media outlets five to six months before the pub date so that editors have enough time to schedule coverage.) All these steps take time, and we'll be exploring them in more detail in later chapters.

On the other end of the spectrum, very small publishers can acquire, edit, and publish a book much more quickly. And, of course, self-publishers can publish their book in a matter of days.

It also depends on the genre. For some nonfiction books that correspond to a strong time peg, production schedules are sometimes shortened and publication dates fast-tracked so that the publisher can take full advantage of the promotional opportunities.

So, yes, it depends.

The Age-Old Question

Each year a lot of attention is paid to "new and emerging" authors under a certain age. Every fall the National Book Foundation honors a group of authors through its 5 Under 35 program, designed to introduce "the next generation" of fiction writers. And in the spring the New York Public Library offers its $10,000 Young Lions Fiction Award to a writer age thirty-five or younger. The hundred-year-old Yale University Press only relatively recently lifted the age restriction for the legendary Yale Series of Younger Poets, which for nearly a century stipulated that the publication award was open only to poets under forty. Every ten years the London-based literary magazine *Granta* names the twenty writers it considers the Best of Young British Novelists, all of them under forty. The *New Yorker* made waves back in 1999 with its first 20 Under 40 list—a popular feature the magazine repeated in 2010—anointing authors such as Michael Chabon, Jhumpa Lahiri, Edwidge Danticat, and George Saunders as "standouts in the diverse and expansive panorama of contemporary fiction," as the *New Yorker*'s fiction editor Deborah Treisman put it. BuzzFeed got in on that action with a feature in 2014, 20 Under 40 Debut Writers You Need to Be Reading, that included the line: "Out with the old, in with the debut."

While there is something undeniably exciting about news of the next big book by a recently discovered talent, *new* does not necessarily mean *young*, no matter how broadly that qualifier is defined. And while popular culture tends to favor youth, there is something equally exciting about the work of those authors who have lived a lot longer—some pursuing alternative careers, others raising families; all of them taking their time, either by choice or by necessity, and collecting valuable life experience that undoubtedly informs and inspires their writing—before publishing a book.

The truth is, it's never too late to start writing and it's never too late to publish your work. Toni Morrison was nearly forty by the time she published her first book, *The Bluest Eye*, a novel she wrote by waking up at 4 a.m. every day while raising two kids alone and working as an editor—the first black woman fiction editor at Random House.

"You have to want to write, and I mean really want it," says Paul Vidich, whose debut novel, *An Honorable Man*, was published when he was sixty-six, after a career at Time Warner. "It is important not to be discouraged by age. You have to inoculate yourself from the perception, however true, that the world only seems to recognize youth and ignores the contributions of later-aged newcomers. You also need self-confidence. One day, feeling down, I put together a list of authors who had debuted later in life. Raymond Chandler wrote *The Big Sleep*, his first book, at fifty-one; Julia Glass wrote her first novel, *Three Junes*, when she was forty-six; and so on. Compiling this list stoked my confidence. If they could do it, then so could I."

And so could you. According to Anne Youngson, whose debut novel, *Meet Me at the Museum*, was published by Flatiron Books in 2018 and went on to be short-listed for the Costa First Novel Award, the only important factor is the quality of your work. "The package has to be right—the book has to be based on a good idea, well constructed, well written, and, of course, finished. If all this comes together, the age of the author turns out to be irrelevant."

Timothy Brandoff, who wrote his debut novel, *Cornelius Sky*, for twelve years while operating a bus for the New York City Transit Authority, finally saw his book published by Akashic Books in 2019. "I'm sixty, but it doesn't matter. The book took twelve years, but it doesn't matter. There is no correlation between those numbers and the work's resonance," he says. "Not so long ago I read *Anna Karenina*. It felt like it was written *that afternoon*. Same with *To the Lighthouse*. Such compelling immediacy, such *nowness*. Human consciousness, captured on the page, seems to live outside time. Knowing the author's age during the period of composition and/or how long the book took might be an interesting aside, amounting to no more than academic gossip."

EIGHT

Writing and Money

There's no money in poetry, but then there's no poetry in money, either.

—ROBERT GRAVES

Some writers stop writing after years of painful rejection. Others lose interest and take up other passions or find that their literary gifts are better suited to working in publishing or running a bookstore. But far too often, writers cannot support themselves on writing alone and simply run out of money—and with it, the time and freedom to write.

Avoiding this fate requires planning and discipline, along with a willingness to navigate the intricacies of federal tax law. But more than anything, surviving as an artist long term means deciding what you can and can't live without and being creative about how you pay for the parts of your life that mean the most to you.

A Little Financial Planning

Writers can gain a measure of control over their fiscal lives even before they embark on a writing career by considering how much debt, if any, they're willing to take on for an MFA, says Arwen Lowbridge, a financial planner and adviser with Massachusetts-based Baystate Financial. An MFA can be a valuable credential if it leads to a full-time teaching job, but those jobs are growing increasingly scarce, and before you enter an MFA program you need to have a clear idea what your monthly loan payments will be after you graduate and have a plan for how you're going to pay them off. "Taking on that much debt without a viable strategy to pay it off aggressively can create financial catastrophe in the long run," says Lowbridge.

The Federal Student Aid website (studentaid.ed.gov) offers a repayment estimator that can help you calculate your future monthly loan payments, along with information on programs that, in some cases, can reduce or eliminate your indebtedness. If you don't qualify for those programs, and aren't offered funding by your university, you may want to delay applying for a few years to build up your savings, Lowbridge says.

Once your formal education is behind you, you'll need to figure out how much you need to earn to pay your bills and still have time to practice your art. Amy Smith, a tax specialist who works with writers and other artists, offers her clients a simple worksheet, reproduced on page 173, that asks writers to calculate their monthly expenses on everything from rent and utilities to student loan debt and estimated tax payments. Those monthly figures, when added up and multiplied by twelve, offer a rough estimate of the writer's annual cost of living.

Then, of course, a writer needs to figure out where that money is going to come from. For freelance writers—not to mention writers who rely on income from giving speeches and lectures, teaching gigs, and book advances—this can be a constant and driving question in their working lives. To calculate how much a freelance writer needs to charge for their work to live comfortably, Smith suggests dividing the annual budget by fifteen hundred to arrive at a reasonable hourly rate. (People working a standard forty-hour week fifty weeks a year work two thousand hours, but artistic work tends to be gig-based, with many hours spent pitching and preparing, so Smith recommends assuming a fifteen-hundred-hour work year.)

Such calculations are by their nature rough estimates, but writers can use them as guidelines when pitching for work, Smith says. If, for instance, you decide you need to make $45,000 a year, you would need to average $30 an hour for your work. If you're offered work that pays significantly less, Smith says, you may want to negotiate a better rate, understanding that you ultimately may have to turn down a job if it doesn't pay enough.

"Just say yes to no," she says. "It's really hard because we internalize all these messages that our time is not valuable, but once you start saying no to opportunities, a magical thing happens, which is that people change their understanding of what your time is worth and start offering you more."

But income is only one side of the ledger. If you're struggling to make ends meet, you can also look for ways to bring your expenses under control. Pop financial advice often focuses on dialing back luxuries like vacations or daily lattes, but most working writers already live fairly frugal lives. Some writers can choose where they live, though, notes Elaine Grogan Luttrull, a Columbus, Ohio–based CPA who works with artists and other creative individuals. Many younger writers gravitate toward New York City, the nation's publishing and cultural hub, but New York is among the world's most expensive cities, and too often young writers sacrifice valuable writing time just to pay their rent.

"Make your choices on purpose," Luttrull advises. "Why are you living in Brooklyn? Why are you living in LA? If your side hustle is writing for film and television and you have to be there during pilot season, you probably don't have a choice. If you have a family obligation that's going to keep you in a particular area and the only sort of creative place nearby is a very expensive city, you might not have a choice. But if you do have options, how willing are you to explore those options?"

Taxes and Insurance

With careful planning and a keen awareness of the rules, you can also reap significant savings by tracking your spending on taxes and insurance, two perennial budget-busters for freelance artists.

The Affordable Care Act has relieved some of the pressure on freelancers needing health insurance, but the cost of coverage remains out of reach for many. If you don't have adequate health insurance through work or government programs, you may want to explore health plans offered through organizations like the National Writers Union (nwu.org) and the Freelancers Union (freelancersunion.org).

But as frustrating as the search for quality health insurance can be, filing tax returns as a freelancer brings its own set of complications. Unlike a traditional employee who receives a single paycheck with taxes and benefits already deducted, freelancers are often paid in lump sums and are responsible for paying their own taxes and insurance.

If a freelance payment is large—a book advance, say, or a major writing award—financial experts advocate spreading it out over more than one tax year, if possible, to avoid jumping tax brackets, and setting aside between fifteen and thirty percent for taxes. In many cases, freelancers have to pay taxes in quarterly installments to avoid penalties.

Writers who are savvy about the tax code and willing to put in the time to collect receipts and itemize business deductions can save a lot of money at tax time. In the eyes of the IRS, your writing is a business for which you can deduct reasonable expenses so long as you consistently make money at it and treat it as a business. Even if your creative work doesn't meet the IRS's definition of a business, you can deduct certain expenses related to your writing up to the amount you earned from it in a given year.

Smith, the independent tax preparer, offers clients a worksheet, reproduced on page 174, listing the most common Schedule C deductions, which range from expenditures on books and research trips to business gifts like sending flowers to your literary agent after signing a book deal. "If it's ordinary in your line of work and it's necessary in your line of work, you can deduct it," she says.

One major expense freelance writers can deduct is office space. If you rent an office or pay for a shared workspace, you can deduct those payments. If you write at home, you can deduct a portion of your rent or mortgage based on how many square feet you're using exclusively as a home office. "It's absolutely ordinary and absolutely necessary to have a space to write so just look at your space," Smith says. "If it's a hundred square feet and you live in a six-hundred-square-foot apartment, one-sixth of your rent and one-sixth of your utilities is now deductible."

Writers who consistently earn a sizable income from their work—more than about $75,000 a year—may want to consider incorporating themselves as a business entity, such as an S corporation, which allows writers to pay themselves a salary and save more money at tax time. Meeting the reporting requirements of a corporation can be time-consuming, and the cost of filing your taxes may go up, but for many top-earning writers the tax savings make the extra time and expense worth it.

The more tangled your finances, the more it may make sense to seek financial help from a professional. Unfortunately, good financial advice doesn't come cheap. Luttrull charges clients $110 per hourlong session through her firm Minerva Financial Arts. Smith, meanwhile, charges $275 to prepare a tax return for a single filer and $400 for a couple filing jointly; but depending on who you work with and the complexity of your finances, your tax prep bill can easily run much higher.

If you hire a financial or tax adviser, look for one who has experience working with artists, either by searching online or by asking mentors and writer friends whom they trust with their taxes and finances. "If you're going to go to H&R Block as a writer, they're probably not going to know what you can deduct, or they're going to do it incorrectly," says Smith. "So if you can find someone who's in the community already, who is an artist or at least familiar with artists' taxes, that's the best."

But Smith, who taught herself nonprofit accounting by keeping the books for a dance company she helped create, says that, with enough work, anyone can manage their own finances. "I'm a big fan of people learning how to do it themselves because it saves money and you feel more empowered, you feel more in control of your financial destiny," she says. "And, frankly, irs.gov is a really good website. People are afraid of the IRS, but you can go in there and type just about any question or keyword and find what you need."

Getting Paid

As we wrote in chapter 1, writers should be paid for their work. Because that's what it is: work. And here we approach the fraught intersection of art and commerce. Writers tend to be well acquainted with the social value of their work: Yes, literature is important. Everyone can—or at least they should—agree on this. But lip service to the value of the writer's art is cheap. Meanwhile, writers need to eat and pay their bills. To do so they must often supplement their earnings from writing with other, more lucrative work. This is the reality of the marketplace, but that doesn't mean writers should ignore the financial value of their work. Indeed, any publisher with resources should compensate its writers fairly. Don't give away your work for free if remuneration is a reasonable option.

Notice we made the distinction of publishers *with resources*. The ecosystem of publishing is filled not only with profitable corporations doing business on the world stage but also with tiny literary journals and nonprofit organizations that offer vital services with very limited resources. Whereas monied publishers can and should be pushed to pay a fair price for your work—and in the case of book publishing, this is where the services of a literary agent come into play in a big way—the smaller entities may not be able to pay, at least not as much as their prosperous counterparts. Therefore, when you're just starting out, trying to make a name for yourself and getting your work out there, it's not uncommon to be confronted with a decision to accept a modest fee from a literary journal or for payment to come in the form of contributor copies.

It's a tricky calculus. On the one hand, there are stories of writers who write something for free—an essay, a review, an article—and the subsequent exposure leads to an e-mail from an agent or an editor asking to see more writing, which in turn leads to a book deal. *Scratch: Writers, Money, and the Art of Making a Living*, edited by Manjula Martin, includes a story like that. "I wrote a piece for free. It led to a book deal. It led to writing a book," writes Nina MacLaughlin, author of *Hammer Head: The Making of a Carpenter*. "This was a combination of events and an outcome that still, in moments, feels unreal, shimmery. I was able to do what I most wanted to do, and get paid for it. The book came out. And now I continue the rush and hustle. Sometimes I write for free; mostly I try not to."

On the other hand, working for free on the off chance that something good will come from it doesn't sound like a fiscally responsible or sustainable plan, at least for the long term. So, we do what almost every writer does:

whatever works. Eyes on the next step in front of us, whether it's next week's groceries, the next rent payment, or the kids' tuition.

Every writer must base these decisions on their own circumstances and comfort level. After all, the writing community is filled with writers from different socioeconomic backgrounds who are dealing with different financial realities. Those with trust funds and wealthy patrons and plump 401(k)s are competing for the same publishing slots and prizes as those carrying mountains of debt, living paycheck to paycheck, and struggling to make ends meet. What is good advice for one of those writers might be lousy advice for another.

There are no easy answers to the money question. There are simply too many factors like luck, chance, and personal experience. But it's always a good idea to establish your own set of expectations and make informed decisions based on what you can reasonably hope to gain.

Eyes on the Prize

Anyone with a subscription to Publishers Lunch, the industry e-mail newsletter that delivers publishing news and the lowdown on the latest book deals each weekday, or the industry magazine *Publishers Weekly*—or anyone who follows a lot of authors on Twitter—can fill up on all the juicy details about which author got what book deal and how high the advance was for which forthcoming book. This can be useful information. (For a monthly fee, the Publishers Lunch Deluxe membership gives you access to a database of dealmakers so that you can see what agents and editors were involved in which book deals.)

Depending on your temperament, this can either be fascinating and fun research—*guitarist Keith Richards got $7.3 million for his drug/rock memoir, really?*—or sobering. It's wise to survey the field and keep abreast of the changing markets for your work, of course. As we've said, a successful writer is an informed one. But research can sometimes tip over into obsession, and that doesn't do anyone any good. And truthfully, there's only so much you can learn from how much someone received as an advance. As with so much else about the intersection of art and commerce, there are too many variables, including luck and chance, that influence those numbers.

Just as a future Hall of Fame quarterback (say, Aaron Rodgers of the Green Bay Packers) can start his professional career by falling to the twenty-fourth pick of the NFL draft and then sit on the bench for three years, a best-selling author can start off with a relatively modest book deal. The only difference is that if a publisher is going to commit to the high six figures or even seven figures as an advance against royalties on a book, then you can bet the full force of their marketing and publicity departments will be working to ensure a return on their investment. But there is no direct correlation between these high advances we read about and the quality of the book in question. It just means that the book and the author checked off the right boxes in the minds of the publisher.

ACTION ITEM 26

Take a deep breath and fill out the Valuing Your Time worksheet, using your best guess at your monthly and annual costs. Even if you don't earn an hourly wage, it's a good idea to keep a budget.

Remember: All those authors whose books sit proudly on our shelves had to start somewhere. And it's a good bet that most of them started out in obscure little literary magazines or being paid a pittance for their early efforts.

And let's not forget that what we're talking about here is how people make a living. Just as one doesn't go around asking everyone they meet at a cocktail party, "So, how much do you make a year?" one shouldn't get too wrapped up in what this or that author is making. Instead, focus on your writing. The money that well-known author received has little to no bearing on your own future payday.

WORKSHEET
VALUING YOUR TIME

To know what your work costs, you need to know what your life costs. So, step one is figuring out: What do you need to earn in a year to live without financial panic?

Monthly rent/mortgage	$_____ x 12 = $_____	per year
Utilities	$_____ x 12 = $_____	per year
Internet	$_____ x 12 = $_____	per year
Car/transportation	$_____ x 12 = $_____	per year
Cell phone	$_____ x 12 = $_____	per year
Groceries	$_____ x 12 = $_____	per year
Childcare/family care	$_____ x 12 = $_____	per year
Recreation, going out, etc.	$_____ x 12 = $_____	per year
Classes/workshops	$_____ x 12 = $_____	per year
Going to shows/artistic research	$_____ x 12 = $_____	per year
Clothes, books, etc.	$_____ x 12 = $_____	per year
Student loan debt	$_____ x 12 = $_____	per year
Savings	$_____ x 12 = $_____	per year
Vacation (annual)	$_____	per year
Health (insurance, prescriptions; annual)	$_____	per year
Estimated taxes (annual)	$_____	per year
MY LIFE COSTS	$_____	per year

Use this number to calculate weekly, daily, and hourly rates. Divide your annual number by 1,500: This is your hourly rate. Multiply that hourly rate by eight to get your daily rate. Multiply that day rate by five to get your weekly rate.

MY WEEKLY RATE IS	$_____	per day
MY DAILY RATE IS	$_____	per day
MY HOURLY RATE IS	$_____	per day

These numbers are for internal use, and can be thought of as an average. In practice, you can always ask for more, and you can work for less. Artists often negotiate more money for certain kinds of work to help balance work that pays less but is closer to their mission. When you budget a project, use these numbers to estimate the real costs of your time, including research and development, working on the project itself, and follow-up. When offered a flat fee, you can use these numbers to determine how much time you would like to spend on the project. And, most important, if you are offered an opportunity that doesn't come close to compensating you adequately, these numbers give you a basis for saying no.

Putting a dollar value on your time helps you know what your work actually costs you to make. You may not be able to get all this time paid for, and it's totally fine to subsidize your work however you need to. But, if you know the real cost, you will have insight into proposing projects, finding new markets for your work, and negotiating better pay and fees for yourself.

Courtesy of Amy Smith with contributions from Andrew Simonet and Aaron Lansman

WORKSHEET

BUSINESS DEDUCTIONS (UNREIMBURSED)

Advertising (cards, mailings) _____

Books/research _____

Business gifts (flowers, wine for agent) _____

Commissions _____

Internet/website _____

Local travel _____

Meals (in town, business related) _____

Office supplies _____

Per diem (use gsa.gov for rates) _____

Photo/video _____

Professional development _____

Rented space (studio) _____

Tax preparation (for previous year) _____

Telephone (business use—can be a % of total cost) _____

Trade publications _____

Travel (not commuting to/from your primary job) _____

HOME OFFICE

Total square footage of home _____

Total footage used for business _____

Total utilities _____ repairs _____ for whole home.

Total rent paid for year _____

Homeowners/renters insurance _____

If own home, property tax paid _____ mortgage interest paid _____

CAR EXPENSES

Make/model _____

Total miles driven in year _____

Total miles driven for business in year (not commuting) _____

AMORTIZABLE EXPENSES (large expenses such as a new computer for work)

What was it? _____

Date purchased/cost _____

OTHER EXPENSES "NECESSARY AND ORDINARY" FOR YOUR WORK

_____

_____

Note: The rules for how much you can deduct vary based on whether your artistic practice
qualifies as a business under IRS standards. For a fuller picture of what the IRS considers a
business, go to the agency's website (irs.gov) or consult a tax or finance professional.

Courtesy of Amy Smith

NINE

Writing and Happiness

And I urge you to please notice when you are happy,
and exclaim or murmur or think at some point,
"If this isn't nice, I don't know what is."

—KURT VONNEGUT

Depending on your experience, your temperament, and your overall world-view, you have arrived at this chapter with either a fully formed understanding and appreciation of the positive effects of writing in your life (why else would you do it?) or you are conversant with the more challenging elements (nothing worth doing is easy). We would venture to argue that there is more time spent, and ink spilled, on the negative, so this chapter is intended to remind us of the virtues of a life spent writing. Of course, we can't fully appreciate those unless we acknowledge the decidedly less appealing but nevertheless common, and in some cases necessary, aspects of being a writer.

The Good

If you're reading this, we can all agree that we love writing, but why, exactly? Is it because of the focus it requires and allows us? The ability to block out the countless distractions that compete for our attention and concentrate on a generative, creative, and therefore beautiful act? When you look around at the state of the world—whether it's politics or the environment or violence or social injustice—perhaps it's no surprise why many of us turn to writing as either sanctuary or battlefield. (We won't back down from our earlier claim that writing can change the world.) Maybe, too, we turn to writing to more fully understand who we are. So often these days our sense of self can be defined in opposition to things, whether it's an opinion thrown at us on social media or the dominant narrative coming at us in the day's headlines, so it's no wonder we savor the ability to turn inward in search of a deeper understanding of who we are and where we stand.

And what about the ability to connect with another human being— another person whom you have never met and who lives nowhere near you and has nothing in common with you except the things you were able to articulate in your writing? The ability to make that person feel things and see things about the world that never occurred to them before? Gold.

There have been a number of studies on the health benefits of writing— so-called expressive writing, which is all about writing through our feelings and experiences and has proven to reduce stress, improve mood disorders, and more. More recently, clinical studies have revealed that by writing one's personal narrative—and then editing it—we can fundamentally change the way we see ourselves. "The concept is based on the idea that we all have a personal narrative that shapes our view of the world and ourselves," wrote Tara Parker-Pope in the *New York Times* back in 2015. "But sometimes our inner voice doesn't get it completely right. Some researchers believe that by writing and then editing our own stories, we can change our perceptions of ourselves and identify obstacles that stand in the way of better health." This is clearly tied to the act of keeping a journal or diary and perhaps less to writing a novel or a poem, but we'd argue that these activities are all con-nected. In both cases, writing is about getting to a deeper understanding of yourself and your world, whether it's in service of your personal narrative or your writing project, and it can have a positive effect on one's mind, body, and spirit. So-called narrative medicine has been used to help physicians, nurses, social workers, mental health professionals, and others to more ef-fectively administer medical treatment with the power of stories.

Back in chapter 2 we mentioned "flow," a phenomenon of optimal produc-tivity that can result in losing track of time or feeling outside yourself, coined by the psychologist Mihaly Csikszentmihalyi. Any writer who has experienced this super-focused state of mind—which is really not unlike the high of a drug—has likely chased that feeling ever since. One of the reasons it's so powerful is the knowledge that you've been so incredibly productive (without even really knowing it). And again, in this day and age of round-the-clock distraction, we shouldn't underestimate the importance and pleasure of periods of generative focus and concentration. It's an achievement—one that plenty of people without a similar creative outlet would be lucky to experience.

Which brings us to pride. This can sometimes sound like a bad word. It doesn't have to be. Be proud. If it doesn't come naturally, practice—give yourself permission. You've written something. It doesn't matter what stage you're at in your career. Maybe you've just finished a poem, a story, or a novel. Maybe you've just published a book. Or your seventh! Or maybe you just started an essay. Whatever it is, take the time to acknowledge yourself. You've accomplished something—probably despite someone telling you, or implying, or you yourself sometimes simply feeling, that it wasn't the best use of your time, that the struggle wasn't worth it. Yet here you are, reading this book, learning more about your craft and the business of writing, having created whole worlds on the page. Be proud of yourself. And, if you're so fortunate, allow others to be proud of you, too. Give yourself permission to brag a bit. Don't automatically dismiss what you're doing if someone brings it up over dinner or in casual conversation. You're a writer. You've written something unique. And there are millions of people out there who cannot say that. It's a special thing you're doing, unique to you. Go ahead, be proud.

The Bad

Now we need to acknowledge some of the more difficult aspects of being a writer, if only so that we can better understand the positive. Because as we'll see, in many cases, the positive and negative are inexorably linked, and sometimes you can't have one without the other. But before we get too far into the bad, let's take a moment to remember the importance of self-care when the writing is hard. This may seem silly to some, but it's not. Don't isolate; take advantage of your community and talk to other writers. Exercise, take walks,

meditate, eat a nourishing meal—you know the drill. As writers we can sometimes forget—we get so engrossed in a writing project, or so blocked when we
are unable to—to attend to our own mental
and physical health. We tend to internalize, which is what makes us
writers, but this can also lead to
getting overloaded with doubt
and anxiety. If these feelings
spill over into despair or another serious mental health
issue, it's crucial that you get
help. We are all familiar with
the long and romanticized literary history of brilliant but
tortured artists. We don't need to
add to it. The idea that you need to be
unhappy to be a good artist is a myth. If
you need help, please don't be afraid to ask for it.

ACTION ITEM 27

Check your humility at the door.
Find some time to list all your literary
accomplishments. If you're just starting out, yes,
you still have accomplishments you can be proud of:
the writing you've done, the courage you've shown in
your journaling. If you're reading this book it's because
you have a high regard for your writing and want to learn
as much as you can about your art and the business of
writing. That can be number one on your list! And if
you've been in the game awhile, take a moment to
review your publication credits, pull your book off
the shelf, remember all the writers you've
met—everything. Spend some time
being proud of yourself.

So many of the challenges of being a writer are rooted in fear. And many
of the fears we have as writers are based in insecurity. Writers are a sensitive
bunch, generally speaking—that's what makes us capable of feeling what we
need to feel in order to create our art, inhabit other lives, practice superhuman
feats of empathy, write from the heart, and move strangers with our words. But
it's also what can lead to insecurity. How many of us have felt like outsiders in
our own homes? Do you know that feeling of being in a gathering of people and
feeling like you're the only one who is "crazy" or "weird" enough to sit alone in
a room for hours just thinking in front of the keyboard? So do we. How often
have you looked into the eyes of the person in front of you and realized they
have no earthly idea what you're talking about when you refer to the narrative
arc or the second quatrain of your pantoum? Have you had that uncomfortable
realization that you're the only one who has thought deeply about what it must
feel like to A, B, or C? It can be unsettling—and, ultimately, silencing.

"Imposter phenomenon" is a term coined by psychologists Suzanne Imes and Pauline Rose Clance in the 1970s to refer to the feeling, the assumption, that despite your many accomplishments you are a fraud. It is perhaps a larger societal issue, common in writers and especially in women, that pushes us to undervalue our own work. Who am I to write this? I'm not good enough or smart enough to get up in front of people and read my story or publish my poetry collection. Much of this is due to our tendency to define ourselves based on what other people think or how other people view us. This is especially prevalent with writers because our value is so often tied to publication, which is ultimately tied to the judgment of others. If no one wants to publish your work then it must mean you're no good. Except it doesn't.

Rejection is a real part of being a writer; there's no getting around it. If you're going to make a go of the writing life, you're going to encounter those who don't see the value in what you're writing. You're going to hear no, a lot. So, it's important to identify ways of dealing with that answer—and coming up with ways to respond that are generative. When she encounters rejection, Chanelle Benz, the author of two books, including the novel *The Gone Dead*, thinks of something the theater director and theorist Jerzy Grotowski said: Whenever the ground shakes beneath your feet, go back to your roots. "I may be paraphrasing there," she says. "I interpret this as whenever you fail or meet with rejection or some experience that saps your heart, that you remember why you started writing, why you fell in love with reading, whatever it was that first inspired you."

Lee Martin, who teaches in the MFA program at Ohio State University and has published two story collections, three memoirs, and five novels, including *The Bright Forever*, a finalist for the 2006 Pulitzer Prize, takes a similar approach. "When I was starting out, I gathered so many rejections, I started to believe that door would never open for me," he says. "I couldn't stop writing, though. It's what gave me pleasure, and I knew even if I never got published, I'd still love moving words around on the page. That's why I tell my students to keep doing what they love as long as they love it."

There are ways of responding to rejection that can take you and your writing in new directions. First, it must be said that rejection can and should be used as a lesson or a teaching tool: If an editor doesn't think the poem you submitted works, take the opportunity to look at that poem with fresh eyes. Maybe you're even lucky enough to have received detailed feedback. If so, don't just hear the no, try to understand the why. Listen to the critique—consider it carefully; it's extremely valuable—and then decide to either heed the advice or ignore it. Either way, it's fuel for what's next: a revision, a rewrite, or another submission to an editor who knows what the hell they're talking about. Or even a completely new approach. Maybe that chapter really isn't working in your novel and it's trying to tell you it's actually a shard of a short story that, if pursued, will open up new opportunities for your fiction. Maybe that story wants to be an essay. Or your memoir wants to be a graphic memoir. Or your novel a collection of linked stories. If no is a stop sign, it means you can turn in any direction you want. And if the rejection didn't come with an explanation, remember that there may be reasons why your submission didn't hit the mark that have nothing to do with the quality of your writing. Maybe it just wasn't right for that specific publication, or they just so happened to accept another sonnet sequence or story about the circus in Alaska last week and can't run two in the same issue.

ACTION ITEM 28

Dig up your last rejection and read it out loud, then read the work you had submitted. If there is constructive criticism to be considered, by all means take it to heart. If not, either revise your work or send it back out there. Turn that no into a yes.

Another challenge of the writer's life is the pressure to produce—that guilty feeling when you're not in the chair banging away at the keys being a writer. While it's true that nothing gets written without putting words down on the page, this is an obvious oversimplification. Some writers are fully comfortable with a strict quota; others not so much. But we've all experienced that stuck feeling—call it writer's block, stuck in the morass, lost in the wild, whatever you want.

The terror of the blank page. And we all have different ways of confronting and overcoming it. "When I have writer's block, I feel trapped in a small, airless box," says Maurice Carlos Ruffin, author of the novel *We Cast a Shadow*. "When I watch movies, I feel free, so it only makes sense that I run to movies when I'm stuck. A few years ago, I decided to watch more classic and foreign films. I haven't suffered significant writer's block since. Sure, I get temporarily jammed from time to time. Who knows why? I suppose the blank page can be terrifying, and sometimes I don't feel particularly brave. But great movies remind me that storytelling can be incredibly fun. Having fun is liberating. Liberation is freedom."

Nafissa Thompson-Spires, whose debut story collection, *Heads of the Colored People*, was long-listed for the National Book Award for Fiction and was a finalist for the Kirkus Prize, says she takes a "low-stakes" approach to writing as a strategy for managing writer's block and the anxiety inherent to writing. "When I'm stuck, if I'm wise enough to take the advice I give to my students, I return to free-writing, often by hand. There's something about moving away from the computer keyboard and back to pen and paper—and a different movement with my hands—that stimulates exploration instead of stress. Free-writing is almost like doodling, a sort of half-conscious and certainly less self-aware method of 'producing' text that shifts my brain back to the playful, drafting mode and away from the pressured, generative mode. I know I will have to transcribe whatever I've handwritten and that in that process it will likely change significantly, so I feel more able to play with ideas on paper than I might while staring at my computer screen."

Others go for a walk or a swim, spend time in a natural setting, listen to music, thumb through the dictionary, look at visual art. And still others refuse to give in to the notion of writer's block at all. "There's no such thing as writer's block," says Akil Kumarasamy, author of a collection of linked stories, *Half Gods*. "Sometimes you go to the computer and nothing valuable comes out and that's okay. It's all about how you see the writing process. You don't need to call it writer's block and you don't need to feel guilty when you're not sitting by the computer. The work requires so much of you that if the guilt doesn't make you more productive, then the feeling is not worth it. You always have a choice in how you are going to perceive something."

Playwright, essayist, and poet Sarah Ruhl says a more apt phrase might be *the studious avoidance of writing*. "To call this writer's block would be like avoiding exercise and calling it 'exercise block.' I have exercise block a lot. Almost every day."

The Ugly

Of the seven deadly sins, envy may be the most common (and potentially harmful) among writers. Aristotle defined *envy* as the pain at seeing the good fortune of others. Dante took care of that, in *The Divine Comedy*, when he depicted the envious with their eyes sewn shut with wire, to prevent them from seeing all that good fortune. To avoid falling into the trap of envy, we'd suggest a good pair of blinders. This is easier said than done, of course. William Giraldi, the author of four books, including *American Audacity: In Defense of Literary Daring*, has written about the plight of the envious writer—and the fruitless pursuit of attaining what others already have:

> Writers, like academics—and for decades now that's been a distinction without much difference—are easily pricked by envy because the criteria for success seem bewilderingly arbitrary, contradictory, even outright unliterary. You'd think that the first benchmark for any successful book would be the beauty of its language and the wisdom of its mind—but no. There's often an echoic canyon between excellence and success. This calls up envy as well as bitterness, envy's grousing twin, in those authors who labor to make their books *dulce et utile*, in Horace's formulation: lovely and useful—lovely in word and form, useful in their intelligence. It also calls up insecurity. You might have noticed that lots of writers suffer from the seemingly paradoxical alloy of insecurity and narcissism, an alloy that enhances envy as nothing else can. I say "seemingly" because insecurity is not the inverse of narcissism; insecurity is its chief ingredient. This puts me in mind of that widely circulated crack, of uncertain provenance, about why academics can be so pettily vicious: "because the stakes are so low."

But the stakes aren't so low for us. This is art, and it's difficult to make a career out of one's art—it's difficult enough just to keep going when the popular culture rarely acknowledges one's work, and there are only so many opportunities to be published and win awards. Which is all the more reason we might try to see another writer's successes in a different light. As difficult as it may be, in this age of social media and Instagram filters, when everyone is seemingly having *the best time ever*, living their ideal life, as writers we should celebrate the accomplishments of our peers. And literary Twitter is full of shining examples of this—authors who are holding one another up and singing one another's praises.

It all goes back to community and being a good literary citizen—an agent of good. After all, those writers who signed the book deals, who won the prizes, whose books were optioned for movies—we're part of the same team. And our team is winning. So don't hate on the good fortune and hard work of others. Let it be further proof that there are rewards for what you're doing, and you'll get yours eventually if you keep going. Use it as an incentive.

Of course, there are those über-successful authors whose accomplishments—*surprise surprise, another week on the bestseller list for Mr. Koontz*—can be a little hard for some of us to swallow. This type of acrimony isn't born out of envy so much as a line in the sand that separates one writer from others in that writer's mind. There are the literary novelists who roll their eyes at the commercial machine that is James Patterson, or the romance writers who regard the experimental novelists with a smirk, or the nonfiction writers who don't seem to notice the poets much at all.

ACTION ITEM 29

Put this book down right now—no, better yet, finish this chapter first then put this book down—and write a letter or an e-mail or a tweet or a Facebook post to an author whose work has made a positive impact on your life. Sometimes those authors whose books are on our shelves seem so distant, as if they live in a different world. But they're not and they don't. They most certainly *will* read your fan letter. And it will make their day. They put their heart and soul into that book; let them know it was worth it.

Depending on one's constitution, this kind of sparring is harmless enough. It relies on a reductive way of thinking, of course, and it's not terribly useful—except, perhaps, as an incentive. In that regard it can be productive. Just as we can and should acknowledge the beauty and mastery in the work of our peers—and strive to match or even exceed it—the achievements of those whose work we can't help but wince at can be their own kind of fuel. Think you can do better? Prove it.

TEN

Writing and Family

As you enter positions of trust and power, dream a little before you think.
— TONI MORRISON

The cliché image of the solitary writer who spends all day and night alone in a room erases one characteristic common to most writers: other people who are dependent on them. A parent or a child, a spouse or a partner, they can all offer and demand a lot of a writer. But we don't often talk about how to manage those obligations while keeping writing a priority in our lives.

Respect and Expectations

Let's start with the people with whom we choose or hope to have relationships. If writing is a priority in your life, make sure that person knows it. Make it clear just how important writing is to you so that they won't be surprised when, instead of spending all day at the park with the dog, like they want to—and assume you do, too—you'd rather be at home working on your novel. Some people might think this kind of planning is silly. It's really not.

Just as you wouldn't want to wait until after the wedding to tell your new spouse that you don't see kids in your future, you don't want to withhold from your partner your true ambition to be a published poet or an award-winning novelist. Both those ambitions will require a significant amount of time and energy to fulfill, and it will shape your lifestyle for the foreseeable future. And make sure the people around you respect not only your ambitions but also your passion for writing, plain and simple. They don't have to share it—surely there are more than a few writers out there who would probably advise you *not* to get involved with another writer—but they need to respect it. This is a simple but important point. Do you want to deal with someone who doesn't respect your writing? How would that affect your ability to write, your ability to realize your dreams, your self-esteem?

Also, consider how important it is for you to be with someone who will support you, not necessarily financially (although that would be nice), but rather emotionally, and on a practical level. Obviously, we all need to pull our own weight—or at least try to—but think about whether you want to be up front about your need for your partner to occasionally shoulder the domestic responsibilities so that you can finish your book. Find yourself someone who will understand, and may even help you prepare, if you want to spend a week away at a writers retreat, or a weekend alone to finish revisions on your poetry collection. Find someone who won't get jealous about the writing group that meets every Tuesday night, who will look after the kids while you prepare submissions tomorrow afternoon, who will listen when you need to talk about which coastal town would be perfect for your novel's protagonist's grandmother to be reunited with her estranged daughter.

You'll be glad you put some thought toward these things when your partner brings you a cup of coffee and a simple word of encouragement nine hours into a writing jag that was supposed to end five hours ago.

If you'll permit us a self-referential case in point: During the writing of this book, on a late-summer Saturday on which we confronted a list of chores and errands that simply had to be done before our kids started school the next week, one of us ran around town checking items off that list while the other wrote. "Thanks for letting me write" was met with the reply "Thanks for writing." Now, it's not always that easy (as a matter of fact, it's almost never that easy), but the point is: Communication is key in any relationship, and that goes double for a relationship that involves a writer (and maybe triple if the relationship is between two writers).

All Expectations Are Not Equal

Before we get too much further, we need to acknowledge that everyone has different obligations. Single mothers of small children have an entirely different set of worries from married women who are caregivers to their elderly parents. A writer whose partner is in medical school is thinking about things entirely differently from a writer whose wife is a poet attending a low-residency MFA program. And a single child is likely contending with a different set of obligations from the second-oldest brother in a family of four. And some of us will always have more opportunity and privilege based on wealth, race, and other factors.

Another thing we need to be clear about is that this is not an issue distributed equally or fairly among genders. A father of two children does not face the same societal pressure as the mother of those same two children. We won't go into all of the historical and sociological reasons for this gender imbalance, but suffice it to say that when it comes to children, men are not under the same obligations to put their children first and their writing second. And when the responsibility of parenting falls heavily on women, it can take away from their writing time.

One writer who recognized this early on is Lauren Groff, two-time National Book Award finalist and best-selling author of three novels and two short story collections. Before she and her husband moved from Madison, Wisconsin, where she received her MFA at the University of Wisconsin, to northern Florida, where her husband wanted to live and raise kids close to his family, she asked her husband to sign a ten-year contract. "I said, 'I'm out of here in ten years,'" she says. "That decade is technically over, and we should renegotiate, but the most important part of the contract wasn't about where we lived. It was about how we live."

This wasn't a hypothetical contract, mind you, this was on paper: "I'm a writer. I'm going to continue to be a writer. I will never be a full-time mother. You will wake up with them. I won't see you or the children in the morning. In the afternoons we'll get a babysitter until I'm ready to come out of my office."

And it worked. Groff admits that her husband sometimes doesn't take the contract as seriously as she does—and schoolteachers still call her first if there's an issue with one of their kids—but the contract certainly got her point across, and no one can argue with her level of productivity and success as an author over that first decade in Florida.

While not everyone is comfortable signing a formal contract, Groff sets a terrific example. By being very clear about her intentions and her expectations before making a significant change to her life, she avoided any resentment that could build up around important things left unsaid. As Groff put it, "Resentment just kills marriage."

Children as Impediment and Inspiration

"A prominent writer once told me, at a barbecue at a friend's house in Maine, that if I wanted to take myself seriously as a writer, I'd better reconsider my desire to have children," says Julie Orringer, the author of three books, including the best-selling story collection *How to Breathe Underwater*. "For each child I had, this writer told me, I was sacrificing a book. Now I can say with certainty that my writing life has been immeasurably enriched and transformed by having become a parent. And if parenthood is demanding, both of time and emotional energy—as of course it is—life with children reminds me always of why writing feels essential: At its best and most rigorous, it illuminates—both for writer and reader—the richness and complexity of the human world, and forces us to make a deep moral consideration of our role in it."

Writers must carve out their creative time from all those things that would take it away from us—not only children but also other family members as well as the minutiae of everyday life, including bills, car maintenance, home repair, taxes, insurance, jury duty, and on and on. "For me it's all about creating psychic, emotional boundaries, so that I have time to feel free and unencumbered while I'm working, no matter what else is going on. That's a real struggle, of course," says Jess Row, the author of four books, including the essay collection *White Flights: Race, Fiction, and the*

American Imagination. "I don't really believe in balance; I believe in trying to sustain a feeling of wholeness, which means, in large part, taking care of other things you need to do so that you can feel free in your work, and also realizing that success in your career is only one part of a larger whole, which involves paying attention to your physical health, your relationships, your children and partner, your religious practice, your financial obligations, and so on."

Having children is bigger than writing, of course—being responsible for and caring for another human life is more important by an order of magnitude that is impossible to calculate. But that doesn't mean a parent should be criticized for taking time away from the kids to concentrate on writing. Unfortunately, the lack of affordable childcare in the United States is a serious issue—one that every parent, whether a writer or not, needs to grapple with—so writer-parents sometimes need to get creative. "I write mostly in bed, with occasional commutes to my kitchen table," says Domenica Ruta, author of the best-selling memoir *With or Without You*. "I try to write every week, sometimes every day, sometimes not. As a mother of a small child, there is no set schedule. I write when I can, usually when the kid is at school, and other pockets I can find." Helen Phillips, the author of five books, including the novel *The Need*, says that when she became a mother, her daily writing schedule shifted from four hours a day to just one hour a day. "But it's a quality-over-quantity thing, or so I tell myself; now I shove the energy of four hours into my single hour," she says. "The biggest impediment to my writing life is also the biggest inspiration for my writing life: my children."

Rosellen Brown, the author of eleven books, including the novel *The Lake on Fire*, says that although her children limited the amount of time she could spend on her writing, the restriction actually boosted her productivity. "When my kids were little and I had to

ACTION ITEM 30

Brainstorm ideas for how to carve a little writing time away from those who depend on you. You work hard and you're there for others, and that's incredibly important, but so is your writing. Make a list of all the people who could watch the kids for an evening while you finish your writers retreat application, or your poem or essay. Try to organize a playdate for your son so you can have an afternoon of writing this Saturday.

take advantage of every minute they were in school, I'll admit I was a lot more disciplined; I published three books in three years."

Thanks to the efforts of nonprofits like the Sustainable Arts Foundation, which gives annual cash awards to individuals and artist residencies for their efforts to make their programs more family friendly, there are options for writers who want to either spend some uninterrupted time away from their kids or bring them along on their residency.

FAMILY-FRIENDLY RESIDENCIES

The following sponsoring organizations, all of which have received grants from the Sustainable Arts Foundation, are making strides toward offering stipends for childcare and/or allowing writers to bring their families with them for a residency:

Brooklyn Arts Exchange in Brooklyn, New York

Cuttyhunk Island Writers' Residency in Cuttyhunk Island, Massachusetts

Elsewhere Studios in Paonia, Colorado

Good Hart Artist Residency in Harbor Springs, Michigan

Hewnoaks in Lovell, Maine

MacDowell Colony in Peterborough, New Hampshire

Marble House Project in Dorset, Vermont

Martha's Vineyard Institute of Creative Writing in Aquinnah, Massachusetts

Mineral School in Mineral, Washington

Popps Packing in Hamtramck, Michigan

Renaissance House in Oak Bluffs, Massachusetts

SPACE on Ryder Farm in Brewster, New York

Vermont Studio Center in Johnson, Vermont

If you need a solid block of uninterrupted time and a formal writers retreat isn't in the cards, however, you may need to get creative. If you have a supportive spouse or partner, think about trying to plan a weekend where you go away to "Mom's Writing Camp" (a local hotel or a friend's empty apartment) and help brainstorm activities to make it a fun weekend for your family back home. If you're a single parent, ask your mother or father, sister, brother, or cousin to watch the kids for a weekend, or even just for a night, so that you can concentrate on something that is important to you. It's okay; you're a writer, and your kids will grow up to understand and respect your dedication to your art.

One of the most important keys to managing your responsibilities and writing is open and honest communication. Be clear with family members, partners, and spouses. When they're old enough to understand, communicate with your children about the important role writing plays in your life. Being the parents of two kids ourselves, we've thought a lot about this. Before we signed on to write this book, for example, we sat down with our kids, who were eleven and thirteen at the time, and talked to them about what it would mean for us to engage with a writing project of this magnitude. We let them know that we would need to work nights and weekends—and sometimes on family vacations—but that it meant a lot to us and we hoped it would help a lot of people and that such a project was part of who we are as creative people. We're not going to claim that it was easy, but it was important enough to us that we figured out a way to make it work. For us, finding time to write—this and the other writing projects we have going on at any given time—is a kind of tag-team affair. We trade off being there for the kids when one of us has a deadline looming. And we've talked to our kids directly about it, established it as a priority—just one of the priorities— in our lives, and that reinforcement has paid off. They are proud of us and think it's kind of cool to have had their own part in creating a book with their parents' names on the cover.

And that's an important thing to keep in mind. Children or other dependent people in a writer's life aren't just obligations that get in the way of a creative life; they also feed it. "I used to be approached in classes by women who felt they shouldn't have children because children were too distracting, or would eat up the vital energies from which art comes. But you have to live your life if you're going to do original work," says Louise Glück, former U.S. poet laureate and winner of a Pulitzer Prize, National Book Award, and

National Humanities Medal. "Your work will come out of an authentic life, and if you suppress all of your most passionate impulses in the service of an art that has not yet declared itself, you're making a terrible mistake."

Poet Geffrey Davis teaches at the University of Arkansas and lives in Fayetteville, Arkansas, with his wife and son. Halfway through writing the poems in his second collection, *Night Angler*, he had a realization: "I was essentially working on a book-length love letter to my son," he says, "one that chronicled and questioned and sometimes intervened upon certain (parental) desires for breaking cycles and discovering new rituals for family. While the stakes and timeliness of the book's address meant that I couldn't have waited to write the book, I had no idea of when/how to place it into my son's hands once it was finished. However, just days after advance copies of *Night Angler* arrived, as sometimes children have the grace of doing, he simply took that impossible in/decision out of my hands. I was taking a late afternoon nap and woke to him reading aloud to my wife from the book. It's been a long time since I've tried that hard to fight back tears so that the voice across from me would keep speaking."

RESOURCES FOR WRITERS WHO ARE PARENTS

THE CENTER FOR PARENTING ARTISTS (centerforparentingartists.wordpress .com) is a nonprofit organization dedicated to encouraging and sharing resources for artists with children.

CULTURAL REPRODUCERS (www.culturalreproducers.org) is a "group of active cultural workers (professional artists, designers, curators, musicians, performers, writers, etc.) who are also parents."

LITERARY MAMA (www.literarymama.com) is an online monthly magazine of writing about "the many faces of motherhood."

PEN PARENTIS (www.penparentis.org) is a nonprofit organization that aims to provide resources to working artists in the literary field who are also parents. Its website "features parenting and writing resources, including an annual fellowship, mentoring opportunities, and online and in-person networking opportunities."

SUSTAINABLE ARTS FOUNDATION (www.sustainableartsfoundation.org) supports artists and writers with children through annual unrestricted cash awards to individuals and grants to support artist residencies for their efforts to make their programs more family friendly.

ELEVEN

Writing and Respect

If we lose love and self-respect for each other, this is how we finally die.

—MAYA ANGELOU

Although it may not always feel like it, we wield power with our words. Talk is cheap, but words on a page have the power to change the world. (Go ahead and challenge that statement: Spend fifteen minutes watching a panel of talking heads on the first twenty-four-hour cable news channel you can find, then spend fifteen minutes reading an essay by Roxane Gay, a novel by Colson Whitehead, a poem by Ocean Vuong, or *anything* by Toni Morrison. After that half hour you'll see what we mean.) If this sounds highfalutin, consider who you'd be without the book or books that made you realize you wanted to be a writer. There's a reason why we sometimes refer to this or that great work of literature as having defined us. The world—our worlds—would not be the same without the words of writers. Writing is powerful.

But this isn't a chapter about admiration, respect's twin sister. Nor is this about censorship. It's not about limitations or capping our creativity to cover only what we know for sure. And it's not about being polite or even kind (although, come on, what's to be gained by being unkind), and it's not about keeping our negative opinions to ourselves.

This is about showing—and demanding—respect for the feelings, wishes, rights, and traditions of others. As writers we owe it to ourselves, our art, and our readers to do whatever we can to make sure our work avoids cultural inaccuracies, biases, stereotypes, or problematic language (and by problematic language we aren't referring to profanity, for fuck's sake, but rather language that dehumanizes or casts in a false light the lives of others). And the first step to avoiding those things is to acknowledge that we may not even know they are in our work in the first place.

Let Your Fear Drive You

In 2014, at the National Book Festival in Washington, D.C., cartoonist and teacher Gene Luen Yang, whose book *American Born Chinese* became the first graphic novel to be nominated for a National Book Award and the first to win the American Library Association's Printz Award, delivered a speech about diversity in literature that every writer, no matter the genre, should read. It says so much of what we're trying to convey in this chapter about respect that we've included an excerpt here with Yang's permission:

> We in the book community are in the middle of a sustained conversation about diversity. We talk about our need for diverse books with diverse characters written by diverse writers. I wholeheartedly agree.
>
> But I have noticed an undercurrent of fear in many of our discussions. We're afraid of writing characters different from ourselves because we're afraid of getting it wrong. We're afraid of what the internet might say.
>
> This fear can be a good thing if it drives us to do our homework, to be meticulous in our cultural research. But this fear crosses the line when we become so intimidated that we quietly make choices against stepping out of our own identities.
>
> After all, our job as writers is to step out of ourselves, and to encourage our readers to do the same. . . .
>
> We have to allow ourselves the freedom to make mistakes, including cultural mistakes, in our first drafts. I believe it's okay to get cultural details wrong in your first draft. It's okay if stereotypes emerge. It just means that your experience is limited, that you're human.
>
> Just make sure you iron them out before the final draft. Make sure you do your homework. Make sure your early readers include people who are a

part of the culture you're writing about. Make sure your editor has the insider knowledge to help you out. If they don't, consider hiring a freelance editor who does.

Also, it's okay if stereotypes emerge in the first drafts of your colleagues. Correct them—definitely correct them—but do so in a spirit of generosity. Remember how soul-wrenching the act of writing is, how much courage it took for that writer to put words down on a page.

And let's say you do your best. You put in all the effort you can. But then when your book comes out, the internet gets angry. You slowly realize that, for once, the internet might be right. You made a cultural misstep. If this happens, take comfort in the fact that even flawed characters can inspire. Apologize if necessary, resolve to do better, and move on.

Let your fear drive you to do your homework. But no matter what, don't ever let your fear stop you.

Sensitivity Readers

Over the past five years or so, the use of sensitivity readers, or authenticity readers, has become common among writers and publishers to identify and avoid a lapse of judgment or unintentional discrimination in a piece of writing. Essentially, it's a professional measure to ensure that the representation of characters—or entire groups of characters—doesn't suffer from an unintentional stereotype, misrepresentation, or just plain error of fact. For instance, if one of the characters in your novel is Jewish, and you are, in fact, not Jewish, do you know the particulars of the Passover meal as it would be celebrated in the home of your character? You might think you do, but unless you have someone who is Jewish read your depiction and point out that actually the Seder plate would not be used that way, how would you know for sure? And the physical descriptions of that woman who doesn't look like you, or the man who grew up on a different continent, or the references to the friend of your main character who happens to identify as queer—when you, yourself, are heterosexual—how do you know you haven't inadvertently written yourself into a homophobic or racist stereotype? Sensitivity readers can point out problematic or incorrect portrayals of race, sexuality, religion, and physical disabilities.

You can explore options for sensitivity readers by visiting Writing Diversely (www.writingdiversely.com) and Write in the Margins (writeinthemargins .org), two databases of sensitivity readers that include rates and qualifications.

ACTION ITEM 31

Reread your latest piece of writing with the idea of a sensitivity or diversity reader in mind. Are you sure you've done justice to your characters, your arguments, your ideas, your art? Consider who you might ask to give it another read. Or check out the databases of sensitivity readers and consider taking advantage of a professional service.

Critics of the use of sensitivity readers argue that this is all a result of liberal, politically correct culture and that it's absurd to hold fictional characters accountable for perceived slights—because they are, after all, fictional. This is absurd in its own right, of course, because it assumes that fictional characters materialize out of thin air and aren't created by real human beings whose work has the power to shape perception and influence new generations of readers. Others argue that it's a slippery slope to censorship, and that it limits a writer's ability to write about experiences or identities other than their own—and still others are just fine with only writing about experiences and identities that align with their own.

At the end of the day, sensitivity readers are not there to ban you from saying something, they're there to show you how your writing might be read by others. As with any editor, you're going to agree with them on some things and hold fast on others—it is up to you what you write.

Quality as a Sign of Respect

No matter where you stand on this issue, we can all agree that the goal is to write the best poem, essay, story, or book we can write. Plain and simple. In our pursuit of that goal, why wouldn't we want our characters to be three-dimensional? Why wouldn't we want our work to have the ring of truth? And why wouldn't we want to have as many readers as possible recognize some aspect of themselves in our writing? This requires work. And careful thought and consideration. And sometimes the help of others who know things we don't. All of this is in service of our writing, because putting out quality work is the best and biggest sign of respect—to ourselves, to our work, and to our readers.

Opinions: Everyone Has Them

A funny/horrifying thing happens when you make the move from writer to author—from having written something to sharing it with others: You open yourself up to the judgments and opinions of others. And this is, of course, fundamental to our work as writers. Unless you are journaling or doing some other kind of diaristic form of writing, the point of sharing or publishing (which means, quite literally, to make public) is to engage others' hearts and minds and, yes, opinions—good or bad, we don't get to choose.

No one is immune to negative reviews. Consider some of the initial reactions to now-classic novels by modern masters such as Kurt Vonnegut and F. Scott Fitzgerald. Writing in the *New Yorker* in 1969, Susan Lardner had a less than flattering opinion of *Slaughterhouse-Five*: "The short, flat sentences of which the novel is composed convey shock and despair better than an array of facts or effusive mourning. Still, deliberate simplicity is as hazardous as the grand style, and Vonnegut occasionally skids into fatuousness." And in the *Chicago Tribune* in 1925, H. L. Mencken wrote, "Scott Fitzgerald's new novel, *The Great Gatsby*, is in form no more than a glorified anecdote, and not too probable at that."

SIX BOOK CRITICS ON THE VALUE OF NEGATIVE REVIEWS

"I think negative reviews, especially of books by well-known authors, are an important contribution to the conversation about art and ideas. The only instance in which I would decide not to write a negative review after reading a book is in the case of an unknown first-time novelist or nonfiction writer. No one knows the book anyway, and the only reason to review that book would be to recommend it to potential readers." —**Maureen Corrigan** of NPR's *Fresh Air*

"Negative reviews are healthy, stimulating, completely necessary. In my view there are fairly stringent moral prohibitions against judging people in life, but art is where one can love and hate at passionate extremes. When I have regrets about my own reviewing, it's usually when I've shied away from negativity into some featureless middle ground. I should say that the best negative reviews are not simply hatchet jobs but pieces that use a book's weaknesses or transgressions to illustrate a larger idea." —**Sam Sacks** of the *Wall Street Journal*

"We don't run a lot of negative reviews, but we do run them when warranted. . . . My philosophy is that we do not trash debut books by unknown writers—what is to be gained by holding up an obscure book and telling the world that it's bad? On the other hand, we have run negative reviews of Stephen King and John Irving and other well-known writers. It seems to me to be a service to readers to let them know which books by their favorite authors might be skippable." —**Laurie Hertzel** of the *Star Tribune* in Minneapolis

"A culture that only cheerleads and celebrates is a vapid culture—a culture of marketing, not thinking. With respect to literature, such marketing is . . . properly the province of publishers and publicists—and that's fine. All writers benefit from publishers' marketing and advertising: I have myself. No shame in that. But precisely because the culture as a whole is so overwhelmingly commercial, it's vital that professional, public, literary, and cultural criticism remain independent. Negative criticism is, in part, what fights against the commercial, or the merely stupid, or vulgar; it is a form of resistance, a reminder that we must think for ourselves and not have our judgments co-opted by advertising and the ephemeral.

Having said that, I would stress urgently that there is a right way to do negative criticism: It has to be reasoned, it cannot be ad hominem, and so forth. Indeed, I'd say that now, with the explosion of vituperative discourse that is the hallmark of much internet culture, doing proper, measured negative criticism importantly models how *not* to like something. In an era in which so many exchanges—literary ones, too—devolve into snark and name-calling, we need good negative criticism perhaps more than ever." —**Daniel Mendelsohn** of the *New York Review of Books*

"You can't trust a critic who doesn't write negative reviews. Most books simply aren't that good. I try to find things to admire even in books I don't like, and I try not to be punitive and to have a sense of humor. But what's a critic for if not to think clearly, make fine discriminations, and speak plainly?" —**Dwight Garner** of the *New York Times*

"I was told when I came to the magazine that we should pick books we think are worthy of coverage and share them with our readers. If we don't like or love a book, we just won't cover it. There are just too many good books to celebrate to devote space to the ones we don't like." —**Leigh Haber** of *O, the Oprah Magazine*

Indeed, reasoned, thoughtful criticism is vital to sustaining and pushing forward healthy intellectual debate and independent thought within the writing and publishing communities. That said, these days it is easier than ever to share—on Twitter, Facebook, personal blogs, etc.—a negative opinion of a piece of writing. Which, of course, is inevitable, unpreventable, and fine. But folks can also tag authors on Twitter or Facebook, forcing those authors to confront the opinions, no matter how constructive the criticism or how personal the attack. A number of authors have tried to bring this up on Twitter (Angie Thomas and Lauren Groff among them) only to be subjected to even harsher criticism by readers who believe, it seems, that part of the author's job is to confront negative responses to their work. While it is true that so much of what we hold dear relies on our ability to say whatever we want about whatever we choose, we must question the point of telling an author we don't like their work in a biting Tweet or brutal Instagram post—unless we have the critical chops to back up our vitriol. A far better, more respectful, and powerful course of action might be to let our money do the talking. If you don't like a writer's work, don't buy their books. Writers aren't the only ones who need to show respect; readers do, too.

TWELVE

Writing and the Law

There are no laws for the novel. There never have been, nor can there ever be.

—DORIS LESSING

As we've said before, a successful writer is an informed writer, and a basic understanding of your rights will help you make better decisions as you approach the marketplace and the business of publishing. In this chapter we will define some common terms that appear in contracts and other legal considerations of a writer's work. With all things concerning rights, contracts, and copyright, of course, the best course of action is to consult a lawyer or your agent. (For an annual fee, writers can join the Authors Guild and gain access to experienced publishing lawyers who will review their contracts and make recommendations.) To learn more on your own, we recommend consulting *How to Be Your Own Literary Agent: An Insider's Guide to Getting Your Book Published* by literary agent and author Richard Curtis, which, though the latest edition was published nearly twenty years ago, explores the basics of book contracts. In this chapter, we will also outline much of what you'll need to know. At the time of this writing, the following information is believed to be accurate and reliable, but we are not legal professionals, nor are we offering legal or professional services on these matters. Again, if legal advice is needed, consult a lawyer or your agent.

Copyright

"Copyright is a form of protection grounded in the U.S. Constitution and granted by law for original works of authorship fixed in a tangible medium of expression," according to the U.S. Copyright Office. Copyright covers both published and unpublished works. You own the copyright to anything you write, but registration with the U.S. Copyright Office will entitle you to monetary damages in cases of infringement, which rarely occur with literary works. The U.S. Copyright Office defines a literary work as "a work that explains, describes, or narrates a particular subject, theme, or idea through the use of narrative, descriptive, or explanatory text, rather than dialog or dramatic action. Generally, literary works are intended to be read; they are not intended to be performed before an audience." Usually it is safe for you to wait until your book has been contracted for publication before worrying about copyright. Because ownership of your work is assumed, it is unnecessary to include a copyright symbol on any manuscript you submit to contests, agents, or publishers. In fact, doing so reflects poorly on you, as it comes off as unprofessional.

When you publish a book, it is standard practice for the publisher to register the copyright with the U.S. Copyright Office on the author's behalf in the author's name. Assuming you want to retain the copyright to your work, you should be sure that the publisher does not register the copyright in its name instead. Also, never sign a contract stipulating that yours is a work "made for hire," which legally makes the publisher the owner of your work—unless, of course, that's exactly what you want to do.

Copyright in the United States extends to any country that has copyright relations with the United States. Although the list of these countries is extensive, it is by no mean exhaustive, which means that your U.S. copyright does not apply in some places around the world. Some people might try to tell you that by mailing yourself a copy of your unpublished manuscript, you have automatically copyrighted that work; this is false. Again, copyright is automatic once you finish a manuscript, but this "poor man's copyright" through the postal mail is not a substitute for registration with the U.S. Copyright Office.

All Rights

The right to publish your work. Avoid granting a publisher all rights to your work; if you do, you can never use the same work again in its current form. For example, if you have sold all rights to a story for publication in a literary magazine and later want to include that story in an anthology, you'll have to purchase the right to do so from the publication that now owns all rights to it. The owner of all rights is free to reprint your material or to sell it elsewhere—and even make a film based on your work, if they so choose—without paying any additional money to you. The owner would also be free to use all the rights listed below.

Electronic Rights

The right to publish or allow others to publish electronic versions of your work, including in e-book format or on a magazine's website. In some book contracts, this may be labeled as "e-book rights." Ideally, this will be limited to verbatim text English-language rights for "electronic rights" or "e-book rights." Other features such as audio or video may be labeled as "enhanced e-book rights" or "multimedia." As new technologies are developed, the definition of electronic rights will continue to evolve.

Exclusive Rights

The right to publish your work without the work appearing elsewhere at the same time. Often, publishers request exclusive rights for a given length of time—three months, six months, or one year, for example. Magazines will often base the exclusivity period on the time any particular issue is available for sale, so for a monthly publication, the exclusivity period may be thirty to forty-five days after the publication of the piece in the magazine; for a bimonthly magazine the exclusivity period may be sixty to ninety days after the publication of the piece. After the exclusivity period has ended, you are free to publish your work elsewhere (assuming the contract doesn't stipulate otherwise).

First Serial Rights

The right to be the first publisher of your work. After the work is published once anywhere, all rights revert back to you. Writers looking to place their work in a literary magazine are selling first serial rights to that work (and sometimes more, depending on the magazine's contract). In the United States, these rights are often called First North American Serial Rights (FNASR) and grant the magazine the right to be the first publisher of your work one time in North America. Granting First North American Serial Rights means you are entitled to sell first serial rights to the same work in places other than North America.

When it comes to book contracts, first serial rights fall under the subsidiary rights clause, which "outlines the rights your publisher is allowed to license to others and what your monetary share of those licenses should be." Often publishers will license first serial rights to a portion of a forthcoming book to magazines, newspapers, and websites, as a way to promote the book and generate word of mouth before it is published.

Reprint Rights

The right to publish a work subsequent to its first publication, also known as second serial rights. For works first published in magazines, these rights usually come into play if you want to reprint your work in an anthology, for example, or on your own website. For books, reprint rights usually refer to those rights that give the publisher permission to negotiate a deal with another publisher to release, say, the paperback edition or the book club edition, for which the author gets a percentage.

Subsidiary Rights

These rights give the holder permission to license your work to others and typically include first and second serial rights, audio rights, film rights, foreign rights, translation rights, book club rights, the right to reprint excerpts of your work, rights to electronic editions and versions, performance rights, and merchandising rights.

World Rights

The translation rights to your work, meaning the holder has the right to publish your work in all languages in all countries.

World English Rights

The right to publish English-language versions of your work in all countries. As more book publishing conglomerates are operating internationally, many publishers seek world English rights.

Film Option

An "option" is a contractual agreement between a potential film or television producer and the author of a book (or story, play, or screenplay) whereby the producer acquires the exclusive yet temporary right to purchase the film rights to the book. An option may be renewed at the end of the contract term. It is essentially a way for a producer to put a hold on the rights of a book while they put together the necessary elements for a film.

Libel

Libel, or defamation, is the publication of false statements of supposed fact that damage one's reputation. The publication of a demonstrably true statement that damages one's reputation is not libel (but it may be invasion of privacy), nor is opinion. Only a statement of fact that can be proven untrue is libel. Generally speaking, it is much easier for a private individual to prove libel; a celebrity, politician, or other public figure will have a much more difficult time. In order for an individual to win a libel case, it must be proven that an author—and by extension that author's publisher—acted negligently, whereas a public figure must prove that the author and publisher acted with malice.

Fair Use

According to Section 107 of the Copyright Act of 1976, even if a work is copyrighted, anyone may reproduce a portion of that work without the author's permission as long as it meets criteria based on four factors: "(1) the purpose and character of the use, including whether such use is of a commercial nature or is for nonprofit educational purposes; (2) the nature of the copyrighted work; (3) the amount and substantiality of the portion used in relation to the copyrighted work as a whole; and (4) the effect of the use upon the potential market for or value of the copyrighted work."

Public Domain

Public domain includes any creative work to which no intellectual property rights apply, either because the copyright has expired or because the work was never protected by copyright in the first place. In most countries, a copyright extends seventy years after the death of the author. In the United States, however, as of 2020, every book published prior to 1925 is in the public domain; the cutoff date advances at the beginning of each new calendar year. Anyone can use work that is in the public domain, but no one can ever own that work.

Basic Parts of a Book Contract

At its most basic level, a book contract spells out your rights and obligations in the following terms:

The work. This defines the work under contract and usually includes approximate word count and the specific forms (print, e-book, audiobook) and markets (domestic/international) in which it will be published.

Subsidiary rights. This outlines the rights (first and second serial rights, audio rights, book club rights, translation

ACTION ITEM 32

Take a closer look at the terms whereby a literary magazine or book publisher is seeking to acquire the rights to publish your work. Do you understand all the legal terms and stipulations? If not, highlight the sections that are confusing and ask questions—never be afraid to ask questions of the publisher—and if you don't get the answers you are looking for, consult a lawyer or your agent before signing.

rights, merchandising rights, and more) that your publisher is able to license to others and what your share of the money would be. Your literary agent can negotiate the terms of these rights so you have approval or consultations over these various licenses.

Payment schedule and royalty rate. This will address your advance and how it will be paid out (traditionally, a third is due to you after both parties have signed the contract, a third when the publisher accepts your final manuscript, and a third on publication, but it can also be quarters, with the final quarter due on paperback publication). This will also outline the royalty rate that you can expect to receive after your publisher has earned back the total amount of your advance on sales of your book. The following rates are standard for a hardcover edition: 10 percent of the retail price on the first five thousand copies, 12.5 percent for the next five thousand copies sold, then 15 percent for all further copies sold. For paperback the rate can go down to 8 percent of retail price on the first 150,000 copies sold, then 10 percent thereafter, though some publishers offer a flat 7.5 percent rate. "Your agent also will know the going—and often changing—rates for every other edition of your book, including audio and electronic rights editions," says literary agent Julie Barer. "She will also know the rates for sales such as foreign; high-discount sales to outlets where the bookseller receives a higher-than-standard discount from the publisher; premium; proprietary editions; and mail order."

Terms for delivery, acceptance, and publication. This sets the dates by which you must turn in your manuscript—and any other ancillary materials—and what happens if the editor deems your manuscript unacceptable. (Remember, that second installment of your advance is contingent on not just your turning in a manuscript but rather turning in a manuscript your publisher deems acceptable.) "Pursuant to this clause, an agent can negotiate the amount of time an editor may take to respond to your manuscript," says Barer. "An agent can also negotiate the amount of time you must be given to revise the work if the publisher finds it unacceptable—anywhere from thirty to ninety days—and the amount of information the publisher must give you about why it is rejecting it, as well as the grounds on which it can contractually reject it." These negotiable terms also outline the time frame in which the publisher is required to publish the accepted manuscript. There will also be a clause about the author's right to consult on or approve the cover design, the catalogue copy, and the biographical information on all editions.

The financial obligations of both parties. By agreeing to publish your book, the publisher is taking a financial risk based on the assumption your book will be profitable. In a traditional publishing agreement, the author should not be asked to forfeit any money. The exceptions occur if the author fails to deliver the manuscript (in which case the author is obligated to return the advance).

The publisher's right to option. Most publishers stipulate in a contract that they be given the first chance to acquire your next book—sometimes called "the right of first refusal." The contract will outline the amount of time the publisher has to consider material from the subsequent book and how much time you have to negotiate before moving on to another publisher if you do not accept the original publisher's terms. Again, this is where an agent can negotiate terms.

III

THIRTEEN

Literary Magazines

Since the first literary magazine was established in the United States—the *North American Review*, founded by William Tudor in Boston in 1815 with the aim of "rivaling the leading British magazines"—literary magazines have served to publish poems, short stories, essays, and criticism that might not otherwise be available to readers. They play a crucial role in introducing both readers and the publishing community to new writing and new writers. As William Carlos Williams put it in his autobiography, "The little magazine is something I have always fostered, for without it, I myself would have been early silenced." Williams goes on to describe the world of literary magazines not as hundreds of publications spread out across the country but as one collective endeavor. "When it is in any way successful it is because it fills a need in someone's mind to keep going. When it dies, someone else takes it up in some other part of the country—quite by accident—out of a desire to get the writing down on paper."

Despite a twenty-four-year pause in publication, from 1940 to 1964, the *North American Review* still exists—it's currently housed at the University of Northern Iowa—and its longevity speaks to the dedication of so many literary magazines like it. Founded in 1819, the *Yale Review* lays claim to being the oldest literary magazine in continuous publication, while *Poet Lore*, founded in 1889, is the longest-running journal dedicated to poetry. The *Sewanee Review*, founded in 1892 by William Peterfield Trent in Tennessee,

211

calls itself "America's oldest continuously published literary quarterly." Throughout the twentieth century it published writing by William Faulkner, Eudora Welty, Saul Bellow, and Katherine Anne Porter, as well as excerpts from first novels by Cormac McCarthy and Flannery O'Connor and early poetry by Robert Penn Warren, Sylvia Plath, and Robert Lowell. And under the editorship of Adam Ross, it continues to publish writing by literary luminaries today, including Richard Russo, Alice McDermott, Donika Kelly, and Kaveh Akbar.

During the early part of the twentieth century, several literary magazines were launched that became venues for some of the most well-known contributions in modernist literature. The *Crisis*, cofounded by W. E. B. Du Bois in 1910, published some of the best-known writers of the Harlem Renaissance, including Countee Cullen, Langston Hughes, Zora Neale Hurston, and Jean Toomer. The *Masses*, founded by Piet Vlag in 1911 in New York City, published the work of Carl Sandburg, Louis Untermeyer, Amy Lowell, Jack London, Upton Sinclair, and Sherwood Anderson; the *Little Review*, founded in Chicago by Margaret Anderson in 1914, with a mission of showcasing experimental writing, was the first to publish sections of James Joyce's *Ulysses* (for which it faced an obscenity trial); and *Others*, founded in 1915 in New York City by Alfred Kreymborg, published the likes of Mina Loy, Marianne Moore, Ezra Pound, Wallace Stevens, and William Carlos Williams. *Poetry: A Magazine of Verse* was founded by Harriet Monroe in Chicago in 1912 and featured writing by Ernest Hemingway, Langston Hughes, Gertrude Stein, and Muriel Rukeyser, among many others. *Poetry* remains one of the highest-circulation poetry magazines in the United States. Other long-lasting stalwarts include the *Kenyon Review* (1939), the *Southern Review* (1935), the *Hudson Review* (1948), and the *Paris Review* (1953).

Along with helping to launch the careers of many of our greatest writers, literary magazines have reflected the political and social climate of the times through the literature they publish. The 1960s saw an increase in the number of so-called littles being published, through what is often referred to as the beginning of the mimeograph revolution, when idealistic editors were driven not only by political activism but also advancements in easy-to-use printing processes. "Direct access to mimeograph machines, letterpress, and inexpensive offset made these publishing ventures possible," write Steven Clay and Rodney Phillips in their book about this period of publishing, *A Secret Location on the Lower East Side: Adventures in Writing 1960–1980*. "For the price of a few reams of paper and a handful of stencils, a poet could produce, by mimeograph, a magazine or booklet in a small edition over the course of several days. Collating, stapling, and mailing parties helped speed up production, but, more significantly, they helped galvanize a literary group. The existence of independent bookstores meant that it was actually possible to find the publications in all their raw homemade beauty."

By the early 1980s, according to the *CCLM Directory of Literary Magazines*, published annually by what was then called the Coordinating Council of Literary Magazines and is now the Community of Literary Magazines and Presses, the number of active literary magazines in the United States was eight or nine hundred. The directory itself included three hundred and forty magazines. By 1989, that number had risen to four hundred.

During the 1990s, the digital revolution changed the literary magazine landscape once again, further democratizing the publication process. Desktop publishing software allowed cost-effective solutions for anyone who wanted to design and publish professional-looking magazines in print. And with the inception of the internet, many more literary magazines were launched in online formats. Today there are well over a thousand literary magazines being published in the United States alone, ranging in formats from high-production print magazines to those reminiscent of the zines of the 1960s and '70s, to those that exist entirely online. Whereas once publishing in print was considered the only legitimate publication credit for a writer, now online magazines offer as much credibility. While print has the history, digital has the reach. And some magazines offer both.

Most literary magazines are mission-driven, not commercially driven, and as such they play a vital role in publishing the work of a diverse range of writers and distributing that work to an equally diverse community of readers. Their aim is to showcase writing that aligns with their editorial mission, not what will sell the most copies on the newsstand. Some magazines focus on a certain aesthetic—publishing innovative writing or formal writing or narrative writing. Others focus on showcasing writing about specific regions, while still others are dedicated to amplifying the voices of traditionally marginalized writers.

First Steps in Publishing

Publishing your work in literary magazines is often considered the first step toward building a platform and starting a writing career. It allows you to accomplish one of the most clear and present goals as a writer: sharing your writing with readers. It also provides professional credentials that can help you reach other goals, such as publishing your work more widely, being accepted to a writers retreat, receiving a grant, finding an agent, or publishing a book.

When submitting your work to any one publication, it always helps to mention in your cover letter the other magazines where your work has appeared. For those editors who read cover letters (and not all do), publication credits can serve as a kind of professional endorsement, giving them a sense of who else in the field has recognized your writing. Publication credits also convey that you're serious about this endeavor, you're engaged in the literary community, and that other professionals have found your work worthy of investment. To an editor considering your work, publication credits can suggest that there's already an existing readership, a factor some consider when weighing whether to accept your work for their pages.

Similarly, when applying to writers residencies and retreats, submitting your writing to contests, and applying for grants and fellowships, a robust publication history indicates that you are an established and engaged writer whose work has been recognized by editors. Some of these kinds of opportunities require that applicants have recent publication credits before they are even considered.

Another significant advantage to publishing in literary magazines is that agents often read them, looking for new writers to represent. This is how Kent Wolf, an agent at Neon Literary, found his client Ingrid Rojas Contreras. After reading a story of hers in *Guernica*, an online magazine focused on the intersection of art and politics, he reached out to her to see if she had a book in the works. Her debut novel, *Fruit of the Drunken Tree*, was published by Doubleday in July 2018. It's also how he found his client Carmen Maria Machado, whom he contacted after reading a story she had written in the *Rumpus*, another online magazine. The debut book that resulted from that connection, *Her Body and Other Parties*, published by Graywolf Press in 2017, went on to be named a finalist for the National Book Award, the Kirkus Prize, the Art Seidenbaum Award for First Fiction, the Dylan Thomas Prize, and the PEN/Robert W. Bingham Prize for Debut Fiction. It won the Bard Fiction Prize, the Lambda Literary Award for Lesbian Fiction, the Brooklyn Public Library Literature Prize, the Shirley Jackson Award, and the National Book Critics Circle's John Leonard Award.

It started with publication in a literary magazine.

Getting Started

Before submitting your work to literary magazines, you first need to settle on a list of the top magazines you aspire to see your work published in, and to determine this list it might be best to consider your overall goals. (Remember the goals from Chapter 1: Getting Started?) Ask yourself why you want your work published in literary magazines at all. Are you trying to build a readership and platform for your writing? Are you trying to directly engage with readers? Do you want to develop a list of publication credits you can cite when applying for a job or a grant or querying an agent? Are you trying to earn money from your writing? Are you interested in becoming more involved in your community's literary scene? Answering these questions will help guide you as you move forward.

If, for example, your focus is on building a *platform*—a publishing term for anything that lends your work credibility and puts you and your name in the public eye—then it would make sense to focus on magazines that have a robust readership and devote resources to marketing and publicity.

If you're interested in engaging directly with readers, you might focus on magazines that also run reading series or other literary events—or focus on online journals, where interaction with readers is often more immediate. If you're a fiction writer looking to find an agent, then focusing on those magazines that agents typically read—often the more high-profile ones like the *Paris Review*, *A Public Space*, and so on—would be a good strategy. If you're trying to earn money from publishing your writing, then prioritize those magazines that pay contributor fees. Or, if you're most interested in becoming active in your local literary community, find the literary magazines in your area that are most engaged and submit your work there.

The best way to familiarize yourself with the overall landscape of literary magazines is to read them yourself. This seems obvious, but not all writers take the time to do so. Regardless of your personal publishing goals, reading literary magazines informs you about your field and introduces you to writing by writers you wouldn't otherwise find. You also get a sense of what magazines are publishing which kind of work and how. Go to the library or your local bookstore and peruse the magazine section looking for magazines that appeal to you. Take a look at online databases of literary magazines. Most databases include information about the magazine's editorial focus, the genres it publishes, its publication frequency, representative authors, how to submit your work, and what it pays, as well as contact information. Take note of where the writers whose work you admire are publishing their pieces. Sign up for magazine newsletters, follow them on social media, and consider subscribing to a few. Not only will you be learning valuable information about their aesthetic and the kinds of work they publish, you'll also be supporting the very magazines you hope to be published in one day. That's just good literary citizenship.

> *"A literary magazine puts a writer in conversation*
> *with other writers and, depending on the magazine,*
> *with a community, with a lineage or tradition."*
> —YUKA IGARASHI

ONLINE DATABASES OF LITERARY MAGAZINES

COMMUNITY OF LITERARY MAGAZINES AND PRESSES DIRECTORY:

www.clmp.org/readers/directory

NEW PAGES: www.newpages.com/magazines

POETS & WRITERS LITERARY MAGAZINES DATABASE:

www.pw.org/literary_magazines

SUBMITTABLE: www.submittable.com

As you start your list of the magazines to which you'd like to submit, take note of other factors that are drawing you to particular titles. Are you impressed with the design? Drawn by the stable of writers featured in the table of contents? The editorial mission of the publication? Make a list of criteria that further defines the kind of publication where you'd like to see your work published. Here are a few more factors to consider:

ACTION ITEM 33

Browse the Literary Magazines database at pw.org, a free resource that includes information about nearly 1,200 magazines, paying attention to the frequency, circulation, editorial focus, and payment rates. Make a list of those you think would be a good fit for your work.

Reputation

Magazines that have earned strong reputations usually have several characteristics in common. They have an established record of publishing high-caliber writing; they have high-quality production value; they devote resources to establishing a wide readership; and they treat writers with respect. Some of these magazines have received recognition for excellence in publishing. You can take a look at which ones have received Literary Magazine Prizes from the Whiting Foundation, Firecracker Awards from the Community of Literary Magazines and Presses, and support from funders such as the National Endowment for the Arts, state arts agencies, and private foundations.

Keep in mind that these magazines also tend to receive the most submissions, so your chances of having your work accepted may be lower, as they only have so much space available in any particular year. The *Paris Review*, for example, which publishes four issues a year, receives approximately nine thousand submissions and publishes about forty pieces per issue. *Poetry* magazine receives about twenty-three thousand submissions, consisting of five to seven poems each, per year. "That means in a given year, we will have received and read between 151,000 to 161,000 individual poems," says editor Don Share. "I should add that there are no screeners, readers, or interns at *Poetry*. Every single submission is read by an editor named on the masthead, something I feel to be very important, and our consulting editor and I do virtually all of that reading between the two of us, which is why our response time is about six or seven months." In 2019, *Poetry* published approximately four hundred poems, or about .25 percent of the submissions they received.

Newly established magazines can present opportunities for writers submitting their work, too, because such outlets in all likelihood aren't yet receiving a high number of unsolicited submissions while they're getting up and running. But before you submit to a new magazine make sure that it has staying power. You wouldn't want to publish what you consider to be your strongest story or poem in a new magazine only to have that magazine fold a year later, likely making your piece unavailable. Remember, once you publish your writing in a magazine, print or online, it's extremely unlikely that other magazines will want to reprint it. You always have the option to submit it to anthologies—or to have it picked up by the Best American series of anthologies, or the Pushcart Prize anthology, but most magazines only consider unpublished work.

Reach

If reaching the widest possible audience is your top priority, then you'll want to submit to magazines with the highest circulation. Circulation for print magazines equals the total number of copies distributed annually, which includes subscriptions (both paid and complimentary), issues sold in bookstores and online, and issues sold or given away at literary events, such as conferences and readings. Some print magazines also publish the work they accept on their affiliate websites, which can increase their reach even more. In the case of magazines that publish exclusively online, their reach is determined by how much web traffic they receive (unique pageviews per month or year). For those literary magazines that share their writers' work through their social media channels—which is easier to do with poems because they can often be shared in full—their number of followers should also be taken into account.

You can find this information in the previously mentioned online databases, and many magazines cite their circulation or distribution on their websites too. If it's not available in the About Us section and they accept advertising, look for it in the advertising section or in the media kit, as they're obligated to share this information so advertisers understand how many potential people will see their ads.

The Company You Keep

Naturally, it is important to you to have your work published alongside the writing of those whose work you most respect and admire. Make a list of your favorite writers and research where they've published their work by searching for them online, visiting their websites, if they have them, and checking the acknowledgments page in their books. The Poets & Writers Directory is also a good resource. Each listing includes where the writer's work has been published and links to the Literary Magazines database.

Consider the masthead of any literary magazine that is on your radar. You can tell a lot about a magazine from the team of dedicated individuals behind it: who is reading and editing submissions, who is designing the magazine, who is publicizing and getting the word out on social media about each issue, and so on. You can also glean details about the diversity of the editorial group in terms of gender and ethnicity. For many writers, a masthead with multiple people of color in editorial roles is important.

"With people of color on the masthead, and in particular when a person of color is at the editorial helm, a magazine is more likely to send a clear message that it's a supportive outlet for writers of color," writes Jenn Scheck-Kahn, founder of Journal of the Month, a subscription service that delivers an assortment of print literary magazines.

Magazines That Pay

With few exceptions, most literary magazines pay their contributors very modest fees or nothing at all. Compensation ranges from contributor copies to a few hundred dollars (unlike commercial magazines, which typically pay upward of a dollar per word). Remember, for the most part, literary magazines are not money-making operations. Rather, they're usually run on a shoestring budget, and the staff is paid well below a working wage, if at all. In some cases, they're staffed by a dedicated group of volunteers. As a result, while many aspire to compensate their contributors, they rarely have the funds to pay cash. Instead, they work on helping writers by doing their best with limited resources to get their magazines into the hands of as many readers as possible.

There are, however, magazines that are dedicated to paying their contributors at least something. You can prioritize those that do, but keep in mind, it's next to impossible to make serious money from contributor fees.

How to Submit Your Work

Now that you've compiled a list of magazines to submit to, the most important thing to do before submitting is to read each magazine's guidelines for submission carefully. Magazines take time and energy to make these guidelines explicit, and those submissions that don't adhere to the guidelines can be swiftly eliminated from consideration, especially when there are so many for editors to read. Most magazines will state how many poems should be included in a submission or, in the case of prose, the number of pages or words they're looking for. Always adhere to these length requirements.

The way most magazines review the unsolicited submissions they receive, commonly referred to as "the slush pile," is to enlist the help of a first round of readers whose job is to eliminate, right off the bat, any submissions that don't fit the magazine's guidelines and standards. These readers then pass along a more curated selection of submissions to the editors. You want to make sure that your submission makes it past this first round so your work is considered by the ultimate decision makers.

Some writers think that by embellishing their submission with a stylized font or with color or, in the case of postal submissions, by including glitter in the envelope it will help their submission stand out. It may do just that, but not in a good way. Rather, this signals to readers and editors a level of unprofessionalism that will almost certainly be a strike against you. Don't do it. It almost never works. Instead, let the quality of your writing speak for itself.

It's best practice to include with your submission a cover letter, unless the guidelines state that it's not necessary. Keep your cover letter short—no longer than a page—and professional. Be sure to address the letter to the appropriate editor. If, for example, you're submitting poetry, find the poetry editor's name on the magazine's masthead and address your letter to them (unless the guidelines give explicit instructions on whom to send your submission to). Consider including a sentence or two that show you're familiar with the magazine and the kind of writing it publishes. This proves to editors that you've taken the time to read the magazine, and you're not simply blanketing the market with your work. If relevant, consider including a sentence or two about why you're submitting this particular piece for a particular issue of the magazine. For example, if a magazine is accepting submissions for a special issue on the environment, you can mention how your submission fits the bill. Include a few sentences about your previous publications, if you have them, and any recent literary accolades. Finally, it's fine to include a detail or two about where you live and your job, but don't go overboard with the personal details. And the following cannot be emphasized enough: Be sure to proofread your cover letter and submission. Remember, any indication—from misspelling an editor's name to typos to other careless mistakes—that you haven't approached your submission professionally gives editors an immediate reason to reject it.

A Note on Reading Fees

Before the onset of online submissions, the standard practice was as follows: Literary magazines accepted unsolicited submissions during open reading periods. Writers sent their work via postal mail and included a self-addressed stamped envelope (SASE) for the editor's response. Typical response time was four to six weeks. Simultaneously submitting—when a writer would send a submission to more than one magazine at a time—was generally frowned upon and considered bad practice. If writers did submit their work to more than one publication at a time, they were expected to note this in their cover letter, which gave editors the option to return the work without considering it (rather than taking the time to read it, only to have it pulled in the final hour when another magazine accepted it).

With the widespread adoption of online submission platforms, such as Submittable, and e-mail submissions, writers are now able to submit their work much more easily (and quickly) with a few simple strokes and clicks. Simultaneous submissions have now become common practice, and writers no longer necessarily incur the costs of paper and postage. Instead, the cost has been passed on to the magazine, which must pay for the use of its online submission platform and pay for paper if they choose to print any submissions. Because most writers submit their work simultaneously, and because it's so easy to submit to literary magazines online, the number of submissions most magazines receive has increased, as has the workload to process these submissions. As a result, many magazines now charge reading fees, typically in the range of $5 to $25, to offset the costs involved in managing submissions. This also becomes a way for literary magazines to limit the number and increase the quality of the submissions they receive.

Some writers feel they should never pay to have their work considered; others accept this shift in the submission process. It's up to you to decide whether you think paying a reading fee is fair. Do your research to see if the advantages of having your work published outweigh the expenditure. Just remember, supporting the publications you hope to be a part of is not a bad way to spend a few dollars. At least your money is going to a good cause—and if you have any hesitation about whether it is one, reconsider whether this is a magazine you want your work to appear in. It is also worth noting that many journals waive reading fees for subscribers, and some will waive the fee in response to an e-mail stating financial hardship or inability to pay.

What to Expect After Submitting

Most literary magazines will state their response time in their submission guidelines, and there is a wide range. Some publications try to adhere to the traditional four to six weeks, while others take four to six months. If you haven't heard back from a magazine within their stated response time, it's perfectly acceptable to send them a polite note inquiring about the status of your submission. If you don't hear back right away, it's probably prudent to wait a few weeks and then politely inquire again. If you still don't hear back, chalk it up to the magazine being overwhelmed with submissions and move on.

If Your Work Is Accepted

Congratulations! You should receive an author agreement letter that outlines the terms of publication, which includes the specific rights the magazine intends on acquiring—for print, most magazines typically acquire First North American Serial Rights (FNASR), which means they have the exclusive right to publish your piece first in North America. These rights also usually include an exclusivity period during which the piece cannot appear anywhere else (including your own website or blog). After the exclusivity period, the rights should revert back to the author, which means you're free to reprint the piece.

Other terms that may be included in the author contract are the exclusive right to reprint the work, the nonexclusive right to reprint the work, the right to reprint the work in subsequent editions or anthologies, and the right to publish the work online or in a replica edition (an exact copy of the print edition but viewable on a screen). If you have any concerns, you should ask the magazine's editor for clarification. You can also contact the Authors Guild or the National Writers Union for guidance. In general, here's what the aforementioned rights mean:

Exclusive right to reprint the work: The magazine holds the right to reprint the work without the author's permission.

Nonexclusive right to reprint the work: You and the magazine share the right to reprint the work. The magazine is free to reprint the work without your permission, although most magazines contact writers for their consent as a courtesy. You also have the right to reprint the work without the magazine's consent, although it is standard to include a credit line citing where it originally appeared.

The right to reprint the work in subsequent editions or anthologies: The magazine has the right to reprint your work in an anthology or special ("best of" or themed) issue.

The right to publish the work online: The magazine has the right to publish your work on its website. Some magazines pay an additional fee for this right.

What to Do with Rejection

Keep in mind, there are many factors editors consider when deciding whether to accept a piece of writing. They have a limited number of spots in their publication per year. They may be trying to include a balance of writing by writers at various stages in their careers or of different backgrounds or pieces about a range of subjects. Plus, editors' tastes are subjective. If your work is rejected by one magazine don't be discouraged. And don't respond to the rejection—it won't change the fact that your work has been rejected, and you could end up burning a bridge that you may need to cross later in your career. Take any feedback they send to heart, consider revising, and send it out again. As author Joey Franklin writes, "A no from an editor can be disappointing, sure, but it can also help us be more honest about the weaknesses in our own writing. On top of that, rejection can help us see more clearly where our work fits into the larger literary conversation and give us confidence to stick with a project."

CHARLES YU ON THE INNER WRITER

INT. KITCHEN - DAY

On a bright fall Thursday morning, I sit down with my inner
writer to ask him a few questions. I slurp from a large mug of
black coffee and nibble on a piece of wheat bread, buttered and
lightly toasted; he has nothing.

ME

Thanks for agreeing to this.

MY INNER WRITER

Not sure I had a choice.

The clouds are low and scattered. A small bird lands in the
backyard fountain, marinating its lower quarters in the burbling
urn, filled with stones.

ME

What kind of bird is that?

MY INNER WRITER

I don't know. A wren?

ME

What do you mean you don't know?

MY INNER WRITER

You don't. Why should I?

ME

Writers are supposed to know the names of birds.

MY INNER WRITER

That's poets. Poets know birds.

ME

What?

MY INNER WRITER

In a poet's world, there are trillions of egrets.
It's like nothing but egrets. Maybe a few terns.

(then)

But you write fiction.

ME

I write fiction?

I think you're confused, buddy.

I don't write fiction.

You write fiction.

A long moment of silence. We stare at each other.

MY INNER WRITER

Holy crap.

(then)

You think *I'm* the writer?

ME

Well who else would it be?

                        MY INNER WRITER
            Oh, I don't know . . . you?
            Why would you think it's me?

                             ME
            Um, you're the one called "My Inner Writer"—

                        MY INNER WRITER
            Because you named me that!
            Because *you're the one writing this*!

I take a gulp of coffee, or fail to. It dribbles all over my
chin and neck and shirt. I wipe my face, try to regain my
composure.

                             ME
                You have a point.

He has a point.

                        MY INNER WRITER
                Man. I just can't believe—

                             ME
                All these years, I thought—

                        MY INNER WRITER
                Unbelievable.

We stare at each other.

                             ME
                So, if you're not—

MY INNER WRITER

And you're not—

We arrive at the question at the same time:

ME AND MY INNER WRITER

Who's been doing all this writing?

ME AND MY INNER WRITER (CONT'D)

And why?

An awkward silence.

ME AND MY INNER WRITER (CONT'D)

This is an awkward silence.

I open the liquor cabinet, reach for the bottle of Jameson and splash some into my coffee mug.

I sit there for a while, sipping, trying to figure out where to go from here.

MY INNER WRITER

You know . . .

ME

Yeah?

MY INNER WRITER

You don't have to do this. No one is making you.

ME

Well, then what?

MY INNER WRITER

You could just . . . not.

ME

Not write?

He doesn't answer.

I wait a minute.

Then another. An hour passes.

He's gone. The dialogue has stopped.

I look at the clock. It's 10:17 a.m. The whole day in front of me. Amazing. I could get my whole to-do list crossed off, and still have time to eat a sandwich before it's time to pick up the kids from school.

I make a list of books I'm going to read. Always meant to read these. Now I'll have the time.

It's 10:19.

I wonder what's on TV.

The house is so quiet. Now that he's gone. It's just me.

I'm lonely.

I need to go find him. Where did he go? Where do inner writers live?

INT. CAR - DAY

I get in the car and drive around my neighborhood. Top 40 radio
isn't helping. I try classical, then NPR, then jazz. I turn off
the radio. I drive for hours, until I'm almost out of gas.

I park the car about a mile from my house. Walk through the park
on the way home. He's not sitting on the bench. We used to sit
on that bench, and I would eat a sandwich while he worked or
read. I took it for granted.

I remember how he and I met. Right here.

I had my head buried in a book, and then I heard something and I
looked up and he was sitting there.

He wasn't my inner writer yet. I think he was maybe my inner
reader? Or maybe not even that. All I know is that I was reading
a short story ("How to Become a Writer" by Lorrie Moore) and
then this guy appeared. And I was less lonely.

EXT. DRIVEWAY - EVENING

By the time I get home, it's dusk. I see the upstairs light is
on. Someone's home.

INT. KITCHEN - CONTINUOUS

I go to the kitchen, grab a steak knife. There's a noise
upstairs.

Whoever broke in is . . . using the bathroom?

I charge up the stairs screaming like a maniac, burst in . . .

INT. BATHROOM - CONTINUOUS

To find the intruder in there, singing, soaped up. He sees me, screams, slips, on his way down grabs for the shampoo caddy, his foot kicks open the shower door, so there are bottles of conditioner and soapy water everywhere.

> MY INNER WRITER
>
> What the hell?

> ME
>
> What are you doing?

> MY INNER WRITER
>
> You know I do my best thinking in here.

> ME
>
> I mean—I thought you were gone.

He starts laughing.

> MY INNER WRITER
>
> Oh, stupid. You thought you could get rid of
> me that easy?

He dries off. I heat water to boil pasta, pour myself a beer into a glass. I was alone. And then I wasn't anymore. He gets back to work.

CHARLES YU *is the author of four books, including his latest novel,* Interior China-town. *His fiction and nonfiction have appeared in a number of publications including the* New Yorker, *the* New York Times, Wired, *the* Wall Street Journal, *and* Time. *He has received two WGA nominations for his work in television, and has written for shows on AMC, FX, HBO, and Cartoon Network.*

FOURTEEN

Writing Contests

If we consider entering the wonderful world of literary magazines as step 1 in the process of building a publishing résumé and hopefully a reading audience, then step 2 might be exploring the realm of writing competitions, which includes prizes for unpublished work, grants to sustain work on any given project, and writing fellowships. Depending on the type, these opportunities frequently offer cash prizes and can include publication, an invitation to give a reading or attend an awards ceremony, time at a residency, and other benefits—including, of course, the honor of having been chosen as winner of the contest or recipient of support from an established and well-regarded organization. Some of the finest nonprofits, presses, magazines, and universities—not to mention government agencies—sponsor writing contests, and having your work associated with them can be a boon to your career.

As with so many other aspects of the writing life, there is what can sometimes seem like an intimidating number of options to consider—and pros and cons to weigh—when trying to decide which contests to enter. But one can relatively easily sort the hundreds of contests out there into categories, starting first with the easiest—genre—then winnowing further by paying attention to things like manuscript requirements. For example, there are a number of contests given for a single unpublished poem, story, or essay that might be right for writers who are in the beginning stages of their careers. (Though it would be a mistake to think these contests are easy to win; indeed, beginning writers who enter such a contest will be putting their work up against that of seasoned veterans.) There are also many prizes given for an unpublished book-length manuscript of poetry or prose, and it's up to you to be honest with yourself about whether your manuscript is ready for prime time. After all, it will be up against hundreds, maybe even thousands, of others that are equally or perhaps more deserving of recognition. Therefore, as with so many other aspects of the writing life, it's important to be patient with your work—push that poem as far as you can, revise that story as many times as necessary before entering it in the competitive arena. Readers you trust—who can critique your work and offer feedback and suggestions—are integral to the process. Otherwise, you may be wasting time, energy, expectations, and money on a contest for which you and your work are not ready.

Other opportunities such as grants and fellowships are open only to writers who have published a certain number of poems or stories in literary journals or who have a published book, or to writers who fall within a certain age range, or fit into any number of other demographic distinctions. And, of course, book prizes—that is, those that are given for published books—have their own guidelines, and writers are sometimes not even involved in the process, with publishers entering their titles into the running for prizes like the Pulitzer and the National Book Award.

Until relatively recently, one common guideline that many writers took for granted or simply overlooked was citizenship. Many contests were open only to U.S. citizens or legal residents until a movement, spearheaded by a group of poets who called themselves "Undocupoets," raised awareness of the guideline, and in response many contests, including those sponsored by the Academy of American Poets and the National Poetry Series, changed their rules.

A Cost-Benefit Analysis

Once you narrow down your choices based on genre and manuscript requirements, you can further sharpen your focus by considering whether the contest is worth the time and attention. This is a simple cost-benefit calculation. An obscure contest, sponsored by an organization you've never heard of, that requires a modest entry fee and offers dozens of prizes might be easy to win, but do you really want your name associated with it? Remember, the journals or presses that publish your work and the contests that reward your writing are putting a stamp on it that can stay there for your entire career. It might be tempting to rack up easy publication credits and contest wins now, but consider how you'll feel a decade down the road, when you start applying to MFA programs, or teaching jobs, and you have a list of credits featuring things like the Gold Star Good Job Prize from a company called Words-n-Stuff that required a $50 entry fee and offered nothing but publication in an onion-skin faux-leather "winner's edition" in which your poem appears in nine-point Comic Sans alongside fifty-six other lucky winners. That's not honoring your work. It all comes back to leading a deliberate writing life: making choices that reflect well on you and your work.

ACTION ITEM 34

Develop a plan for submitting your work to writing contests. Compile a list of contests (start with single-piece contests, then book publication contests, then grants and fellowships) that have deadlines in the next few months and plot these dates on a submissions calendar. As the deadlines approach, read through your work and revise if necessary—use the contests as incentives to polish up your writing.

So how to think about a cost-benefit analysis of contests? Let's start with the issue of cost. The most obvious cost associated with a contest is the entry fee, and about eighty percent of the contests that are worth your time and attention do charge some kind of fee, typically between $10 and $25, that is used by the sponsoring organization to pay the judges and fund the cash prize. It's a good idea to carefully look at how the contest is run and to consider the simple financial implications of the prize versus the entry fee. For instance, if a contest charges an entry fee of $50 and only offers a $1,000 prize, do the math: That contest would need to attract only twenty writers who are willing to submit and pay the fee in order to make up that cash prize. That would lead us to wonder whether this sponsoring organization is in it to make money or to truly honor deserving writers.

Literary magazines that sponsor contests sometimes offer incentives by giving a free subscription as part of the entry fee. Similarly, small presses sometimes offer entrants a copy of the winning book.

Of course, many contests offer more than a cash prize or even publication of a poem, story, essay, or book. Take, for instance, Cave Canem's Toi Derricotte & Cornelius Eady Chapbook Prize, given annually for a poetry chapbook by a black poet. The winner receives $500, publication by Jai-Alai Books, and a weeklong residency at the Writer's Room at the Betsy Hotel in Miami, Florida. The winner is also invited to give a reading at the O, Miami Poetry Festival. There is a $12 entry fee, but this contest is clearly designed to give a deserving poet not only some money and the publication of a chapbook, but also time to write, exposure, and networking opportunities at a world-class literary event. Contests like this one—and there are many—showcase why literary contests are such an attractive way for poets and writers to gain accolades, publication credits, and potentially career-changing experiences.

Entry fees are not necessarily something to be avoided. Free is always best, of course, but if the entry fee seems like a fair price to pay for having your work considered by a well-known judge or a well-regarded sponsoring organization, then by all means enter the contest if it's a good match for your work. By paying it you are also supporting a worthy organization and maintaining the health of this particular region of the literary ecosystem. Of course, entry fees are prohibitive for some writers, but there are a few contests that will accommodate writers who are unable to pay.

Depending on the type of sponsoring organization—a literary magazine, a small press, a nonprofit organization, a private company, a university, or a government agency—a writing contest can be administered a number of different ways, but there are some pretty common elements that can be useful for a beginning writer to be familiar with, especially as they relate to entry fees. An awareness of how contests are run can help writers avoid those that are unethical or scam operations. The carefully vetted Grants & Awards section of *Poets & Writers Magazine* and its related online Writing Contests database are also resources that list only legitimate contests offering prizes that would further a writer's career.

The costs associated with contests depend in large part on the prize being offered, but they can include: the cash prize, the judges' fees, the readers' fees, the online submission portal's (Submittable's) fee, the contest coordinator's salary (typically a percentage of that person's annual salary allocated for the specific contest), advertising and promotion, and so on. But if the prize includes, say, the publication of a book, then you have to factor in all the costs associated with that book's publication. (It should be pointed out, however, that while the typical contest offering book publication should come with a standard book contract, it often does not come with an advance against royalties; the cash that accompanies the prize replaces the advance.) Other contests also offer an invitation to read at a specific venue, in which case one needs to add the cost of the winner's travel to the reading.

One of the more interesting things to consider when you start thinking about entering writing contests is who, exactly, is going to be reading your submission. It's easy to think about the judge reading your work—and you should certainly research this to determine whether the judge might respond to your work—but the judge will likely only see a very small percentage of the submissions, the best of the best, the cream of the crop: the finalists. All the rest of the submissions are typically sorted and read by screeners, or first readers. The front line in any writing contest, the first readers are often interns, students, or staff of the sponsoring organization, and depending on the writing contest, they may not even be paid for their work.

This is why it's so important to research the sponsoring organization and determine whether it's a group you can trust. If you feel confident that it's a professional organization that does consistently high-quality work, then you can probably feel confident that they are employing competent first readers for their contest. But the fact is, you just never know, which is why it only makes sense not to place too much importance on winning. It's what we all want, of course, but if you don't win, it could mean any number of things, including the possibility that your work just didn't resonate with an undergraduate English student or unpaid intern.

THE SMART APPROACH TO CONTEST SUBMISSIONS

1. **FINISH FIRST.** It sounds obvious, but so does most valuable advice. Before you submit your manuscript make sure you've pushed it as far as it can go. Revise, revise, and revise some more. Send it to five friends and ask them for constructive criticism. Pass it around your writing group. Workshop it. Stick it in a drawer for a week and then read it. It's still brilliant? Great. Stick it back in the drawer and submit it next week after you've reread it again and asked yourself, *Is this better than the five hundred other manuscripts that have already been submitted to this contest?* If you're paying an entry fee, there should be no doubt in your mind.

2. **KNOW YOUR SPONSORING ORGANIZATION.** Do you read the magazine that sponsors the contest? Do you subscribe? Have you read the books published in the past year by the press that's putting on the contest? Do you disagree with any of the editorial policies of that magazine or press? Familiarize yourself with the organization's website and read some of the marketing copy. Does it present itself as an organization you'd like to be associated with? Are you comfortable with the idea of having your name—not to mention your writing—associated with that sponsor for the rest of your career? The Deadlines section of *Poets & Writers Magazine*, or the Writing Contests database at pw.org, are the perfect places to start gathering information about legitimate contests with upcoming deadlines. They provide all the details you need to know (how much, for what, by when, and so on) in order to make a decision about whether you should research the contest further.

3. **JUDGE YOUR JUDGE.** Read that famous poet's work as well as the work of winners that judge has chosen in the past. Read interviews with that

well-known novelist, reviews of her latest book, and articles and essays she has published in magazines. Try to figure out not only how she writes but also how she thinks, how she reads. Never heard of the judge? Double your efforts and proceed with caution. (See no. 2.)

4. **FOLLOW THE RULES.** You may have written a story for the ages, but it won't matter if you printed your last name on the top of every page when the rules explicitly forbid any identifying information on your manuscript. Don't e-mail it as an attachment when you're supposed to upload it to an online submissions manager. Follow the guidelines to perfection.

5. **DON'T GET FANCY.** Let your words win the contest, not your paper or your ink or your fonts or your formatting. Don't print your manuscript on special paper. Keep it in a standard font—for the love of God, no script fonts—and don't include an Oscar-worthy thank-you speech on an acknowledgments page. (Save that for the published book.) Don't include the endearing anecdote in your cover letter about the first time you picked up a crayon and realized you wanted to be a writer. If you're submitting a paper manuscript, don't recycle the folded-up, fingered-through, and rejected copy from the last contest. Save that for your doodles and your grocery lists; consider the extra money you're going to spend on ink and paper as an investment in a submission with a better chance at winning. No reader or judge wants proof that an entry has already been rejected. Don't plant doubt: It will grow.

6. **KEEP TRACK.** Start logging your submissions on some sort of spreadsheet. It doesn't need to be complicated (we've included a sample on pages 244–45); just keep a record of which contests you enter, how much you paid, when you were notified of the result, and so on. Not only will you have a better sense of how much you are investing in writing contests, you will also allay some anxiety about when you'll get that e-mail or letter of congratulations.

7. **KEEP WRITING.** Your writing career does not necessarily hinge on winning or losing a contest—winning can help, no doubt, but there are plenty of brilliant, well-respected writers who publish book after book and never win a contest. The most important thing to focus on is your writing. But don't fall into the trap

of writing for contests. If you want to use a contest deadline as a deadline for your revision, that's okay; however, the two should be related but separate activities. Submit your work to contests when the writing is finished (see no. 1). And when you're done, start writing again.

On Winning

The benefits of winning a contest can far exceed the short-term gains of a bit of money or the publication of your work. Those things are great, of course, but writers who have won contests—single-piece awards, book-publication prizes, or life-changing fellowships and grants—consistently say there are more meaningful ways of measuring the impact on their careers than how it affected the number in their bank account or added a line on their résumé. Things like affirmation, validation, exposure, visibility, and the gift of more time to work on the next project are among the intangible benefits we've heard winning writers describe.

"Any time I've won an award, whether for an individual poem or as an emerging writer, it has felt like the poetry gods were conferring a blessing on me," says Ama Codjoe, winner of a 2019 NEA Creative Writing Fellowship, the 2019 Drinking Gourd Chapbook Poetry Prize, the 2018 Georgia Review Loraine Williams Poetry Prize, and the 2017 Rona Jaffe Writer's Award. "And though the money has materially changed my life, it's the affirmation that is the true gift."

Emily Skaja, winner of a $25,000 NEA Creative Writing Fellowship as well as the 2018 Academy of American Poets Walt Whitman Award, among other prizes, says winning the Walt Whitman Award, which came with publication of her debut poetry collection by Graywolf Press, changed her life. "On a personal level, it marked a meaningful vote of confidence from Joy Harjo, the prize judge. Knowing that a poet I admire so much believed in my book gave me courage and renewed my faith in myself and in my work at a time when I really needed a positive sign from the universe. I used to have the sense that I was writing poems into a void, or writing something that ultimately would matter only to me or to my closest friends. Winning a book prize has changed that because I'm gaining an audience of strangers, some of whom are writers I deeply admire." Of course, that greater level of attention also comes at a cost. "It's thrilling, but it's also unexpectedly intimidating," she adds. "I guess the stakes for speaking are higher when you know someone is listening."

Lillian Yvonne-Bertram, winner of the 2018 Noemi Press Poetry Award, the 2018 Sonora Review Poetry Prize, and the 2016 Narrative Magazine Poetry Prize, knows all about the exposure that winning a contest can bring a writer. "Winning contests provides greater exposure, which can have a big impact on your career, the size of your audience, and the distribution of your work," she says, while also acknowledging that the financial remuneration is a significant factor.

Megan Giddings, winner of a 2018 Barbara Deming Memorial Fund grant worth $1,500, agrees. "Winning the grant gave me two things when I really needed them: confidence and time to write," she says. "The money allowed me to take time off from work without having to do a desperate scramble to pay my bills or feel guilty that I was putting my writing over life stability. And I wish I could say I'm a person who is patient and assured in her abilities, but as embarrassing as it feels to admit, I needed the validation a lot."

As much as money matters—and there's no point in trying to act like it doesn't—it also doesn't last. And it certainly doesn't last as long as a feeling of validation or a vote of confidence when it's given at just the right moment in one's career.

On Losing

Of course, for every writer who receives a shot of confidence with a contest win, there are many more who suffer the rejection that comes with not winning. But as with many things about the writing life, weathering those storms is a matter of perspective.

While Sophie Klahr knows about winning—she is the winner of Bucknell University's 2019 Philip Roth Residence in Creative Writing—she also knows plenty about coming close but not quite close enough. "Just in the last seven years I've submitted to around thirty contests, won two of them, been a finalist for four others, and been nominated for five prizes. That's a lot of rejection on record, which isn't even close to the number of rejections I've received from regular submissions," she says. "No rejection or acceptance has ever changed my writing practices—I do my work, and step back."

"It's such a crapshoot," says Mark Wagenaar, winner of the 2019 December Magazine Jeff Marks Memorial Poetry Prize, the 2018 Press 53/Prime Number Magazine Flash Fiction Award, the 2018 Frontier Poetry Open Prize, the 2018 Tupelo Quarterly Poetry Prize, the 2017 Southern Indiana Review Mary C. Mohr Poetry Award, and the 2017 Nimrod Pablo Neruda Prize for Poetry. "Rejections have to be water off a duck's back if you're going to survive. I'm always interested in the work of the winners and finalists. I'm often blown away. Sometimes that's daunting, sometimes inspiring."

Codjoe, the winner of the NEA fellowship, chalks up losing to a necessary part of being a writer who is working to find a way to winning. "I wish I could show you my Submittable page, chock-full of rejections. Most writers, dare I say all, experience more rejections than acceptances. This is part of the terrain of being a writer. My attitude toward rejections is that they are invitations to send out more work. I acknowledge my

ACTION ITEM 35

Fill out the Submission Tracker on pages 244–45. For an interactive version, visit pw.org /submissions.

disappointment and then get back to writing. Strange as it may seem, rejections are generative for me."

"A rejection isn't always a no; it can also be a 'not right now,' or a 'not yet,'" adds Klahr. "Let go of the results. Just keep writing poems (or stories or essays) that you feel have integrity, and when they find their true form, offer them to the world. The rest will fall into place."

SUBMISSION TRACKER

CONTEST	DEADLINE	FEE	TITLE OF ENTRY
		Total	

SUBMISSION TRACKER

DATE SENT	RESULT	NOTES

DANI SHAPIRO RECOMMENDS

Five Books to Read When You're Feeling Lonely,
Solitary, and Out of Step with the World

A WRITER'S DIARY by Virginia Woolf

I keep this book near me and open it at random when I'm feeling lost. Like a guide from beyond, Woolf always brings something I didn't know I needed.

DAYBOOK by Ann Truitt

Another book that's never far out of reach. I once was at Yaddo at the same time as Truitt and was too intimidated to approach her. I now regret that. Always approach your idols!

LIFE WORK by Donald Hall

This slim, marvelous memoir is a paean to humility and discipline.

THOUGHTS IN SOLITUDE by Thomas Merton

Lest the world grow so noisy and fast-paced that we forget, here's a reminder that quiet reflection is a necessity.

THE PARIS REVIEW INTERVIEWS, VOLUMES 1–4, edited by Philip Gourevitch

These interviews with writers including Elizabeth Bishop, Joan Didion, Maya Angelou, Gabriel García Márquez, and many others are an art form unto themselves. It's so use-ful to read about the craft, process, and lives of great writers.

DANI SHAPIRO *is the author of the memoirs* Inheritance, Hourglass, Still Writing, Devotion, *and* Slow Motion, *as well as five novels, including* Black & White *and* Family History. *She is the cofounder of the Sirenland Writers Conference in Positano, Italy.*

FIFTEEN

Self-Publishing

Two roads diverged in a yellow wood . . .

—ROBERT FROST, "THE ROAD NOT TAKEN"

If you will excuse the extended metaphor, here we have arrived at a fork in the road.

To our right there is a path along which there are a number of gates, and in order to pass you need to possess not a key but rather sufficient evidence of literary merit to persuade the keepers of these gates, the so-called gatekeepers, to let you pass. These gatekeepers go by many names, but the most common are agent and editor and publisher. It is worth pointing out that these gatekeepers want nothing more than to let you continue along this well-worn path, but unfortunately there is only so much room here, and they can't let everyone proceed. No one quite knows where the road ahead leads, but if you get far enough along you will see familiar landmarks such as brick-and-mortar bookstores, well-established and curated book review sections, and fancy awards ceremonies—each with their own gates and gatekeepers. Some writers are committed to as many attempts as it takes to show the required materials and gain entry to this path. Others, not so much.

Fortunately, to our left there is another path, and this one has only one gate, right at the start. One needn't have a key or evidence of literary merit to pass, or really anything in particular except one important thing: money. No one really knows what lies ahead on this path, either, but one thing is certain: Everyone who chooses to travel this path will have a book to carry with them.

In this chapter we will take a look at the path on the left.

A Brief History

Before the internet, an aspiring author didn't have many choices if a publisher rejected their book. They could abandon their manuscript, relegating it to the back of the desk drawer. Or, if they could afford it, they could pay to have their book printed and try to sell the copies themselves à la Walt Whitman, who made a lifelong commitment to publishing his collection *Leaves of Grass*. He produced the first edition of twelve poems in 1855, followed by several revised editions, the final one including almost four hundred. It should be noted, though, that Whitman was trained in the art of printing and was a committed self-promoter, even writing anonymous reviews of his own book (pro tip: don't do that).

If they didn't want to go that route, they could pay to have their book published by a "vanity" publisher, with the promise that the book would not only be printed but also promoted. The most famous—or perhaps infamous—example of a vanity publisher is Vantage Press, which often advertised in the back of the *New York Times Book Review*. But in 1990 the New York State Supreme Court ordered Vantage to pay $3.5 million in damages to more than two thousand authors who, the court said, were defrauded after paying for the press's services but never received the promotional efforts they were promised. Vantage Press closed in 2012 after more than sixty years in business.

With the advent of the internet and the arrival of technology solutions for designing, printing, and distributing books, self-publishing has become not only a viable option for authors but a booming market. While not every self-published author may turn a profit, the self-publishing platforms offering their services are. According to a recent report from Bowker, the official ISBN agency for the United States and Australia, the number of self-published titles per year surpassed 1,000,000 in 2017, growing from 786,935 the previous year to 1,009,188.

That's a lot of books.

First, Some Questions

Just because so many authors choose this road to publication doesn't mean it's right for everyone. To determine whether this is the right path for you, there are a few questions to consider.

Who is your audience? If you can identify a niche audience that you can promote to effectively (if you're a real estate agent, say, and you have a suspenseful novel with a protagonist who is a real estate agent that you just know other real estate agents in your trade organization would love) then self-publishing might be a worthwhile choice. Imagine: You can print as many as you'd like to bring with you to that real estate convention in Cleveland in two months, and after you sell enough copies to recoup your initial investment, you could be staring at a nice little profit.

Do you have a strong platform? Let's say you have a well-trafficked blog where you write about your passion for vintage Volkswagens, you have ten thousand subscribers to your monthly newsletter, and you've been traveling around to auto shows for a decade, during which you've shaken hands with hundreds of people who are just as enthusiastic about 1967 Volkswagen Beetles—and story collections featuring the iconic cars—as you are. Perhaps you can use that platform to sell your self-published story collection, *Abbey Road*.

How hands-on do you want to be? If the answer isn't "very," then you might want to skip to the next chapter, because if you're not hands-on, there will be no hands on your book at all. Self-publishing is ideal for micromanagers—those who want complete creative and business control and who want to be in on every little decision, right down to the font size on the copyright page. And there's a lot to manage, including developmental editing, line editing, copyediting, proofreading, legal vetting, cover design, interior design, promotional copy, blurbs, and more.

How comfortable are you selling your own wares? While all authors, even traditionally published ones, must do the difficult work of self-promoting and publicizing their books these days, self-published authors shoulder all the weight of selling their wares. Unless you want to hire your own publicist, you won't be able to rely on a well-known publisher or a department full of highly educated folks whose jobs are to let readers know about your book.

What skills do you bring to the table? Obviously, we mean skills beyond those it takes to be a brilliant writer. If you have experience with graphic design, or you're a copywriter for a PR firm, consider whether you have skills that can be applied effectively to a self-publishing project—and perhaps save you money that would otherwise be going to professionals to do that part of the project for you.

How much money do you want to spend? Most self-publishing platforms offer bundled or packages of services, from the most basic (just upload the text and print) to the more inclusive (editing, design, promotion, and so on), including an à la carte menu of options. Whether you go with a bundled service plan or you farm out the various elements of a successful self-publishing project to freelancers, expect to pay for it.

Are you in a hurry? If the answer is yes, then self-publishing is certainly a good option.

What do you really want out of it? Do you dream of winning a National Book Award? Do you envision tens of thousands of readers? Front page of the *New York Times Book Review*? Well, those things are long shots even in traditional publishing, but the odds are significantly steeper if you go with self-publishing. That's not necessarily a reason to avoid it—you can self-publish one book and then go on to work with a traditional publisher later—but it's important to be honest about your expectations and choose a path to publishing accordingly.

Advantages and Drawbacks

As long as you're comfortable with handling the details yourself or assembling a team of professionals to help, there are a number of benefits to self-publishing:

- **Speed in getting to market:** It is possible to publish within three to four months compared to the typical nine- to twelve-month schedule of most traditional publishers.

- **More control:** You decide on the title, price, cover design, and cover copy as well as final content. A traditional publisher will typically give you final say on the content, but you will still most likely be sharing these decisions, which some writers consider a downside (while others are happy to learn from their editor's expertise).

- **Higher profits:** Publishers generally pay royalties ranging from ten to fifteen percent of the cover price of a hardcover book once the advance is earned back. If you self-publish, any earnings beyond the cost of producing the book are yours.

Despite these benefits, most authors prefer traditional publishing over self-publishing. Apart from the financial backing, which is obviously beneficial, the credibility and prestige that is associated with traditional publishers are significant factors, especially for authors in the academic field, says Marcia Layton Turner, an author and founding director of the Association of Ghostwriters. "Career decisions are based on whether they have published, so those authors should sign with a traditional publisher."

Jeffrey Blount self-published *Hating Heidi Foster*, a young adult novel in 2012. His second novel, *The Emancipation of Evan Walls*, was published by Koehler Books, a traditional publisher, in 2019. "In my opinion, the most important thing a publisher provides a writer is access." He continues:

So many necessary avenues are closed to self-published authors. Many bookstores won't allow a launch event or stock your books. Some literary prizes refuse to accept self-published work. And access to many of the most important review and marketing avenues is summarily shut in your face. It's troubling to put your heart and soul into your work only to find yourself a second-class citizen within the literary world. Being with a publisher has opened doors and legitimized my work in a way that I couldn't have done on my own. As a self-published author, you can find yourself alone and unsure. Yes, you give up a lot, including creative control over the cover and interior design, but with a publisher you have a partner with the necessary resources that is committed to making your book a success. There is comfort in that when, if you're like me, you really just want to write and leave the business end to the professionals.

Other authors question the benefits of traditional publishing. "Why would you want to be traditionally published if you're doing well on your own? Last time I worked with a traditional publisher, the title and the cover changed and the publisher insisted that I remove one chapter to shorten the book. I will never let that happen again," says Stephanie Chandler, author and CEO of the Nonfiction Authors Association. "If you have a budget, inclination, and the drive to do it yourself, I don't think you need a traditional publisher." It is difficult but not impossible for you to get your books into specialty stores and wholesalers, according to Chandler, who suggests sending your self-published books to the Small Press Department of Barnes & Noble.

Not a Sure Stepping-Stone

While a handful of well-known self-published novelists such as Lisa Genova (*Still Alice*) and Andy Weir (*The Martian*) received large advances from traditional publishers for books after they were already successfully self-published, they are the exception. The concern from traditional publishers is that popular self-published authors have already saturated their target readership, so there's no reason for them to repackage the same book. "When it does happen, it's because the authors are well known in a particular subject area and have a large social media following," says Martha Bullen, a book publishing/marketing consultant and editor. "But it's not something that happens consistently."

The Logistics of Self-Publishing

If you're comfortable with basic formatting and design programs, you can handle uploading your manuscript online, but there's much more involved in creating a professional book. In fact, self-publishing isn't necessarily a do-it-yourself enterprise—or at least it doesn't have to be. A cottage industry of consultants and companies is available to guide you through the self-publishing process, for a price. And it's usually worth paying for this expertise. You don't want your book to look amateurish. "The worst thing you can do is to hit Publish on a Word document without careful preparation," says Scott Lorenz, president of Westwind Communications. "Your book should be professionally edited, copyedited, typeset, and proofread by experts, not friends and family. And you need a great cover designed by a book designer."

Other industry insiders agree that quality content and design are critical to a book's success. "The two most important elements of a successful self-published book are cover design and editing," says Chandler of the Nonfiction Authors Association. "When those two elements are skipped or aren't invested in properly, book sales and reader reviews will be affected. A handful of errors are expected and forgivable, but more than five or six typos will be noticed." While Chandler recommends using beta readers early on to provide editorial feedback and catch grammatical errors, she warns writers that they still need to hire a professional editor and proofreader. "Also, don't try to cut corners by laying out your pages in Word. That's not a publishing software. You need a graphic design program for pagination, or your pages just won't look good," she says.

Unfortunately, some dodgy firms have targeted inexperienced authors. "With authors desiring a one-stop solution, there has been a surge in self-publishing entities that promise a streamlined service. But the design may be low quality," says Michele DeFilippo, owner of 1106Design.com, a full-service design firm. "Authors are often drawn to a company's low price, rationalizing that their content is so strong that readers will overlook mistakes. That's simply not the case. When authors say they can't afford to pay for other services, I recommend they save up and wait to publish until they can."

One very straightforward way to find reputable companies is to do an internet search for "*self-publishing company name* + complaints." You can also ask other authors for recommendations of services they've used. But before you sign anything, or type in your credit card number, carefully review your contract so you understand the specific services the vendor is providing. For example, will your manuscript be copyedited and proofread? Will you hold all the rights to the work? The answer to the latter had better be yes; if it's no, move on.

Reliable companies include Lulu and BookBaby, both of which provide cover design, print and e-book formatting, purchase of ISBNs, print-on-demand services, and other support. Other reliable options include Barnes & Noble Press, Amazon Kindle Direct Publishing (KDP), and IngramSpark, which is part of Ingram, the major book distributor in the United States. Authors often use more than one service so that their books aren't limited to a single platform, like Barnes & Noble or Amazon. With Amazon KDP, your books are available in paperback POD (print on demand) and on Kindle. Amazon KDP is the quickest and least expensive option, and your book is available on Amazon sites around the world (but not, it should be pointed out, in brick-and-mortar bookstores). However, if you want a hardcover book, then you can consider IngramSpark, which also allows you to produce an e-book that is compatible with Apple, Nook, Kobo, and Amazon formats.

How Much It Costs

Having a budget in mind ahead of time as you're planning for publication is helpful. Costs vary depending on word count, illustrations, and so on, but the actual production/printing is a relatively small portion of the total expense. You can upload your book on IngramSpark for $25 for an e-book and $49 for a print book. However, the prepublication costs will account for a larger portion of your expenses. You need to account for editing—perhaps a developmental edit but certainly a line edit, as well as a copyedit. For a novel of eighty thousand words, for example, you could expect to pay approximately $3,200 for line editing and another $2,240 for copyediting using BookBaby. A developmental edit with Lulu costs 9 cents per word, or $7,200, and could take an estimated four to five months. There's also the jacket design, which with Lulu and BookBaby starts at $399. And don't forget formatting, including interior design and typesetting, which will cost at least $500 but likely more. And, of course, you should also set aside some money for publicity and marketing.

ACTION ITEM 36

Visit some of the websites of the self-publishing services we just mentioned. Explore the different options with your particular project in mind. Some of them even have free e-books you can download that will explain how it all works.

"If you only focus on price, you may be disappointed," says Meryl Moss of Meryl Moss Media, which has a concierge publishing division that helps a handful of authors self-publish each year, providing step-by-step help from editing through publicity. "Your book needs to have a cover that makes sense, a sophisticated interior layout, and engaging back cover copy. You need the right type and size of font and to know what the book spine should look like. If you're planning to share your book only with your family, that's one thing, but if you plan to make a career out of writing, you have to keep up with the standards of the industry. Get honest feedback from people and work on getting blurbs from others in the writing world, including other authors." Readers, warns Moss, are very unforgiving and will quickly point out errors in your book by commenting online.

Publicity Efforts for Self-Published Books

"With so many books being published there are simply more books clamoring for attention," says Mike Onorato, vice president at Smith Publicity, who works with both traditionally published and self-published authors. Regardless of whether the book is self-published or traditionally published, his focus is on the book's message. "Sometimes I don't say the book is self-published. If I'm pitching to media with whom I have worked before, they trust me and trust that the book has quality content. You need to have a good story that is targeted at a specific group of readers," adds Onorato, who says you shouldn't only focus on national media. There are many influential targeted blogs that you can approach to do a Q&A or a feature on you and your book. "Also, it's important that you don't get distracted by book sales or your Amazon ranking. Your book is not a failure if it doesn't make 'best-seller' ranking," he says.

If you're on a limited budget, you need to find ways to get free publicity. "Learn how to create hooks, pitch local media, and reach out yourself by phone and in person," says Martha Bullen. "Time and creativity can be more effective than money." Bullen is a big fan of Goodreads, the book community site where you can interact with readers in several ways, including book giveaways and interviews.

You should have a launch plan that leads up to your official release, advises Stephanie Chandler. It should include a list of who you will notify, including friends, colleagues, and anyone who can provide support. "I don't recommend hiring a publicist in most cases because it's hard to earn back your investment. However, it can work for nonfiction authors who have universal topics such as leadership or women's issues that are media worthy," she says.

If you decide to work with a publicist and you're planning a major launch campaign, the publicist will want to start months ahead of your pub date, often four months ahead but sometimes even earlier. "For a robust campaign that includes bookstores and speaking engagements, we need six to seven months. The sooner we can begin, the better. Doing things right takes lead time," says Meryl Moss, who also founded BookTrib.com, a reader site that features author interviews, book reviews, giveaways, and news about upcoming titles. The site's newsletter, which is free, has about fifty thousand subscribers. BookTrib offers promotional packages for authors, including a big-mouth mailing, a book review, promotion of your book on BookTrib's social media channels, and a promo page on the company's website, for $375.

As for social media, authors and publishing insiders agree that you need to have an online presence. But rather than a scattershot approach of occasionally posting on every platform, experts say, you should pick out the one or two platforms on which you're most comfortable and build a following on those.

Looking Ahead

"Audiobooks are growing in importance and popularity, to a pretty extraordinary degree," says Clayton Smith, who has self-published several books. "The discussion used to be, 'Should an author have both e-book and paperback?' Now it's 'What's the most efficient way to get high quality e-book, paperback, and audiobook versions into the marketplace?' Ignoring audio right now is a pretty huge—and pretty common—mistake." Another aspect to self-publishing that has changed, according to Smith, is the frequency of publishing. "There are so many indie authors publishing their work now so it's more challenging than ever to stand out. One of the ways Amazon's algorithm can be used to set an author apart from others is by publishing as often as you can. Amazon is going to look at an author who publishes a book every four weeks and give him or her preference, in terms of additional promotion, over an author who publishes one book a year. The more often you publish, the more the algorithm will notice you, and the more it notices you, the more comfortable it feels promoting you," he says. Smith took sections of his 150,000-word novel *IF* and published a new one every two weeks. After releasing two parts, he saw an influx of new readers to the series, without doing any additional paid promotion.

"Five to eight years ago e-book publishing seemed to threaten print books. But now print is selling well again. The good news is that there are new ways to deliver content. The primary thing is that people love reading and learning in different forms," says Martha Bullen.

Hybrid Publishers

Another option for independent authors looking into self-publishing are hybrid publishers. Similar to traditional publishers, hybrid publishers provide retail distribution and generally produce high-quality books. One key difference: Hybrids usually publish a book within six to nine months of receiving a completed manuscript, which is quicker than traditional publishers. Under this model, a writer makes a contractual commitment either to purchase a certain number of books or to utilize the company's marketing or publicity services. Writers who already have a following—either from speaking engagements, social media, or newsletters, or who need to have their books available soon—have found hybrid publishing to be effective, particularly if they're not interested in managing the many details of self-publishing.

Not all hybrids are reputable, unfortunately, so authors need to do their due diligence. Look at sample books published by the hybrid; talk to authors published by the company. Ask where and how your books will be distributed. Avoid making an up-front payment covering all services including printing. Reputable hybrid companies include She Writes Press and Greenleaf Book Group. She Writes Press only publishes manuscripts that are deemed to be of high quality and publish-ready. The hybrid publisher's primary publishing package costs $7,500, which includes interior design for up to 100,000 words, cover design, e-book file conversion, traditional distribution through Ingram Publisher Services, proofreading, copyright filing, and warehousing and fulfillment of short-run printed books. Copyediting and developmental editing are not included. Authors must invest in their project up-front, but retain sixty percent of the net profits of print books and seventy percent of the net profit of e-books (minus a distribution fee).

Parting Thoughts

As we've seen, there are plenty of options for independent authors with some money to spend. It all comes down to establishing expectations, determining a budget, researching your options, and making decisions that will put you in the best position to meet your goals. Self-publishing can be a viable option for those who want complete control over their book, including financial and editorial decisions as well as design, promotion, and sales. To do this successfully, however, you need to keep a lot of plates spinning at once.

As with any part of the business of writing that requires spending money, it is imperative that you approach your options with a critical eye. If you do your research as you should, you will likely encounter scams and companies that engage in unethical business practices. These companies know that for the most part you are on your own and may try to take advantage of your lack of legal and literary representation. If you're going to go down this path, tread carefully.

While we believe that self-publishing is a viable alternative to traditional publishing—as long as your expectations match the likely outcome—traditional publishers do offer three major benefits that bear repeating: money, promotion, and distribution. A publisher can essentially act like a bank, able to deliver the financial backing that your project deserves, and it will bear the financial risk of publishing your book well if it believes in the value of your work. It can also offer you access to a publicity machine that has the ability to connect your book with the mainstream media—a sector that, for better or worse, continues to see publication by a traditional publisher as a seal of approval that can open doors that are, for all intents and purposes, closed to self-published authors. Until Oprah picks a high-quality self-published book to champion or the National Book Foundation bestows one of its awards on a self-published title, this will remain the case. And a traditional publisher can offer a level of distribution both in the United States and around the world that far exceeds the abilities of the typical self-published author.

There truly are publishing options for everyone. It's up to you to decide which are the best ones for you and your work.

JANE HIRSHFIELD ON THE POEM
AS A FIELD OF POSSIBILITY

During his years as a political prisoner, Nâzim Hikmet (1902–1963) wrote the following lines from his poem "Some Advice to Those Who Will Serve Time in Prison," translated from Turkish by Randy Blasing and Mutlu Konuk:

> Part of you may live alone inside,
>   like a stone at the bottom of a well.
> But the other part
>   must be so caught up
>   in the flurry of the world
>   that you shiver there, inside,
> when outside, at forty days' distance, a leaf moves.

Hikmet's lines describe actual imprisonment. They describe the human condition as well. They do the work of increase that all good poems do, in the life of a person, in the life of a culture. They begin as private sounding and create public hearing. They record and witness both our elemental human solitude and our foundational connection. They prove that an agile, committed attention can unmute and transform the spirit's deepest abyss. They demonstrate that language can turn flat, ink-marked paper into a three-dimensional world of wellbore and tree; can bring to a moment's perception almost inexhaustible furtherance—in time, emotion, knowledge, nuance, mystery. They bring to our words the expansions of singing and they bring to our singing the hived, precise experience that all words portage within them. They recalibrate the compass's east-west of beauty and justice away from the simple and toward the multiple, nuanced, complex. They show that within whatever circumstances a person might find themselves, a changed world can be brought into being.

Good poems increase the field of the possible in our lives. A person writing is not passive or choiceless before their fate; they are maker, agent. Hikmet's prison was real, his advice to others hard-won, and still, any life will know its imprisonment, will feel the severities of unchosen walls. Each person will see in their own and others' bodies and stories the inexorability of time, of losses that fall beyond cliff edge. Each person will see as well, in their own and others' stories and bodies, moments that—while we live— carry gifts of existence beyond counting or limit.

The work of poetry, in a life, in a culture, may seem at first quiet, peripheral as a person jailed. The work of amplitude is inner, not a matter of literal amplification. Literal volume can distort, can deafen; the world's myths, in every tradition, warn against simplistic greed for more. Yet creative amplitude, both in the trust of it and in its making, is always available, omnipresent, changing everything. It is the ants and bushes and birds that come to help Psyche in the dark hours of her impossible labor— already there, only needing enlistment.

How, then, is Hikmet's leaf seen?

Mostly, a person must draw on a lifetime's accumulated reservoir of choices, choices that build—or fail to build—a spirit strong enough to bear the fractures of being and continue. Some large part of that resilience is made by becoming a person present, awake, permeable, willing to look and willing to enter the condition of shivering.

Poets follow the first rule of improvisational theater: They say yes to the given, agree to what is, without any assumption of stasis. The improvisational *yes* speaks into both present and future. Consider Richard Hugo's *31 Letters and 13 Dreams*, its chiasmic, balancing count. Letters— their day-to-day life and thoughts—and dreams: A good poem, however subtly, is faithful to both. It will take in, speak to, speak of, the actual granite and griefs of a life, and it will claim the kite lift of dream mind as an inalienable part of that life.

Good poems take the real as window, not limitation. Like a painter holding a palette of separate colors, good poems mix, intensify, exceed, in the service of enlarging what can be seen. Reading Hikmet's "outside, at forty days' distance," you are already a person who has stepped beyond ordinary vision. The sleight of hand mixing of time and space is so quick, you almost don't notice the trick. But the spirit expands within even that single, small reminder of slipped-between bars.

The instruction of good poems is infinite; it cannot be held in a single statement, idea, or description. But for a while, it is good to rest in Hikmet's offered instruction and solace: that anywhere a poet writes is a place of freedom.

JANE HIRSHFIELD *is the author of nine books of poetry, including* Ledger, The Beauty, Come, Thief, *and* Given Sugar, Given Salt. *She is also the author of two collections of essays,* Nine Gates: Entering the Mind of Poetry *and* Ten Windows: How Great Poems Transform the World, *and has edited and co-translated four books presenting the work of world poets from the past. Her books have received the Poetry Center Book Award, the California Book Award, and the Hall-Kenyon Prize in American Poetry, have been finalists for the National Book Critics Circle Award and England's T. S. Eliot Prize, and long-listed for the National Book Award.*

SIXTEEN

Literary Agents

A curious thing happens when you finish a book. For years, you've been working as an artist crafting a work of art, worrying only about nailing down your characters' motivations and excising lazy verbs and flaccid metaphors from your prose. Then one day you hit Save on your final edits and find yourself faced with navigating a strange new world peopled by agents and editors talking breezily of elevator pitches and comp titles, platforms and blurb hunts. For many first-time authors this can be an intimidating—even disorienting—experience.

In this chapter, and in the next one about book deals, we will do our best to demystify the process of publishing a book, from your decision to find an agent or seek a publisher on your own, to the tools and tactics involved in finding a home for your work, and finally to the nitty-gritty details of the book contract itself. When we're done, we hope to leave you with the knowledge, and the confidence, to take your work from a file on your hard drive to a published book.

The first thing to understand about the world of publishing is how very small it is. Nearly all large American publishing houses are headquartered in New York City, and after decades of corporate mergers, commercial publishing has consolidated into five primary conglomerates—Hachette, Harper-Collins, Macmillan, Penguin Random House, and Simon & Schuster—each of which publishes thousands of books a year via a stable of smaller imprints.

Add to this the fact that New York–based editors and agents often jump between firms, and you have a clubby little world in which just about everyone goes to the same parties, follows the same industry publications and social media feeds, and has often worked with one another at some point.

Midsize independents like W. W. Norton and Grove Atlantic in New York—and even the larger but still independent Boston-based Houghton Mifflin Harcourt—make up a second tier of publishers, while smaller presses, many of which are located outside New York and often have far tighter budgets, make up a separate, though still deeply interconnected, club. Broadly speaking, these presses fall into two categories. In one are more established presses like Graywolf Press, Milkweed Editions, Coffee House Press, Tin House Books, and Algonquin Books, which are much smaller than the so-called Big Five houses in New York, and are known for taking on riskier, more literary authors, but mostly work with agented writers. A second group are academic and even smaller indie presses, many of which have tiny staffs and smaller print runs, but which accept unsolicited manuscripts, sometimes through open submissions and more often through contests or paid submissions portals. Poetry presses likewise mostly stand outside the commercial publishing industry and tend to find authors via contests or open submissions. There are exceptions, of course. "More literary agents are coming into the field and more literary agents are accepting poets," says Carey Salerno, the executive editor of Alice James Books, an independent press in Farmington, Maine, that publishes around eight poetry titles per year. "Some of the agents who are new and trying to forge their own businesses are starting to see poetry as a place where they can grow their business, they can grow their opportunities, and they can grow the voices of poets as well."

Whether it's a Big Five house or a tiny indie press, publishing remains a club, and your job as a new writer is to find a way into that club. That's the bad news. The good news is that this isn't high school. What matters most to editors and agents is the quality of your work. Publishers are always searching for new talent, and they compete fiercely for the rights to publish the next big book. Connections matter, hugely, but you make connections by writing well, being an active member of the community in person or online—showing up at other writers' readings, supporting your peers, attending book festivals and writers conferences—and building an audience for your work among other writers and readers. Ibrahim Ahmad, the editorial director of Akashic Books, an independent press in Brooklyn, New York, cautions against the impersonal approach to querying or submitting your work to an agent or editor. "There's this kind of cold and clinical approach to querying where you are kind of in a vacuum, sending out your thoughts into the void and hoping for a positive outcome," he says. "There's something about it that feels both passive but also one step removed from being an active member of the literary community." Instead, Ahmad advises, writers should put the time and effort into "being an engaged participant in your local literary culture or subculture. . . . Take an honest and fully engaged step into that world. If your goal is to be a writer and live the life of the writer, you have to participate in this community. It's all well and good to be querying people from your laptop in your living room or whatever, but it's another thing entirely to be out there going to readings, talking to people, going to workshops, talking to agents, talking to editors. We don't just exist as monolithic entities on the other side of the digital barrier. There are ways to gracefully ingratiate yourself into the publishing world."

Going It Alone: Contests and Small Presses

For all intents and purposes, the Big Five and the larger independents are out of reach for writers without agents. This was not always the case. Before World War II, according to book-industry historian Eric de Bellaigue, just one in ten published authors had an agent. As the industry grew, that number climbed to roughly fifty percent by the 1960s and then to ninety percent by the late 1990s. By 2008, close to 99.5 percent of all authors with books at major houses had worked with an agent.

So, if you're seeking a wide audience and think your book has commercial potential, you're better off looking for an agent. But if your interactions with agents have convinced you there's little commercial interest in your book, or if you think your book is simply better suited to a small press, you can always go it alone. It's not easy, and you aren't likely to find a big audience for your work, but in some cases it's the wiser option.

If you're trying to publish a debut poetry collection, you will almost certainly be going it alone, either by submitting directly to publishers or by entering contests. Increasingly, the same is true for debut story collections unless you have a novel in the works. The reasons are simple. In our hyperfast world of social media feeds and streaming services, the market for novels and book-length nonfiction is extremely tight, but at least there's still a viable market. More and more today, books of poetry and short story collections require subsidy—from donors or contest fees, or both—to survive.

With some digging, you can still find a publisher for a book of poems without paying a fee. The venerable Four Way Books in New York City holds a monthlong open reading period in June, while lesser-known publishers like Plan B Press, based in Alexandria, Virginia, publish chapbooks by emerging writers. It's slightly easier to find small presses accepting submissions for novels and story collections without a fee. Coffee House Press in Minneapolis, Minnesota, holds occasional open reading periods, each capped at three hundred submissions, while smaller presses like Two Dollar Radio in Columbus, Ohio, and Unsolicited Press in Portland, Oregon, take unagented fiction with a $3 submission fee.

ACTION ITEM 37

Scout small presses at pw.org/small_presses as well as other online sites like New Pages (newpages.com/books/publishers) and Bookfox (thejohnfox.com).

But for the most part, submitting a debut poetry or story collection requires a reading fee or contest fee ranging from $5 to $30 or more per submission. This irritates some writers, who feel they shouldn't have to pay a publisher to read their work, but contests and fee-based submissions can be a good way for a new writer to break in, says poet Victoria Chang, whose debut collection, *Circle*, won the Crab Orchard Series in Poetry Open Competition Award in 2004. Like many prizewinning poets, before she published *Circle*, Chang had been publishing her poems for years, working her way up from obscure journals to better-known magazines, building a network of editors who admired her work. "I'd sent a bunch of poems to the *Crab Orchard Review* because they were publishing writers of color," Chang recalls. "I didn't realize it at the time, but they have a publication arm, and the editors are the same people. They're reading the slush, not always, but usually, and they're going to push your work through the slush pile [for the book contest]."

Chang's journal publications paid off again four years later with her second book, *Salvinia Molesta*, when Ted Genoways, then the editor of the *Virginia Quarterly Review*, e-mailed her asking if she would like to submit to a new poetry imprint he planned to launch at the University of Georgia Press. "With the editors at these literary journals, you never know what other projects they have up their sleeves," she says. "You never know how they're associated with book presses that are related to the literary journals."

This strategy of building a reputation among editors of literary magazines before branching out first into book contests and then small presses has worked for Chang, whose two most recent collections were published by Copper Canyon, one of the country's more prestigious poetry presses. Novelist Shane Jones followed a similar path to publishing his first novel, *Light Boxes*, with indie house Publishing Genius in 2009. Like Chang, Jones had been steadily publishing poems in small magazines before he began sending *Light Boxes* to small presses. Even so, he says, more than thirty presses passed on the book before Atlanta-based Publishing Genius took it on.

At that point, Jones's nascent career took a storybook turn. Publishing Genius had printed fewer than six hundred copies of *Light Boxes*, but one found its way into the hands of filmmaker Spike Jonze, director of *Being John Malkovich* and *Adaptation*, who optioned it for film—meaning he paid Jones a fee to secure the exclusive yet temporary right to purchase the film rights to the book. In the end, no film was ever made—which is not uncommon; it's called a film "option" for a reason—but Jonze's interest drew the attention of literary agents. "I was in a unique situation where agents were coming to me and then I was able to talk to them and see what my options were," Jones says.

With the help of literary agent Bill Clegg, whose clients include Emma Cline, Lauren Groff, and Ottessa Moshfegh, Jones resold *Light Boxes* to Penguin Books, which also bought his next novel, *Daniel Fights a Hurricane*. But Jones and his work weren't a perfect fit for Penguin, and before long he returned to the small-press world, selling his next two books to indie presses—*Crystal Eaters*, published by Two Dollar Radio in 2014, and *Vincent and Alice and Alice*, published by Tyrant Books in 2019.

The lesson is clear. Whether you're submitting a poetry collection to contests or sending a novel or story collection out to indie presses, the path to publication is the same: First and foremost, you have to write a good book, but it also helps to build a reputation among editors of journals and small presses, and to be prepared to send out large numbers of submissions, knowing you'll get many more rejections than acceptances.

"I think it's just being relentless and having a thick skin and sending it to as many places as possible," says Jones. "You have to take a lot of shots and get a lot of rejection and be okay with it."

Finding an Agent: Preparing the Ground

For most writers, the path to mainstream press publication begins with finding an agent, which in turn begins with drafting a query letter, the short, professional letter that introduces a writer's work to an agent. So much of the discussion about approaching agents focuses on queries, how to structure them, what tone to adopt, how to write a compelling pitch, and so on. These are important questions, and they will all be covered in this chapter, but writers' obsessive focus on the minutiae of writing query letters obscures what a long shot a cold query really is.

Matt McGowan of the Frances Goldin Literary Agency, whose clients include essayists Eula Biss and John D'Agata, says he receives about five thousand queries a year. Miriam Altshuler, an agent with DeFiore & Company, whose clients include novelist Maya Lang and children's book author Walter Dean Myers, estimates she gets between five thousand and ten thousand a year. Back in 2012, Scott Hoffman, cofounder of Folio Literary

Management, said the nine agents at his firm reading unsolicited submissions received roughly one hundred thousand queries that year. Hoffman said he'd taken on four new writers the previous year, just one of whom he'd found through the slush pile, putting the odds of an author without connections getting Hoffman to take on their book at roughly 1 in 11,111.

Agents aren't rejecting all those queries simply because they're written badly. Often, the real problem is that writers haven't properly researched the agents they're contacting. Most agents specialize in a select number of genres—literary fiction, say, or narrative nonfiction—and use their websites to list authors they've worked with and genres they do and do not represent. Ignoring this information wastes the agent's time and yours. The old adage "time is money" is especially true for an agent. After all, an agent isn't paid unless a book is sold to a publisher, so all the work of finding a new client, including reading through all those queries—not to mention working with an author to develop a proposal, preparing the work for submission, and finding an editor who is the right fit—is unpaid labor. It's no surprise, then, that agents tend to develop a rather cutthroat approach to the queries they receive.

"A lot of queries get filtered out pretty quickly," says McGowan. "I'd say that's about sixty percent of them. I've gotten pretty ruthless about not responding. The ones that catch my eye are the ones where they've taken some effort to explain why I'm possibly the right agent for them. If there's any sense that they haven't done their homework, I just don't feel like I have to respond."

So, before you approach an agent, do your homework. Start with your own bookshelves. Find the contemporary books you love most, or that most closely match the book you've written in style or subject matter, and check the acknowledgments to see if the author has thanked their agent. Then start googling, checking the agent's website to see who else they've worked with and reading any interviews or Q&As the agent has done. You're looking for points of contact between your work and the agent's literary sensibility, which you can then put in the opening lines of your query letter.

Once you exhaust your bookshelves, try the Literary Agents Database on the Poets & Writers website (pw.org). Using the site's search tools, you can find agents who represent books in your genre and then click through to agents' websites to read more about authors they've worked with. Generally speaking, great authors are represented by great agents, and you can tell a lot about the quality of an agent by the names on that agent's client list. Other listing sites include Agent Query (agentquery.com), the Association of Authors' Representatives (aaronline .org), and MS WishList (mswishlist.com), where agents post calls for types of manuscripts they'd like to see. For a more in-depth understanding of the publishing industry, you can subscribe to Publishers Marketplace (publish ersmarketplace.com), which offers, among other things, agent bios and listings of their recent sales.

ACTION ITEM 38

Go to your bookshelves and take down five books that have been published in the last few years, find the acknowledgments section of each, and locate the name of the agents. Write them down in your notebook or journal and find out more about what genres they're interested in and whom they represent.

But web sleuthing will only get you so far. This is a club, remember, and a good query letter demonstrates that you are already partway in it. The most important element in this, of course, is the work itself. Most agents now ask writers to paste a few pages from their manuscript at the bottom of an e-mailed query, and if those pages don't make an agent want to read more, nothing else really matters. If your book only starts to get interesting in chapter two, you need to find a way to get there quicker. Agents are first and foremost readers, and just as you wouldn't keep reading a book that bored you in the first chapter, neither will they.

So, getting your work, not just the opening pages, but the whole book, into the best possible shape *before* you submit is priority number one. Most agents will work with writers to polish their books, but like everyone else in publishing, they're strapped for time—and, as we mentioned earlier, they are essentially working for free at this stage. "If I get a manuscript that needs a tremendous amount of work, even though I see the beautiful writing, even though I see the value of it, I will do that work if I feel I can, but if I'm in a particularly busy time, it may be overwhelming for me and I will have to think, 'Do I have the time to put in the editing it needs?'" says Altshuler. "But if something further along in that process, because that person has been able to share their work with other writers and get valuable feedback that has allowed them to move the book further along, helps them, it helps me, it helps the entire process."

Be ruthless with yourself. Ask five readers you trust to read the book and let their feedback guide your revisions. Sign up for creative writing classes. Attend writing conferences. Hire a freelance editor. If the book has sections that can stand alone as essays or stories, consider submitting them to magazines.

Done right, these steps will not only improve your book, but also give you contacts and exposure that will help you attract an agent. Agents, especially newer ones, read literary journals searching for unsigned talent—this is how Julia Kardon of the Hannigan Salky Getzler Agency found Brit Bennett, who went on to publish the acclaimed novel *Mothers*, for instance—and all agents look for a track record of publication when they're considering taking on a new client. In writing classes, you will meet other writers who may one day be able to refer you to their own agents, and at conferences, you can meet with agents to pitch your book in person.

This is key. As they sift through those thousands of queries, agents—or more accurately, the assistants and interns assigned to read their queries—are looking for any reason to reject a query and move on. A referral from an existing client or a reference to a conversation you had with an agent at a writers conference or pitch event makes that much harder.

If you don't have the time or money to attend conferences or writing classes, you can leverage the power of social media and the open web to get on an agent's radar. A personal website with links to your published work is hardly required but it can be an easy reference for an agent reading your letter. (Simple websites are inexpensive and easy to create on platforms like WordPress and Squarespace.) But if you're publishing your work, even on small, lightly trafficked websites, posting links on social media can get an agent's attention.

"I follow a ton of writers on Twitter, and occasionally I'll see a comment someone made that sounds smart or interesting," says McGowan. "I'll click on their bio and if they say they're an MFA student or 'I'm working on my first book,' I'll follow them and hope that they'll notice that I'm following them so that when they're done they'll send it to me, or maybe they'll publish a piece of it and I'll track that down."

You can also use the internet to create a platform for yourself that can attract agents and make it easier for your publisher to find readers for your books. Celebrity is a platform, which is why you see so many celebrity memoirs. But a large Twitter following can also be a platform, as can a popular podcast or blog. In fact, some agents regularly comb the internet looking for interesting blogs or podcasts that might, with some work, make a publishable book. A platform is more crucial for nonfiction than for fiction, but anything that helps your work cut through the digital noise and builds a bridge between yourself and potential readers will make your agent search that much easier.

EIGHTY-FOUR AGENTS ACTIVE ON TWITTER

Laurie Abkemeier @LaurieAbkemeier

Miriam Altshuler @MiriamAltshuler

Amelia Atlas @ameliaatlas

Noah Ballard @NoahBallard

Julie Barer @juliebarer

Vicky Bijur @VBLA

Iris Blasi @IrisBlasi

Brettne Bloom @Brettne

Sarah Bowlin @svbowlin

Sarah Burnes @sarahburnes

Lucy Carson @LucyACarson

Farley Chase @farleychase

Elyse Cheney @ElyseCheney

Ginger Clark @Ginger_Clark

William Clark @william_m_clark

Bill Clegg @TheCleggAgency

Laura Dail @LCDail

Liza Dawson @LizaDawsonAssoc

Brian DeFiore @DeFiore

Adam Eaglin @aeaglin

Melissa Edwards @MelissaLaurenE

Caroline Eisenmann @CarolineMEisen

Mary Evans @MaryEvansInc

Katherine Fausset @Kfauss

Jenni Ferrari-Adler @JenFerrariAdler

Ryan Fischer-Harbage
  @fischerharbage

Seth Fishman @sethasfishman

Melissa Flashman @melflashman

Christy Fletcher @FletcherChristy

Emily Forland @EmilyForland

Kate Garrick @kategarrick

Katie Grimm @grimmlit

Alia Hanna Habib @AliaHanna

Jordan Hamessley @thejordache

Joy Harris @JoyHarrisAgency

Ross Harris @rossharris1

David Haviland @davidhaviland

Carrie Howland @ECarrieHowland

Allison Hunter @AllisonSHunter

Dorian Karchmar @DorianKarchmar

Julia Kardon @jlkardon

Kirby Kim @PantherFirst

Kim-Mei Kirtland @kmkirtland

Jeff Kleinman @FolioLiterary

Stuart Krichevsky @skagency

Natalie M. Lakosil @Natalie_Lakosil

Daniel Lazar @DanLazarAgent

Thao Le @ThaoLe8

Betsy Lerner @BetsyLerner

Sarah Levitt @slevittslevitt

Andrew Lownie @andrewlownie

Carol Mann @carolmannagency

Gary Morris @garymmorris

Kiki Nguyen @kianangu

Duvall Osteen @AragiAuthors

Zoë Pagnamenta @zoepagnamenta

Ayesha Pande @agent_ayesha

Jessica Papin @jkpapin

Emma Patterson @EmPat222

Beth Phelan @beth_phelan

Soumeya B. Roberts @soumeya_b

Rena Rossner @renarossner

Curtis Russell @CurtisPSLA

Rayhané Sanders
  @rayhanesanders

Deborah Schneider
  @deborschneider

Meredith Kaffel Simonoff
  @mere215

Dongwon Son @dongwon

Peter Steinberg @PeterSteinberg1

Uwe Stender @UweStenderPhD

Rachel Sussman @SussmanRachel

Danielle Svetcov @dsvetcov

Emma Sweeney
  @EmmaSweeneyESA

Alice Tasman @AliceTasman

Michelle Tessler @tessleragency

Joe Veltre @veltre

Rachel Vogel @Vogelrachelm

Carly Watters @carlywatters

Elisabeth Weed @elisabethweed

Kimberly Witherspoon @kwspoon

Kent D. Wolf @kentdwolf

Monika Woods @booksijustread

Joanne Wyckoff @JoanneWyckoff

Sarah Yake @slyyake

Renée Zuckerbrot @RZAgent

Approaching an Agent: The Query Letter

Once you've refined your manuscript to a high polish, tapped all your connections in the book world, and researched the agents most likely to represent the book you've written, you're ready to write a query letter. Queries are now almost exclusively sent digitally, mostly by e-mail, though some agencies are starting to use submission portals. You should write a single template query, which you can then tailor to fit each agent. Feel free to query multiple agents, but keep the numbers to a manageable level (no more than, say, five to ten active queries at one time) and focus on quality rather than quantity.

For each agent, read the directions posted online and follow them to the letter. If an agent asks you to paste the first three pages of your book below your letter, paste exactly three pages from the first chapter, not from later in the book, and don't use an attachment unless the agent explicitly requests it. Any deviation from these directions is an invitation to instant deletion.

A good query letter should cover no more than one single-spaced page (about three hundred to four hundred words) and include these elements in roughly the following order. (Note: Agency submission portals, which are becoming more common, typically contain all these elements and you can cut and paste from your template letter to fill the boxes on the online form.)

Opening: This is where you establish your connection to the agent and make clear why you're querying them and not another agent. If someone has referred you or if you've interacted with the agent in person or online, lead with this. (Also mention this in the subject line of your e-mail.) If you don't have a personal connection to the agent, you can mention one or more of their authors and draw a connection between their work and yours. "One of the very important things in a query is to say, 'I am writing you because of your list,'" says Sarah Burnes, an agent with The Gernert Company. "In my case, a writer could say they're writing me because I represent Alice McDermott or Heather Havrilesky or whoever it is, and I know there's a reason they're writing me, as opposed to just blanketing the agenting community."

If you have no connection to the agent or the authors they represent, you can skip the opening and go right to the pitch, but this sends a clear message that you couldn't find a meaningful connection to the agent or their authors—not a great way to kick off a potential working relationship.

Project description: This should be less about plot summary and more about giving the agent a reason to read the book. In publishing, this is called the *elevator pitch*, the fifty to one hundred words you would use to recommend a book to someone between stops on an elevator. "It's not just the synopsis, like saying 'This book is about a girl who . . .' It's what I call the heart of the book. 'This book focuses on . . .' or 'It explores the . . .' I want to know what you're trying to say in this book," says Altshuler. "That will help me understand both if it's right for me and how to read the book, too."

You do need to give the who, what, when, where of the book, but rather than summarizing the entire plot, try to answer the question *Why would a reader pick up this book?* If it has a catchy premise or hook, focus on that. If the book's central characters or relationship are tantalizing, make the reader feel how that might be so. If voice is going to drive the narrative, give the reader a taste of that. Keep it to one paragraph. Altshuler suggests reading the marketing copy on the inside flap of your favorite novels for tips on how it should sound. The copy on the back cover of the paperback edition can be even more useful, because in many cases it is a refined version of the original text.

Context: In publishing circles, books are often sold based on how they relate to other books. An agent might tell an editor, "This book is *Little Fires Everywhere* meets *The Nest*." Or: "This book is *Bad Blood*, but about cancer drugs." These are called *comps*, or comparables, and they help publishing professionals orient an unknown book among books that people do know. If you can make a case that your work mirrors that of a successful author or title, either thematically or stylistically, it helps an agent understand what you're trying to do and how to sell your book.

Writers put off by this marketing-driven approach can instead try to clarify who they are as writers and where they see themselves in the contemporary literary scene, says Burnes. "I think a more interesting way for a writer to think about this is inspiration," she says. "I'm much more interested in a book when a writer says, 'I love Meg Wolitzer. She's an inspiration. My book is very different from hers but . . . ,' and then I understand that they think about literature in a complex way."

Author bio: Keep it brief and professional. If you've published in journals or newspapers, say where. Ditto for awards and contest prizes. Many fiction writers have MFAs these days, but it's still a good idea to mention it, especially if you attended a prestigious program or if you think your professors might blurb your book (e.g., "I studied under George Saunders and Dana Spiotta in the MFA program at Syracuse University"). If your life outside of writing lends credibility to your book, mention it. If you are, say, a teacher at a school that serves at-risk kids, that's relevant if your book touches on issues facing those kids or those schools. Otherwise, simply say you're a teacher, or leave it out entirely.

Coda: This is a final sentence or two that says how long the book is, whether it's complete, and invites the agent to read more. For length, always use word count rather than page count. And, it should go without saying, sincerely thank the agent for their time and attention. You don't have to get saccharine about it but acknowledging that you appreciate their consideration is not only polite but can also make a difference to an agent (or assistant) on a long, difficult workday afternoon.

ACTION ITEM 39

Even if you aren't quite ready to query an agent, try writing a query letter now. It's good practice to write about your project with the market in mind and to think about where your book would fit on a shelf with other similar books. And it's always good to hone your author bio—you never know when you're going to need it.

CASE STUDY: NANA KWAME ADJEI-BRENYAH'S *FRIDAY BLACK*

In January 2017, Nana Kwame Adjei-Brenyah, a recent MFA grad with solid publication credits in an eclectic mix of literary magazines, sent the following query letter to Meredith Kaffel Simonoff, an agent at DeFiore & Company who seeks "arresting voices across a spectrum of genres" and "writing steeped in ferocity of language, purpose, intellect, and heart." Of particular note is the straightforward manner in which Adjei-Brenyah conveys his accomplishments (his MFA, awards, and publication credits), his experience working with a well-known author (George Saunders), the themes explored in his work, and his gratitude for the agent's time.

January 8, 2017

Dear Meredith Simonoff,

My name is Nana Kwame Adjei-Brenyah and I recently received an MFA from Syracuse University. There I worked closely with George Saunders in completing my debut collection of short fiction. I felt I might query you specifically because I think my work might be bold in a way that it seems you look for.

I hope you will consider representing my manuscript, titled *How to Sell a Jacket*. In one story, a school shooter and his victim are paired together in the afterlife—hopefully to a transcendent result. In another, a protagonist is forced to consider who he is in a world where five young black children can be murdered via chainsaw while their murderer goes free.

The first story in the collection, "The Finkelstein 5," was chosen as a finalist out of 4,200 applicants for the Nelsen Algren Literary Award hosted by the *Chicago Tribune*. I was also chosen as the 2016 O'Connor Fellow in Fiction at Colgate University, where I am currently about to begin the semester as writer-in-residence. Besides this complete manuscript I am also in the very early stages of a new novel.

My publication history is as follows:

"Cardigan Blues," *Broken Pencil Magazine*, Issue #59, Summer 2013

"Coughs," *Gravel Online Journal*, January 2014

"Things my Mother Said," *Foliate Oak Literary Magazine*, September 2014

"In Retail," *Compose: A Journal of Simply Good Writing*, Fall 2014

"Winter Break," *Every Writer*, June 2015

"Thunder With Him," *Pembroke*, Spring 2016

"The Finkelstein 5," *Printer's Row*, Summer 2016

Thank you for your time and kind consideration. Please find the first five pages of the first story of the collection below.

Best,

Nana Kwame Adjei-Brenyah

———————————————

On the strength and intrigue of that query letter, Meredith Kaffel Simonoff requested Nana Kwame Adjei-Brenyah's manuscript and eventually agreed to represent him. About six weeks later she sent the following pitch letter to Naomi Gibbs at Houghton Mifflin Harcourt. Note how the agent pulls details straight from the author's query letter for use in her pitch letter and adds vivid description and valuable context to sell the author's project.

February 21, 2017

As promised—I am thrilled to share with you 25-year-old Syracuse MFA graduate and Colgate Creative Writing Fellow Nana Kwame Adjei-Brenyah's debut story collection. *How to Sell a Jacket* is a treacherously surreal and, at times, heartbreakingly satirical look at what it's like to be young and black in America. It is also an excoriation of consumerism, and the ways in which it can distract us from those who mean the most. It is a book steeped in fearless storytelling and ferocious imagination.

How to Sell a Jacket's stories hold the reader accountable for the fact that our country has long been nothing short of a tragic caricature of itself. By dropping ordinary, relatable characters into increasingly extraordinary situations and worlds, Adjei-Brenyah, over the course of these stories, reveals the extraordinary strength and vision so often required of his characters if they hope to survive at all. This book fills me with a keenly alert sense of pain, anger, and wonder, and the vibrating desire to press Adjei-Brenyah's work into as many readers' hands as possible.

So many moments throughout these stories will stay with me. Sometimes, they're memorable because of the way their line by line beauty dissonantly highlights injustice ("Under the unspectacular sky Emmanuel felt the story of the Finkelstein Five on his fingers and in his chest and in each of his breaths."). Sometimes, it's the way they eerily skewer and hold up to the light existing cultural realities simply by ever so slightly tilting fact ("Friday Black," "The Era," "The Justice Park," "The Finkelstein 5"). Sometimes, it's their naked, earnest searching for connection and exploration of the lengths we go for the family we love: "Things My Mother Said," "In Retail." And sometimes, it's the manner in which they artfully and discomfitingly literalize emotional pain that devastates the reader ("Lark Street," "Through the Flash"). In all cases, each story is, as must be the case in any excellent collection, in its own way unforgettable. By the book's end, we are confronted with a complicated, furious, insistent, and wrenching chorus of emotions, the final note of which, remarkably, is hope.

These stories embody everything I look for in a debut writer. Together, the pieces comprise a book of profound heart that demands ongoing conversation. The first story in the collection, "The Finkelstein 5," was chosen as a finalist out of 4,200 applicants for the Nelsen Algren Literary Award hosted by the *Chicago Tribune*, and published in *Printer's Row*. Other stories have appeared to date in *Broken Pencil*, *Gravel*, and *Foliate Oak*. Adjei-Brenyah was also chosen as the 2016 O'Connor Fellow in Fiction at Colgate University, where he has just begun the semester as writer-in-residence after graduating from Syracuse (where he worked closely with George Saunders). Adjei-Brenyah was born in 1991 and is from Spring Valley, New York.

I will eagerly await your thoughts on *How to Sell a Jacket*. With thanks, as ever, for your consideration.

Yours,

Meredith

In response to Meredith's pitch letter, Gibbs bought the book in a two-book deal, and Mariner Books, an imprint of Houghton Mifflin Harcourt, published Adjei-Brenyah's debut story collection under the title Friday Black *in October 2018. It was a* New York Times *bestseller, won the PEN/Jean Stein Book Award, and was named a best book by the* New York Times, TIME, Elle, Entertainment Weekly, *the* Huffington Post, *the* Guardian, Newsweek, O, the Oprah Magazine, *and a dozen other publications.*

Five Key Query Questions

Your first conversation with an agent interested in your work will probably focus on the work itself, and those discussions are by far the most important you can have with a prospective agent. You'll be working with this agent not just on this book, but potentially on every book you write, and it's essential that an agent understands what you're trying to do and can communicate that to editors.

Those conversations will likely carry on well past the first phone call, but as you get closer to signing an agency agreement, a legal document that lays out the agent's fiduciary obligation to you as well as other terms related to the scope of representation (some agents offer an agency agreement while others rely on the publishing contract's agency clause, which includes similar information), you'll want to get a better idea of how you and your agent will work together. Here are five questions you may want to raise, either on that first phone call or in later conversations.

1. **How do you communicate?** Some agents spend their days on the phone while others put more focus on reading and responding to client manuscripts. Try to get a sense of where your agent stands on this spectrum and how much time they will have for you if you hit a snag. Are they a phone person or an e-mail/text person? Do their assistants screen their calls, or do you have their direct line? How long do they typically take to respond to e-mails? You want an agent who is responsive to your questions and concerns, but you need to be respectful of their time as well. You aren't this agent's only client, and their time is money.

2. **What is your submission strategy?** This is a crucial question because it will help you understand, first, how your agent plans to position your book, and, second, whom the agent feels most comfortable pitching projects to. Does your agent have a particular editor in mind for your manuscript, and if so, why? Are they planning a broad set of submissions aimed at sparking an auction or will they target only a few editors at a time? What is their Plan B if the first round of editors pass? What about after that? How willing is the agent to sell your book to smaller indie presses where advances are smaller?

    When the agent mentions names, write them down and google them later. Most editors now have some presence online, and with a few mouse clicks, you can get a sense of the books they've edited and where they stand in the hierarchy of their publishing house. Are they senior editors with shelves full of bestsellers to their names, or are they twentysomething assistant editors still building a list? Do you like the books they've edited? An agent's submission plan will tell you more about how they think about your work than anything they say or don't say in your early conversations.

3. **How much responsibility do you give to your assistant?** A literary agency is an office like any other, and it helps to know how work flows

through that office. Is the agent primarily a figurehead who will make a few calls and drop your name at lunches with key editors, but leave the work of marking up manuscripts and haggling over contracts to assistants? Is the agent a sole proprietor with little or no staff to track submissions and oversee the details of contracts?

As with the other questions, there are no right or wrong answers. Some large agencies operate on the "rainmaker" model, in which a prominent agent draws in the big clients and handles relationships at publishing houses but leaves the details to assistants. If the rainmaker can indeed make rain, and they hire competent assistants, this can work just fine. By the same token, a highly organized solo practitioner can do all the work of a larger, full-service agency, provided their client list is small enough. But an emerging writer can get lost at a big agency and a solo practitioner can get swamped and miss important things. You need to find an agency arrangement you feel comfortable with.

4. **How does your agency handle foreign rights, film rights, and other ancillary rights?** Going in, your big questions are whether the agent understands your work and whether they can sell it to an American publishing house, but once these are answered, you'll want to know how the agent will handle foreign sales, film and television rights, and other ancillary rights. You may also want to ask who will negotiate the finer points of the contract you ultimately strike with your publisher. A large full-service agency will handle all of this in-house. Other agencies subcontract out some or all of these functions to other agencies or specialists, while some smaller agencies lack the capacity to handle these rights in a systematic way. If you think your book could sell overseas or might attract the attention of film or television producers, it would be smart to talk this through with an agent before you sign on.

5. **How involved are you going to be after the book is sold?** Ultimately, an agent gets paid to find a publisher for your work and hammer out the contract you sign with that publisher, but a good agent will keep fighting for you as your book wends its way through the publishing process, checking that everything's on schedule, making sure you

have at least some say in the cover of your book, and ensuring that the publishing house is doing everything it should be to publicize and market your book. No agent will admit they'll do nothing for you after the book contract is signed, so listen to *how* they answer your questions, keeping an ear out for signs that they enjoy the publishing process and have good contacts in the industry. Another sign is how well their clients' books are published—or not—so pay attention to recently published books by the agent's clients: Did they get media attention? Lots of reviews? Were they launched with a bang, or a murmur?

CASE STUDY: NATHAN HILL'S *THE NIX*

In late 2010 Nathan Hill, a graduate of the MFA program at the University of Massachusetts in Amherst, sent an e-mail to Emily Forland, who at the time was an agent at the Wendy Weil Agency. He reached out because he had read Susanna Daniel's novel Stiltsville, *noted that Forland was Daniel's agent, and thought she would like his collection of linked stories. Notice in his e-mail how he mentions Forland's client in the first paragraph, followed by a description of his project as well as a bit about himself and his experience as a writer, editor, and teacher.*

From: Nathan Hill
Date: Sun, Dec 12, 2010 at 1:30 PM
Subject: query
To: Emily Forland

Dear Ms. Emily Forland,

I'm writing you today because I recently came across the book *Stiltsville* and really enjoyed it. I believe my own project shares much in common with Ms. Daniel's.

I'm a literary fiction writer seeking agency representation for a book called

Mistakes I've Made So Far. A collection of linked stories, the book traces the bumpy evolution of a marriage, from its intense courtship through its later growing pains, from a blown wedding proposal to the uneasy plateau reached after the birth of a child. It's a book about a couple trying to love each other the right way, and doing stupid things in the process. Each story is a chronicle of these mistakes: He tries to protect her from a stalker, but gets a little too obsessed; he takes her to Venice to make up for his secret infidelities; he struggles to remain relevant in the days after his newborn son comes home.

I'm including a story from the collection. If you'd like to read the whole book, I'd be happy to send it.

I hold a BA from the University of Iowa, an MFA from the University of Massachusetts, and I teach writing at Florida Gulf Coast University. My stories have appeared in *Fiction*, *AGNI*, *The Denver Quarterly*, *Pleiades*, *The Sycamore Review*, and several other journals. I was the winner of the Short Story Prize from *Fiction*, and I was nominated for the "Best New American Voices in Fiction" series by the University of Massachusetts.

Before joining the faculty at FGCU, I edited the website Poets.org for the Academy of American Poets. I've also worked as a reporter, writing stories for daily newspapers, magazines, and the Associated Press.

Thanks very much for your time. I look forward to hearing from you.

All best,

Nathan Hill

Fully aware that a collection of stories is a hard sell for most editors, Forland nevertheless wrote to Hill after reading the first few pages of his story, requested the full manuscript, and eventually sent it out on submission in 2011. Hill didn't get an offer for his story collection, but rather than let the rejection derail him, he told Forland about a novel he'd been working on for the past six years, and they stayed in touch for two more years while he took his time to finish it. In the meantime, Forland had moved to Brandt & Hochman Literary Agents, where she remains today, and gladly read the full manuscript—all 275,000 words of it—when he was finally ready to show it to her. After an additional six months of revising and editing between agent and author, Forland submitted the novel to twelve editors at the end of January 2015, over four years after Hill's original query. Tim O'Connell, an editor at Alfred A. Knopf, was not one of the twelve editors she had sent it to, but after he inquired about the big book she was shopping around—word spreads quickly in the world of publishing—she sent it to him along with the following e-mail.

From: Emily Forland
Sent: Wednesday, January 28, 2015 3:20 PM
To: O'Connell, Timothy
Subject: The Nix by Nathan Hill

Dear Tim:

Thanks for being in touch, and for your interest in Nathan Hill's novel. I'm delighted to send you *The Nix*, an ambitious, bittersweet, wholly inventive debut that transports the reader through one family's experience over generations and disparate geographies, and through cultural moments such as World War II Norway, the Chicago Riots of 1968, the Gulf War, Occupy Wall Street, and the virtual tundra of the Wintersaber Glaciers in the multiplayer online gaming world of "Elfquest."

Samuel Andresen-Anderson's mother left his family when he was a boy. So it is a surprise when she reenters his life some twenty years later, having made headlines for hurling stones at a conservative presidential candidate at a rally. Stalled as a writer who peaked early, he spends his days playing video games and teaching literature, poorly. Under pressure from his publisher to deliver on a ten-year-old book contract, Samuel sets out instead to write the story of his mother's life—a plan that will capitalize on her fame, and give him the satisfaction of portraying her publicly in the worst possible way. Instead, as he researches her story and excavates through family history, he finds answers that force him to reevaluate all that he thought he knew about his mother, and himself.

A moving and often funny novel of mothers and sons, of teenage love triangles, of the Midwestern suburbs, and Choose Your Own Adventure stories, *The Nix* is a book of wide narrative sweep that reaches all the way to Hammerfest, Norway, the northernmost city on the planet, where we meet the titular Nix of Norse mythology.

Nathan Hill's short stories have appeared in the *Iowa Review, Fiction, AGNI,* the *Denver Quarterly,* the *Gettysburg Review, Gulf Coast, Fugue,* and many other journals. He was the winner of *Fiction*'s annual Story Prize, the winner of a 2015 artist grant from the Minnesota State Arts Board, and a finalist for the Donald Barthelme Prize. In 2014, the *Iowa Review* nominated him for a Pushcart Prize, his second nomination. He holds an MFA from the University of Massachusetts, and is now an assistant professor of English at the University of St. Thomas in Saint Paul, Minnesota.

I hope you are as taken with this one as I am, and look forward to hearing from you.

All best,

Emily

After reading the manuscript, O'Connell made a preemptive bid, the purpose of which is to end a bidding war immediately by offering a significant advance, and Knopf published the book in August 2016. It landed on all the big year-end lists—the New York Times, Entertainment Weekly, *the* Washington Post, Slate— *and it has since been published in more than two dozen countries.*

Selling Nonfiction: Book Proposals

Few agents will consider a debut novel before it's finished, but with nonfiction, you can often sell a book with a partial manuscript and/or a book proposal. There are no hard and fast rules, but in general, the more a nonfiction book relies on the quality of its writing, as opposed to its subject matter or premise, the more likely you'll need to finish it before you can sell it. Thus, a book on links between childhood trauma and addiction that could take years to report and write could well be sold as a proposal while a memoir about overcoming addiction and a traumatic childhood will probably need to be complete before it sells.

Most book proposals contain the following elements in roughly this order:

Overview: A capsule description of your book that demonstrates that you have an original, marketable idea and gives the reader a sense of what the finished book will feel like. Like an executive summary of a technical report, it lays out everything a reader needs to know—the purpose of the book, the highlights of the story, the central issues it grapples with, the characters, the world of the book, and so on—in one to three pages, though it can often be longer depending on the project.

Detailed outline: Often this takes the form of an annotated table of contents, with each chapter described in a paragraph or two. If your book doesn't use chapters, you can substitute a detailed synopsis covering the major characters and plot elements. However you structure it, you need to show that the book is fully conceived, and that all you need is time to finish researching and writing it.

Extended author bio: This goes beyond the standard one-paragraph biography to demonstrate that you have the expertise and contacts to finish researching your material and the experience to turn it into a publishable and marketable book.

Marketing: This section combines an analysis of the book's target readership and an in-depth discussion of how you can help the publisher reach that audience, including writing articles in magazines, tapping famous authors to provide blurbs, and identifying bookstores and other locations you might visit on a book tour.

Comparable and competitive titles: Comparable titles are published books that have done well with readers you're targeting with your book, even if they're not necessarily on exactly the same subject, while competitive titles are books that will directly compete with your book for readers. With the comparable titles, you're trying to show that there is a plausible path to success for your book, and with the competitive titles, you're trying to show that the other books on a similar topic won't steal readers from yours because they're outdated or in some important way different from what you've done.

Writing sample: This varies from project to project, but typically includes one or more chapters from the book you're proposing to write.

You don't necessarily have to have all these elements written before you approach an agent. Matt McGowan says he likes to see the overview and outline, along with at least one sample chapter, with a query letter; if those elements promise a book he can sell, he can help the writer shape the more marketing-oriented sections of the proposal. But, he says, first-time writers should take their proposal as far as they possibly can before they start submitting to agents. "You can sense it if something's coming in half-baked," he says. "You want the feeling that the writer has to write this book. It's this book and no other book. They've been thinking about this for years and they've thought about everything ten times. Those are the ones that feel serious and professional."

CASE STUDY: POLLY ROSENWAIKE'S *LOOK HOW HAPPY I'M MAKING YOU*

After Polly Rosenwaike, a freelance editor and teacher living in Ann Arbor, Michigan, finished a collection of linked stories about pregnancy and new motherhood, she sent the following query letter, along with three stories, to Renée Zuckerbrot, an agent at Massie & McQuilkin Literary Agents. Note how Rosenwaike references two items that appear in Zuckerbrot's bio on the agency website, which signals to Zuckerbrot that this author has done her homework and tailored her query specifically for her. The author also conveys important information—word count, publication credits, a description of the plots and themes of her stories, comparison titles, and bio—without being overbearing or going on for too long.

January 30, 2017

Dear Renée Zuckerbrot,

I so much appreciate the enthusiasm you expressed for short stories in your interview with *Poets & Writers Magazine*, and I loved seeing your list of top-ten stories on Storyville. (It's so hard to choose, but "Sea Oak" and "Memory Wall" might be on my list too.) I hope you find my story collection to be a good fit for your interests; I'd be thrilled if you might consider me for representation.

Baby Person consists of eleven thematically linked stories (55,775 words) exploring women's experiences with pregnancy and the challenges of caring for a new baby in their lives. Eight of these stories are published or forthcoming in literary magazines, including *Glimmer Train*, *Prairie Schooner*, *Colorado Review*, *Copper Nickel*, and *Indiana Review*. "White Carnations" was also selected for the *O. Henry Prize Stories 2013*.

The collection begins with a couple struggling with infertility and ends with the parents of a ten-month-old desperate to sleep train their baby and get something of their pre-parenthood identities back. The stories in between follow a chronology of complications in women's reproductive lives: abortion, miscarriage, postpartum depression, tensions among couples trying to figure out how to adjust to their new roles as parents. As a whole, the collection offers a portrait of how new and impending motherhood, as well as cultural perceptions about motherhood, impact women's work, relationships, and sense of self.

When I was expecting, and after I had my first child, I pored over books that imparted practical information on birthing and caring for a new baby. But the reading material I craved most—and which meant the most to me—offered honest, emotionally charged reflection about the complexities of becoming a mother, such as Helen Simpson's *Getting a Life*, Rachel Cusk's *A Life's Work*, Jenny Offill's *Dept. of Speculation*, and Jennifer Senior's *All Joy and No Fun*. I hope that my book, with its particular focus on intimate stories about reproductive choices, pregnancy, and caring for an infant, might contribute to the conversation, as well as provide an enjoyable immersive experience for readers with and without children.

In addition to fiction, I've published book reviews and essays in the *New York Times Book Review*, *San Francisco Chronicle*, *The Millions*, and elsewhere. After receiving my MFA from The New School in 2009, I began teaching creative writing at Eastern Michigan University, and I also currently work as a freelance editor.

Thanks very much for your consideration. I've attached three stories from the collection.

Sincerely yours,

Polly Rosenwaike

––––––––––––––––

About ten months later, after Zuckerbrot agreed to represent Rosenwaike and worked with her on her manuscript, ultimately changing the title to Look How Happy I'm Making You, *she sent the following pitch letter to Margo Shickmanter at Doubleday. Note how certain details from the author's query letter show up in the agent's pitch letter, with additional contextual information and description written by Zuckerbrot.*

October 16, 2017

Dear Margo,

The new mothers in *Look How Happy I'm Making You* are overwhelmed by exhaustion—and completely in love. "She's a narcissistic insomniac, preventing others from sleeping if she cannot," is the way one frazzled mom describes her baby. "The most grating of alarm clocks: no radio option, no snooze button. But here are her trump cards: she smiles as if she herself had discovered joy, and she never holds a grudge."

Imagine if Jenny Offill and Lorrie Moore were to elope; their love child might resemble the poignant and voicey stories in Polly Rosenwaike's debut collection. The eleven thematically linked tales explore the minefield and the magic of pregnancy, childbirth, and motherhood, and grapple with the challenges that arise in women's reproductive lives: infertility, miscarriage, postpartum depression, and the tension of couples struggling to adjust to their roles as parents. Together, these stories offer a stunning composite portrayal—hip, funny, harrowing, passionate, and *real*—of how impending and new motherhood impact women's work, relationships, and their sense of self.

One woman, determined at thirty-five to start a family with her younger, less committed boyfriend, faces the daunting prospect of single motherhood when the relationship falters. "I thought that I could handle being a single parent, but what had I done to prepare for such a formidable status?" she asks. Another newly expectant mother finds her happiness nearly extinguished by devastating grief when her beloved aunt—a single mother, successful lawyer, and her niece's role model—is diagnosed with stage four stomach cancer that coincides with the pregnancy. In another tale, a group of childless, motherless women seek refuge on Mother's Day in a bar, where, in their pain and wry humor and mutual criticism and support, they take on the role of mothers and daughters to each other.

I'm proud to be representing Rosenwaike, an emerging writer of short fiction as sharp and smart as they come. In her own words: "When I was expecting, and after I had my first child, the reading material I craved most—and which meant the most to me—offered honest, emotionally charged reflection about the complexities of becoming a mother, such as Helen Simpson's *Getting a Life* and Rachel Cusk's *A Life's Work*. I hope that my book might contribute to the conversation." Indeed, the stories are written with wit and panache, and evoke the endeavor of bringing new life into the world in all its raw emotion, anxiety and absurdity, darkness and wonder.

Polly Rosenwaike's fiction has been published in *Glimmer Train, Prairie Schooner, New England Review, Colorado Review, Copper Nickel,* and *Indiana Review.* Her story "White Carnations" was published in the *O. Henry Prize Stories 2013,* edited by Lauren Groff, Edith Pearlman, and Jim Shepard. She teaches creative writing at Eastern Michigan University and has published book reviews and essays in the *New York Times Book Review, San Francisco Chronicle,* and *The Millions.*

Delighted to share *Look How Happy I'm Making You* with you. Please note: I am offering North American rights.

All best wishes,

Renée Zuckerbrot

Polly Rosenwaike's Look How Happy I'm Making You *was published by Doubleday in March 2019. Writing in the* Washington Post*'s* The Lily, *reviewer Cathy Alter praised the book as "required reading for all women of childbearing years."* Publishers Weekly *called the stories "endearingly honest, excruciatingly detailed, and irresistibly intimate, expertly depicting what motherhood means to millennials."*

Getting to the Submission: Working with an Agent

Once you begin talking with an agent about representation, you should let any other agents who have expressed interest know. It's up to you how to play this but be professional. As is the case with so many situations, the Golden Rule applies: Treat others as you'd like to be treated. If you think you're definitely going to work with this agent, sincerely thank the others for their interest and move on. If you're unsure where the discussions will lead and want to know what other offers you might get, you can use the interest from the first agent to spur the others to read your manuscript more quickly. Agents may not love having to compete against one another for clients, but they use similar tactics with editors every day.

Once you commit to one agent, you may be asked to sign a contract agreeing to work exclusively with that agent, though some agencies skip this step and rely on the agency clause in the standard book contract to determine how payments will be made. It's not a red flag if an agent doesn't ask you to sign an agency agreement, but it's probably wise to talk through your agreement to guard against surprises. It's also worth reading the Authors Guild's commonsense "An Author's Guide to Agency Agreements" at authorsguild.org.

Agents work exclusively on commission, typically taking fifteen percent of any domestic earnings from your books, twenty percent of any foreign earnings, and fifteen to twenty percent of earnings from film rights. They may also deduct any direct expenses for copying or transmitting manuscripts from your book earnings, though these expenses have become increasingly rare in the digital age. Under no circumstances should you ever pay an agent to read your manuscript, nor should you pay any expenses before an agent has sold your book.

Any contract you sign should leave you free to break off the relationship if things don't work out, though many agents reserve the right to collect on any money you make from a book within a few months of leaving, to protect against losing out on a sale they helped set up. Typically, if you leave an agent after selling one or more books, any future commissions from those books will stay with the agent who sold them originally.

THE AGENCY AGREEMENT

Some agents provide a written agreement that a writer is asked to sign before an agency will agree to enter into a relationship, effectively turning that writer into a client. Others rely on the agency clause that is inserted into a specific agreement with a publisher.

The agency clause will usually set forth terms stating that all sums payable to the author will be paid to the agent (who will deduct the specified percentage for their commission then send the remainder to the author) and that the agent is entitled to act on the author's behalf in all matters related to the publishing agreement.

An agency agreement is specific to the agency that has drawn up the agreement, but there are some common provisions that should be carefully considered before signing on the dotted line. These include the points from the agency clause above but may also stipulate: *Works Covered* (some agents wish to represent only a single work by a client, others wish to represent everything written by the client, and still others wish to represent a client for works created during a specific time period), *Rights Granted* (often an agent is appointed the exclusive worldwide agent who has the right to sell all rights everywhere, but sometimes an agent requests the right to appoint sub-agents who can handle rights outside their purview, such as foreign-language rights and motion picture rights), *Commission Rates* (fifteen percent of any domestic earnings, twenty percent of foreign earnings, and fifteen to twenty percent of earnings from film rights), and *Expenses* (an agent may deduct money from sums owed to the author in order to cover things such as photocopying, postage, bank charges, and so on).

As with any legally binding document, it is imperative that you take your time to read it carefully and ask questions to clear up any confusion you may have about what you're being asked to sign.

Once you sign with an agent, you will start working together to polish your book for submission. In recent years, as publishing houses have downsized, agents have taken over some of the developmental editing that editors used to do, with the understanding that publishers will pay a premium for highly polished manuscripts. For this process to work, you have to find an agent whose editorial judgment you trust, which is why your early discussions with an agent about your book are crucial.

To get the most out of revisions, Altshuler says, writers would do well to resist the urge to race against the clock to turn out new drafts. "I will read and edit a book numerous times, but the more times I read it, the harder it is to have that fresh eye, so the further you can bring a book along before I step into the process the better, and even in the process, once you've done another draft, show it to your readers before you even send another draft to me," she says.

When you and your agent have a draft ready for submission, your agent will draft a brief pitch letter, similar in form and purpose to your original query, and present it to editors, either over the phone, by e-mail, or both. Depending on their strategy, an agent may submit a manuscript widely to as many as twenty editors at once or focus on just a few editors who have done well with this kind of book in the past.

> *"The writer who's outside of the business views the business as this fortress designed to keep him or her out. And in fact, what I see is an industry in which we want nothing more than to discover an amazing new voice."*
> —ERIC SIMONOFF, LITERARY AGENT

And then you wait. Book editors generally take less time to respond to manuscripts than agents or editors at literary journals do (editors are eager to snatch up a brilliant manuscript, and especially in the world of the Big Five, competition is fierce; no one wants to miss out on the next big book) but it can still take a few weeks to hear back, especially if your book isn't at the top of the editor's to-be-read pile. But as your agent will likely tell you, approximately one million times in the days before and after your book goes out on submission, all it takes is one editor to say yes.

ANTHONY DOERR RECOMMENDS

Five Books That Might Save You When Your Writing Starts to Feel
Dry and Dull and You Consider Becoming a Full-Time Dog-Walker

OVID'S METAMORPHOSES, translated by Ted Hughes
First published in 8 AD, Ovid's tales of bodies turning into other bodies glow mega-
bright in this translation: They are speedy, shocking, vibrant, and electric with desire,
and you'll find a tablespoon of inspiration in every stanza.

AUTOBIOGRAPHY OF RED by Anne Carson
Is it a novel? A long poem? Maybe an essay? Whimsical or serious? A fairy tale or a
realistic coming-of-age story? Whatever it is, it's dazzling, weird, and super-strange.
Our main character, Geryon, is a boy who is also a red demon with wings, though you
forget about the wings most of the time. His story is devastatingly sad but told in language that offers continuous zings of pleasure.

PLATERO AND I by Juan Ramón Jiménez
I love mosaics, literary and otherwise, and *Platero and I* by Spanish Nobelist Juan
Ramón Jiménez is a glittering mosaic: a 1914 novel constructed out of little vignettes
that are as much prose poems as they are chapters. In each, the poet relates an adventure in the Andalusian countryside with his remarkable silver donkey, Platero. Along
the road, Jiménez's prose carries you back to a slower time, when humans were more
connected to the birds and animals they lived beside and the seasons glimmered with
meaning.

MEMOIRS OF HADRIAN by Marguerite Yourcenar
Every page of this book rings with bright, deep wisdom: about love, sleep, beauty,
impermanence. This is a demanding novel, so you'll want to leave your smartphone
somewhere else (preferably drowned at the bottom of a Roman aqueduct), but it is utterly rewarding; one of the most soulful, skillful novels ever written.

THE RINGS OF SATURN by W. G. Sebald

Unsettling, drifting, dreamlike, and haunted by the deaths of those who have gone before us, *The Rings of Saturn* is a book that inevitably reminds me of the mysterious, soul-shaking power of literature. Sebald's ability to layer meaning on top of meaning is sheer witchcraft.

ANTHONY DOERR *is the author of the story collections* The Shell Collector *and* Memory Wall, *the memoir* Four Seasons in Rome, *and the novels* About Grace *and* All the Light We Cannot See, *which was awarded the 2015 Pulitzer Prize for Fiction and the 2015 Andrew Carnegie Medal for Excellence in Fiction. He served as guest editor for* Best American Short Stories 2019.

SEVENTEEN

The Book Deal

So you've written a great book, found the right agent to represent it, and at long last you have an editor—or, possibly, multiple editors—who wants to work with you to publish it.

Now, not to put too fine a point on it, you'd like to get paid. So, how does that work?

The short answer? It's complicated. Depending on how many editors are vying for your book and whether the editor you ultimately choose works at an indie press or a larger publishing house, your book advance could range from a token sum of a few hundred dollars to $1 million or more. But if you're looking to build a lasting writing career rather than simply earn a big onetime payday, you would be wise to pay attention to more than just the size of your advance.

How Publishers Make Decisions

Before we step into the particulars of a book deal, let's take a look at what's happening behind the scenes at the publishing house leading up to an offer. Depending on the size of the publisher, decisions about whether to publish a book involve the time, effort, and judgment of a group of people. The bigger the publisher, the more people in the group. In the case of a Big Five house, acquiring editors need the approval of the publisher before making an offer on a book. And the best way to get that approval is to build support from colleagues first.

Every publisher is structured and operates a little differently; some are more formal and others are rather more informal. One editor at a Big Five publishing house describes his imprint's acquisitions process this way: If he loves a manuscript and can get supportive reads from colleagues, then his editor in chief will give him the green light to circulate the manuscript more widely in the company, and it will be discussed in the weekly acquisitions board meeting. The acquisitions board is composed of the editorial staff, including the publisher and editor in chief, as well as the heads of other departments such as publicity, marketing, and subsidiary rights (commonly referred to as subrights, which covers translation and foreign rights, book clubs, and so on). When a manuscript makes it to the acquisitions board, the editor says, the conversation is less about whether it should be published and more about how it can be published well. Occasionally there will be an instance when the publisher decides the house should stand aside and not pursue the manuscript, but the meeting is more about how successfully the book could be pitched and published, which affects the decision of what level the advance offered will be.

Of course, every system has its exceptions, and the editor at the Big Five house acknowledged that sometimes a manuscript submission arrives with greater urgency attached to it, in which case a quicker response is required and the methodical scenario above is circumvented or hastened. Let's say the submission comes from an agent with whom the editor has done a lot of business before, or is about a subject of special interest to the editor. Or there's already some buzz around this manuscript: People in the business are already talking. Maybe there was an early version of it, a long story, that appeared in a high-circulation magazine that was shared widely and got all the industry insiders excited. Or perhaps the literary scouts, or book scouts, as they're sometimes called, have gotten hold of it and sent e-mails to publishers about this rising new talent. (Book scouts are a little like literary spies; essentially consultants, they are paid a monthly retainer by a book publisher, usually one based in a different country, to keep them abreast of what's hot and who's selling what and to whom.) The point is, sometimes submissions that come in from an agent command more attention than others. When this happens, it behooves editors to drop what they're doing and read the manuscript as soon as possible. If it lives up to the hype—and it seems likely that other editors will be interested and may try to make a preemptive offer—the editor can fast-track the process and go straight to his editor in chief and publisher. If he makes a convincing argument that the manuscript is worth taking quick action to acquire, the editor in chief will read it quickly and, if in agreement, forward it to the publisher for a swift decision.

At small presses and even medium-sized independent publishing houses, the process is often less formal. At Alice James Books, executive editor Carey Salerno makes all the decisions about which books to publish. The only exception is the manuscript that wins the annual Alice James Award, which is reviewed by an editorial board. At Akashic Books, editorial director Ibrahim Ahmad is one of four senior staffers (including Johanna Ingalls, the managing editor and director of foreign rights; production editor Aaron Petrovich; and Johnny Temple, the publisher and editor in chief; all of whom have worked at the press for at least fifteen years) who field queries from agents, investigate promising leads for projects, read through unsolicited submissions, and decide what to publish. "This core editorial team has worked together for fifteen years, which means that we have a kind of shorthand language that we can use to communicate," Ahmad says. "We also implicitly and explicitly trust one another, so it is very easy for us to make quick decisions because we have a shared understanding. But this also means that if one of us reads something and wants to jump on it and doesn't want to wait for any other person to weigh in on it that's totally fine, but there are other times where if I have any bit of hesitation I might say, 'Hey, Johnny, can you give this a second read?' And usually there's a degree of consensus in the publishing decisions that we make."

Profit and Loss: How Editors Think About Your Work

Before an editor at one of the larger houses decides to acquire a book by a new author, they will create a profit and loss projection, or P&L, which compares the manuscript they want to buy to a handful of similar books already on the market to determine whether the book can make a profit, given the cost of publishing and publicizing it. On one side of the ledger, the editor adds up the costs of producing and marketing the book, including office overhead, payments to freelance copyeditors and proofreaders, the cost of manufacturing the book—in hardcover, paperback, e-book, and/or audio formats—and shipping it to stores, along with any spending on publicity such as ads or author book tours. On the other side of the ledger, the editor tries to predict how much the publisher can make from sales of the book under consideration by comparing it to similar titles tracked by BookScan, a sales-data service owned by the NPD Group, which records roughly eighty-five percent of all hardcover and paperback book sales (e-book sales are recorded instantaneously, and are therefore fully accounted for).

So, if you've written a sweeping historical epic set in World War II Europe, an editor will calculate the costs of producing a book of that length—and longer books do cost more to produce and ship—along with the costs of publicizing it. Then she will look at sales figures for half a dozen recent novels set during the war years, leaving out mediocre books that didn't sell and breakout bestsellers like Anthony Doerr's *All the Light We Cannot See*, which may be overambitious, to arrive at an estimated market value of contemporary novels set during World War II. If she can make a case to her bosses that the potential profits have a reasonable chance of outweighing the costs, then she will make an offer, using the calculations of her P&L to help her arrive at an advance generous enough to entice you into signing but reasonable enough to leave the publisher room to make money on the book.

For books in well-defined categories like cookbooks or self-help manuals, using a P&L to determine an advance can be a fairly straightforward process. Using BookScan, the editor looks up sales figures for recent books similar to the one they're planning to buy, tweaks the numbers to account for the prominence of the author or the angle the book takes, and arrives at an advance that, with luck, makes everybody happy. Similarly, if a writer has published previous books, the editor can look up sales figures for those books, and if there's an upward trend, the editor may bump up the advance. But if the author's earlier books have lost money, and there's no compelling reason to think this new one will buck that trend, the editor may offer a lower advance—or not make an offer at all.

The system breaks down, though, when an editor wants to take on a new author, especially if that author writes literary fiction or creative non-fiction, whose sales are driven by factors like reviews and bookseller interest that a publisher can't predict or control. The editor will plug in comparable titles that they think will draw a similar readership to the one they want to publish, but often this is little more than educated guesswork.

"The science isn't infallible," admits one veteran editor at a Big Five publisher. "I mean, it usually doesn't work. Two-thirds of the time it doesn't. We put numbers into a P&L, but it's based on historical evidence of books in a similar category. Who's to say if a hundred thousand people bought a book set in dystopian America that those same hundred thousand people will buy a new book in the same category two years later?" Another editor at a different Big Five publisher jokingly calls the P&L a form of "licensed gambling."

You will almost certainly never see the P&L an editor creates for your book, so there's no way for you to gauge the accuracy of the assumptions the publisher is making. Nevertheless, once an editor has created a P&L for your book, they will present it to their boss—typically the editor in chief or the publisher—as part of their argument for taking on the book. The editor and their boss will then arrive at an opening offer, based in part on the P&L, but also taking into account the track record of the agent representing your book, the publishing house's need for this kind of book on its list, the chances your book could win a major award—and, above all, how hard the editor fell in love with your book.

But there's a wild card: If editors at other publishing houses also want your book, all that analysis can quickly fly out the window. And if there's an auction involving multiple publishers, the winning editor could end up paying you hundreds of thousands more than anyone ever imagined.

"I've had editors call and make me an offer," says literary agent Nicole Aragi, of Aragi Inc., whose clients include Junot Díaz, Colson Whitehead, and Edwidge Danticat. "I say, 'Well, I've got someone else who's offered, you know, zeroes more,' and they say, 'Hang on, let me talk to my boss,' and they come back and suddenly they can offer the extra zeroes. That's not because they've run a P&L and suddenly they've discovered that there's a huge audience that they'd forgotten to count in. It's because they've decided they really, really want it and other people really want it and they're going to have to pay more than they planned."

The Bids: Individual, Preemptive, and Auction

Broadly speaking, an editor can acquire your book in one of three ways: via an individual bid, a preemptive bid, or an auction.

An individual bid, in which only one editor makes a serious offer on your book, is the simplest of these scenarios, though it's usually the least lucrative for you as the author. Since no other editors are bidding on the book, the acquiring editor holds most of the leverage, not only on the size of the advance, but on the myriad ancillary issues covered by the contract, such as cover approval and rights to sell the book overseas. Advances vary wildly, but in general, if only one Big Five publisher bids on your debut literary novel or memoir, you can expect to be offered anywhere from about $20,000 to about $100,000, with most offers falling in the mid five figures. With an indie press, single-bid advances on debuts tend to be much smaller, ranging from $1,000 to about $25,000—that is, if there's an advance at all. Small presses, or micropresses, often don't have the resources

ACTION ITEM 40

Just as you did to identify agents, go to your bookshelves and take down five of your favorite books by contemporary authors, find the acknowledgments section, and locate the name of the editor. Get in the habit of paying attention to the people who are publishing your favorite books.

to offer any money up front. If you're in a position to have your book published by one of these presses, and you feel like it's the best opportunity for you and your work—perhaps you're writing in a form that doesn't typically draw a lot of interest from major publishers—don't worry about the lack of advance. Again, it's all about expectations and being deliberate, and patient, with your decisions.

If an editor at one of the big publishers really wants to buy your book, they may make a preemptive bid, offering terms they hope will persuade you to take the book off the market before other editors have a chance to make their bids. "If you get a preemptive offer, you can't shop it around," explains Renée Zuckerbrot of Massie & McQuilkin Literary Agents. "You can't call all the other editors who have that book and say, 'Guess what, I have this preemptive offer.' What you can do with a preemptive offer is negotiate with the editor who made it." These negotiations must move fast, however, since preemptive bids typically expire quickly, often after a single day.

If these negotiations fail, and other editors want to publish your work, the book will go to auction. Auctions can take many forms, but typically an agent will send a manuscript to a large pool of editors at the same time, and then, if more than one wants the book, the agent has them bid against one another for the right to publish it. In a round-robin-style auction, the agent sends the auction rules to all the interested editors, telling them what rights they're bidding on, the minimum amount of money they can raise the offer, and so on. In the first round everyone makes their initial bids, and then the agent calls the lowest bidder and tells that editor what the highest bidder's number was, and the editor with the lowest bid has to become the new high bidder or drop out. Then the agent calls the next-lowest bidder and tells that editor the new high bid—and so on, until only the highest bidder remains.

Auctions can produce truly eye-popping advances. Consider the more than $1 million that Little, Brown paid to outbid about a dozen other publishers on Whitney Scharer's 2019 debut novel, *Age of Light*, or the more than $2 million Random House paid for three novels by Emma Cline, including her 2016 bestseller *The Girls*. But just because your book goes to auction doesn't necessarily mean you're going to get rich. Competition nearly always boosts a manuscript's purchase price, but if there are only two or three bidders, or if your book is a collection of stories or for some reason has a naturally limited readership, the advance may remain relatively small and publishers may try to win over the author with other, nonfinancial inducements.

Among the inducements editors can offer is a multiple-book deal, in which the publisher buys not only the completed manuscript you're submitting now, but your next book (or two or three) before it's written—though, in truth, it helps if you already have an outline or some polished pages of the future books for the editor to read. Multiple-book deals are by no means limited to auctions. You see them most often when an author is selling the first in a planned series or when a debut writer is submitting a collection of short stories and has started work on a novel. In the latter case, the multiple-book deal can serve as a sort of insurance policy for the publisher, which is hedging its risky bet on the story collection by guaranteeing itself the rights to the writer's follow-up novel, which it hopes will sell better than the collection.

This is often, though not always, a good deal for writers. A multiple-book deal not only guarantees you will have a publisher for your next book, but that that you'll be paid in advance to write it. And in today's sales-data-obsessed publishing world, in which a disappointing debut can prematurely doom an author's second book, a multiple-book deal can be a vital safety net if your first book doesn't sell as well as you'd hoped. But a multiple-book deal also locks you into a relationship with one publisher, which can be a problem if your editor moves to another house or if the first book does much better than anyone expected and your publisher isn't inclined to sweeten the original deal. Obviously, it's also a problem if you can't finish the second book and have to pay back an advance you've already spent.

Advances: How the Money Works

A book advance is an advance payment against the royalties you will earn from sales of your book. Advance payments typically come in three installments, the first when you sign the contract, the second when revisions are complete and the book goes into production—a process that includes copyediting, design, and formatting—and the third when your book is published. (If your advance is relatively small, you might get paid in two installments, and if your advance is large, payments may be spaced out over four installments, with the fourth sometimes coinciding with paperback publication.)

This is great for writers because it means you get paid up front no matter how well your book sells, but it also means that, for many writers, the advance is the only money they will ever make from their book. In a standard book contract, the author earns 10 percent of the book's cover price on the first five thousand hardback copies sold, 12.5 percent of the next five thousand copies, and 15 percent on any copies sold after the first ten thousand. When the book goes into paperback, typically a year after the hardback comes out, the writer earns 7.5 percent of the cover price of each trade paperback copy sold and 8 to 10 percent on copies of mass-market paperbacks. With e-books, writers typically earn 25 percent of any revenue publishers receive.

For you to make any money over and above your advance, your book has to sell enough copies that your royalties exceed your advance payment. In industry parlance, this is called "earning out," and only about a third of all authors ever pull it off. Industry veterans are quick to point out that this does not mean that two-thirds of books lose money. Since the publisher's revenue per sale is higher than the author's royalty, a publisher that has done a good job of managing costs can start making money long before the author earns out.

It's also important to remember that, in publishing, money isn't just money. The more cash a publisher pays you in advance, the more copies of your book the house needs to sell to see a profit, making it more likely to throw its full resources into publicizing and marketing your book, including buying newspaper and magazine ads, sending you on a book tour, and pushing for reviews and feature profiles in prominent publications.

But you don't have to rely on the publisher's self-interest to get what you want out of the relationship. In a book contract, literally everything is on the table, and if you've written a book that an editor really wants—and especially if you've written a book a bunch of editors really want—you can ask for more than just a hefty advance.

Ancillary Rights: What's in the Fine Print?

At the most basic level, when you sign a book contract, you're accepting cash in exchange for the right to publish your work across a number of formats—hardcover, paperback, e-book, and audiobook—in various parts of the world. But all of this is negotiable. Let's say a publisher wants the right to publish your work in all formats everywhere in the world. In most cases, this means the house will publish your work in the U.S. and Canada, and then, if there's interest, sell the rights to publish your book to publishers in the UK and elsewhere around the world.

ACTION ITEM 41

If you're really interested in keeping track of who's getting the big book deals, consider signing up for the free daily newsletter offered by Publishers Marketplace. For $25 per month, you can get premium access to the site, including a longer, more detailed newsletter and the ability to search the huge online database of deals as well as information about the agents and editors involved in those deals.

This may be fine with you. You're just happy to see your book in print, and anyway, you don't anticipate there being much interest in your work outside North America. But if you think there may be money in a foreign edition, and your American publisher wants your book badly enough, you can agree to sell only the U.S. publication rights and keep the foreign rights for yourself. That way you, and not your publisher, will earn money from the sale of the foreign rights.

But it's not just territorial rights that may be up for grabs in a book contract. Until fairly recently, book publishers routinely negotiated away audio rights. Now, as audiobooks have caught on, most Big Five publishers have their own audio divisions and won't sign a book deal that doesn't include audio rights. Most smaller presses don't have an audio division, and if you're making a deal with an indie press it may be wise to retain audio rights, so you can make an audiobook yourself or sell the rights to do so to Audible or another audiobook publisher.

With the right leverage, you may also be able to gain some control over how your book is marketed and publicized. You can, for instance, ask the publisher to commit to financing an extended book tour or giving you a featured role at an industry trade fair. Publishers rarely grant authors veto power over their book cover, and most writers will have to be satisfied with "meaningful cover consultation." But, says Renée Zuckerbrot, "if you're in an auction, it is possible to get cover approval. The thing you have to ask for, because in an auction things are heated and they're moving quickly, is cover approval for the hardcover and the paperback."

Nonfiction: Selling the Truth

Selling a nonfiction book is much the same as selling a novel, with two important exceptions. First, nonfiction is often sold in the form of a book proposal rather than as a completed manuscript, and second, with a nonfiction book, you are promising your reader—and your publisher—that what you've written is true and not invented. (As a general rule, the more literary and personal a manuscript is, the more likely you will need to finish the book before selling it. Thus a memoir or a deeply personal work of literary nonfiction, where the quality of the writing is a prime selling point, will probably be sold as a complete manuscript like a novel. A work of popular science or a celebrity memoir, on the other hand, where the "hook" or premise can sell the book, is more likely to be sold on a proposal.)

Whether it's a memoir or a novel, when you sell a finished manuscript, your contract will lay out a detailed revision schedule, but assuming the book is in decent shape, the deadlines will be relatively tight and your publication date will depend as much on how the publisher wants to position the book in a particular season as anything else. If you sell a book on a proposal, however, then the contract will give you time to finish writing the book— eighteen months is a typical time frame—and you can use your advance to pay yourself while you write it. If you miss the deadline for delivering the finished manuscript, the publisher can technically revoke your contract and ask for its advance back, but editors usually grant extensions if the writer seems to be making progress on the book.

When you turn in the final draft, you're responsible for delivering any photographs, maps, and diagrams you want to include in the finished book and for clearing permission to use any copyrighted material. If you're required to include an index, you will probably have the choice to create one yourself or pay the publisher to do so (usually, the fee is around $1,000, which gets deducted from royalties). Larger publishers employ freelancers to compile indices, and some will do this on behalf of their authors, free of charge.

And then there are the facts you're using, which are your responsibility, not your publisher's. "Publishers do not fact-check," explains Michelle Tessler, founder of Tessler Literary Agency. Most large publishing houses have legal departments that vet books for libel and other potential legal problems, but a standard book contract contains a long list of warranties asserting that nothing in the book is plagiarized, infringes on anyone else's copyright, and that you've done all you can to ensure that your facts are accurate. "The publisher will do a legal vetting, and if they see anything alarming, they will ask the writer to vouch for it and make sure that something that needs to be changed will be changed," Tessler notes.

Beyond the Book Contract

Ultimately, a book contract is just a legal document, but a book deal should be about something more: the start of an artistic and business relationship that, ideally, will last an entire career. Too often, writers get caught up in the excitement of striking a deal, and in an auction, simply take the bid promising the largest advance.

"It can't just be about money," says Zuckerbrot. "You want someone who gets the book, who sees it in the marketplace and has a real vision for how to publish it and has an idea for what kinds of publicity and marketing campaigns their colleagues will run. You don't want someone just throwing money at a book and then figuring this stuff out later."

Typically, if an editor shows interest in acquiring your book, your agent will arrange for you to talk with the editor—by phone, in most cases, unless you happen to live in the same city as the editor. These are essential conversations. You want to know, first and foremost, whether the editor understands your work on an artistic level. Do they want you to make a lot of revisions? If so, what kinds? Are their ideas smart and interesting? Can you envision working with this editor not just on this book, but on your next one and the one after that?

But when you sign with an editor, you are also signing with an entire publishing house, and you want to find out what plans they have for marketing and publicizing your work. Whom do they see as the target audience for your book? How do they plan to reach those readers? What resources are they willing to put behind their marketing push?

In this case, whom you talk to may be as important as what they say. Is it only the editor who speaks with you, or do members of the marketing and publicity teams also join the call? Is it clear that the whole office has read your book and is excited to publish it? Whom do they see as your book's target readers, and what do they plan to do to help you reach those readers before and after your book is released?

"You want to get a sense that the enthusiasm runs deep," says Zuckerbrot. "The last thing you ever want is a cheerleading squad of one, meaning for some reason the editor is able to make a big offer, but you find out when things are moving along and you're working with the editor that there doesn't seem to be a ton of in-house enthusiasm."

Inking the Deal

The bids are in, you've spoken to all the editors who want to publish your book, and in consultation with your agent and trusted advisers you've picked the one who seems right for you and your work. You and your agent have fought for the best deal you could get, but at some point, you will have to sign on the dotted line. Pour yourself a drink. Post a photo of the contract for all your writer friends on Facebook and Twitter. Take a victory lap. You deserve it. You are now officially an author. And, starting tomorrow, you're going to have to start acting like one, which means being the best publishing partner you can be.

ADAM HASLETT ON FAITH AND WONDER

It is late in the day for the planet, as Toni Morrison once said. Our technical civilization, in its relentless greed, is quite literally consuming the world. In its latest phase of digital capitalism, it has morphed into a machine-driven conspiracy to consume our minds as well. Our ability to focus is daily slaughtered by the speed and virulence of the forces seeking to monetize ever-smaller fractions of our attention. Under these conditions, people either keep trying to will their brains to operate at digital speeds or shut down and dissociate. Most of us do a bit of both. Writing well is hard in the best of circumstances. Doing it in the age of mass distraction often seems not only irrelevant but close to impossible.

And yet, on as many mornings as I can manage, I sit at my desk with my earplugs in, hour after hour, writing and rewriting sentences and paragraphs, reading them back to myself over and over, frequently despondent at the pace of my (non)progress, not infrequently bored, and only occasionally, upon hearing the sound of a particular phrase, am I shot through with that fleeting, minor ecstasy of exactitude. Of not just saying but singing some little figment of my imagination that has managed to escape the general dull-headedness of a writing day. By now, many years of my life have been spent in this fashion. Why do it? Why persist?

The most direct answer I can give is that the only thing I find more frustrating, maddening, and difficult than writing is not writing. If writing is a trial, not writing is a horror. And I do a lot of not writing. So one, perhaps counterintuitive reason I persist is because I'm scared not to. How so? I'm scared that if I don't keep track of the dead they will haunt me in less loving ways. I'm scared that if I don't resist distraction and mental drift it will immiserate me. Or rather, I know that it will, and so I resist it. If these seem like negative motivations, it's because they are. I think all writers want to hide, just like all serious readers do. We want to disappear into imagined lives, to escape the little dystopias of daily existence and the big ones. To skip up out of the phenomenal world into the noumenal, into the realm of meaning. The irony for writers being that we hide in order to be found. All writing is a communicative act, an attempt to reach another person. And yet we pursue it in solitude. We retreat from the world in the keen hope of one day being understood by it. Writing is, among other things, the practice of that hope.

Bearing this in mind might let us put aside the plaguing question *Does writing fiction and poetry matter?* Particularly now, in the seemingly perpetual emergency of toxic politics and a toxic environment. To me, this is akin to asking, *Does faith matter, or wonder?* The answer is obviously no, if by "matter" you mean alter in clear and definitive ways the course of history. But do they matter as modes of being fully human in an economy that treats us as otherwise? Do they matter as a means of resistance to the commodification of absolutely everything, including our own selves? Yes actually, they do. Because faith and wonder, and the writing of poetry and prose are acts of contemplation and reflection. And these are human capacities that will only survive if we practice them. Avarice would just as soon see them die.

It is clear by now that technical civilization does not know the secret of its own cure. And it now seeks to extract our attention from our minds just as it extracts natural resources from the earth. In the solitude of writing, and the seemingly endless privacy of the desire to be understood, it is easy to feel as if what you are doing is selfish or self-aggrandizing or merely pointless. But when you wrest back your attention from the system that seeks to exploit it, you aren't just doing it for yourself. You are creating the means for others to step with you out of that force field. We know this because we benefit daily from others who have done it for us—we read. And in doing so we are slowed to the point of reflection, of feeling, of intuiting our connections to the lives of others.

God knows most mornings at my desk such high-mindedness seems distant at best and at worst no more than a kind of hortatory nonsense ginned up to glorify the utter mundaneness of trying for the thousandth time to describe the weather. But then, I suppose prayer grows dry for the monk, too. Faith is no promise of constant conviction. But for me, as with the practice of writing itself, the only thing more difficult these days than maintaining my faith in the power of our well-wrought imaginations is giving it up.

ADAM HASLETT *is the author of the novel* Imagine Me Gone, *winner of the Los Angeles Times Book Prize and a finalist for the Pulitzer Prize, the National Book Critics Circle Award, and long-listed for the National Book Award; the short story collection* You Are Not a Stranger Here, *a finalist for the Pulitzer Prize and the National Book Award and winner of the PEN/Malamud Award; and the novel* Union Atlantic, *winner of the Lambda Literary Award and finalist for the Commonwealth Prize. His books have been translated into twenty-four languages, and he has received fellowships from the American Academy of Arts and Letters, the Guggenheim Foundation, and the American Academy in Berlin. He lives in New York City.*

EIGHTEEN

Independent Publishers

After decades of mergers, major New York publishing houses have become increasingly attuned to the corporate bottom line, leaving smaller independent presses to take on writers whose work is more overtly literary or experimental. Minneapolis-based Graywolf Press, for instance, has had great success with innovative creative nonfiction like Leslie Jamison's essay collection *The Empathy Exams* and Eula Biss's *On Immunity*, both published in 2014. Meanwhile, Tin House Books, spawned by the now-shuttered Portland, Oregon–based literary magazine, has published well-regarded novels like Kristen Arnett's *Mostly Dead Things* (2019), Pamela Erens's *Eleven Hours* (2016), and Sean Michaels's *Us Conductors* (2014).

Many smaller presses also take a more idealistic approach to publishing books. Some of them are run as nonprofits, which means they have a mission to fulfill in addition to recouping their expenses and hopefully making a profit that they can then funnel back into their publishing program. And others are so small that they are able to make decisions about what to publish without as much focus on the bottom line. "Our value as independent publishers lies in the authors we can say yes to when others may be turning them down; our greatest triumphs therefore lie in our discoveries," writes Fiona McCrae, publisher of Graywolf Press. "Roberto Bolaño, Karl Ove Knausgaard, and Valeria Luiselli are all now published within large conglomerates, yet my principal respect remains with the small houses—New

Directions, Archipelago, and Coffee House Press—that first introduced their work to American readers. Conversely, I define failure at Graywolf not so much as the book that has underperformed (one can still hope) but as the book turned away because there was something in the manuscript that we were not open to exploring."

Jamia Wilson has a similarly inspiring approach to the work she does as executive director and publisher of the Feminist Press, the world's longest-running women's publisher. "From our earliest years we have considered ourselves a press of discovery, backing books and writers considered too niche, risky, or controversial," she writes. "Some of our earliest authors felt they had never before been given the permission to write; many of our new authors find themselves outside of the agented, university-trained, and debt-filled system. In our commitment to specificity of voice and urgency of story, rather than narrowly focusing on sales indicators (known to be biased against writers of color), we provide genuine, sustained support to our authors in ways that are unique to an independent press with a passionate activist ethos."

The world of small presses is filled with hundreds of incredibly hardworking, idealistic, and courageous publishers who have their eyes on a prize some might consider far greater than dollar signs. But because smaller presses can't afford the large advances their corporate counterparts sometimes lavish on their authors, some writers steer away from submitting to indie houses until it becomes clear no Big Five house will buy their book. While most single-offer deals with major New York houses earn their writers in the mid five figures, it's rare for an indie house to offer more than $25,000 for a debut, and most of the time advances are far smaller—and

> ### ACTION ITEM 42
>
> Go back to your bookshelves and look at the colophons on the spines of your books. How many are published by Big Five publishers? How many of them feature that recognizable borzoi that signifies a book published by Knopf, or the little house logo of Random House, the sower of Simon & Schuster, or the three fish of Farrar, Straus and Giroux? And how many are published by smaller presses? Be aware of who is publishing what—this kind of information will come in handy as you face the marketplace with your own book.

in some cases, the publisher's budget is so tight it can't offer any advance at all.

But agent Renée Zuckerbrot says seeing small presses only as a publisher of last resort is a mistake. "Indie presses are a really important part of the publishing ecosystem," she says. "They serve a real function. It's not just, 'A big house won't take my book.' Every once in a while I hear a writer say, 'So I guess I'll have to go to an indie press because I couldn't get a deal with a big house,' and it makes me really angry. They're not sloppy seconds. They have a very different business model and a very different approach to publishing books."

Not all agents share Zuckerbrot's view, however, and some may discourage their writers from submitting to smaller houses, particularly micropresses that offer little or no advances. If your book is experimental or in some other way not especially commercial, this may be a topic you want to broach with your agent before you work with them.

BEFORE YOU SIGN A SMALL-PRESS CONTRACT

"My advice is to ask a lot of questions; don't be afraid to ask questions," says Carey Salerno, executive editor of Alice James Books. "Any editor worth their salt and any editor interested in working with an author is not going to pull the contract or pull interest if you ask questions. Make a list of the things that are important to you as you're sending your manuscript out so that when the call comes or the acceptance letter comes, you know what you want. Don't get caught up in the moment and think, 'I'm just going to accept this.' Have your wish list and have questions that you can ask. Ask about the contract. Ask about the production process. Think about everything you want, because there are so many places where you could get surprised. 'Oh, I didn't realize that you don't do galleys. I didn't realize that you don't do print ads or that you don't have a social media presence. I didn't realize that you will offer me a thousand dollars to do a book tour.' Ask questions. Ask for things. The worst that anyone is going to say is no. Think about what it is that you want and ask questions."

If you reach a book deal with a smaller house without an agent, consider hiring a publishing lawyer to vet your contract before you sign. (If you go this route, be sure to search for a literary attorney who works in your state. Ask other writers in your community for recommendations. Do an online search—the website Avvo.com allows you to filter by city and state as well as specialty, but be skeptical of the reviews and ratings—and always google the lawyer's name and "complaint" to see unfiltered opinions. Maybe contact your state's bar association or reach out to a local law school for suggestions.) Most small-press publishers are honorable businesspeople who have their writers' best interests in mind, but you should be on the lookout for onerous contract terms such as substandard royalty rates or sweeping claims to all ancillary rights. (The Authors Guild offers members, who pay annual dues, a free contract review.) If a small press can't offer you much money up front, try to hold on to the audio rights as well as the rights to publish the book overseas. That way, if your book becomes a hit, the small press will still make money from selling your book in the United States, but you alone will benefit from selling the rights to the audiobook and foreign editions. Also, never sign over film rights. While it's unlikely that Hollywood is going to come knocking, in the event someone does want to make a film based on your book, you want to make sure you have retained those rights—otherwise you would be cut out of the deal.

Still, for many literary writers, smaller presses represent an attractive publishing option. While indie houses can't match a corporate publisher's marketing and publicity muscle, small presses take on fewer books so their editorial and publicity staff may have more time to focus on each of their authors. And while the initial payout may be lower at a smaller press, indie presses often serve as a launching pad for emerging writers looking to build an audience.

This is what happened for novelist Emily St. John Mandel, who published her first three novels with Unbridled Books, receiving advances that ranged from $7,000 for her first novel, *Last Night in Montreal* (2009), to $15,000 for her third, *The Lola Quartet* (2012). By the summer of 2013, when she finished her fourth novel, *Station Eleven*, Mandel was still working part-time as an administrative assistant and was ready for a change.

"I was tired of barely scraping by and wanted to see if I could make more money at a larger house, and I felt that moving to a Big Five publisher was the only way I could take my career to the next level," she says. "I recognized that *Station Eleven* had a somewhat more commercial premise than my three previous novels, so it seemed like a good moment to make a move. My editor at Unbridled could not have been more gracious about it."

The gamble paid off handsomely for Mandel, who received a $210,000 advance from Knopf for the U.S. rights to *Station Eleven*, along with a $20,000 bonus if the book earned back its advance within a year, which it did. (She signed separate contracts for Canada and the UK.) *Station Eleven*, which was a breakout hit and nominated for the National Book Award, has earned back its U.S. advance six times over. Knopf gave Mandel an $800,000 advance for the U.S. rights to her new novel, *The Glass Hotel*.

BENJAMIN PERCY RECOMMENDS

Five Books That Will Change the Way You Think About Writing

HOUSE OF LEAVES by Mark Z. Danielewski
Yes, Shirley Jackson owns the haunted house story, and we all kneel and quake before her awesomeness, but Danielewski reinvents the genre in this postmodern masterpiece that uses footnotes within footnotes, coded pages, found objects, tipped and backward text to make you feel like a participant (not just an observer) in this unsettling labyrinth of story.

THE BLOODY CHAMBER by Angela Carter
According to legend, when asked to describe her writing, Carter once said, "Imagine a razor blade drawn across the shaft of a penis." In this collection of stories, she does exactly that with these bold, exquisite, terrifying feminist revisions of classic fairy tales like Bluebeard and Little Red Riding Hood. What's old is new again.

MRS. BRIDGE by Evan S. Connell
This novel comes together like a mosaic—consisting of nonlinear conversations, images, and scenes—and makes you want to question the familiar architecture of storytelling.

RIDDLEY WALKER by Russell Hoban
This postapocalyptic novel does not hold the reader's hand, and that's both the challenge and the pleasure of it. It's narrated in an imagined English dialect that you have to figure out on your own, and part of the suspense you experience as a reader is immersing yourself in a world that feels truly alien. I would be remiss not to mention that Hoban's sweet, strange *The Mole Family's Christmas* is one of my favorite holiday reads.

CEREMONY by Leslie Marmon Silko
This novel, which is inspired by the Laguna oral tradition, always excites me with its surprising form and knockout poetry. Silko shows that language can be a weapon

and a form of healing as she brilliantly defies the standardized notion of what a novel can be.

BENJAMIN PERCY *is the author of four novels, including* The Dark Net, The Dead Lands, Red Moon, *and* The Wilding, *as well as three books of short stories,* Suicide Woods; Refresh, Refresh; *and* The Language of Elk. *His craft book,* Thrill Me: Essays on Fiction, *is widely taught in creative writing classrooms. He writes comics for Marvel and DC.*

NINETEEN

Working with Your Editor

As an unpublished writer sitting in your living room, or your home office, or your basement—or whatever corner of your apartment or house or coffee shop you've designated as the place where you conduct your literary business—the dream, or the finish line, is the book deal. Finally, after years of hard work and determination, someone has recognized your talent and determined that your manuscript deserves to be published and placed alongside those books you grew up reading. And, certainly, this is an achievement worth celebrating. Your life as a writer, it's really happening, it's paying off, and you have a shot at making an impact in the world of books.

But here's the thing: This isn't the finish line. It's the beginning of an entirely new process. You have signed on as a critical member of a team whose collective goal is to not only publish your book but publish it well. What does that mean? In an ideal situation, when the whole operation is firing on all cylinders, the author, the agent (if there is one), the editor, the publisher, the publicity and marketing team, the jacket designer, the copyeditor, the proofreaders, and the sales force all share a unifying vision of your book and agree on strategies for how to get it in the hands of as many readers as possible. This requires three key ingredients: communication, trust, and a whole lot of patience.

In this chapter we'll look at arguably the most important and dynamic relationship you'll have throughout the process—the one with your editor.

Your editor is your go-to point of contact at the publishing house throughout the publishing experience. And this relationship begins well before you sign on the dotted line of a book contract. Most editors will be in touch with you before they agree to publish your book. Good editors will want to make sure that they fully convey their vision for your book to make sure it matches your vision and expectations, and to bring up any suggestions they have for editing before entering into a long-term business relationship with you. These could be relatively minor suggestions, such as expanding a minor character a bit further, or cutting one character's backstory—or it could be a more substantial proposition.

Types of Editing

There are essentially two kinds of edits that your editor will likely give your manuscript, depending on the number and extent of areas of improvement that your editor has identified. Your editor may perform more than one round of each, or just one round in which both kinds of editing are applied to your manuscript. *Developmental editing* often involves big-picture changes such as reordering chapters, structural changes to the arc of the book, the expansion of characters, a new introduction, a new ending, or even shifting a point of view. Depending on the scope of the developmental edit, this macro level of editing could necessitate another substantial investment of your time and energy for revision and additional writing. A developmental edit will typically result in a comprehensive conversation with your editor, or at the very least a detailed editorial letter in which they lay out their case and point to specific areas of the manuscript that need work. *Line editing* is, as the term implies, a micro level of editing during which your editor will go through your manuscript line by line, scrutinizing everything from word choice and grammar to punctuation. (Copyediting and proofreading come later, typically after the heavy lifting on a manuscript is finished; these rounds of editing, in which each word is put under the microscope, are often done by specialized editors.)

Every editor works a little differently, so it's important to ask questions up front about the process: Can we hop on the phone to discuss the edits? Will I see the document with your edits clearly marked, in Track Changes perhaps? What are your expectations for my response?

The Author-Editor Relationship

It is worth slowing down here to consider the relationship that naturally and necessarily develops between an author and editor during these phases of editing. It is unlikely that anyone in your life up to this point has studied your manuscript so closely, which is why it is incredibly important that your editor has earned your trust before you sign a contract. This is a business relationship, of course—anyone who doubts that hasn't read the fine print carefully—but it's about to get quite personal. The manuscript that you've devoted a significant portion of your life to creating is passing from your hands into the hands of your editor, who is tasked with making it the best possible book it can be—and that will require an openness to suggestions. It doesn't mean you need to surrender all creative control; it just means you now have a publishing *partner*—in every sense of the word. You can sometimes get a sense of just how much the editor was involved in a particular book by reading the acknowledgments at the back. For instance, Jake Wolff, whose debut novel, *The History of Living Forever*, was published by Farrar, Straus and Giroux in 2019, includes more than a standard line of thanks for the editorial help he received: "My editor at FSG, Jenna Johnson, who helped me find the beating heart of this story and never let me settle for anything but my best. I also thank editorial assistants Sara Birmingham and Lydia Zoells, who kept me on schedule and provided valuable insights during the many months of revision."

Ben George, a senior editor at Little, Brown, recalls a recent submission— a novel that really knocked his socks off in terms of the quality of the writing but that clearly, in his estimation, had significant problems that needed solving. "It seemed so far away from being done, in a kind of big-picture sense, but I thought the writer was so extraordinary," he says. "I got on the phone with her and said, 'I think you're basically the greatest thing since sliced bread when it comes to your writing, and here are all the ways in which you totally bowled me over. But in this case, for us to work together—I have such a radically different vision of what's actually possible with this book and what you should be doing that I think we would need to have a meeting of the minds in order to proceed.' And we talked all that through and she was on board with all that." In this case, George got approval to make an offer on the book—a relatively modest offer, given the amount of work he estimated needed to be done—and the author ended up signing with another editor at a different house. But this illustrates how willing some editors are to sign a book based not just on what's on the page but also the potential for what could, with a little help and encouragement, be on the page. This is an important thing to keep in mind: Just because an editor has agreed to publish your book doesn't mean the writing is finished. It is imperative that you and your editor are in agreement about this before you sign a contract.

At Alice James Books, Carey Salerno always has a conversation with a poet before signing a contract. "I try to lay everything out on the table, because I think it's really important for poets to get the best fit. You want to be happy with the publisher you have and you want to understand what the expectations are and what you can expect of your publisher," she says. In some cases, this conversation involves suggestions for how to improve the manuscript. "I'll say, I think this probably could benefit from a bit of structural reorganization or reimagining, and maybe we can work on that together, and if you have a few more poems and you want to send those over to me if you think they might be good candidates, we can talk about putting some in or maybe taking some out—maybe there's some room to grow or there's some room to pull back, and we can talk about those things."

Depending on the publisher, editors may be more or less willing to relent on a specific point of contention in the manuscript. This is why it's critical to have a conversation with your editor before signing a contract. It may be that your work has been accepted under the condition that you agree to work with the editor to revise it according to more or less specific editorial points. Here's an important point to remember: In the instance of a book deal that includes an advance, most contracts stipulate that the second installment of your advance is paid only after the manuscript has been accepted by the publisher. This usually does *not* mean the manuscript as it was written when you received the contract; rather, it means that you have revised and/or addressed the suggestions of your editor to the satisfaction of the publisher. Editors only want what's best for the book, of course, so it's worth keeping that in mind as you work through the edits. Try not to take changes too personally.

At Akashic Books, editors are up front with authors about their expectations, especially when a manuscript needs significant editing. "We edit our books as aggressively as we need to, and there are some manuscripts that we get on submission and acquire that end up needing full-scale surgery—they need to be fully formed and realized in the editorial process," says editorial director Ibrahim Ahmad. "In those cases we go into it with open eyes, knowing what we're getting into. Our editorial process, on a textual level, involves multiple stages, and each work may or may not be subject to all these different stages. Some manuscripts still need some developmental editing, yet we sign them up and we will put in that work, we will do that heavy lifting on the conceptual side of things to make sure that the author is fully articulating their vision for the book—that's obviously fundamental and foundational to what we're doing."

At small presses, the author may have even more editorial input than at a large publisher. At Alice James, for example, Salerno says she gives every poet the same words of introduction, comparing the book to the poet's own home. "I say, 'This is *your* house, and you've invited me in. I'm a guest inside your house. And it's not appropriate for me to come in and just start moving your furniture around and putting everything where I think it should go. I can make suggestions to you that range and vary in strength. What I ask of you is to consider those suggestions, to consider where they're coming from, and to dialogue with me about them where you feel like we need to talk about those things. And if you do that and you make your own decisions based on the feedback I've given you—and you make the decisions you feel are best for the book—that's all I ask.'"

WHAT HAPPENS IF YOUR EDITOR LEAVES?

It's not something an author should expect, or even plan for, but it can happen: Your editor could potentially leave the publishing house before your book has been published. Especially in commercial publishing, with so many imprints filled with editors jockeying for better, more senior-level jobs, experiencing burnout, or just deciding on regular, run-of-the-mill life adjustments, it is possible for an author or a book to be "orphaned" upon the departure of an editor. If this happens to you, don't panic. You have a contract; your book will be published sooner or later. (Unless, of course, the entire publishing house is going out of business, which is more likely in the world of independent and small presses; in this case, get as much information as you can and consult your agent or even a lawyer, if necessary. There may be a plan in place for another press to take over the defunct press's backlist, including books still in the pipeline; or, at the very least, the rights to your work will revert back to you.)

The fact is, the larger publishers are prepared for such a situation, and there are other editors there who can step in to take over at whatever step in the process you were when your original editor left. This is what happened to Rachel Khong, whose debut novel, *Goodbye, Vitamin*, was published by Henry Holt in 2017, but not before the acquiring editor, Sarah Bowlin, left the world of New York publishing altogether and moved to Los Angeles, where she is now an agent at Aevitas Creative Management. After her departure, the book was reassigned to another editor at Holt, Barbara Jones. "I could think of no better editor to take up the mantle than her," says Khong's agent, Marya Spence of Janklow & Nesbit Associates. "She had said that she was the first person to raise her hand to take it on because she read it and cried during submission."

While the departure of an editor can be disruptive, it needn't spell disaster. This is where a good agent will earn every dollar of their fifteen percent, ensuring that an equally talented and committed editor takes over and guides the book through to publication.

The Editing Process

Every publisher, and every editor, has a different editorial process, which is why it's important to ask questions so you know what to expect. The most valuable piece of advice you can get during this part of the process is likely this: Be patient. Editors are ridiculously busy. "People think editors go around and have fancy lunches and just kick back with our feet on our desks and read manuscripts, which is nothing like what the job requires," says Little, Brown's Ben George, who at any given time is juggling a nearly impossibly full schedule of meetings, responsibilities, and tasks that don't include editing, which is usually done outside the office, at night and on weekends. "I try to be as fast as I can but it just all depends on what else is going on. I feel like my authors have had to learn to be patient, and then eventually they get the edit and they realize, 'Oh, that's why it took a while.' But at the same time I really feel for them. I was in an MFA program; I know that feeling when you give someone your work and you're in agony, thinking, 'Oh my God, I really need to know what you think of it.' But my attitude is, well, you decided to come on board with me. I have my strengths and my weaknesses. If you want the deep edit I can give you, you just have to be patient. And some people are more patient than others."

WHAT WAS THE MOST UNEXPECTED THING ABOUT THE PUBLICATION PROCESS?

"The inestimable benefit of sharing a very early draft with my editor, Jordan Pavlin. Jordan edited my two previous books, but I'd never before shown her anything that hadn't been revised six or seven times. This novel involved so much risk, and took so long to complete, that I felt I needed her insight and support long before I'd written three or four versions," says Julie Orringer of her novel *The Flight Portfolio*. "Did the novel strike the right balance between history and fiction? Had I captured the characters' essential struggles clearly? How to address problems of pacing, continuity, clarity? Jordan's exacting readings—not just one, but three

or four—echoed my own doubts and provided necessary perspective and reas-
surance. And her comments pulled no punches. She was scrupulously honest.
She was rigorous. She challenged me to do better. And my desire to meet her
standards was, as it always is, fueled as much by my ardent admiration for her as
a human being as by my deep respect for her literary mind."

Salerno, too, must escape the demands of the office—its constant
e-mails, phone calls, and other distractions—to get any editing done. After
her initial conversation with the poet, during which the two talk about possible additions and potential cuts, the poet is asked to e-mail the revised
manuscript to the editor, at which point Salerno will schedule time to do
any necessary developmental and line editing. "I usually take what's called
my editing day," she says. "I don't allow anything else to come into the bubble of the editing day. So no e-mails, no phone calls unless it's an emergency.
And I just immerse myself. I use that day to immerse myself in the world of
the manuscript."

Once she has had a chance to go through a poetry manuscript, making
detailed notes about the structure of the collection, the titles of the poems,
recurring themes, and other editorial issues, Salerno typically schedules a
phone call with the poet so that they can go over every proposed change
together. Salerno's process is unique in that she does not share her marked-
up manuscript with the poet; instead, she simply talks through her notes
and asks that the poet have a copy of the revised manuscript on which to
follow along. In the end, the poet has veto power over any changes, but
Salerno says more often there's agreement. Still, there can be unexpected
roadblocks. "There have definitely been instances where we had to schedule
another session and discuss it again," she says. "And what I say is, ultimately,
it's your book. We did this contract together and we're going to do it, but it
can be disappointing. I always have the book's best interests at heart, and I
think any writer worth their salt should listen to their editor, at least consider their editor's ideas and their thinking."

HOW LONG DO YOU NEED TO WAIT BEFORE YOUR BOOK IS PUBLISHED?

There are a number of determining factors, including who your publisher is and how many books they have scheduled for publication; the state of your manuscript and how much work you and your editor still need to do in order to get it into shape; the amount of editing and copyediting that needs to be done; and whether there are special promotional factors, such as an election or an anniversary, with which your book's publication would ideally coincide.

When you deliver your final manuscript—and sometimes even before you've finished—your editor will have a conversation with the publisher and the marketing director about when they think your book should be published. At all but the very smallest of small presses, the publication date will be positioned in one of two or sometimes three seasonal catalogues. Hachette Book Group, for example, presents new books in either Fall/Winter, which covers September through the following March, or Spring/Summer, which spans April through August.

At the Big Five publishers, there are typically two big meetings for each season's list at which certain people will pitch books to the company's sales representatives, who have gathered from all over the country. The first is the launch meeting (sometimes called a "focus" meeting), which is the first time the books are presented—typically with the editor delivering a sixty- to ninety-second summation of the book and its intended audience along with a draft of the cover—to the sales reps. (Such a quick pitch—summarizing a work of art that took an author many years to create in a minute and a half—may seem reductive, but it's important to realize that the sales reps will likely have even less time talking about the book to the booksellers. And a customer at a bookstore will likely take even less time than that when deciding whether or not to pick up a book and give it a closer look.) Books published from April 2020 through August 2020, for example, were pitched at this focus meeting back in May 2019—and some of those books, specifically nonfiction titles, may not have even been finished when they were pitched to the reps. The second meeting is a full sales conference—for those April 2020 through August 2020 books, this took place in September 2019—at which the same books are pitched again, this time by the marketing and publicity teams. Typically there are blurbs for the books, and the sales reps may have had a chance to read the final manuscript prior to the meeting.

Ben George of Little, Brown says that a year and a half is a pretty typical amount of time between the signing of a contract and the publication of the book, but it can obviously get longer if the manuscript ends up requiring more work, or there are other setbacks in the schedule. In the summer of 2019 Cary Salerno at Alice James Books said she had books scheduled through 2022, which means a poet who has just signed on with the press will need to wait approximately three years. Ibrahim Ahmad of Akashic Books reported a similar timeline.

As we mentioned at the beginning of this chapter, the editorial process requires three key ingredients: communication, trust, and a whole lot of patience. The good news is that at this point you are part of a team of people whose unified goal is to do right by you and your vision for the book. Although some of their feedback might be difficult to hear, take a deep breath and try to look at the issue as objectively as possible. Always act professionally. Push back when you feel like you need to push back.

"A writer wants her book to be as good as it can be before it goes out to what we both hope will be many thousands of readers," says George. "But I also don't think a writer should ever make a change to a book that doesn't in her gut feel like the right change to make. In an editorial letter from the novelist and *New Yorker* editor William Maxwell to Eudora Welty, Maxwell once said, simply, 'I trust you to be firm about the unhelpful suggestions.' I've always remembered that. While an editor can sometimes see something in a manuscript that a writer can't, the editor is never as smart as the writer about her own book."

Through it all, keep the lines of communication clear. If you're unsure about something, ask either your agent or your editor. And if you don't hear back from them by the end of the day, be patient. As one New York literary agent advises, "You want to pace the follow-ups." In the meantime, there are many other items on the publication checklist to think about, as we'll explore in the next chapter.

LUIS ALBERTO URREA ON TRUST AND POWER

I didn't have money, but I had a library card. I had vivid conversationalists at the helm of my family, Mom in English and Dad in Spanish. I had the border: barrio on this side and our beloved dirt street in Tijuana on the other. And I had the gift of friends and family this country did not respect or listen to, but who wished I could tell their stories for them in my "pretty talk." (*"Hablas tan bonito."*)

Later, I had a new neighborhood (white), cheapo records and used paperbacks, and the gift of despair. I was hiding in plain sight. Wrote pretty talk in notebooks late at night. I hid my writing and wondered why the kids at school didn't really know who I was. The burning ember in the writer's heart to become something/someone, to be heard and read, glowed inside me.

And yeah, I was naïve—I thought if I wrote really good poems to my girlfriends (since words were the only things I could afford) I'd get famous like Leonard Cohen or even better, Robert Plant. I'd get a jetliner with my name on the side and I'd be greeted by fans and that would show Colette and Becky and Lyn and my cousin Irma Cristina. I didn't know then that I was trying to show myself that I merited some small square of this world on which to stand.

You and I both know, or should know, that the Led Zeppelin Starship doesn't land on our street to whisk us away. But we are in the business of ascension. We are bent to these keyboards and notebooks and we are summoning wings made of words to etch themselves in the air above our shoulders. We have joined the ancient migration, the most human ritual. Shawn Phillips once sang, "Deep down, we all are butterflies." You monarchs, you rule the world.

Or not. Let's not get too grandiose. Editors hate that.

But you know what I mean: Sometimes, if you're well caffeinated, and got some sleep at last, you fell back suddenly because you wrote the most amazing sentence that irradiated a fine paragraph with inexplicable mojo. You know this. You dare not ask yourself why the paragraph has such power because you can't find the trick you must have pulled to hypnotize yourself, and you might actually risk a crash when you show your partner or Mom or writing group or agent. But something inside you knows: The power you have unleashed is so right, so strong, because it cannot be easily parsed. Sister, you have tapped into the profound shadows of writing. You shaman.

Read haiku. Seriously. Even if you write horror stories. I always have haiku near me. Mary Oliver read Rumi every day, and I have him nearby as well. But Bashō and Buson and especially Issa teach me over and over to get out of my own way and let the tree talk, let the bird talk, let the river talk, let the snail be the snail and the mountain be the mountain. Because I learned from those poets to let Luis be Luis. I never liked him much, but I sure grew to like his words. My words. Not hubristically, though I was sure I could get rich by typing. What I like is that I have words, and the Zen masters and my indigenous teachers and Ursula K. Le Guin, my first mentor, taught me that having words was a miraculous thing. I am grateful for them. Words are my friends.

Yeah, I curse them. Yeah, I throw fits and give the computer the finger and announce I am *through* with writing and go binge-watch *Below Deck Mediterranean* on Bravo. But that happens when I allow myself to try to dominate the words. What kind of friend is that? How do you feel when your high school pal shows up on Facebook and suddenly asks you for money? How do you feel when a close friend makes fat jokes at your expense? I am not always as good a friend to writing as writing is to me.

My hardest lesson was drummed into me by relentless teachers. I was taught to stop competing—I was never going to write a sentence as sinuous and amusing as Thomas McGuane because I was Luis Urrea and had my own garden to grow. That writing wasn't a career; it was a lifeway. That writer's block was not failure but evidence that writing is seasonal, and the right seeds had not yet germinated or sprouted. (This is how I settled into a cross-genre writing practice. Mo' seeds everywhere.) I was after a black belt; I just didn't know it.

Here's a tip: Writing is on your side. Writing, story, poem, words, they need you if they are to survive. You are part of the life support system of story. I happen to believe that makes you part of the life support system of the world. You know this is true, deep inside: Just listen to the toxic lies flying all around you, and you know who you are and why you're here.

Bear witness.

Issa had a rule for life and art. It really irritated me. So I leave it with you. Because it is a message of love. Love for you. Because you really do talk pretty, even if you rage. Issa said: "Simply trust."

Get to work. Though for us, work is play—and we don't need a uniform. We don't even need clothes.

Or disagree with me: It'll give you something to write.

LUIS ALBERTO URREA *is the best-selling author of seventeen books of poetry, fiction, and nonfiction, including the novel* The House of Broken Angels, *nominated for a National Book Critics Circle Award, and the nonfiction book* The Devil's Highway, *which won the Lannan Literary Award and was a finalist for the Pulitzer Prize and the Pacific Rim Kiriyama Prize. A member of the Latino Literary Hall of Fame, Urrea is a distinguished professor of creative writing at the University of Illinois in Chicago.*

TWENTY

Publication Checklist

Up to this point we've been discussing all the work that goes into your manuscript—for good reason, of course, as that will be the meat of the book—but it is far from the only material you will be asked to deliver or weigh in on. All publishers are different, but the following is a list of just some of the things your editor may be asking you to think about and/or submit at some point in the process.

Cover art

Your editor will likely ask you for your thoughts on a cover for your book. Depending on who you are and how you envision your work, you may have very specific suggestions—a photograph or piece of art you think is perfect—or you may be at a total loss about visual representations of your writing. Either approach is fine, but if you want something specific on the cover, just remember that there may be rights issues. (Perhaps that Robert Mapplethorpe photograph *would* look great on your cover, but that doesn't mean you can secure the rights to reproduce it.) And keep in mind, too, that your publisher's art director, or the freelance designers your publisher employs, are professionals, and they probably have years, even decades, of experience. So, they likely know what makes an effective cover and what doesn't. Remember that the whole point of the cover is to get readers who have no idea who you are to pick up your book and give it a closer look. At its best it is a work of art, but it also serves as a sales tool, and the professionals who work at this for a living have valuable opinions about which colors, fonts, and artwork will create the best cover. They have experience with the size, color, and placement of the title, your name, and the art. Listen to them. Give your feedback in a professional, polite manner. Remember that this is a relationship, and everyone wants what's best for your work. In an ideal situation, both sides are extremely happy with the cover design—and many publishers will do whatever they can to make sure you're satisfied—but in the end, many contracts stipulate that the final decision on a cover rests with the publisher. That said, even the biggest publishers work hard to make their authors happy. And, it's worth noting, the authors being published by those big houses typically have agents whom the publishers have a vested interest in satisfying. (Their enduring professional relationship, which will likely result in future books, depends on it.)

Some publishers—often smaller, independent presses—have a slightly different approach to the cover. At Alice James Books, Carey Salerno and her team of freelance designers will solicit suggestions from the poet and offer multiple designs—both interior and exterior—from which the poet can choose. "We ask all our authors to look for cover art and to send us a lot of different choices. It takes a special kind of image to be a book cover," Salerno says. "When they get the cover designs and the interior designs they can say, 'I really like this cover, but I hate yellow.' Or 'I really want to see what that font looks like in pink,' or 'I like the font on this cover, but I don't like that color.' They get a lot of agency in the process. But there's also a lot of trust that they have to put in us that we know what we're talking about and that we are the professionals in publishing."

Unlike at a larger publishing house,

ACTION ITEM 43

Study the covers of some of your favorite books. What do they have in common? Is the title clear and easy to read? Is it successful because of the cover art or the graphic design? Pay attention to the font choices and the colors. Make notes about what you'd love your cover to look like. This isn't just daydreaming; these notes could come in handy when you're having a conversation with your editor about the cover of your book.

at Alice James the poet always wins. This can be an appealing facet of small-press publishing—the author having more agency, and ultimately, decision-making power, in the process—but Salerno says it's also a unique and important element of publishing poetry specifically. "So much of poetry and the sales of poetry are driven by the writer's connection with their audience and the writer's connection with their book and the way that they perceive their book and the way they want to talk about their book, and a lot of it is very emotionally driven." In the end, Salerno says, happy poets are better promoters of their books.

Promotional copy

The copy that will be used throughout your book's publication—from the catalogue copy to the data fields at electronic retail sites to the book's jacket copy—will be written by some combination of you, your editor, and the marketing team. Some publishers will send authors a publicity questionnaire that includes not only questions about you and your platform (where you work, your social media accounts, etc.) but also prompts for you to write about your work, describing the style of your book, the themes, what inspired you to write it, and so on. The publisher will then use these descriptions to write promotional copy that is true to your intentions. The editor will share this text, sometimes called catalogue copy, with you and ask for your comments and feedback. At other publishing houses, the editor will create a fact sheet, sometimes called a tip sheet, that includes a brief pitch of the book, a longer description, specifications such as format and length, your bio, any sales history you may have, your previous titles, blurbs, comparison titles, and so on. This internal document is used by the sales and marketing staff to orient themselves to your book. A version of this will be used as a galley letter that may accompany advance reading copies (ARCs), which many publishers send out to reviewers and editors ahead of your publication date. (An ARC is a little like an early, bound paperback edition of your book that is produced—sometimes before the text is final, before copyediting or proofreading—without all the frills of a finished copy. Depending on your publisher, it can be beautifully produced and feature final cover art, or it can be pretty simple and straightforward.) A press release is intended to give the editor or producer at a TV network an easy way to quickly learn about your book and discern whether it's worth a closer look and potentially provide media coverage. (See pages 358–59 for the press release for Jami Attenberg's novel *All This Could Be Yours*.)

Blurbs

Sometimes referred to as prepublication praise, blurbs are those quotes from well-known authors on the back—and sometimes the front—of a book. These aren't excerpts from reviews—often seen on paperback reprints—but rather gushing enthusiasm from authors (or sometimes experts in your field, if you're a nonfiction writer) that is designed to add credibility to your book, or an air of authority to your writing. Your editor or publicist will likely ask you for a list of names of people whom you think would be appropriate to ask if they are willing to write a blurb. Give this list your careful consideration: These people could be friends, former teachers, or other professional acquaintances, but ideally, they have names that will be easily recognizable to a reader browsing the new release table at the local independent bookstore or clicking around the Barnes & Noble website. Your publisher will likely ask you to reach out to these potential blurbers personally, as it increases the chances they'll say yes, but it's important to coordinate this with your editor and/or publicist. They may be aware of an author who has already offered a blurb for another title on next season's list, or who has blurbed a dozen books in the last six months and whose praise may be considered a bit less potent than they would like. Your editor or publicist will likely have ideas of their own as well. The process of requesting a blurb from an author you know or whom you've always admired can sometimes be an anxious proposition. Not only are you putting your unpublished work out there for your hero to see, but you're also asking for a kindness from someone whom you may not know very well. This is a big ask, too. You're asking someone to make time to read an unpublished book (for this reason, the requests should go out as soon as your editor approves the list) and vouch for it to the reading public. It needn't be so fraught, though. The writer may be flattered that you thought of them, or more than happy to attach their name to yours. Remember, the worst they can say is no.

Author photo(s)

If you don't have a great digital photo of yourself—up close, in color, in focus, large (at least five by seven, preferably larger), high-resolution (at least 300 dpi, or dots per inch), against a background that doesn't distract from your face—do everyone a favor and get one taken. For now, don't spend a bunch of money on a professional photo shoot; just grab your digital camera or your cell phone and either ask someone to take a dozen or so shots, or just take them yourself (try not to make it look too much like a selfie). You are a writer, and you will soon be a published author, so there is no excuse for not having a good, relatively recent photo of yourself that you can immediately fire off to an editor or blogger or anyone interested in paying a little attention to your work. Like it or not, most readers like to see a photograph of who wrote the book, the essay, or the blog post they are reading. At some point your editor or publicist is going to ask you for a recent photo so they can include it on some combination of the publisher's website or in the publisher's catalogue, on web pages of online retailers, and of course in the book itself. Talk to your editor or publicist about what they want in an author photo (three-quarter length, how close up, smiling or serious?) and then get as many as you can. You only need one, but it's best to have several that you like, because as we'll see in the next chapter, they may come into play during your publicity and promotional efforts. Digital photography makes it easy to get both color and black-and-white versions of any given shot. If you know someone who is a good photographer, buy them lunch and ask them to do

ACTION ITEM 44

Get a photo of yourself. Even if you don't have a book under contract or forthcoming, get a photo. You never know when an editor of a newspaper or a magazine, or a website or a blog, might ask you for that photo. You want to be prepared.

an informal photo shoot; always offer to credit their work. Or, if you feel it's worth it, get in touch with a professional photographer. Rates vary, but you can expect to pay several hundred dollars or more. Take a look at other books and look for the photo credit. These days getting an author photo is easier than ever, but it's an important asset for you and your publisher.

Publication Credits

If you are publishing a collection of poems, stories, or essays—or if you've had excerpts of your novel or nonfiction book previously published—you'll want to make sure you have an up-to-date list of the magazines, websites, or newspapers that gave your work its first home. This is not only a professional courtesy, a nod to the publications that gave you an early boost, but it is also quite possibly a contractual obligation. Many magazine contracts request that you acknowledge the publication in the event of a reprint, even if you have revised or substantially changed the piece for your book. This information could also end up appearing in your bio or catalogue copy.

Permissions

Do you have photographs that you didn't take in your book? Maps, illustrations? Have you quoted song lyrics or included excerpts from other people's books? If so, you need to address the issue of getting permission to use this material. It may require money, and it will most definitely require time. Consult the Library of Congress or talk to your editor about whether the quoted material falls within the public domain (in the United States, every book published at least ninety-five years ago is in the public domain) or is considered fair use (in general, not more than a couple of short paragraphs from a published piece of prose or a couple of lines from a song or poem). For everything else, you'll likely need to request permission—which is often up to the author or their publisher. The Authors Guild can also offer advice and provides standard permissions forms.

Parts of the Manuscript

Every published book has certain obvious elements—a cover, a title page, and a copyright page, for instance—but depending on your publisher and your particular book, there are a number of other items a book might contain. It's worth taking a look at them sooner rather than later so you can be thinking about whether your book will include any or all. Of course, communicate with your editor about whether these pieces are appropriate for your book and how your publisher would like them delivered and in what format and style.

Previously published books: These are typically listed in reverse chronological order and/or by series.

Title page: Created by your publisher, it includes the title, subtitle, any necessary series information, the publisher's name and location, and often the company's logo (sometimes called a colophon).

Copyright page: Also created by your publisher, it features a copyright statement and may include permissions information and a disclaimer that characters are fictional (if it's fiction) or a disclaimer that limits liability if the book includes medical, financial, or professional advice.

Dedication: Not to be confused with the acknowledgments page, the dedication is typically a concise line or two honoring a special individual or individuals who offered either extraordinary inspiration or help.

Acknowledgments: Typically located at the back of the book, this is where you get to thank everyone who had a hand—literally, metaphorically, spiritually, whatever—in helping you bring your words to print. Family, friends, colleagues, teachers—they're all fair game, but don't forget to acknowledge the people in publishing who helped you realize your dream: your agent, your editor, the editorial assistants, the publisher, the publicist, the designer, the copyeditor, the proofreaders, the production crew—anyone and everyone who formed your team. If you've made it this far, to be writing your acknowledgments page, then you owe it to all those people to take your time and think carefully about the network of folks who contributed to the life of your book. Alternatively, some writers see the inherently incomplete nature of such a task and take a minimal approach. It's a matter of style, and no approach is wrong. But this is your chance to give back, if only as a small gesture, to those who have given something—time, attention, resources, emotional or even financial support—to you. It's worth keeping in mind that including these names can also make those people more invested in your book. It's a big deal for most folks to see their names in a book, and they will likely be stronger advocates of your work if their names are in print for all to see.

Quotation page or epigraph: There is an art to the epigraph, and it is particular to each book. Suffice it to say that if you remember an epigraph it was a successful one; if not, there was likely no harm done. It can strike a powerful note in the silence before a reader gets to the first chapter, and it has the potential to resonate until the very last page. It is, for the most part, unnecessary—and it is sometimes even overlooked—but if you have one in mind it likely means a great deal to you. At its best, it can be poignant and prescient; at its worst, it can be trivial and undermining. Consider it carefully.

Preface or introduction: Usually included in a nonfiction book, these synonymous terms refer to the early pages that explain the purpose or scope of the book.

Foreword: Typical in a nonfiction book, a foreword is written by someone other than the author, sometimes under separate copyright, whose platform lends credibility to the book.

Table of contents: This usually lists all chapter titles and page numbers, sometimes broken into parts, and is frequently created by the publisher (as page numbers are rarely final until the final book).

List of illustrations, figures, or maps: If necessary, this list sometimes appears in the front of the book, sometimes in the back, and can contain names and dates of the copyright holder.

Dramatis personae: A list of the main characters, especially useful if your book spans generations and introduces many characters.

Prologue: Not to be confused with a preface, a prologue is mostly used in fiction, to set the stage for the narrative or theme.

Appendix: Supplemental material that augments the text of your nonfiction book, an appendix or appendices sometimes list resources for more information about a given topic.

Glossary: This is sometimes included in nonfiction books, but it's also useful in fiction or poetry that incorporates a dialect or foreign (or invented) language that is likely unfamiliar to the average reader.

Endnotes: Citations of quoted or paraphrased material may be included at the back of the book. Hot tip: Compile these as you're writing the book, not after.

Bibliography: This is a list of books, articles, videos, and anything else that aided in research for the book.

Index: If it is determined to be necessary, sometimes the publisher will prepare the index at its own expense and other times the author is expected to prepare it and/or pay to have it compiled.

NICOLE DENNIS-BENN RECOMMENDS

Five Books to Read if You're Unaccustomed, Queer, and Alien in a World Too Stuck on Labels to Read Between Lines and Across Borders

THE NAMESAKE by Jhumpa Lahiri

This novel, one of the first books I read about immigrants, is a coming-of-age story that delves into identity and acculturation. I fell in love with the way Lahiri writes about the painful assimilation process we immigrants go through. I'm captivated by Jhumpa Lahiri's writing and the care and compassion she gives to her characters.

WE NEED NEW NAMES by NoViolet Bulawayo

This is another coming-of-age story. I love NoViolet Bulawayo's characters and how she uses the voice of a young girl, Darling, to unflinchingly relay issues that many of us would rather look away from. Bulawayo depicts the beauty as well as the ugliness of a country ravaged by poverty and shows the hopelessness of a girl arriving in America only to lose her way in life, as well as the people she loves.

BREATH, EYES, MEMORY by Edwidge Danticat

Edwidge Danticat, who writes about Haiti with compassion and beauty, is my biggest inspiration. I've learned much from her, particularly in how she draws clear pictures of people's lives, both before and after leaving the island. In *Breath, Eyes, Memory*, a young girl leaves Haiti to live with her mother, who is as foreign to her as America itself. It's a riveting novel that taps into the generational traumas we carry, even across oceans.

ANOTHER BROOKLYN by Jacqueline Woodson

This novel about girlhood, set in Brooklyn in the 1970s, captivated me. I appreciate the poetry in Woodson's writing, and especially the sparseness with which this story is told. It's about a young Tennessee transplant named August who, after moving to Brooklyn following her mother's death, forged an intimate relationship with three other girls in a quest for companionship and survival in a place with "teeth as sharp as razors."

ZAMI: A NEW SPELLING OF MY NAME by Audre Lorde

This book did more than liberate me as a college student, coming into my identity as black, immigrant, and lesbian; it showed me how fundamental it is to write all my identities on the page. Audre Lorde crafts a semiautobiographical tale about a young woman trying to navigate the throes of identity as she comes of age in the country of her parents' sojourn, discovering the challenges of being a black woman who loves women in a world that was not ready.

NICOLE DENNIS-BENN *is the author of the novel* Patsy *(Liveright, 2019), which was selected as a* New York Times *Editors' Choice, a* Financial Times *Critics' Choice, and a* Today Show *Read With Jenna Book Club pick, and* Here Comes the Sun *(Liveright, 2016), a* New York Times *Notable Book of the Year, winner of the Lambda Literary Award for Fiction, and a finalist for the National Book Critics Circle John Leonard Award, the New York Public Library Young Lions Fiction Award, and the Center for Fiction's First Novel Prize.*

TWENTY-ONE

Publicity and Promotion

Despite the placement of this chapter after those about agents, editors, and book deals, the conversation about promoting yourself as a writer and publicizing a project you're excited about is not something you should turn to only after good things start happening for you, such as a forthcoming book or journal publication. The time to start thinking about how you want to communicate, share ideas, support others—and, yes, promote your work and position yourself in the local, state, regional, national, and even global literary community—is right now.

We are not suggesting every emerging writer needs to immediately design and launch a website. And we're not advising beginning writers to go out and hire a freelance publicist. Nor are we espousing that disingenuous brand of "shameless self-promotion" that we've all encountered on social media (though, as we'll see a little later in this chapter, a bit of that is inevitable—and perfectly acceptable if it's delivered in the appropriate context). Instead, we're suggesting a more holistic approach to the notion of attempting to tell the world about yourself and your work.

Let's pause to recalibrate, because it's important to consider what we really mean by publicity and promotion—and how we see it fitting into the life of the writer, no matter where you're at in the writing life. Just as firing off a dozen cold submissions to agents or presses or magazines without first doing your research is a pretty lousy (and usually ineffective) way of approaching publication, getting the word out about something you've dedicated years of your life to creating in a manner that is artificial or insincere is just as lousy and ineffective. Promoting yourself and your work should be more than just a box you check off or a rote task performed with only the immediate self-serving goal in mind.

Here's what Michael Taeckens, an independent publicist and cofounder of Broadside: Expert Literary PR, says about a healthy, integrated approach to the world of publicity: "I always tell authors to get involved in their local literary community. In whatever city they're in or near, there is going to be stuff happening on a local level. There are going to be other authors who live there, there may be an independent bookstore nearby, there may be librarians, there may be a literary festival on the state level. Get to know those people. When you befriend other people in the literary community, you help lift them up, and they will, in turn, help lift you up. When authors are visiting, when they're coming through your city, make a point of showing up to their events. You need to give a lot and support a lot before you're going to get a lot of support yourself."

Take a deep breath and shake off the notion of approaching the steps to (and through) publication as tasks that, once accomplished, will automatically result in a specific desired outcome—at which point you move on to the next one and the next. There's no instruction manual for the literary life. (This book is probably the closest you'll get to one.) That's not to say there aren't choices that need to be made—there most certainly are—but many of those choices are about being a good literary citizen, an engaged, generous, and open-minded member of your literary community who takes the time to see who and what is around you, and enters relationships with other writers in a spirit of communication and collaboration. We've seen how this approach is critical to the process of finding an agent and working with your editor. And as we're about to see, publicity and promotion are no different.

Working with Your Publicist

If your book is being considered for publication at one of the major publishing houses, then part of the acquisition process typically involves the director of publicity and marketing (and others from these departments) weighing in on the strengths of the manuscript under consideration. "When an editor is considering a manuscript for publication they will often come in and speak with us to look at publicity potential and media potential," says Sarita Varma, the director of publicity at Farrar, Straus and Giroux (FSG). "The main perspective they're looking for is any kind of insight or questions I might have in terms of the author's platform, their connections, and making those connections to the media landscape or current news climate." Although people other than the editors can and do offer their opinions on the editorial merits of any given manuscript ("We have conversations around the structure of books and direction as well," Varma says), the decision about whether to publish a book or not is really the purview of the editors, especially at a place like FSG, which Varma describes as an "editorially driven house."

At W. W. Norton, a large independent house that has been owned by its employees since the early 1960s and publishes four hundred books annually through its trade, college, and professional departments, publicity director Erin Sinesky Lovett says at least one person from publicity is privy to book proposals and participates in conversations with editors about the acquisition.

Once the decision is made to publish a book, the focus shifts to *how* to publish that book. This is where the publicity department (and the marketing department, which handles things like advertising and the placement of your book in paid promotional opportunities), along with your editor, comes into the picture in a big way. Anyone can publish a book—the goal is to publish a book well, and this requires an extended, coordinated effort involving a number of people, including you.

Remember in chapter 19 when we learned about the launch meeting, at which editors present a season's forthcoming titles to representatives from sales, marketing, and publicity? Varma says this meeting—which at FSG and most big publishers typically happens between a year and a year and a half before publication—is the signal to her and her team to reach out for their first direct communication with the author since the book deal was signed.

So what can you expect from that initial phone call or meeting with the publicity team? "First we'd want to be finding out about the author's background, their connections, what drew them to the work," says Varma. "If they're not a first-time author, we explore how the work fits into the arc of their career and their other published works, or how it may be a departure. The debut story can be equally fascinating. These meetings are really valuable, from a publicity perspective, and we glean a lot of interesting information from them."

At this first publicity meeting the team will begin to develop a strategy for how to pitch your book to booksellers and the media: review outlets as well as newspapers, magazines, websites, radio programs, podcasts, and blogs that may be inclined to run a story about you and your book. There's also discussion about social media, of course, as well as opportunities for events and partnerships with organizations that might be fruitful in building a conversation around the book. "It's not just strictly limited to media," says Varma. "Our contacts vary across many fields."

This is where the promotional muscle of the large publishers starts to flex, opening windows of opportunity for the right kind of book at venues such as NBC's *Late Night with Seth Meyers*, Comedy Central's *The Daily Show* with Trevor Noah, or NPR's *Fresh Air* with Terry Gross. This kind of media attention can be a game changer, and the publicity teams at the major publishers have the contacts and resources to make it happen for a lucky, talented few. Anyone who has been paying attention over the last few decades knows that coverage of books in regional and national newspapers and magazines is shrinking (gone is the stand-alone *Sunday Book Review* at the *Los Angeles Times*, significant books coverage has dried up at the *Boston Globe*, and many other dailies big and small have shifted away from books coverage), and even the casual observer of the national literary conversation felt the absence of Oprah's daytime talk show and her original book club (her current book club can deliver a powerful boost in sales but not quite the way the original could alter the national conversation). As the media landscape continues to change, however, there are countless new websites, newsletters, podcasts, and late-night TV shows that can still expand an author's reach significantly.

Sinesky Lovett acknowledges the changing landscape but marvels at the ability of industry leaders to adapt. "Not too long ago, book *influencers*, blogs, and podcasts weren't something that publicists relied on to get the word out about books, and now they play a key role in many campaigns," she says. "I continue to be amazed at how the book industry is able to transform and evolve as new technology comes into play. And even with all the technology in play, of course it's still the people—particularly the booksellers and librarians and critics and interviewers—who establish, support, and recommend books and give those books lives."

"In every decade or cycle of publishing there is that kind of media moment that becomes like a sea change and suddenly that is the cornerstone of every publication campaign going forward," says Varma, who adds that a creative publisher is flexible enough to pivot toward whatever opportunities are available.

But what about at a much smaller press—one that doesn't have the resources of a multinational media conglomerate at its disposal? Nightboat Books is a small poetry press, based in New York City, publishing eighteen to twenty-four books a year. It has only three full-time staffers: the publisher, a managing editor, and a publicist. But the initial process of developing a publishing strategy and how to position a book is much the same as at FSG—just on a different scale. Andrea Abi-Karam, Nightboat's editor-at-large, says they typically get their hands on a manuscript about a year ahead of publication, at which point they begin cataloguing it with the press's distributor, Consortium Book Sales and Distribution, and scheduling it for one of their two annual seasons: fall/winter or spring/summer. When this process is complete, usually about eight months ahead of publication, publicist Caelan Nardone, along with publisher Stephen Motika and sometimes the press's team of interns, gets on the phone with the author for the first publicity meeting. "We get to know the author a little bit and learn about the communities they're a part of," says Abi-Karam. "We have a brainstorming session about where to send galleys, people who we feel confident will cover the book." This includes media such as *Publishers Weekly*, *Poets & Writers Magazine*, and other magazines, newspapers, and websites.

But this initial conversation is about more than just the usual suspects; it's about thinking creatively about the author's personal and professional contacts and making connections that could spark interest in the book. To the uninitiated, it can be a rather intense undertaking. "You meet so many people in your life, it can be overwhelming to try to write an e-mail and put together everyone you've ever met who might read your book or talk about your book," says Abi-Karam. "So sometimes getting authors on the phone and talking and saying names out loud is really helpful, especially for first-time authors who haven't been through this kind of publication process before."

The process goes much the same way at Copper Canyon Press, the poetry publisher in Port Townsend, Washington, where publicist Laura Buccieri says her relationships with authors typically begin about a year before publication. "I usually set up a call or an in-person meeting with the author to get a sense of how they see the book and how the book came to be, to understand their hopes and dreams for the project," she says. But the line of communication doesn't flow only from the author to the publicist. Buccieri makes a point of saying that she tries to be transparent about her perspective, too. "I let them know how I see the book, *my* hopes and dreams for the project."

ACTION ITEM 45

Take a moment to start a list of people you know who might be useful in your publicity efforts. It's never too early to start thinking about your network of connections and making notes that might come in handy when you're meeting with your publicist down the road.

Communication and Collaboration

Talk to any publicist long enough and these twin themes emerge. It's worth pausing here to consider what can be a difficult shift for a first-time author to make. You've likely been working for years, in relative seclusion, on a project that probably feels like part of your body and soul at this point, so accustomed are you to thinking about it and working on it—one of the first things you think about when you wake up and one of the last things you turn over in your mind before falling asleep. But now you're on your way to making this previously private thing public, hopefully in a big way. You opened up enough to work with your editor on this book, but even that can feel like an intensely private relationship—no one knows this thing better than you and your editor—and now there is a publicist asking questions and you are expected to talk about it intelligently and carefully and to strategically consider how to get other people, strangers, to read it and care about it. It's a massive shift in thinking.

Varma is quick to try to alleviate any nerves that a first-time author might be feeling about this step of the process. "At that first meeting, especially for first-time authors, there can be some anxiety, but we really try to put them at ease and say, this is the just the beginning of a long relationship." And this long relationship—if it's to be a successful one—is characterized by an openness to not only share all your thoughts and feelings about the work but also to consider what your publishing partners are sharing. This requires a spirit of communication and collaboration on the part of the author, and, as Varma says, "thinking strategically about their connections, their background, and really having that sense of openness."

Broadly speaking, the initial conversation with your publicist—or publicity team—is designed to give them a better sense of who you are and how you relate to your book. They've already read your book and love it; now it's up to you to talk about how and why you wrote it, what personal and professional affiliations helped you write it, and whom you *know*, in every sense of the word. Your publicist wants to leave no stone unturned in terms of compiling a list of people who may be interested in your book. If you belong to any groups either locally or regionally, they want to know about them. Even if it's just your quarterly meeting of local amateur beekeepers, or an affiliation with your city's collective of professional doulas, or perhaps you're an alumnus of a writers workshop, or you were a fellow at a well-known writers retreat—anything that can be used to identify groups of people that can be targeted for special promotions or outreach. Maybe all these names will appear on a list of people who will receive an e-blast announcing your book's upcoming publication, or maybe they'll receive an advance reading copy. Your publicist will also have names to add to the list—"the big-mouth list," industry insiders call it. "Big mouths" are anyone in a position of influence—writers, editors, bloggers, and people with a large following on social media—to spread the word about a book. They're often on a list that the publicity department uses for a targeted mailing of finished copies of a book, sometimes accompanied by a personal note from the author or editor. The more people who learn about your book, the greater the chance it will start to generate word of mouth—and that is the name of the game. Word of mouth sells books. It's what causes customers to pause for an extra second or two and pick up your book on the New Releases table at their local bookstore and think to themselves, *I've heard about this book*. Word of mouth is what leads to a reader clicking on the Preorder button. It's what gets an editor to consider not just a review but also a feature-length magazine profile with a photo shoot and a line on the cover.

Another thing publicists are listening for and thinking about during this critical process is any part of your story—as a person, a writer, the author of this book—that can be framed and pitched to media outlets as a story worth covering. Also of critical importance is the subject or themes of your book, which can be similarly pitched to editors of magazines and newspapers, curators of websites and podcasts, and producers of radio and TV programs. So, if the protagonist of your novel happens to follow a similar trajectory as the nominee of a major political party in the next national election, for example, your publicist can pitch that in such a way as to be attractive to an editor or producer. "You can find so many nuggets of gold in impromptu conversation," says Varma. "We've had authors who stumbled on their strange and varied path to becoming a writer—they may have had a variety of really odd jobs . . . and that builds into a feature story. Maybe they were the only female carpenter in this tiny town, and suddenly that's another tactic one could take to pitch a feature story."

As all of this is making abundantly clear, your job isn't over when you hand in the final manuscript. Once you do, there's a whole phase of work that begins—work that can include more writing. "The writing doesn't end with the manuscript," Varma says. "In terms of publicity there are so many opportunities for original pieces, maybe an opinion piece, tying the book or the topic of the book to the current news climate— that could be a huge opportunity. On a more personal level: personal essays or literary criticism. There's a variety of original writing that can be done in support of a book. Authors may have had ideas or gone off on different tangents during the process of writing their book, and those pieces may not have made it into the book, but they should think about saving all that additional information because there may be another way to fold it into the promotion of the book that may form the nugget of an essay or a short story that could be placed elsewhere and tie in to publication."

ACTION ITEM 46

Consider the story behind your book and whether your background or the process of writing your book could be pitched to media outlets. Make notes and do some thinking about this before you meet with your publicist.

Nightboat's Abi-Karam says original pieces published online can be helpful for poets, especially those publishing with a small press, whose online profile may not be as large as their counterparts in prose. So think about writing a personal essay or a think piece and trying to place it in your favorite online journal, website, or blog. "That way if you get googled, you're visible as a poet and findable in some way," Abi-Karam says.

Throughout the process, the best thing an author can do is remain open to whatever opportunities present themselves. "Whether it's talking up their book at a cocktail party, or handing a friend in a book club their business card, or making sure they're staying on top of the news in case there's a breaking news story that relates to their own expertise, there's never an opportunity too small to pursue," says Sinesky Lovett. "Engaged authors are willing to do many things for their book but savvy enough to determine the best use of their time and energy."

Media outreach is one of the avenues a good publicity team will be exploring—and this often involves in-person meetings with editors and producers. Prior to each season a good publicist will reach out to their contacts and ensure that they know about their upcoming titles, often scheduling in-person meetings during which the publicist pitches each book, referring to the catalogue or, in many cases, copies of an ARC that they've brought along. In addition to media outreach there are events that might be planned, and those can run the gamut from a simple reading at a local bookstore to a regional author tour consisting of a number of events. This is where affiliation with organizations, especially ones with robust mailing lists and event spaces, can come into play. Conferences, festivals, bookfairs, reading series—all of these opportunities can and should be explored. Abi-Karam sees the author reading as especially fruitful, and each poet published by Nightboat gets a launch event in New York City, where the press is based, sooner or later, depending on where the poet lives.

While many small presses—and even many major publishers—do not have the resources to plan and pay for a reading tour, some, like Copper Canyon Press, will do what they can to ensure that your readings are successful. "If an author is touring, I try to make sure there are some local publicity hits along the route," says Buccieri. "As soon as the author has tour dates scheduled, I ask them to send those to me so I can get started pitching and making sure books are there. Same goes for festivals."

A FEW THOUGHTS ON ENGAGING READINGS

We've all gone to a reading with high hopes that we will be entertained and inspired—losing ourselves in the performance just as we are able to lose ourselves in a book—only to be a little disappointed as the author fails to live up to our expectations either because they're an awkward public speaker or they chose to read for an hour straight without interruption. It's a tough assignment for any author—to engage with an audience and hold their attention in a live, unpredictable setting. While there is no formula for an engaging author event, here are some general tips that will help you think about how to present yourself and your work on stages both big and small.

FIRST, LET PEOPLE KNOW ABOUT IT. Spread the word on social media well in advance. Post details for free on the Literary Events Calendar at pw.org.

MAKE SURE THEY CAN HEAR YOU. Whether it's making sure the microphone is on or speaking loudly so you can be heard over the espresso machine in the corner of the room, it's imperative that your audience is able to hear you.

PRACTICE, PRACTICE, PRACTICE. Pretend your dog is your audience. Read to your mirror. Do not let a public reading be the first time you ever utter the words in your book aloud.

ENGAGE WITH YOUR AUDIENCE. Break down the barrier between you and them. If they wanted only to engage with the words in your book, they could have stayed home and read it. Show them you're human. Share your personality. Don't get too hung up on the persona of capital-A Author and instead engage with them as a human being who is absolutely thrilled and honored to be standing in front of them and sharing this work.

LESS IS MORE. You may really want to read the entire first chapter of your novel, but if it's thirty pages, it's likely too long to keep your audience enthralled. Remember that they're probably sitting in chairs that aren't all that comfortable, it may be hot and stuffy, people do need to occasionally use the restroom, and it's just plain hard to follow along when you don't have the text in front of you—it only takes one momentary lapse of attention to lose the entire thread of your narrative.

LIFT THE CURTAIN. Let's be honest: Readings can be pretty dull. Instead of filling the whole time with reading, tell the story of your book: why you wrote it, what the purpose is, the challenges you overcame to finish it. Connect with your audience. Show them who you are. They didn't come to listen to an audiobook; they came to hear *you*.

STICK TO THE SCHEDULE. Never, ever go over the allotted time. The schedule is your contract with the audience; don't break it.

TRY TO HAVE FUN. If it looks like you're having fun, odds are your audience will have fun. If you're nervous, it's okay, let them know! They'll likely lift you up and encourage you. They're in front of you because they want to support you—let them.

BREAK THE ICE. Tell a funny story before you begin reading, or tell the story of the book's creation, or the story of preparing for the reading—anything that may allow the audience to identify with you as a person, as a writer, or a reader.

BE THANKFUL. Despite having a lot to do—probably something more important than listening to you—they are supporting you. Let them know you appreciate it.

DON'T SHOW UP EMPTY-HANDED. You better have copies of your book to sell. Coordinate with your publisher to make sure a bookseller is on hand or be prepared to sell your own. And don't forget to sign copies.

The first time reviewers, editors, producers, freelance writers, and book-sellers see your book, it will most likely be in the form of a galley or ARC. These are sent out months prior to publication so that coverage of the book can be considered in line with the production schedule of the magazine, newspaper, or radio program—and so booksellers have a chance to read the book, place orders, and be prepared to talk about it with (and recommend it to) their customers. Along with the ARC, publicists will include press mate-rials, which can take the form of a letter from them, a press release (see the sample press release for Jami Attenberg's latest novel on pages 358–59), or in some cases a letter from the book's editor.

This material—sometimes just a page long; other times several pages—includes the book's title, format, price, genre or category, the ISBN, the publication date, a short description of the book, the target audience, the author's biography, tour information, any special promotions, and perhaps some comparison titles. Also included are any advance reviews or praise that the book has garnered, contact information for the publicist, and sometimes a Q&A, typically done with either the editor or publicist, to give reviewers a sense of you as a writer and thinker. Sometimes the editor or publicist will write a personal letter to accompany the ARC, especially if they have a spe-cial connection to the book.

SAMPLE PRESS RELEASE SENT TO MEDIA OUTLETS

Houghton Mifflin Harcourt

FOR IMMEDIATE RELEASE

Contact: Taryn Roeder, Director of Publicity

A "Best of Fall" Book from

*BuzzFeed * People * Entertainment Weekly * USA Today ***
*New York Magazine * Vogue * Good Housekeeping * Woman's Day*
** AARP * Nylon * The Millions * Lit Hub * Bustle * PopSugar ***
*Bust * CBC * New York Post * The Observer * Newsday**

"Dazzling . . . A delectable family saga."
—*Publishers Weekly*, starred review

*"The novel takes place in one very long day but encompasses the
entirety of lifetimes. . . . Prickly and unsentimental, but never quite
hopeless, Attenberg, poet laureate of difficult families, captures the
relentlessly lonely beauty of being alive. Not a gentle novel but a
deeply tender one."*
—*Kirkus*, starred review

*"Attenberg writes with a deeply human understanding of her
characters, and the fact that, when it comes to family,
things are rarely well enough to leave alone."*
—*Booklist*, starred review

ALL THIS COULD BE YOURS
A Novel
JAMI ATTENBERG

From *New York Times* best-selling author **Jami Attenberg** comes a sharp, funny, and emotionally powerful novel about a family reuniting at the deathbed of its patriarch. **ALL THIS COULD BE YOURS** (On-sale date: October 22, 2019), HMH's lead fall novel, is the drama of *Big Little Lies* set in the heat of a New Orleans summer.

Power-hungry real estate developer Victor Tuchman was, by all accounts, a bad man, and he is dying. Strong-headed lawyer and daughter Alex Tuchman wants the truth about her father. She travels to New Orleans to be with her family, but mostly to interrogate her tight-lipped mother, Barbra. Attenberg's tightly written and epic story reveals Victor's wife, son, and daughter-in-law reckoning with the impacts of his secret past, to see if they can rebuild and begin anew.

In **ALL THIS COULD BE YOURS** Attenberg is charting the course of a family—and the Tuchman clan overflows with secrets and misdeeds. In looking at this family, we also see our society as a whole: the things we overlook and sweep under the rug, the men we celebrate, the money we chase. Like the Tuchmans we all want to know where we can find forgiveness—and where we can't—and how these insights can illuminate the future.

Jami Attenberg is the *New York Times* best-selling author of six novels, including *The Middlesteins* and *All Grown Up*. She has contributed essays to the *New York Times Magazine*, the *Wall Street Journal*, the *Sunday Times*, and *Longreads*, among other publications. She is available for interviews and will tour to **New York, Boston, Washington, DC, Chicago, Los Angeles, San Francisco**, and of course **New Orleans**, where she lives.

ALL THIS COULD BE YOURS: A Novel
By Jami Attenberg; On-sale Date: October 22, 2019; Price: $26.00; Pages: 304
ISBN: 978-0-544-82425-6

Considering a Freelance Publicist

Whether or not you have the pleasure of working with an in-house publicist in the lead-up to the publication of your book, you may want to consider hiring a freelance publicist who will be able to either work with your existing publicity team on a more expansive campaign (or a more targeted one, depending on your situation) or provide some much-needed promotional power if you're going it alone. It is important to note, however, that in order for this step to be worthwhile, you should not hire a publicist anywhere near your publication date. Instead, you need to decide a good six months prior to that date. To assess whether a freelance publicist is right for you, it's essential that you put some time into carefully considering your position and what your goals and aspirations are as an author. Certainly, you should talk to your agent, if you have one, as well as your publisher, about this question. "I always make a point of telling both the author and the agent, talk to your publisher and communicate with them—and let me know what they say," says Michael Taeckens of Broadside PR. "Most of the time it works out well, because in-house publicists are so overworked that typically they welcome having an extra member of the team—if they know it's somebody who has a good track record and is very communicative and plays nice." Taeckens has proven to be all these things, having worked with clients such as Nicole Dennis-Benn, Natasha Trethewey, Leslie Jamison, Mark Doty, Kevin Young, Luis Alberto Urrea, Ada Limón, Tom Perrotta, Max Porter, and many others. "When I take on a project it has to be something I not only feel passionate about but also that I feel like I can get a lot of publicity for," he says. "I can see different ways in which I can pitch the book and the different kinds of media that would be interested in the book."

But how do you know whether you even need a freelance publicist? There is no simple answer, of course, because everyone is at different points in their careers—but here are some general points to consider:

1. Unless you're a household name, or at least a name that is familiar to the book-buying public, your publisher will likely have somewhat

limited resources to devote to your book. In the case of a Big Five publisher, keep in mind that yours is one of a dozen or more books that a particular imprint is trying to promote in any given season. So, unless your book has been identified as a lead title—and if it is, you'll know—and unless great things are already happening for you, it's likely there is more that can be done for your book.

2. Many small presses have very few staffers, often consisting of just one publicist working with an intern or two, or perhaps student volunteers. Some micropresses don't have a publicist at all. In this case, getting the word out about your book is almost entirely up to you (though it should be said that many micropresses exist, and even thrive, because of the nearly superhuman enthusiasm and energy of their founding editors or publishers, and many of them try as hard as they can to promote their press's titles).

3. Freelance publicists cost money. Many of them charge a minimum fee per month for a minimum number of months, and depending on the publicist, it would not be unreasonable to expect to pay at least $10,000 for their services. Michael Taeckens charges between $4,000 and $5,000 per month for a six-month campaign. Freelance publicists who specialize in authors published by small presses will likely charge less, but you should still expect to pay a significant amount of money for their services.

4. Do you have a compelling story to tell? The answer to this question is yes, of course, and if you have a book coming out it's probably because a publisher has recognized the appeal of that story. But does your book have a story? Is the story of your writing the book compelling? Does the subject of your book tie in to current events—cultural, political, environmental—in a way that is compelling to a significant number of people? If so, and you feel like your publisher's limited resources won't be enough to get this story out there, then a freelance publicist might be right for you.

5. Pay attention to whether the freelancer is offering publicity or marketing or both. Remember, marketing is, in general terms, paid

promotion such as advertising, whereas publicity is trying to get a reviewer, an editor, or a producer to promote your book for free.

If you've decided that you need—and can afford—a freelance publicist, how can you identify the right one for you? You'll want to do your research. Take a look at the clients the publicist has worked with in the past. Are they names you recognize? Do an internet search on the publicist's name and read everything you can about them. Most freelance publicists will have testimonials from satisfied clients, and those are important to read, of course, but search for complaints about that publicist, too. Ask other writers whether they've heard of this person. Maybe try to reach out to one of the publicist's clients and—very politely—ask for a quick opinion (just don't demand an answer; always be respectful of a writer's time).

Be wary of any publicist who guarantees specific results. Publicists can promise to do a specific set of things to promote your book, but they cannot guarantee how the world will respond to those things. The reaction to a pitch is beyond a publicist's control, but a good one will know whether a pitch is likely to resonate with a specific editor or producer. Publicists are only as good as their contacts at media outlets, so you'll want to ask questions about who they know. Also, carefully scrutinize the contract with your publicist; send it to your agent or lawyer and make sure you are aware of exactly what is expected of you and what you can reasonably expect from your publicist.

Social Media

Most writers fall into one of three camps: those who love social media, those who hate it, and those who spend half their time in the first camp and half their time in the second, depending on what's trending that day. "Some authors are naturals on social media; others abhor it," says FSG's Varma. "But any good publisher, any creative publisher, can work with that whole spectrum." Twitter, Facebook, Instagram, Pinterest, Tumblr, and all those social media apps and platforms with clever names—love them or hate them, they are powerful tools that put the power of promotion directly in the hands of an author. And all publicists, whether they are freelance or in-house, recognize their potential for powerful messaging. But as with any potentially powerful tool, it's important to know how to use it; otherwise, you could end up hurting yourself.

"I think the number one mistake authors make when it comes to social media is to say, 'Oh my book is publishing in four months, I guess I should set up a Twitter account.' It's not that it's too late, but if you want your Twitter account to be something that makes a difference in the publication of your book it's really something you have to do much earlier, because so much of social media, and especially Twitter, when it comes to literary publishing, is about community, and it's about being seen as somebody who engages with that community," says Taeckens. "A lot of authors make the mistake of getting on Twitter three or four months before the pub date and only sharing information about their book, and it becomes the equivalent of a spam channel—it's not going to make much of an impression, and chances are that people who follow you are probably going to mute you, if not unfollow you, if they see that all you do is talk about yourself and your forthcoming book."

ACTION ITEM 47

If you're not on Twitter, sign up now. Don't forget to create a username (or handle) that is as close to your name as possible. Few will likely remember if you tell them "Follow me on Twitter, @lu2938elleke" after your reading (unless your name is Lu2938 Elleke, of course).

The trick, then, is to not be tricky. It's fine to go on Instagram, Facebook, or Twitter and promote yourself and your forthcoming book—you'd be silly not to do that—but it can't be the only thing you do there. We've all seen it done, and it never fails to leave a bad impression. Instead, find a way of supporting your community that feels most natural. Maybe it's giving advice about some area of writing or publishing you feel especially equipped to weigh in on. Perhaps it's sharing quotes from novels or poetry collections. Maybe it's letting folks know about this or that opportunity—or all the great literary events that are always happening in your city. The point is not to avoid talking about yourself at all—sharing facets of your personality (the best ones) can be very attractive to your followers. And speaking of followers, follow all your heroes, follow all the authors you've read, all the ones you hope to read, all the literary magazines that have published your work, the publishers, the literary organizations, and so on.

"It's basically the equivalent of everybody being at a literary conference together," says Taeckens of the writing community on Twitter. "If you were at a conference, you wouldn't go up to people and just say, 'Hi my name is Fred and my book is this and da da da da.' A lot of what you need to do is interact with other people and comment on different things. It's really important to be seen as a good literary citizen, that you're helping lift up other authors, you're helping lift up literary organizations." Of course, it's also a personal platform, as is Facebook and the rest of them. Not to apply a formula to a mode of social interaction that resists one, but twenty-five percent about you and seventy-five percent about others is a pretty good split, according to Taeckens. "Don't make it a one-dimensional promotional channel; show the full you, the full dimensionality of your personality. And that will get you somewhere," he says.

TEN OF THE BEST WRITERS ON TWITTER

"I don't give my authors ongoing training on what you should do on Twitter, but I do tell them, 'Here's why it's important. Here are ten authors who use Twitter in really useful and engaging ways, and they all have completely different styles and voices.' And I do that to show that it can be a fun and creative thing," says Michael Taeckens of Broadside PR. "I not only suggest they check out their voices and how they're using Twitter but also to be sure to click on tweets and replies to see how they are engaging with other people."

Megan Abbott @meganeabbott

Hanif Abdurraqib @NifMuhammad

Alexander Chee @alexanderchee

Roxane Gay @rgay

Garth Greenwell @GarthGreenwell

Lauren Groff @legroff

Ada Limón @adalimon

Helen Macdonald @HelenJMacdonald

Celeste Ng @pronounced_ing

Jeff VanderMeer @jeffvandermeer

The main thing to keep in mind is that building an audience on social media—and with it a readership for your future books—takes time. Don't rush it; be patient. Cultivate your following. It's not going to happen overnight. There are real people on the other end of those tweets and posts— and if you treat them as such (if you mingle among them as you would attendees of a conference), they'll be more likely to respond when you have something you need to ask of them (like spreading the word about your book and maybe even buying it). And when that time comes—when you really do need to start ramping up your self-promotion, it's okay. It's common for authors to acknowledge to their followers that they're going to be putting their salesperson hat on more often in the weeks leading to and away from publication day, like "Howdy folks, apologies for the coming onslaught of personal and publication news but I'm really excited that my novel is coming out next month!" If you've put the time in on the front end and established your account as a multidimensional outlet for your personality and an extension of your supportive nature, odds are your followers will love the heavy period of self-promotion—and rejoice with you in your good fortune.

And after your book is published, after you've seen how your followers have supported you throughout the process, take the time to thank them— repeatedly. José Olivarez, whose debut book of poems, *Citizen Illegal*, was published by Haymarket Books in 2018 and was a finalist for the PEN/Jean Stein Award and a winner of the 2018 Chicago Review of Books Poetry Prize—it was also named a top book of 2018 by NPR and the New York Public Library—took to Twitter to thank his more than twelve thousand followers for their part in the book's success.

But don't expect too much. If you engage on social media with your expectations in check, you might just enjoy it. You might even truly feel

josé olivarez @_joseolivarez · Aug 11

it still blows my mind that almost a year later people are still reading and re-reading my book. i'm blown away. thank you

💬 14   🔁 14   ♡ 389

supported and lifted up when you need lifting up. And we all need lifting up from time to time. "Within the literary community I think by and large Twitter is a group of people who are really warm and caring and funny and creative and largely supportive of one another," says Taeckens. "Why wouldn't you want to be a part of that?"

GOOD THINGS CAN HAPPEN ON GOODREADS

Goodreads, the social networking site and app for readers that was launched in 2007 and acquired by Amazon in 2013, has become an incredibly powerful promotional tool utilized by authors and publishers alike. While anyone can create an account for free on the site and start cataloguing the books they've read and interacting with others on the site, published authors with a book that can be found in the site's powerful database can create an official author profile and use their profile page to promote their book and engage with readers. While authors can do something similar on Facebook and other social networking sites, Goodreads has proven especially effective for authors with books coming out. One such author is Celeste Ng, who joined the site well before the publication of her debut novel, *Everything I Never Told You*, to keep track of the books she'd read. When her own first book came out, she created an official author page, participated in online conversations, and answered questions from readers. Goodreads was so effective in helping to spread the word about her book, in fact, that her publisher, Penguin Press, made the site a big part of the promotional campaign for her 2017 follow-up, *Little Fires Everywhere*, raffling off galleys to Goodreads users and placing targeted ads on the site. "I think the site has helped people discover the book," Ng told fellow novelist Jonathan Vatner. "My sense is that it's an amplified version of friends recommending books to other friends."

Author Websites

There is no denying the potential power and reach of social media and other third-party sites, but if you're serious about publishing a book—or you have a book already scheduled for publication—you should consider launching your own website. "I think it's really an essential part of having a brand out there, just having a destination where people can read about you," says Taeckens. Even more important, it is a portal through which readers can buy your book, contact you or your representatives, and find out about your upcoming events. If you're working with one of the big publishers, talk with your editor or publicist about this—some of the large houses can offer help and guidance, and some will even offer some financial help. But these days an author website can be created for relatively little money, depending on what you envision.

If you've gone the traditional route, working with a publisher that is either large or small—or somewhere in between—your publisher will have a website that includes information about you and your book (some even have pages dedicated to each author), but it can still be beneficial to have your own website where people can find you, for search engine optimization (SEO) if nothing else. If you have your own website it will show up at or near the top of the search results for your name.

Here are a few things to keep in mind:

Domain Name: Before you start thinking too long and hard about what your site will look like or what it will contain, you need to choose and buy a domain name. Keep it simple. The most obvious domain is YourName.com. If that's not available—and you may be surprised at how often domain names have already been snatched up; all the more reason to consider this on the early side—try something like YourNameAuthor.com

ACTION ITEM 48

Search for the websites of some of your favorite contemporary authors. What do you like about them? What don't you like about them? How do they use art and other imagery to convey a mood or personality? Can you easily find a list of their books? Are there links to booksellers and online clips? What does their contact page look like? Take notes and compile a list of features that will one day be a part of your website.

or YourNameBooks.com. Or try a hyphen between your names. You want to avoid naming it around your specific book title, as ideally there will be more to come and you don't want to be forever known by your first book (unless you really do). There are a number of domain registration services out there: GoDaddy, Wix, and Network Solutions among them. Do some research and compare prices, terms, and expiration dates (you often need to renew the domain name every year or two). Some companies also offer to create an e-mail address associated with the website for an additional cost. (You've likely seen these somewhere: AuthorName@AuthorName.com.)

Website Design: You can either hire a web development company to design your website for what will likely be thousands of dollars, or you can choose a more do-it-yourself approach. There are a number of DIY website platforms from which to choose—popular ones include Wix, WordPress, Squarespace, Jimdo, and others. If you go this route you will also be able to update your website whenever you want. These services typically have templates you can choose from, all of which should have been designed with mobile optimization in mind. You don't have to break the bank on website design. If you want to have a complete hands-off experience—if you have a specific vision for your website and you want nothing to do with the actual creation of it—by all means pay someone to do it. But if you are on a limited budget and want control over the whole thing—and the ability to change it whenever you want—consider one of the DIY platforms. They can look every bit as good as the expensive ones.

Ingredients: You should have all the basic information about you and your book, of course, but beyond that, you should have anything you want on your website. Just keep in mind: This is your brand, your calling card, and first impressions are important. Here are the key ingredients:

- Author bio with at least one great color photo that can be easily downloaded by editors and producers who want to promote you and your book.
- List of books with high-resolution, downloadable jacket images, each linking to its own page that goes into detail about the book, including

summary, praise, publication date, format, page count, and so on. Each of these pages should include clear and obvious links to multiple retail outlets, including preorder buttons prior to publication.

- Contact information for you and/or your agent, publicist, and so on. Sometimes the author contact includes a form that readers can fill out and submit by clicking a button—especially useful if you're the kind of person who doesn't want your personal e-mail address shared around the globe. And be sure to include Follow Me buttons for your social media accounts. You want to make sure readers have every available access point so they can become fans and supporters of your work.

- Media page with excerpts from reviews, prepublication praise, links to online publications, and more.

- Upcoming events. Whether you have a full-on author tour with dates around the country or just one-off readings that you've been able to schedule, this list should include everything anyone needs to know, including date and time, location, address, etc.

- A blog—but consider this one carefully. A blog can be a great way to keep your website fresh and stay in regular contact with your readers, but think long and hard about whether you have the stamina to keep a blog current. Nothing will make a website look more stagnant than a blog post at the top dated three years ago. If you're going to have a blog—and this goes for the entire website—keep it current.

- Mailing list sign-up. If you want to stay in regular touch with your readers consider creating a newsletter (this is often a free service offered by the DIY platforms) that you can send to your readers either on a regular basis or when you have special news for them—like an upcoming book. When readers sign up, they'll be giving you their e-mail address, which is also valuable information for your publicist to have.

As with all things publicity and promotion, keep your publicist and/or marketing team apprised of your activities. Remember: Collaborate and communicate.

JENNIFER ACKER ON PROMOTING A BOOK AS AN AUTHOR WITH A DISABILITY

In all writers' lives there's an inherent tension between the public and private. We spend months and years dreaming and crafting largely in solitude and then one day everyone knows about our once-secret imaginings. This is at once an explosion of joy and validation (I wasn't just practicing my penmanship all those years) and a source of shame (what if people think I'm weird/aggressive/unhappy/sentimental/crude/delusional like my characters?). To the exposed-nerve process of publishing we masochistically add readings, putting not only the writing but also the writer in front of audiences. Neither the book nor the author is ever perfect, and so there's solid reason for apprehension and awkwardness. This was true for me as well, but for additional, unexpected reasons.

When it came time to plan a tour for my debut novel, at the end of a ten-year journey of writing and revising, I wasn't particularly nervous about public speaking; I've appeared before audiences of all shapes and sizes as a teacher and editor for more than a decade. Instead, I was worried about my body. Not how it looks—it looks fine. But therein lies the problem. I look normal, but below the surface dark forces are at work. I have an invisible chronic illness, and it affects me every day. It affects what activities I can do, in what order, and how many of them. It affects what I eat, when I eat, where I go, how long I stay, and how I get there. While I can't say I was ever a highly flexible or spontaneous person, I used to be an active and adventurous one. I ran, I canoed, I hiked; I traveled to distant places and walked all over them. When I was seventeen, I lived in a mud hut in Kenya and traveled solo across Mexico. At thirty, I launched and learned to sustain a new literary magazine on hope, good faith, and adrenaline. My whole life I ate whatever I wanted: I liked the spicy, the untried, the raw; the stronger smelling, the more exotic, the better. While the demands of adult life often curb our adventures, most people retain their independence. What they do, whether it's commuting to work, taking care of children, or visiting friends, they do on their own and without much thought about their physical ability to do them.

After I got sick five years ago, much freedom and flexibility were stripped from me. I have myalgic encephalomyelitis/chronic fatigue syndrome (ME/CFS), a disease largely under the radar and poorly understood. It took two years to be diagnosed. People with ME inhabit a range of prognoses—from complete recovery to years of being bedridden—and a similarly frustrating range of symptoms, including profound fatigue unrelieved by rest, immune sensitivity, GI disturbances, sore throat, unexplained muscle and joint pain, headaches, and difficulty thinking and remembering. In the beginning I suffered from all of these; these days, it is primarily the headaches and the fatigue. Sometimes the sore throat and the achiness if I get run-down or overexert myself. Within the last year, the cause of the fatigue has been pinpointed as something called "preload failure" in the right ventricle of my heart. This chamber doesn't maintain enough pressure to keep my blood circulating everywhere it needs to go. To keep the blood flowing, I take medication and adhere to a prescribed physiotherapy routine that incrementally increases my stamina. What all of this means for my public life is that I have to arrange my events and appearances very carefully. When it came time to plan my book tour, it suddenly seemed delusional that I would be able to visit several cities in the span of a few weeks when taking a shower often exhausted me. I needed a personal set of guidelines that would allow me to participate in the long-anticipated joy of publishing my first book while also setting realistic expectations.

A lot of these rules boil down to "plan ahead" and "ask for help." Simple, right? But when the new ways of doing things run counter to the deeply ingrained old ones, such rules need repeating. My close friends and colleagues know my situation, but it is embarrassing and awkward to tell strangers and professional acquaintances that you are going home from the party because there is no place to sit down. That you are not as fine as you look, and you need their help. So I inscribe these notes here not only as reminders to myself, but as encouragement and support to all those who are limited by forces beyond their control. As a reminder of what is still possible, even if you used to do things differently, and on your own.

1. **Ask yourself these questions.** When does the event start, and how far ahead of time do you need to be there, to reassure your host and to rest, relax, and prepare? How will you get there, and how long will it take? What time will the event end? When will you eat? Where will you eat? Whom will you eat with? How will you get home and by what time do you need to leave to get a good night's rest?

    A book tour is a wonderful opportunity to escape the tedium of your own head, reunite with friends and family, and commune with readerly strangers. But often there are more people you want to hang out with than you have energy to talk to. A too-long or too-lively conversation before an event could tire you out for the reading, which really is a full-throttle performance complete with bad lighting and sweating. So, allot no more than an hour for dinner, and ask a few select friends to meet you at whatever restaurant is closest to the venue. Map locations in advance, making sure the distance is no more than a five-minute walk. Plan transportation down to identifying the subway stops with elevators.

2. **Make accounts with Uber, Seamless, Grubhub,** or whatever newfangled come-to-you conveniences exist in your area. Uber, you are loathsome for the damage cars do to our atmosphere, the unpredictable presence of nauseating air fresheners, and the way you treat your workers, but for someone who can't walk for more than a few minutes at a time, you are close to a miracle.

3. **Don't overschedule.** Plan rest days between events, and between events and travel. Maybe this means not traveling on the day of an event—getting in the night before and/or staying a night extra. Maybe it means limiting extracurriculars on the day of an event—as in limiting your activities to staying on the couch and reading, or listening to an audiobook if your

head hurts, catching up on e-mails, and pretending to stay off Twitter. Sometimes you can meet friends or family for a meal. Sometimes you find a gym to do your prescribed physiotherapy. Sometimes not. Don't plan anything that can't be easily canceled. Know you are fortunate to have the resources to cover an extra night away as well as a flexible job.

4. **Ask your host for what you need.** Learn from experience. Maybe your very first book event, in front of your hometown crowd, sprouted butterflies in your belly and threw your body into overdrive, causing your heart to race and pound throughout the fifteen minutes you were standing, leaving you with a week's worth of the peculiar soreness and post-exertional malaise that comes with your condition. After that, you ask your hosts, at bookstores, universities, and community centers, to provide a chair and a microphone, no matter how intimate the venue.

5. **Ask your host for what you need, Part II.** Sometimes you ask in advance but there are curveballs. For example, an otherwise wonderful bookfair provides golf carts to transport writers and moderators to the venue, but forgets to provide them for the way back. When you ask a T-shirted staff member if you could get a cart back to the hotel you're told, "The carts are only for people with disabilities." Then you screw up your courage and say, face reddening, starting to sweat, "I *have* a disability," and he apologizes and arranges a cart for you right away. If people know what you need, they will usually try to help.

6. **Skip the party.** This is some tough love advice. Because you like parties. You like drinking. You really like dancing. But maybe you can't do any of those things right now, and noise and shouting bother you more than they used to. As do bratty children, people talking on cell phones in train cars, anyone who says *bro*. . . . Maybe your disability is Being Over Forty? It can be painful to eat dinner by yourself at a mediocre hotel bar, or in your room, because everyone else is doing trivia at the lit crawl, so just remind yourself that there's always something on Netflix, and no one is there to see how much guacamole you eat with your tacos.

7. **Ask your friends to come to you.** This can be hard at big conferences and bookfairs especially, when everyone is overstretched and

overwhelmed, but it's moving and heartening how many friends will come to you if you simply ask and are honest about how you're feeling. When you're young and healthy, you can go out of your way for people, get to their readings at 10:00 p.m. on the other side of town. When your heart isn't pumping properly, you cannot. A lot of people have something they're working around, it's just that some excuses are easier to say out loud, like the ones you often hear from parents: The kid isn't sleeping, the babysitter fell through, the kid will throw brussels sprouts at the waitstaff and blow snot bubbles into your drink. You hope people understand that you wouldn't ask if you didn't have to, and that you wish you didn't have to ask. If they don't, they are not your close friends for now.

8. **Know your limits; and learn how to cancel if necessary.** You've had frequent migraines for nearly twenty years, but they've worsened with your illness. You've learned to do book events with lightning bolting through your head because the distraction of reading and conversations is better than a dim room full of regret. But if it's one of those migraines with nausea, you must cancel. Or else you will throw up on the floor. You hate not being unfailingly reliable. You worry your community will lose faith in you. But then you compare your excuse with those of others: sick kid, elderly parent hospitalized, car accident from sexting your husband. Illness is surely no more embarrassing than any of these.

9. **Get a wheelchair.** When you book a ticket, ask the airline for a wheelchair. Maybe you don't need a chair to board the plane, but you do need it to cover the long distances between gates and terminals. You nicely get picked up near the ticket counter and wheeled all the way to the gate. The pushers ask if you need to use the restroom, or to pick up something to eat. But still, you have to ask questions. Like, *How do I get out of here?* Maybe you have been dropped off in baggage claim near your suitcase, but far from the exit for ground transportation. Or maybe you encounter an asshole, someone from that airline who looks at you, disbelieving, and says, "Why don't you just walk?" Again the red face, the heart pounding, the embarrassment, the frustration. You want to punch him. Other times you are humbled by your wheelchair experiences, aware

of how other people look at you, with both curiosity and indifference. You pass an elevator line of dozens of veterans, men in their nineties flown to the nation's capital for free to see the monuments. One old man waves to you in general friendliness or solidarity, and you wave back. Remember that your pushers are usually immigrants and some of the lowest wage-earners at the airport, so don't forget to tip.

10. **Do one extracurricular, if you can.** Because you need to steward energy for the essential, work trips and book tours can become both monotonous and isolating if you spend too much time in the three As: Airbnbs, airports, and air-freshened cars. In the past, you would've gone for long walks, visited unfrequented neighborhoods, chosen interesting restaurants as destinations. Spent some portion of time on your own to absorb the rhythm, observe the people, maybe scribble in a notebook. Now, because you rely on friends and family to travel with you, you are rarely alone in the world, and if you are with company for too long, you will lose your mind. You were raised as an only child in the Maine woods, and writers are solitary creatures. So occasionally, try to do one thing, maybe a very simple thing, to remind yourself what's important to you beyond your profession.

　　One week it's a museum. The Tintoretto exhibit at the National Gallery. Excuse yourself early from lunch at the house of your mother's friend to take a nap on the friend's couch, to gather some reserves. Then take an Uber and spend an hour doing the museum shuffle, gazing at luminous faces staring out from shrouded backgrounds, eyeing the marvelously detailed brushstrokes, being mesmerized. True, you won't actually be alone, but museums foster silence and introspection, which are your most natural states. All the standing might wipe you out, but that's okay. It feeds you in a different way, and following the rules above, you haven't planned anything else for the next twenty-four hours before the reading, so afterward you can just lie around, listen to music, order in, and go to bed early.

11. **Ignore conventional wisdom.** It may not apply to you. "Pushing through it" is rubbish advice. So is "Take every opportunity, do everything

possible." You are not a slave to a schedule. This is life, not a factory, and lives are not measured by productivity.

12. **Don't be afraid to look a little ridiculous.** Usually you look put together, although in the last few years you've adjusted your style to accommodate tired days of tunics and leggings, which you used to think of as clothing for lazy people and your friends now call your "invalid chic." But now you're told that compression garments aid your circulatory system by pushing blood back up from your feet, legs, and abdomen. So you wear them: an abdominal binder under large sweaters, or tall black knee-highs with neon accent colors. You wear them always at home, and sometimes, with a long day ahead, or in the heat that exacerbates your condition, you also wear them with skirts, leggings, and other unlikely or unfashionable combinations. You look weird, but maybe it's time people knew how strange you really are on the inside.

13. **Bring your mom.** It's hard at first, taking your mom up on her offers to help. To drive you places, run your errands, especially when you know she cares too much for others and not enough for herself. Yet you need her for some of your trips. To fetch breakfast foods from Trader Joe's, to scout the shortest path to the subway stop, and to refuse to take it personally when you snap at her in frustration. She and your husband drive you to and from events, expertly catching your *I'm tired and need to go home now* glances. (Some trips you do manage on your own, successfully, even if those trips are harder, more tiring, but you keep your family's counsel in your head and build in rest days on the other side.) It doesn't always feel good to have your white-haired, seventy-three-year-old mother pushing you and all your bags in an overloaded wheelchair through airport terminals, though you both giggle when she's mistaken for an airport official and is asked for directions from travelers with all manner of international accents. You try to remember your friends with kids who travel with their mothers, and no one seems to think that's shameful. (How else are today's iPad children going to learn eye contact and table manners if their grandmothers don't teach them?) Also, everyone should be so lucky to have a mom like yours. When you tell her that the day of

your book launch was the happiest day of your life, she looks at you and beams. She says, "It was the happiest day of *my* life." When you later tell this to your husband you make sure to emphasize, as any good editor would, that the book launch was only *one* of your all-time happiest days.

And now, at the end of the first round of the book tour, having avoided colds and flus and serious fatigue setback, and with another year's worth of events ahead, and feeling, some days, a little stronger, you know that there are good, and perhaps even better, days ahead. You will savor them, even if they are not what you once imagined.

JENNIFER ACKER *is the founder and editor in chief of* The Common *and the author of the debut novel* The Limits of the World. *Her short stories, essays, translations, and reviews have appeared in Amazon Original Stories, the* Washington Post, *Literary Hub, n+1, Guernica, the* Yale Review, *and* Ploughshares, *among other places. Acker has an MFA from the Bennington Writing Seminars and teaches writing and editing at Amherst College, where she directs the Literary Publishing Internship and LitFest. She lives in western Massachusetts with her husband.*

IV

TWENTY-TWO

Surviving Success and Failure

No matter how consciously or carefully we articulate them or even acknowledge them in our daily lives, we've all internalized ideas of success and failure to such a degree that they are indelible features of our own literary landscape. One of the challenges of navigating these slippery slopes and dark valleys is that we tend to map them, or at least formulate responses to them, in absolute terms, as if success and failure were two different countries, on the shores of which we arrive after much hard work. Congratulations, you've arrived in Success, take a load off! Or: Welcome to Failure, here's your shovel. Ask any writer who has just published a book, or won an award, or cracked the bestseller list. Talk to any writer who has received the ubiquitous sheaf of rejection slips (or folder of rejection e-mails) or whose novel was just crucified by a critic. Success, however you define it, is great; failure, whatever that means to you, is not. But both of these empires are built on shifting sands. Success, as they say, is fleeting, but so is failure.

But there we go again with those absolute terms. So, what do we really mean when we talk about failure? Before we go any further, we need to acknowledge that much depends on the context in which this question is asked. After all, there is a very real difference between "failure" for writers who are relying on writing for their livelihoods, whose sense of safety and well-being, and perhaps the security of their families and loved ones, depends on it—and those who are able to be a bit more idealistic in their perspectives. We would do well to remember this when we consider just how painful the sting of rejection, how bright the glow of accomplishment.

F Is for Failure

Throughout your life as a writer you will encounter many challenges—so many ways to fall flat on the page and in the marketplace. You already know this. Anyone who has tried to convey in writing a thought, a feeling, an idea, a scene—the simple way a single slant of light in the corner of a room on an early summer Sunday morning makes dust motes sparkle like winter's first snow—knows just how difficult it can be. And anyone who hits Submit on a submission that's been nine months in the making only to receive a boilerplate rejection e-mail the very next day can relate. Despite how it feels in the moment, however, we wouldn't really want it any other way—at least in the early going—because in the face of adversity writers grow, they learn, they adapt by pushing their craft, refining and revising and polishing, until they overcome whatever is in their way—or they find a different way. The way you respond to these challenges and setbacks says a lot about you as a writer and as a person, and a healthy attitude about the inherent challenges of the writing life will allow you to avoid an endless cycle of negativity.

Aimee Nezhukumatathil says her poem "Sea Church" was rejected nineteen times before a revised version—she made minor tweaks along the way—was accepted by *Poetry* magazine. "Just goes to show: Be humble—be willing to edit and revise—but also to not give up and to believe in yourself even when it seems bleak," she adds. One could argue that those rejections were a necessary route to the eventual acceptance. That's not failure. It's progress. And "Sea Church" is now a part of Nezhukumatathil's fourth poetry collection, *Oceanic*, published by Copper Canyon Press in 2018.

Over the years we've spoken with countless authors in various stages of their careers, and they've all talked about the various challenges and setbacks that can all too often be lumped together as capital-F Failure—rejection, poor sales, bad reviews, unfinished manuscripts, and so on. We've heard from a crowd of writers on social media who tweet of similar "failures." But let's try to put those negative results into perspective.

The kind of failure we're talking about here doesn't fall under any hard-line definition of the word—as in, you have failed; you are a failure—but rather a local type of failure, specific to an individual project. A failure to live up to either our own or others' expectations, for example, whether it's those of the publishing industry or our readers. But here's the thing: We're writers, which means that by definition we are creators (which is a hell of a great thing to be, by the way), so as long as we are creating in some way—no matter the external or internal responses to the creation—there's really no such thing as failure, is there? Challenges yes, setbacks definitely, specific failings, okay. But you have not arrived in Failure.

"The problems of failure are problems of discouragement, of hopeless-ness, of hunger," said Neil Gaiman in his 2012 commencement address at Philadelphia's University of the Arts—the so-called Make Good Art speech. "You want everything to happen and you want it now. And things go wrong." But things going wrong, Gaiman would certainly agree, does not constitute failure.

"Failure is part of the process, and you have to trust the process," says poet January Gill O'Neil. "There's something to be learned from each rejec-tion, each project that didn't quite work out. Bad writing is still writing. Failure is still a necessary evil and a powerful teaching tool—but it doesn't define me."

This is a good time to dispel a myth that is frequently tossed around as truth. While nothing was ever written without a significant amount of time spent, you know, *writing*, you should not feel a constant sense of guilt if you're not in that chair writing at every available moment of every day. Reading about career authors and how they're able to plant themselves in the writing chair every day can be inspiring, but it can also give beginning writers the impression that everyone works that way. Or that everyone should *want* to work that way.

We also need to guard against the assumption that if you don't keep a rigorous writing schedule you must not want it enough, that you must not be serious about writing if you aren't dedicating a set number of hours to the act of writing. This is nonsense. It ignores the reality for many of us—the reality that is composed of varying levels, degrees, and amounts of responsibility, of inequality, of privilege, of access. Your level of passion and commitment to writing is not commensurate with the number of hours per day/week/month that you write.

Being a writer is about more than just writing. There's a reason we refer to it as "the writing life." An important part of being a writer is living—and truly living is not being chained to a desk staring at a computer at the expense of lived experience. "When I was young I led the life I thought writers were supposed to lead, in which you repudiate the world, ostentatiously consecrating all of your energies to the task of making art," says former U.S. poet laureate and award-winning poet Louise Glück. "I just sat in Provincetown at a desk and it was ghastly—the more I sat there not writing the more I thought that I just hadn't given up the world enough. After two years of that, I came to the conclusion that I wasn't going to be a writer. So I took a teaching job in Vermont, though I had spent my life till that point thinking that real poets don't teach. But I took this job, and the minute I started teaching—the minute I had obligations in the world—I started to write again."

So, live a little off the page—in the end your readers will thank you for it. "Creativity arises from playfulness, not from relentless concentration," says Helen Phillips, author of the novel *The Need*. "Insight will arrive during a walk or a shower or a tumble on the floor with my kids; while I'm scrubbing the toilet or strolling around the visible storage gallery at the Brooklyn Museum or reading a science article or going through airport security. When I'm in an idea drought, I try to experience as many random things as possible. I want unfamiliar scenes and sounds clattering around in my head. I want to be catapulted out of my own clichés. I want to have a sense of myself more as a human than as a writer. Being in a situation that interferes with my writing time often breeds ideas. I'll be visiting extended family for a week, forgoing my writing hours, and that's when the ideas start to hit. I'll have epic dreams every night, and I'll become desperate to get back to writing, to play around freely in the mud; I'll feel again that old urgency that is the basis of any good writing I've ever done."

"The feeling that the work is magnificent, and the feeling that it is abominable, are both mosquitoes to be repelled, ignored, or killed, but not indulged."
—ANNIE DILLARD

But what about quitting—as in no longer writing? Is that failure? There have been plenty of famous authors who made the decision to stop writing: Think of Philip Roth, who decided to stop writing in 2012, six years before he died, or Alice Munro, who said it's better to retire on a high note (and we can all agree that winning the Nobel Prize, as she did in 2013, is a high note). No one in their right mind would label them failures. And even someone who isn't a famous author and who decides to stop writing—for whatever reason—can't be considered a failure. Maybe the fire inside just goes out for some people; that's not a failure, it's a decision—or perhaps a realization. Now, if one still wants to write, and is able to write, but doesn't? A writer who doesn't try?

"The only kind of failure that matters is giving up; the failure to keep listening to and honoring and checking in with whatever wild impulse and voice brought you to this path to begin with," says poet Tess Taylor, the author of *Rift Zone*.

The "Loser" List

Let's try a simple exercise—just to flesh out what it is we're talking about here and put our "failings" as writers into perspective. Let's make a list of what we might possibly mean by "failure."

- Trying and failing to come up with or execute an idea
- Struggling with a specific element of a writing project—the fourth chapter, the second stanza, or a turn in the personal essay
- Getting rejected—by an editor or an agent
- Not winning the contest or receiving a grant or award for which you submitted your work
- Missing a deadline
- Getting a "bad" review
- Getting few reviews
- Giving a "poor" performance at a reading or on a panel or talk, however you qualify that
- Not being invited to give a reading or be on a panel or deliver a talk
- Any of the countless permutations of problems that arise when you write—everything from a line of poetry that doesn't sing to an ineffectual plot device to a tone-deaf point in an essay

This is by no means an exhaustive list; there are plenty of others. But all these things are either part of the job of being a writer and can be navigated, avoided, or fixed; or they are a result of external judgments (of an editor or an agent or, quite literally, a judge) that may be completely out of your control. And if you've encountered a setback or challenge that either you can turn around or overcome—or that is completely out of your hands—you can't consider that a failure, can you? To return to an earlier point: We are creators, and if we're creating, no matter the reaction to your creation, one could argue—and we are—we're right on track.

Kevin Wilson, the author of two story collections and three novels, including *Nothing to See Here*, says literary culture can too often make us feel like there is one way of doing things, and if we don't succeed in a certain way, of course we feel like we've failed. "In the world of writing we're constantly

ACTION ITEM 49

Revisit your folder (or shoebox) of rejection e-mails or slips. Note how they represent just one person's opinion or judgment. Consider counting them up and posting your total on social media—always a crowd favorite—with an uplifting message of resilience in the face of rejection.

told that you *need* to find an agent, the implication being that nothing good will ever come of your writing if you don't find an agent," he writes. "We're told that if your first book doesn't sell, you'll probably never get another chance, because the book world is run by sales numbers and there's less interest in growing a writer's career. We're told that you need publications to be taken seriously. And that's fine; I think it's good for writers to have some sense of the business behind writing. But the real focus should be on the writing itself, the work you're either making or not making."

> *"Ever tried. Ever failed. No matter. Try*
> *again. Fail again. Fail better."*
> —SAMUEL BECKETT

Failure Is Forever

Failure is not something experienced only by beginning and emerging writers, of course. No matter how accomplished you are, no matter how many accolades you collect or how much money you make, failure is only one step behind you. This isn't meant to be a depressing notion, or a pessimistic approach to the writing life. Instead, it should give us no small amount of confidence—after all, we're walking the same line as that of our literary heroes!

But, okay, those famous authors whose books are on our shelves may not be toiling in obscurity like many of us. They might be collecting royalty checks while the rest of us are catching the 7:30 a.m. train or warming up the pickup at dawn in order to arrive on time for our nine-to-five job. That distinction is real (although the dream of being a writer who sits around collecting royalty checks is just that, a dream), and again, context counts for a lot, but the point is: The specter of failure doesn't buzz off just because you achieve some success.

Jonathan Lethem is a MacArthur ("Genius") Fellow and the best-selling author of nearly twenty novels and collections of essays and stories, but he started out like so many authors—writing in obscurity and struggling to break into publishing for years. For ten years, in fact, while living in Berkeley, California, and working at two of the area's iconic bookstores, Pegasus and Moe's, he wrote and revised and submitted his work to little or no success. "I was just dreaming in the dark," he says of those days. "And I love that time now in retrospect. I love the freedom I found in that anonymity—the hunger I felt to connect was extraordinary, and every day there was nothing back in my self-addressed stamped envelopes and my mailbox was empty, it felt like another eternity to me."

But then, in 1994, when he was thirty years old, Lethem published his first novel, *Gun, With Occasional Music*. That book, and the three that followed, sold steadily and were well reviewed, but it was his fifth novel, *Motherless Brooklyn*, published in 1999, that catapulted him to an entirely different level of success. It won the National Book Critics Circle Award for Fiction, the Macallan Gold Dagger for crime fiction, and the Salon Book Award; actor Edward Norton adapted it for a 2019 film starring Norton, Bruce Willis, and Willem Dafoe. And since that book was published, each of his subsequent novels—*The Fortress of Solitude*, *Chronic City*, *The Feral Detective*, and more—has solidified his status as a writer who, in the words of the MacArthur Foundation's citation, "heightens emotional engagement with his characters, blurs boundaries across a broad spectrum of cultural creations, and expands the frontier of American fiction." In other words, over the past twenty years Lethem has achieved a level of success that pretty much eliminates an entire category of possible failures that haunt the beginning, emerging, and even midlist author. "I have this incredible privilege, which I might even call a luxury, that on the strength of some of what happened to me in the first ten years of publishing . . . the chances are somebody will publish my novels until I drop dead."

Easy street, right? Isn't that what we're all working so hard to achieve, what we're all dreaming about? The creative freedom to write what we want to write, secure in the notion that a publisher will likely run with it no matter what? Well, sure, but just because Lethem's books are published "doesn't mean everyone is going to care about them," he says. Which brings us to a different kind of challenge, one that falls on the same line as the kind of failure we discussed earlier. No longer as dependent on agents, editors, and other "gatekeepers" to grant access to mainstream publishing, an author like Lethem must wrestle with a fresh set of concerns that has more to do with time and expectations—both his readers' and his own.

"I worked in bookstores, so I was always very aware of how there are a lot of books published that no one really cares a whole lot about," says Lethem, who now teaches at Pomona College in Claremont, California. He continues:

> And there's an ocean of writers who were fashionable, who were a flavor of the month for maybe a few months or even a few years, and then there's this unbelievable harvesting. Time is merciless. And I know this from so many different angles. I know this from putting remainder stickers on books and I know it from talking to younger readers in my classrooms and saying a name that I think of as canonical, like Robert Stone—I mean, he won the National Book Award—and their eyes just glaze over; they don't know who I'm talking about. The stuff that's rushing into the rearview mirror at any given moment is terrifying. And you know there comes a day . . . when you can feel that you are long past being anyone's flavor of the month. What do you do with being alive and writing and still feeling like you're getting better, but no one can pretend you're breaking news? It's like, "Oh yeah, okay, you wrote another one. That's very nice. There's another one of those."

Lethem talks about "the shrug"—the reaction of readers to work that conforms to expectations, that is pleasantly safe within the confines of what has come before it. He says he has always been very adamant that he didn't want to repeat himself, that he always wanted to push into new creative territory with each new book, that he didn't want to do things he already knew how to do. To be surprising, to find new ways to make a reader laugh and cry. "Early on that sounded pretentious because nobody cared what I was doing at all," he says. "Now it sounds pretentious because people are like, 'Oh come on, we all know what you do and it's really obvious,' which is fair enough. I have to write against that undertow of the implicit shrug. People are shrugging all the time. If you focus on that you could be crushed by it."

Still, Lethem acknowledges he's extremely fortunate to have had his talent recognized and supported the way it has been over the years. "I've had just such an amazing ride in so many ways and I try every single day to keep in mind how crazy it is that I get to walk around under that kind of nominal success—but it is nominal, it doesn't sink into your bones, it doesn't alter your sense of self unless it does so in really regrettable and idiotic ways. You are still just an insecure human animal who likes to try to make things out of words, and every day, if you're doing it for real, you wake up as confused and helpless and insecure as ever."

S Is for Success

The only way of guaranteeing success as a writer is to derive your definition of success from within, from the act of writing, rather than any external validation such as publication, praise, and prizes. It's fine and normal and healthy to pursue those things—let's call them the three Ps—but if they are our sole indicators of success, we're going to be setting ourselves up for . . . you guessed it—more failure. Here's Tess Taylor again: "The prizes, the world's notice, the outward trimmings, those come and go, and you're largely not in charge of them. The part of success you are in charge of is nourishing the voice that can help you go on." Just as there are challenges or setbacks (or failure) that we're not in control of, there are just as many things about success that are out of our hands.

"The moments when things that other people regard as success kind of come over you, whether it's someone telling you that you've won an award or been on some list or something, those are really intriguing, but they pass like weird dreams, and then your hunger to connect is always still with you," says Lethem.

"For a long time, I had trouble believing this, and you might not believe me, either, but the real joy's in the writing," says R. O. Kwon, author of the novel *The Incendiaries*. "None of the rest of it, no publication or public recognition, will bring you more joy than the act of writing itself."

Elizabeth Gilbert said some interesting things about the difference between success and failure after the publication of *Eat, Pray, Love,* her 2006 memoir about traveling alone around the world following a difficult divorce. In case you didn't hear: It did pretty well. Over twelve million copies have been sold worldwide; it has been translated into more than thirty languages. In a TED Talk she gave back in 2014, "Success, Failure, and the Drive to Keep Creating," Gilbert explained that the only thing she ever wanted to be in life was a writer. After college she got a job as a waitress at a diner and wrote—and wrote and wrote—and for six years she tried to get published and failed. Still she wrote. And still her writing was rejected. And the way she got through it was to keep writing. "I loved writing more than I hated failing at writing," she said.

Flash forward to 2010 and Julia Roberts is playing her in the movie adaption of her memoir. One of those celebrity websites estimated her net worth at $25 million. That's a level of success the vast majority of us will never taste. But Gilbert says she still relates to the writer she was when she was an unpublished waitress, not a mega-best-selling author. The reason, she learned, is because of the psychological similarities of experiencing great failure and great success in our lives.

So think of it like this: For most of your life, you live out your existence here in the middle of the chain of human experience where everything is normal and reassuring and regular, but failure catapults you abruptly way out over here into the blinding darkness of disappointment. Success catapults you just as abruptly but just as far away out over here into the equally blinding glare of fame and recognition and praise. And one of these fates is objectively seen by the world as bad, and the other one is objectively seen by the world as good, but your subconscious is completely incapable of discerning the difference between bad and good. The only thing that it is capable of feeling is the absolute value of this emotional equation, the exact distance that you have been flung from yourself. And there's a real equal danger in both cases of getting lost out there in the hinterlands of the psyche.

Gilbert's remedy was simple: She found her way back to the middle, to what she calls home, which she defines for herself—for anybody—as the one thing that you love more than you love yourself. For her that was writing. If you concentrate on the act and art of writing, she seems to be saying, you can more easily weather the storms of failure (rejection, criticism, disregard) as well as success (expectations, definitions, criticism).

WHAT IS YOUR DEFINITION OF SUCCESS?

It's all well and good to get perspective on success from someone like Elizabeth Gilbert, an author who has sold more than twelve million copies of her breakout book. But what about the rest of us? We took to Twitter to ask the big question: How do you define success for yourself? The following are a selection of responses:

"Scaring myself on the page. Giving everything I have. Writing up, above my weight—to an ideal imagined reader more intelligent, more wise, more compassionate, more illuminated, & more tender than I am. Everything else is ego & out of my control." —**Joy Castro**

"When the work I'm doing today is stronger, more daring, a bit deeper, tighter, more peculiar and surprising, more meaningful than the work I was doing six months ago." —**Dinty W. Moore**

"Success for me is creating something from nothing. It's adding a little beauty to the world or being part of a larger conversation. It's based on actions I can control—writing, submitting, helping another poet, finishing a manuscript—not on an outcome I can't control such as publication." —**Kelli Russell Agodon**

"When I'm challenging myself and working on what feels urgent and trying as hard as I can. Also, when I'm loving other writers, when I'm part of a larger conversation about books and keeping culture alive in these scary times." —**Sonya Huber**

"For me, if I can maintain that magic + wonder I felt when I got my first typewriter and wrote and 'published' my first novel (sold to my parents) + want to get up + do it every day, that's artistic success." —**Marie Myung-Ok Lee**

"The hardest part of the gambit, I think, of writing a novel is getting the final project to meet the lofty goals you set for the project. So for me success is: does the book look anything close to what I'd set out to write." —**Daniel Torday**

"If I have time to write and read poetry each day, to sometimes create a poem that resonates with someone else's heart and is beautifully crafted, to reach out and help another writer, that is success." —**Erin Coughlin Hollowell**

"If I get the opportunity in this life to occasionally use my imagination and channel that through writing. All the other things are noise. Books are nice but that's not success. Success is the gift of writing. And at my age, if I can help others, build community, that's success." —**Victoria Chang**

"I'm a short story writer, so if I defined success through money, I'd be a very sad human. Instead, I ask myself: Am I making progress? Have I published more, written things I think are better than things I wrote last year, continuing to challenge myself? Then I'm succeeding." —**Amber Sparks**

Playing the Game

On the first evening of the 2018 Kachemak Bay Writers' Conference in Homer, Alaska, Pulitzer Prize–winning novelist Anthony Doerr delivered a keynote that addressed in a really inspiring way some common notions of success as a writer. His perspective proved extremely useful for the dozens of beginning and emerging writers

ACTION ITEM 50

What is your definition of success? Take a moment to consider and then try to articulate what it is you hope to achieve. Maybe write it in the front cover of your journal as a reminder of what's important.

in the audience that June night. "In my thesaurus, believe it or not, the word 'success' is matched, amongst other groaners, to: *bestseller, megahit, winner, big name, superstar,* and—shiver—*celebrity*," Doerr said. "To succeed is to be desired. To succeed is to be celebrated. To succeed is to sell. But is that the sort of success we—and our children—should always chase? An equation that correlates higher levels of commercial success with higher levels of happiness suggests a graph that I've almost never seen come true in real life. Did selling lots of paintings make Mark Rothko happy? Did selling lots of albums make Kurt Cobain happy? Did selling lots of books make Hemingway happy? If we rely on extrinsic yardsticks to measure our success—if we count how many promotions we've won, how well we score on standardized tests, how many site visits we got, or how many followers we have, are we setting ourselves up to be our best selves?"

Doerr went on to propose a different approach to writing—one that we've probably all taken before, maybe when we were younger and just starting out or, if we're lucky, one we use to this very day—which is to think of writing as play. To get back to that feeling of being a dreamer and to write because it gives us pleasure, not because there is some specific outcome attached to it. And just because you experience failure doesn't mean you lose. You wait your turn and you keep playing the game. And if you experience success? The game's not over. You don't win at writing. You keep playing the game.

> Now, as a working writer who sits at a keyboard every morning, I have to remind myself every day that it is okay to accept failure—that language is only an arbitrary system of semblances and symbols, that languages live alongside living people, billowing around us in an ever-changing, naturally selecting cloud. Words mean more than one thing to more than one person, and they mean one thing one day and another thing the next. 'In practice,' as Bertrand Russell said, "language is always more or less vague, so that what we assert is never quite precise." And he was right. Can the word *tree* ever do any more than *approximate* the great shivering, growing, clattering, blooming, steadfast thing that is a tree? Can the word *marriage*

ever come remotely close to suggesting the fortifying, confusing, exhilarating journey that is a marriage? In the spaces between words and sentences and paragraphs lurk snags and silences and pits into which we all as writers inevitably must fall. You can never control all the possible outcomes of any sentence you write; the best you can do is to make the thing as carefully as you can, then let go.

R Is for Reading the Reviews

The ability to digest rejection is one thing—once you accept the fact that your poem won't be in the next issue of *Poetry* magazine, or that your essay is not destined for the Best American series next year, or that your dream agent will not be shopping your novel around to editors (*not yet*, anyway), you can mine that rejection for lessons, perhaps weighing any advice in the rejection letter (if you're one of the lucky few to have received more than just a curt no), or you can set it aside and forge ahead, maybe exploring new avenues. But once you move past rejection (for a specific project, anyway; writers never really move *beyond rejection*) and get something published, there's a whole different level of responses to digest. We're talking about critical and popular responses to your work. We often try so hard and focus so long on getting something published that we can forget there's a whole different realm of feedback on the other side.

Just as the way in which you respond to rejection says a lot about your constitution as a writer, the way you respond to a negative review or snarky comment on social media reflects just how deep your commitment is to your art. Will you be derailed by negativity, or will you learn something from it?

Some writers make a conscious decision to not read reviews, whether they're good or bad. This approach likely worked a lot better back in the day when authors could rely on a publicist or agent to collect clippings and either share them or not. But these days, when everyone is a critic and social media makes the dissemination of those opinions as easy as tapping your finger on glass, ignoring reviews can be difficult. When Angie Thomas, the author of *The Hate U Give* and *On the Come Up*, tweeted a reminder that authors have feelings and questioned why anyone would want to tag an author in a negative review, she unleashed a storm of criticism—and support—from the young adult book community. "We have to protect our mental space," she tweeted. "Too many opinions, good or bad, can affect that. . . . Getting feedback from too many sources can harm your writing process. I have a group of people whose feedback I value—my editor, my agent, other authors who act as beta readers. With the position I'm in, social media is for interacting with readers, not for getting critiques."

A year earlier, Lauren Groff, the author of three novels and two story collections, most recently *Florida*, tweeted a similar reminder. "You're entitled to your opinion, and to shouting it loudly. But tweeting it to a writer is like grabbing their cheeks and shouting it into their face."

On the other hand, fiction writer and creativity coach Shelly Oria says she knows writers who find reading reviews helpful. "You need to figure out what works best for you," she writes. "But I *would* argue that mindfulness is crucial with this: Check in with yourself after you read a review (even if it's a rave). See if you might need to talk to a friend, or if taking a kickboxing class suddenly seems super appealing. Stay in that kind of conversation instead of pretending that what you just read (again, good or bad—in some ways it's all the same) has not affected you. And even if you decide to follow the mainstream reviews, there is never, ever a reason for a writer to read the reviews of random people on the internet. Amazon, Goodreads, and certainly any and all comment fields are always 100 percent none of your business."

NAOMI SHIHAB NYE RECOMMENDS

Five Books of Poetry to Turn to When the Going Gets Rough

ASK ME: 100 ESSENTIAL POEMS OF WILLIAM STAFFORD, edited by Kim
Stafford
William Stafford always puts my head back on straight, even when it's really tipped.

THE ESSENTIAL W. S. MERWIN, edited by Michael Wiegers
W. S. Merwin's voice of attention and care is so crucial to our crazy moment—read just
one poem out loud, maybe twice, and feel your compass swing back to center.

DELIGHTS & SHADOWS by Ted Kooser
Ted Kooser is still my president—more than ever! Details, little things, wake up, world!

ODES by Sharon Olds
Sharon Olds's unadulterated, honest joy in praise feels like a cleanser after a few toxic
news reports.

POEMS TO LEARN BY HEART, edited by Caroline Kennedy
Regularly reading books like this to a three-year-old becomes a restful, delicious oasis.

NAOMI SHIHAB NYE *is the author and/or editor of more than thirty books, including*
19 Varieties of Gazelle: Poems of the Middle East, *a finalist for the National Book
Award, and* Honeybee, *which won an Arab American Book Award. She is the first
Arab American author to serve as Young People's Poet Laureate.*

TWENTY-THREE

Careers

Several times a year the venerable book-trade publication *Publishers Weekly* breathlessly reports yet another seven-figure advance for a debut novel by an unknown author. If you are yourself an unknown author at work on a debut book, you can be excused for thinking that untold riches await you once an agent and an editor fall in love with your work.

The cold reality, however, is that it's nearly impossible to make a living solely by writing books. While a handful of hardworking fiction writers, blessed with an outsized literary gift or an eye for the popular taste, do earn a steady income from royalties, the vast majority of prose writers, and virtually all poets, subsidize their creative practice with other, better-paying work. Which is another way of saying that if you plan to make a life writing poetry or literary fiction, you'll probably need a day job. The question is: Which day job? Or perhaps more accurately: Which day *jobs*?

Elaine Grogan Luttrull, the Columbus, Ohio–based CPA who works with artists and other creative people, uses a performing arts analogy to help her clients find a happy balance between making art and making rent. First, Luttrull says, there's your core artistic pursuit, which feeds your soul but only rarely pays the bills. In Luttrull's analogy, this central labor of love occupies the "starring role" in artists' lives, while the jobs that subsidize it fall into two categories: "supporting-cast work," which are jobs like copywriting or teaching that are related to your art but pay better, and "production-assistance work," which are jobs that have nothing whatever to do with one's art but can be relied on for steady income.

The key, Luttrull says, is to choose the mix that works best for you, rather than have your choices made for you by circumstances or lack of foresight. "Some people want all starring role and supporting-cast role work, and that's awesome," she says. "But I've worked with writers who say whenever they're writing something that they don't want to be writing, they're too tired to write what they want to write, so for them, the ideal mix is starring role and production-assistance work. You want a job where you don't have to tax the writing part of your brain so you can save that for your writing."

This chapter is for writers looking to explore jobs that fall into the category Luttrull calls supporting-cast work. We'll look at your prospects for finding full-time jobs in academia, publishing, and at literary nonprofits, as well as more part-time gig work in freelance writing and editing and delivering speeches. First, though, a few general themes stand out:

- Art isn't especially valued in our society, so the more overtly artful the work you're doing, the less it's likely to pay. If you're writing freelance, for instance, it's hard to get paid more than a nominal fee to write literary essays, but less glamorous freelance work like advertising and copywriting can offer something closer to a living wage. A similar rule of thumb is at play in publishing. While a few literary agents have forged lucrative careers representing literary fiction, most agents finance their more literary projects by taking on highly commercial books.

- Because literature is so rarely profitable, much of the work available to writers requires long apprenticeship periods where you're making very little money or none at all. This is especially true in publishing, where future editors, agents, and publicists build contacts and skills through years of assistantships and internships. But it's true in academia as well, which requires at least two years of graduate school, plus, for many writers, years of low-paid adjunct teaching before they can land a tenure-track job. Freelance writers, too, have to cut their teeth writing for smaller, web-based publications for little or no pay before they have the contacts and experience to write for better-paying print magazines and high-traffic websites.

- The gig economy has hit literary work, and then some. While MFA programs, publishing, and literary nonprofits offer full-time jobs, these fields are all to one degree or another outsourcing work to part-timers— adjuncts in academia, freelance editors in publishing, and consultants at literary nonprofits. Other fields open to writers, like freelance writing, are by their very nature gig-based, and in fact exist in large part because journalism and publishing are shedding full-time employees.

- These factors—the low pay, long apprenticeships, and unpredictable nature of the work—tend to skew the job market in literary professions away from people from less privileged backgrounds. A 2018 study by *Publishers Weekly* found that eighty-six percent of people working in publishing were white, while a survey conducted the same year by Americans for the Arts found that eighty-two percent of staffers at local arts agencies were white. These figures are slowly beginning to change as publishing and the nonprofit sector, along with academia and journalism, make a concerted effort to diversify, but the road to success remains steeper for writers of color and those from working-class backgrounds.

- Finally, even if you can't live on book royalties alone, the better your work performs in the marketplace, the more the *other* kinds of work you do will pay. This is most obvious in the freelance world, where critical acclaim can attract offers to write for glossy magazines and make lucrative speaking appearances. But critical attention and, yes, book sales matter in MFA programs, too, which depend on "name" authors to draw students to their programs.

If you're considering a career in a writing-related field, you need to know going in that the competition is stiff, and even once you find a job you like, you're not likely to get rich, but that obscures the reasons why writers go into these fields in the first place: The work is more engaging and fulfilling than most other kinds of paid work; it connects writers to other writers and the writing community at large; it allows writers to help fulfill a mission they believe in; and done right, it leaves writers time to focus on their writing.

Academia

University teaching is perhaps the most common career path for writers coming out of MFA programs. There's no great mystery why. If you're lucky enough to land a tenure-track job at a reputable MFA program, you can make between $50,000 and $65,000 a year to start, with a substantial bump after six or seven years if you make tenure. If you climb the ladder to make full professor at one of the more prestigious graduate writing programs, you can earn $200,000 or more a year. And, of course, professors can take their summers off to write.

But these are very, very tough gigs to get. Today, there are roughly 250 MFA programs and fifty PhD programs offering degrees in creative writing, but according to the Modern Language Association (MLA), which hosts a prime job posting site, there were just 119 openings for full-time jobs in creative writing in 2018, down from 195 in 2009. Thus, if creative writing programs graduate, on average, ten writers with MFAs or PhDs a year, the system is pumping out roughly twenty-five qualified applicants for each job opening.

Writers looking to go "on the market" for creative writing jobs can check online listings hosted by the MLA (mla.org) or AWP (awpwriter.org) as well as online sources like HigherEdJobs (higheredjobs.com) and Academic Jobs Wiki (academicjobs.wikia.org). Each posting is different, but nearly all require an MFA or doctorate in the genre the professor is being hired to teach. Some listings flatly require candidates have a book published or under contract while others refer more vaguely to "a significant record of original publication," but most jobs are out of reach for writers who haven't published a book or don't at least have one due out from a reputable publisher.

Given the dearth of tenure-track job openings, many writers start out as adjunct instructors or non-tenured lecturers teaching introductory creative writing and composition courses. Full-time lecturers can earn a reasonable salary—think mid five figures—and enjoy a degree of job security, but these positions remain relatively rare. Adjuncts, on the other hand, are hired on short-term contracts and are often poorly paid, sometimes scandalously so. According to a recent report by the American Association of University Professors, "earnings for adjuncts range from about $31,000 a year at top doctorate-granting universities to just $16,000 a year at community colleges."

Writers teaching full-time in MFA programs enjoy far better pay and benefits, but like all professors, they must publish or perish. Most creative writing departments expect new professors to have at least one book out before they're hired, and then, after five or six years, when the writer comes up for tenure, she has to publish another book or face the prospect of looking for a new job.

And whether you're an adjunct at a community college or hold tenure in a prestigious MFA program, teaching is itself hard work, requiring talent, dedication, and a genuine interest in students and their problems. Your summers may be your own, but for nine months of the year, teaching is a full-time job, and for those teaching in MFA programs, the rigors of the tenure process can make it a nerve-racking one.

"There are a lot of people who get into this work thinking it's not work and those folks usually are not successful," says poet A. Van Jordan, who directs the MFA program at the University of Michigan. "The people you see who are doing well and have had successful academic jobs and have been publishing, they got that way by showing up for work. I think that's something that's really not talked about enough."

The Publishing Industry

Say you're a young writer just finishing school. You love books and you know you have a long way to go before you can make money writing them. You want to earn a steady living and make professional connections as you hone your craft, so you figure you'll go straight to the source and find work at a publishing house or literary agency.

This line of thinking has sent waves of aspiring writers to New York City for nearly as long as there has been a publishing industry. If you follow that path today, however, you'll find a fiercely competitive market for jobs—one that's shrinking. Over the past two decades, according to the U.S. Bureau of Labor Statistics, the number of people working in book publishing has dropped from about 91,000 in 1997 to a little over 60,000 today, with the steepest dip coming in the wake of the 2008 fiscal crisis.

Because publishing jobs are scarce and highly sought after, people in the industry are highly educated and often underpaid, particularly early on when young editors, agents, and publicists pick up on-the-job training through internships and assistant positions. According to the employment website Glassdoor, editorial assistants in New York average about $39,000 a year, which sounds reasonable until you factor in the long hours most assistants put in and the city's exorbitant rents. Internships, which serve as gateways to assistant jobs, often pay very little, and sometimes not at all. (The Fair Labor Standards Act of 1938, or FLSA, states that any employee of a for-profit company must be paid for their work, but interns are not considered employees under the FLSA as long as the intern is the "primary beneficiary" of the work arrangement, a subjective phrase that is open to interpretation.)

Of course, not all publishing jobs are based in New York. Indie presses like Tin House Books (Portland, Oregon), Coffee House Press (Minneapolis), Hub City Press (Spartanburg, North Carolina), and McSweeney's Publishing (San Francisco) are spread out across the country, and a number of literary agents live and work outside New York. But these tend to be small operations, and people working in publishing have long gravitated toward New York, where there are more jobs and it's easier to jump between firms without having to move to a new city.

For writers working in publishing, the flip side to the long hours and middling pay, especially for those based in New York, is the chance to learn the book business from the inside out and rub shoulders with powerful editors and agents. But while a career in publishing can give a young writer invaluable contacts and insight, writers who work in the industry warn that it's in no way a surefire shortcut to a book contract.

"Obviously, you learn a tremendous amount about the business," says Sloane Crosley, the best-selling essayist who worked for many years as a publicist at Vintage Books. "It would be disingenuous of me to suggest that I got nothing from my career in publishing. But I wouldn't necessarily say, 'Hey, go work at a really good publishing house for nine years on the off chance you might publish a zeitgeisty collection of essays.' That doesn't seem like a good financial plan."

Freelance Editing

The sharp drop in employment in the publishing industry, combined with a growing number of writers trying their hand at fiction and memoir, has opened up opportunities for authors with strong editing skills and an entrepreneurial streak.

Writers in the United States, spurred by innovations in e-book and print-on-demand technology, self-published more than a million books in 2017, according to a report by Bowker, an affiliate of the database firm Pro-Quest. With fewer editors at publishing houses to take on new work, and with those who remain having less time to guide manuscripts into print, freelance editors are picking up some of the slack, working either for agents and editors or directly for aspiring authors looking to revise a manuscript.

To earn money as an editorial freelancer, it helps to have a book or two out, or deep connections in publishing, or both, but even for writers with long publishing track records, it's hardly a matter of throwing up a website and waiting for clients to sign up. Competition for editing work is stiff, in part because layoffs in the industry have pushed many former book editors into the freelance ranks, and clients can be slow to materialize, especially in the beginning.

Many editorial freelancers advertise their services in the classified pages of *Poets & Writers Magazine* or in the member directory on the Editorial Freelancers Association website (the-efa.org), while others build visibility by joining Facebook writers groups or websites like Inked Voices or Writers Helping Writers. But writers who have been working as freelance editors for years say the bulk of their clients still come through word of mouth, most often from writing workshops they've taught or from referrals by agents and editors.

Because the field is relatively new, few formal rules govern how freelance editors work with their clients or how much they can charge. Typically, prospective clients send short excerpts of their work to an editor, who will offer a critique for free or a limited fee. If the writer is impressed with the editor's feedback, they can hire the editor to read the remainder of the book. The Editorial Freelancers Association (EFA) publishes a guide on its website that suggests a rate of $45 to $55 per hour (at a rate of one to five pages per hour) for a developmental edit, with slightly different rates for line editing, but while the EFA rate sheet serves as an unofficial industry standard, every editor ultimately sets their own rate.

Marcy Dermansky, a longtime editorial freelancer and author of four novels, including *Very Nice*, typically charges 4 cents a word, which comes out to $3,200 for an eighty-thousand-word book, though she says a client's ability to pay can play a role in pricing. "If I get a really great book by a struggling person who reaches out to me personally, I have lowered my rates," she says. "On the other hand, I've gotten queries from lawyers from really fancy offices, and I've been like, 'Maybe I won't lower my rates for them.'"

In her busiest year, Dermansky made $60,000 from editing, though she says most years she has earned closer to $30,000. For the better part of a decade, steady editing work enabled Dermansky to support herself and her young daughter while giving her time for her own fiction. Ultimately, though, she has her doubts about whether freelancing makes sense as a lifelong career. "Sometimes I would say to myself, 'This really isn't a sustainable way to live,'" she says.

Indeed, given the unpredictable paydays and constant hustling for clients, freelance editing *isn't* a very sustainable career, and according to a 2018 Authors Guild survey, few writers do it full-time. Just seven percent of writers in that survey who reported working as editors earned more than

$20,000 a year and a scant two percent made more than $40,000 annually. By contrast, nearly three-quarters of freelance editors in the survey earned less than $5,000 a year from the work and more than half made less than $2,000 annually.

Freelance Writing

Click on virtually any website, pick up any print publication, and you will find words. Whether it's a deeply reported feature story, a car ad, an opinion piece, a set of instructions, or travel advice, someone had to write it, and in today's world, chances are that someone was a freelancer.

Before the internet, freelance writers looking for work drew on contacts built up over years of writing for local newspapers or regional magazines. Today, with the blogosphere adding new digital-native publications daily and print magazines like the *New Yorker* and the *Paris Review* launching their own content-hungry websites, an enterprising freelancer needs little more than a good idea and a serviceable prose style to get that first by-line. But because so many websites are competing for readers—and because much of the advertising revenue that used to go to news outlets has migrated to platforms like Facebook and Google—it's hard for a writer breaking in to turn a sideline into a paying profession. Still, if you're willing to put in the time, and especially if you're open to writing marketing and technical copy, you can make freelance writing pay.

Both in print and online, longer articles that involve extensive reporting pay better than personal essays or reviews, but print publications typically pay more than digital sites even for the same type of article. For instance, a humor piece that appears on the *New Yorker* website's Daily Shouts page will pay a few hundred dollars while a similar piece in the print magazine's Shouts & Murmurs column will pay many times more. And of course, many smaller web-only publications pay nothing at all, offering their contributors online exposure in lieu of payment.

Add it all up and for most writers, freelancing is less a job than an interesting side hustle that can be juggled around a full-time job or slotted in with other part-time gigs and childcare. But, says freelancer David Hill, writers willing to take on less glamorous corporate writing assignments can piece together a living.

"I would not suggest anybody quit their day job on a lark and give it a shot," says Hill, who left a job as a union organizer to freelance full-time in 2015. "I think everybody has to figure it out on the side. What I did to get to this point is what I think a lot of people have to do, which is do it on the side until you can figure it out and then you can make the jump once you've got your sea legs."

Hill, a vice president of the National Writers Union, which advocates on behalf of freelance writers, cautions new writers against accepting lower pay to get their foot in the door. But it's an unavoidable fact of the freelance market that most new writers have to start out writing for smaller publications that pay little or nothing, in the hopes of using those early bylines to open doors with editors at more prominent outlets.

As with freelance editing, there are no formal job requirements to meet or applications to fill out. Online and in print, the universal entry point for nearly every freelance piece is the pitch—a brief letter, usually e-mailed to an editor, that includes a pithy capsule of the story you plan to write, along with your qualifications for writing it and links to similar stories you've written for other publications. If an editor takes your pitch, you'll agree on a deadline and a price for the finished piece and begin writing.

PITCH WRITING 101

The first task of writing a successful pitch is deciding where to send it. If you haven't written for pay before, you may want to start small—a blog you read regularly or the website of a print publication you respect. Spend some time reading the site to make sure it runs stories like the one you have in mind and to see how those stories are written.

If possible, send the pitch directly to an editor rather than an open submissions portal. Most publications list their editors on their masthead or on the

"Contact Us" page. If those pages don't list individual e-mails, many editors now maintain personal websites, which will give their e-mail address.

The pitch itself begins with the subject line of your e-mail. If you have a legitimate connection to the editor—as someone you met at the AWP conference last year, or you come recommended by a friend who writes for this publication—you can reference that in the subject line. Otherwise write it as if it were the headline of the piece you're proposing. As editors are deciding whether to take on a piece, they're thinking how to put a label on it that will attract readers. If you can sum up your piece in a few punchy words, you're already halfway to showing an editor that it can work for the publication.

In the body of the e-mail, if you don't have a professional connection to the editor, dive straight into your pitch. If you're not sure how to frame the story, write the pitch as if it were the opening paragraph of the piece you're proposing. Drop the reader into the story, but be sure to give all the necessary information: whom you plan to interview, what trends or news events you're jumping off from, what point or argument you're planning to make. And be brief—a paragraph or two at most.

Follow this up with a quick summary of your professional writing experience and any special expertise you bring to the story. Editors need to know two things: that you have a great idea that's right for their publication and that you can write it without huge amounts of editing on their part. If your work has appeared online before, include links to your best two or three pieces, but don't be surprised if the editors don't read them that closely. A good pitch is all the introduction an editor needs.

But while a byline in a glossy magazine can bring prestige, and occasionally a decent payday, even the most talented freelancers struggle to string together enough assignments to guarantee a stable income. This is where corporate work comes in. Savvy freelancers can use a portfolio of articles in a particular field—travel, say, or men's fashion—to help win more lucrative work writing "branded content," a hybrid form of advertising in which a company commissions articles, often unbylined, that tout its products.

These corporate-sponsored articles often pay double the word rate of an unbranded piece. Other freelancers pay the bills by writing marketing copy and scripts for corporate training videos, while many more churn out short blog posts and other web copy for so-called content mills like iWriter and WritingBunny.

Hill himself mixes heavily reported features for *Vice* and the *New Yorker* with work for a roster of corporate clients and earns between $38,000 and $70,000 a year. "The writers that you're reading who write those long-form features, very few of them are making their entire living from doing that," he says. "Some of them may have partners who earn money and that may help them out, but a lot of writers do this kind of stuff on the side, or they work in television, or they sell scripts."

OTHER WRITING GIGS TO CONSIDER

GHOSTWRITING: As a ghostwriter, you are paid to write something—a book, an article, anything—under someone else's name. While this probably isn't a great arrangement for the egocentric among us, since ghostwriters do not own or get credit for anything they write, it can nevertheless be a lucrative gig. Start your research with the Association of Ghostwriters (associationofghostwriters.org).

TECHNICAL WRITING: Just about every technical and occupational field— engineering, chemistry, aeronautics, robotics, finance, medical, consumer electronics, biotechnology, and forestry—requires writers to draft technical communications for web pages, fact sheets, and so on. A college degree is usually required, as is knowledge of or experience in the given field.

COPYWRITING: Even more common than technical writing, copywriting requires writing text for the purpose of advertising or other forms of marketing. A copywriter is focused on increasing brand awareness. Google "copywriting" and the name of your city and you'll likely find some results.

BUSINESS WRITING: Sometimes called corporate writing or business communication, business writing involves crafting newsletters, in-house magazines, memos, e-mails, and intranet sites for an audience within a company. Business writers also sometimes write for an external audience comprised of shareholders, analysts, or the public. Learn more at the International Association of Business Communicators (www.iabc.com).

MEDICAL WRITING: A technical writer for the medical field, a medical writer works with doctors, scientists, and other experts to create documents that convey research results, product use, and other medical information. The American Medical Writers Association (www.amwa.org) offers an educational certificate that can give you credibility as a medical writer.

PUBLIC RELATIONS WRITING: A public relations writer, or PR writer, produces content to promote or convey information about a company or organization in the form of press releases, web copy, articles, mailings, and so on. Learn more at PRNEWS (www.prnewsonline.com).

Speaking Engagements

As newspaper book pages have slowly withered, book tours have become an increasingly important way for writers to get their books in front of interested readers. An author gets behind the wheel of a car—or if they're extremely fortunate, their publisher picks up the bill for airfare—and visits as many bookstores, libraries, and book festivals as time and budget allow, reading from the new book and signing copies for readers.

Touring can be a great way to sell books and forge personal relationships with booksellers who, with any luck, will still be putting your book in the hands of readers long after you leave, but for the most part, these are unpaid gigs. However, if you have a flair for performing and enough of a following to attract a crowd, you can earn serious money as a speaker at universities, arts and culture lecture series, corporate events, and sales conferences.

Most major publishers now have in-house speakers bureaus that book speaking engagements for their writers, but many writers choose to work with independent bureaus like the Lavin Agency, which represents acclaimed novelists Margaret Atwood and Salman Rushdie, and the redBrick

Agency, which has best-selling memoirists Mary Karr and Tobias Wolff among its clients.

Much as literary agencies mediate between writers and publishers, speakers bureaus help writers find and book speaking gigs, negotiate fees and travel arrangements, oversee the logistics and planning, and make sure the hosts pay up. And like a literary agent, a speakers agent works on commission, typically twenty to twenty-five percent of the speaking fee.

At the higher end, these events can be extremely lucrative. Most speakers agents won't take on a client who can't routinely command a fee of at least $5,000 and rates for well-known authors can range up to $35,000, says Jamie Brickhouse, founder and CEO of the redBrick Agency. Very busy speakers may do as many as two or three events a month, while others average between ten and twelve a year, he says.

But to command these kinds of fees, you have to be able to draw—and entertain—a fairly large crowd, which means you have to both be good behind the microphone and have a wide audience for your books or an expertise in a subject that would interest a paying audience. "It doesn't necessarily mean you have to be Malcolm Gladwell, or that you have to be a mega-bestselling author," Brickhouse says. "You can be an expert in your field, in your niche, and there's all kinds of venues for that, but you have to have a little bit of name recognition or at least be a top expert in your field for a speakers bureau to be able to book you."

While it takes a certain level of celebrity or recognized expertise to win top-dollar speaking engagements, writers just starting out can gain experience and exposure by looking for speaking gigs on their own, Brickhouse says. You can start in your local area, he says, pitching yourself as a speaker for a library reading series or book festival or seek out organizations gathering to discuss a topic that you cover in your books. If, for instance, you've written a memoir about overcoming a life-threatening illness, you might be able to offer yourself as a speaker for groups of people battling the disease or medical conferences devoted to finding better ways of treating it.

If you book speaking gigs on your own, Brickhouse says, be sure to have someone film it with a video camera or an iPhone, and if the speech goes well, ask for testimonials from the event's organizers. Reports of how you wowed a crowd, along with video of the event itself, can help you get more gigs—and when you're ready, help attract the interest of speakers agents.

Literary Nonprofits

Some writers are comfortable cobbling together a living from part-time gigs—a class or two at the local university, combined with private writing clients and the occasional high-paying speaking engagement. But that kind of freelance life isn't for everyone, and if you need a regular job, one with traditional hours and a benefits package, your best bet outside publishing and the MFA world is a job at a literary nonprofit. Literary nonprofits range from local institutions like the Loft Literary Center in Minneapolis or Seattle's Hugo House, which host writing classes and literary events, to national organizations like Poets & Writers and the Academy of American Poets, both of which are based in New York and provide information and support to writers.

In many ways, working at a literary nonprofit is like working in any office—staffers manage budgets, fill out spreadsheets, and sit in on a lot of meetings—except that the work isn't selling office supplies or insurance benefits, but supporting writers, writing, and literature. Unfortunately, these jobs tend to pay less than corporate work—as much as thirty to forty percent less than similar positions at for-profit firms, according to Britt Udesen, executive director at the Loft Literary Center. "I've done a little bit of corporate work in my life," says Udesen. "I think one of the reasons that some of us stay with nonprofits is that we believe in the work we do, and we believe that if we have to spend fifty or sixty hours a week doing something, it may as well be something that makes us feel like we're serving our community."

While salaries vary depending on the size of the organization and where it's located, executive directors at local arts organizations earn about $81,400 a year on average, according to a 2018 report by Americans for the Arts, which surveyed more than eleven hundred employees at government arts agencies and private arts nonprofits. Lower down the org chart, communications and public relations staffers at arts organizations make about $51,400 a year on average, while those overseeing arts education earn an average of about $52,400 a year, according to the study.

In return for the lower pay, literary nonprofits offer writers the satisfaction of helping other writers, along with writer-centric perks they could never find at a regular office job. At most literary nonprofits, staff can participate in classes and other programs the organization offers for free or at greatly reduced cost. At the Sewanee Writers' Conference in Tennessee, for instance, associate director Adam Latham not only sits in on readings and craft talks during the annual twelve-day conference but is also entitled to a one-on-one session with a workshop leader each summer to discuss his own fiction. "Every time I go through the conference, it helps refill the well," he says. "We're sponges and we absorb more than we realize. My writing gets a bump every time I go through that cycle."

Parting Thoughts

To prescribe a specific line of employment as more or less ideal for writers would be a bit like saying that in order to make it as a writer you need to live in New York City or Los Angeles, which is rubbish, of course. As we have illustrated throughout this book, there is no single path through the writing life.

In this chapter we've touched on how the academic, nonprofit, and publishing sectors are common sources of employment for writers (and in the process shared information about a number of potential jobs; additional positions can of course be found in magazine publishing, university administration, bookselling, web development, library science, and other specialized areas). But literary history is filled with examples of authors who did not follow any of these paths. How you earn money to pay the bills is a highly personal and idiosyncratic choice—as is how you juggle writing with the other priorities in your life. If you are fulfilling your responsibilities—to yourself and others—while feeling content with your writing practice, don't let anyone tell you you're doing it wrong.

ADA LIMÓN ON SADNESS AND SUCCULENTS

To live in my mind is to always be asking *Am I having an experience?* And the answer is most often, *Yes.* Getting a lift home from the Blue Grass Airport in Lexington last night, I was looking out the window on New Circle Road and noticed that all the trees were so dry. We usually get a great deal more rain than we have lately and so now the horse pastures, the lawns, the trees, everything looks brittle and smells like dust and decay. It made me want to take out an enormous watering can and run water over everything. To drench the world. A way of bringing everything back to life. A beckoning toward return.

Poetry does that to me. Brings everything back, pours water over the dry and needy parts of the brain, the body, the world, and asks it to live again. Quite simply, writing is my way of loving the world, to see it with great attention. To watch the browning leaves and to nod to them, to say to them, *You and I, we are dying. I see you aching on the hillside by the side of the road.* Does it make me feel better to notice things? Yes. Am I having an experience? Yes.

Here's an example taken from this exact moment that I am writing this. I apologize if it is maudlin or mundane, but I am trying to be true. Today I am a little sad. I woke up from a deliciously long sleep after days of travel, and I am tired and I am sad. Also, the very lack of rain, the dryness, the dying season of fall, of us all, it's too much.

It is an experience, though I'd prefer to be having a different experience. Swimming in a clear, cool lake in the mountains somewhere, making love in the afternoon without any obligations afterward but daydreaming and napping, sitting on my parents' patio. But that is not the experience I am having. I am having this one. Leaves are curling up on their branches, birds sound desperate and mournful, and only the succulents on the porch seem fine.

I am looking now at the succulents and examining the way they are flowering, how the purple one in the middle is practically glowing. It is called a *Graptoveria Debbie*. Which I think is a great name, especially if you say it out loud. We could name it something else more dramatic like *Amethyst Desert Star* or *Terrible Stubborn Frosty Heart*. Does it make my sadness go away a bit if I tell you about this succulent? A little. Could I tell you that my sadness is this succulent? Sure.

Why am I sad? Mostly, I don't want to tell you. One reason is not public and not allowed to be shared. One reason is not important and feels selfish to even bring up. But all you need to know is that it is about failure. I have failed at two projects that I thought might, well, not be failures. Still, I am glad I made them. I am not saying I like failed things, but I do think it is useful to fail. Even if it makes you sad for a whole morning. What have we to say for ourselves if not *I have tried*?

When I was much younger, I thought writing was an ecstatic act. A way of exclaiming and pointing out something important to a friend or a stranger or to myself. Now, I think it's different. It is quieter to me. There's a way in which it feels both more intimate and secretive than before, while still feeling essential to how I love myself and the world. Maybe it is that I am both less desperate and more desperate at the same time. I want to tell you something, but if you don't read it, that's okay, too. I will still be here, telling you about this succulent.

Terrance Hayes once gave a talk at a conference I was also teaching at and he kept emphasizing the importance of making things that allow you to play. He plays the piano, paints, and makes short films. The only thing he doesn't do—it seems—is write novels. He's pretty adamant about that. I, myself, have written three novels. I should say, "three failed novels." But are they failures if they gave me a place to play? A place to be free for a while despite the constraints of life and living? The failed novels are all living in my basement being smug and indifferent about my needs. Failing is a way of being free. After all, what's really the difference between a weed and a flower?

C. D. Wright said, "It is a function of poetry to locate those zones inside us that would be free, and declare them so." I have always loved that quote. Because it is how I feel. It is a place where I can be free, not just on the page, but in my too-heavy heart. I lean into the page so that I can lean back into life, to write myself back into the moment, to be here again, to commit to being here again. There she is again, a woman on the page that is me living.

They say that succulents are drought resistant and that the best way to care for them is to let them dry out entirely between waterings. To practice a deluge and then a drought. Abundance and scarcity. Writing can be that way for me. It comes and then it doesn't come, just like joy, or grief, it is a great pendulum that swings back and forth. I wish I could tell you how truly healthy this succulent looks, sun on its plump rosette core. Forgive the personification, but it almost looks happy. Or maybe it is simply that it has been brought into the light of the page, dragging my humming mind with it. Am I having an experience? Yes. Am I being saved by these words? Again and again.

ADA LIMÓN *is the author of five books of poetry, including* The Carrying, *which won the National Book Critics Circle Award for Poetry and was named one of the top five poetry books of the year by the* Washington Post. *Her fourth book,* Bright Dead Things, *was named a finalist for the National Book Award, the Kingsley Tufts Poetry Award, and the National Book Critics Circle Award. She serves on the faculty of the Queens University of Charlotte low-residency MFA program and the online and summer programs for the Provincetown Fine Arts Work Center. She also works as a freelance writer in Lexington, Kentucky.*

TWENTY-FOUR

The End of the Book

Having gone through the process of writing and publishing a book, we know there are a few things about this great undertaking that writers don't talk about, at least not often or in public. There are likely a couple different reasons for this. Unless you've been through the process yourself, you wouldn't necessarily know to ask authors you meet about this stuff. The other reason is that some of it can be really personal. It can even be a little embarrassing.

We're here to tell you: Don't be embarrassed. Although it may sometimes feel like it, you're not alone. If you recently finished writing your book, or if you are going through the many steps in the lead-up to publication, or if your book is just making its way out in the world—you are likely feeling a lot of different things. Relief, excitement, and happiness are what you may have expected. And surely you are feeling some of those things. So maybe you need to acknowledge them now. After all, you worked really hard on this. You likely suffered untold rejection and doubt, yet you persevered and accomplished something incredible. Allow yourself to feel proud. For some of us, this is easier said than done. If you tend to downplay your contributions and accomplishments, for example, or if you grew up in an environment where modesty was held up as a principle—if you know this about yourself, you need to take a minute and give yourself permission to beam a little bit. No, scratch that. Beam a lot.

Be proud of yourself, because you are entering a period when you will likely start to question yourself—others will certainly question you; your private project is now public—and you need to give yourself what you may not get from those who don't know you: a break. When you type the last period of the manuscript that will someday become your book, when you're finally able to take a step back and turn that pile of pages in to your editor or your agent, or pick your newly printed book out of the box, it can be an emotional moment. And not all of those emotions feel very good. Sometimes it's a rather unpleasant mixture of feelings. Don't ignore it—this is part of the journey. Is it sadness that you've reached the end of something you've lived with for so long? Exhaustion? Or maybe it's nerves. Perhaps it's simply a kind of physiological response to shifting gears on such a big project, like finally stopping the car after having driven on a highway for six hours in the dark. The silence feels a little odd, doesn't it, the still world so strange after watching it rush by at seventy-five miles per hour for so long. You're finally able to relax your muscles a little bit. We've all had the experience of getting through a momentous occasion, a big day or a big week or an important project or a business trip—so physically and emotionally intense, but you did it!—only to come down with a cold or the flu the very next day. Your body, your mind, was fighting the fight, perhaps without your even being aware of it, but at some point it succumbs. Hitting a big milestone in your writing career can be a similar experience. You've finished the book; your editor finally has it. Or the long publishing process is over; your novel is in bookstores. The wave you were riding has hit the shore. It's good to be on dry land again, but your knees still feel a little shaky.

Fortunately, there are people on your team who can help—your agent, your editor—but they are not therapists, and it's unfair to expect them to predict the emotional needs you have at this point in the process. Depending on your relationship, they may give you exactly what you need—they may say the perfect things as they read your manuscript—or not. While it's important for them to be communicative and to be good partners through the publication process, avoid putting too much pressure on what are, in the end, professional relationships. We all need to find our own confidantes— those people whom you can call up or DM or meet for a quick coffee and talk through the less technical, more human side of this endeavor. And, of course, we can do what we've always done with the more complicated thoughts and feelings we've carried around with us: We can write them down.

Fear and doubt can also be frequent companions in the lead-up to publication. This is almost never talked about, and perhaps for good reason. What writer in his right mind will admit to being worried about his book when so much of the conversation is about enticing people to buy it and read it? And who wants to talk to other writers about being afraid of the very thing, publication, that we all work so hard to achieve? We are here to tell you that it's okay to be afraid. Why wouldn't you be—you're about to go public with something that you've kept relatively private probably for years. And doubt is perfectly natural. There are so many pieces to any book—so many things to get right. You'd have to be made of steel not to feel a few niggling doubts. This is where you can lean on your editor. Your editor wants this book to be as perfect as you do. Trust her to do her job. She's got your back.

On the other hand, you may feel nothing but joy now that the challenge of writing a book is over, and you worked through every ounce of your fear and doubt during the many years of hard work. That's perfectly normal, too—and good for you! The point here is that we all experience the writing life differently, and there is no wrong way or correct way or weird way to feel about all of this. At the beginning of this book we pointed out that writing allows for a clarity of thought, that it makes possible an illumination of emotion and feeling, and that it holds the potential for personal transformation. These are big words—because they're true. You are engaged in something really big. Keep that in mind as you work your way from inspiration to publication and beyond. This work involves every part of you—your heart, your mind, your body—and there are highs and lows at every step. Feel all of it, and use every piece to fuel and empower your writing.

NAFISSA THOMPSON-SPIRES
RECOMMENDS

Five Books to Remind You Why You Started Writing When the World Is
Too Much and Not Enough and Expatriation or Giving Up Isn't an Option

DRINKING COFFEE ELSEWHERE by ZZ Packer
Wry, dark, hilarious, and heartfelt, this is my favorite short story collection, and I'd
venture to say, a perfect book.

SONG OF SOLOMON by Toni Morrison
No one could write a sentence, a town, a world, and a mind like Morrison, and her third
novel is, like all of her canon, a masterpiece. My recent reread of this novel sustained
me through a very dark time—not only her recent passing, but my own attempt at
making sense of the racism and darkness in this world.

LONG DIVISION by Kiese Laymon
Kiese is among my favorite living writers and truth-tellers, and his debut novel, *Long
Division*, is as structurally impressive as its humor and brilliant critique.

UNDER THE FEET OF JESUS by Helena Maria Viramontes
This devastating novel is very close to my heart. Viramontes writes with such love for
her characters and their plight as migrant farm workers that you won't be able to look
away.

WHAT DOESN'T KILL YOU MAKES YOU BLACKER by Damon Young
Damon Young, the editor and cofounder of *Very Smart Brothas*, brings his signature
wit and eviscerating critique to long-form in his memoir in essays. I know I will return
to this book again and again as both a teaching tool and a coping mechanism in the
coming days.

NAFISSA THOMPSON-SPIRES *is the author of the story collection* Heads of the
Colored People, *which was long-listed for the 2018 National Book Award, the PEN/
Robert W. Bingham Prize, the PEN Open Book Award, and the Aspen Words Literary
Prize, and was a finalist for the Kirkus Prize.*

TWENTY-FIVE

The End Is Just the Beginning

What we call the beginning is often the end.
And to make an end is to make a beginning.
The end is where we start from.

—T. S. ELIOT, "LITTLE GIDDING," FROM FOUR QUARTETS

When we are just starting out as writers, the path up ahead can look impossibly long and winding, receding from view on the horizon where it disappears up a great mountain range that rises into the sky, its peaks obscured by clouds. And as we walk, or crawl, or jog, or run further up that path, the horizon never seems to get any closer, even as we pass significant markers along the way: the first finished story or poem, the first open-mic reading, the first workshop critique, the first literary magazine credit, the first novel draft, the first response from an agent, the first book. So much work to get as far as we've gone, but the path ahead looks just as long as it does winding.

But turn around, look behind you. What a view!

Early on in this book, George Saunders shared his thoughts on a writer's motivations and the forces that push us further up that artistic path. And along the way he discussed the very real and necessary parts of the writing process that don't feel as good as perhaps we think they might or ought, including the beginning of a project, which for him is filled with feelings like *Ah crap, I have no ideas, I'm washed-up,* and the end: *There will never come a time when I get to the ending without feeling like crap first.* Now keep in mind, this is coming from a guy who has published nine really well-received books. His novel, *Lincoln in the Bardo,* won the Man Booker Prize. He's a

MacArthur "Genius" Fellow, for goodness' sake! And yet he starts projects with the thought, *Ah crap, I have no ideas, I'm washed-up*. Or consider Jonathan Lethem's remark a few chapters back: "You are still just an insecure human animal who likes to try to make things out of words, and every day, if you're doing it for real, you wake up as confused and helpless and insecure as ever." The path ahead looks impossibly long for everyone.

And it's true, of course. The path never ends. We're not going to make it to the horizon, it just keeps extending into the distance. Finish a book, there's revision and editing to do. Publish that book, there's publicity and promotion to do. Repeat as necessary. And for a true writer, it never ceases to be necessary. There is something incredibly freeing and empowering when you look at the writing life this way (this is the reason it can be called the writing *life*, by the way), because there is always a new project up ahead, always something else to engage our senses, our intellect, our imaginations.

"We want to be part of something bigger than ourselves," Richard Powers said about the prospect of writing a novel, about eight months before his latest, *The Overstory*, won a Pulitzer Prize. He went on to paraphrase Peter Brooks, the author of *Reading for the Plot: Design and Intention in Narrative*, and his theory on our relationship to the logic of time in a novel: "We read in anticipation of retrospect, and we know that page 400 is going to change page 20 forever. And we love the fact that page 20 is disappearing under our feet as we move forward to this ending that has already been written. It reverses our relationship to the fixity of future and past. We want that immersion. We want to feel like we've gone into a world, and when we turn that last page it's hard for us to come back from that world into this world."

Perhaps there is something in that experience of reading—the full immersion of it—that is instructive about the life of the writer as well. The two are inextricably linked, after all. When we talk about the experience of writing and the magic that is happening in the mind of the writer at the moment of creation (excuse that rather mystical word, *magic*, but really, there is something nearly supernatural about it), the only corresponding experience that can do it justice is happening in the minds of readers, as we engage with those words and live in those worlds unfolding on the page.

Just as readers we love that page twenty is disappearing under our feet, as writers we love first the act of bushwhacking our way through page twenty, then going back over it and over it, each time clearing the path a little more until there is a passage that shines in the morning light. (Even if we don't love it, exactly, we are drawn to it, inexorably, as artists to our art.) And when that page is finished there is the next word and the next line, next passage, next page, all of which leads to brand-new openings through which we can glimpse vistas that were unimaginable a few pages ago. This is the inexhaustible and ever-changing life of the writer.

So often we view our work one project at a time, and that's only natural. Indeed, it may be the only way to find our way—eyes down, mind focused on the project at hand. There is always a goal in front of us, whether it's a poem in a journal or a line on our résumé or a book on the shelf. And that's how we move along the path.

This isn't intended as some kind of banal platitude to illustrate the bigger picture but rather a reminder of the incredible freedom and power afforded the creative writer. Because if we can agree that there is no summit, no highest peak upon which a writer, after years of struggle, can rest, having accomplished it all—and the perspectives of many of the authors in this book bear that out—then suddenly the path takes on different dimensions. Indeed, the path becomes as wide as your imagination will allow. There are no wrong turns, as long as we continue moving. And suddenly there is time, and there is good reason, to be there for the community of writers around us—all of whom are traveling similarly unique paths.

There are countless ideas, scenes, emotions, characters, and arguments to write; countless ways to write them; and countless methods of sharing them with others. We hope this book has offered some examples that will inspire and guide you on your own path—some sparks that have caught fire somewhere inside you.

Thank you for being a writer. Your writing is important. It is creative, generative, and the world needs more of it. We wish you the very best of luck with your writing and publishing. And now that we're at the end, it's time to get started. The end is just the beginning.

About Poets & Writers, Inc.

For fifty years Poets & Writers has been a trusted companion on what often is a long and lonely journey to publication. The organization was founded by Galen Williams in 1970 with an initial grant from the New York State Council on the Arts for a program now called Readings & Workshops, which helps provide income to writers by paying them to give readings and lead writing workshops.

The money was important. But Poets & Writers understood from the start that writers need more than financial support to create a life in literature. They need access to reliable information and guidance. They need opportunities to connect with peers, publishing professionals, and readers. And they need encouragement.

Five decades later, the organization has grown and its programs have evolved, but these core needs—information, encouragement, community, and cash—haven't changed.

Readings & Workshops is going strong in its fiftieth year, providing mini grants to support some two thousand literary events annually. That's five events a day, on average. Collectively, these events help writers reach an audience of over eighty thousand annually.

Writers turn to our flagship publication, *Poets & Writers Magazine*, for trust-worthy information and guidance on the business of writing, including the most extensive list of writing contests available in print. Since its launch in 1987, the magazine has also become a beloved source of inspiration and connection for its more than one hundred thousand readers.

Online, writers rely on pw.org for news, information, and community. A suite of databases provides accurate, timely, and comprehensive information about writing contests, small presses, literary magazines, literary agents, book review outlets, MFA programs, and more. Select content from *Poets & Writers Magazine* is also posted on pw.org, along with a range of online-only content, updated daily. Poets & Writers is committed to keeping its extraordinary online resources free for all writers and continues to invest in the development of new online features.

Looking ahead, Poets & Writers will empower creative writers and strengthen literary communities throughout the country. Without a doubt, its programs and services will continue to evolve, but meeting the needs of writers will remain its singular mission. Learn more at pw.org.

Free Resources at pw.org

Poets & Writers Directory: www.pw.org/directory. Browse well over ten thousand profiles of poets, fiction writers, creative nonfiction writers, and translators to find contact information and links to new markets for your work. Writers who have publication credits can also apply to be listed and open up opportunities to connect with reading series coordinators, agents, and editors.

Tools for Writers: This suite of databases includes a wealth of practical information about hundreds of opportunities for writers: Writing Contests, Grants & Awards (www.pw.org/grants), Literary Magazines (www.pw.org/literary_magazines), Small Presses (www.pw.org/small_presses), Literary Agents (www.pw.org/literary_agents), MFA Programs (www.pw.org/mfa), Conferences and Residencies (www.pw.org/conferences_and_residencies), Literary Places (www.pw.org/literary_places), Reading Venues (www.pw.org/reading_venues), and Book Review Outlets (www.pw.org/book_review_outlets).

Submission Calendar: www.pw.org/submission_calendar. Peruse upcoming deadlines for writing contests with this monthly calendar.

Submission Tracker: www.pw.org/submissions. Keep track of your submissions to writing contests, literary magazines, small presses, literary agents, and applications to MFA programs and writers retreats.

Literary Events Calendar: www.pw.org/calendar. Writers can list their own events or browse listings of readings, workshops, and other literary events held in cities across the country.

Poets & Writers Local: www.pw.org/local. Download the app to find readings and author events near you; explore indie bookstores, libraries, and other places of interest to writers; and connect with the literary community in your city or town.

Top Topics for Writers: www.pw.org/top10_faq. Since 1970 Poets & Writers has served as an information clearinghouse on all matters related to writing. While the range of inquiries has been broad, common themes have emerged over time. Top Topics for Writers addresses the most popular and pressing issues, including copyright information, self-publishing, and publishing your book. If you have a question that isn't answered, writers may e-mail us at info_services@pw.org and the editorial staff will assist you.

The Time Is Now: www.pw.org/writing-prompts-exercises. A series of weekly writing prompts—poetry on Tuesdays, fiction on Wednesdays, and nonfiction on Thursdays—to help you stay committed to your writing practice throughout the year. Also included is a selection of recommended books on writing—both the newly published and the classics. Sign up for the newsletter to get all of it every Friday.

Poets & Writers Theater: www.pw.org/theater. A clip is added daily to this sizable archive of author readings, book trailers, publishing panels, craft talks, and more.

Writers Recommend: www.pw.org/writers_recommend. Authors share books, art, music, writing prompts, films—anything and everything that has inspired them in their writing in this weekly feature.

Agents & Editors Recommend: www.pw.org/agents_and_editors_recommend. Publishing professionals share advice, anecdotes, insights, and suggestions for books, movies, music, and more in this weekly feature.

Ten Questions: www.pw.org/ten_questions. Timed to coincide with a new book's publication every Tuesday, authors talk about their writing process, their reading habits, their publishing experience, favorite advice, and more.

City Guides: www.pw.org/city_guides. Authors, booksellers, publishers, editors, and others take readers on a tour of some of the most active literary cities in the country, visiting the places they go to connect with writers of the past, to the bars and cafés where today's authors give readings, and to those sites that are most inspiring for writing.

Jobs for Writers: www.pw.org/joblistings. Whether you're looking for a job in publishing, academia, or the nonprofit sector, these frequently updated listings can help you find the perfect job. Writers can browse openings by area and e-mail listings to friends and colleagues; and hiring managers can post details of positions they need filled.

Agents & Editors: www.pw.org/content/agents_editors_the_complete_series. This series of in-depth interviews with book editors, publishers, and agents offers a unique look at the past, present, and future of the book industry and what writers can do to thrive in today's publishing world.

Agent Advice: www.pw.org/content/agent_advice_the_complete_series. The industry's best and brightest agents respond directly to readers' questions about how to find an agent, how to craft a query letter, and best practices in this regular column dating back to 2010.

Reviewers & Critics: www.pw.org/content/reviewers_critics_the_complete_series. The professional writers, readers, and thinkers whose job is to start conversations about contemporary literature share their insights about the world of books in this series of interviews.

Daily News: www.pw.org/daily_news. Every day *Poets & Writers Magazine* editors scan the headlines—publishing reports, literary dispatches, academic announcements, and more—for all the news that creative writers need to know.

Craft Capsules: www.pw.org/craft_capsules. This series of micro craft essays by authors such as Kimberly King Parsons, Simon Van Booy, Christina Baker Kline, Tayari Jones, and others explores the finer points of writing.

15 National Organizations Serving Writers and Writing

ACADEMY OF AMERICAN POETS

poets.org

The Academy of American Poets supports American poets at all stages of their careers and fosters the appreciation of contemporary poetry. Its programs include the American Poets Prizes; the website poets.org, which features an extensive collection of poems and biographies of poets; its digital series Poem-a-Day; its education initiatives; as well as its readings and special events. The organization also coordinates the work of the Poetry Coalition, a national alliance of more than twenty organizations dedicated to working together to promote the value poets bring to our culture and the important contribution poetry makes in the lives of people of all ages and backgrounds.

ASIAN AMERICAN WRITERS' WORKSHOP

www.aaww.org

AAWW is a national organization devoted to the creation, publication, development, and dissemination of creative writing by Asian Americans. Its programs include a New York City event series, the publication of the online magazines *The Margins* and *Open City*, and other editorial initiatives.

AMERICAN SOCIETY OF JOURNALISTS AND AUTHORS

www.asja.org

The nation's largest professional organization of independent nonfiction writers, the ASJA represents freelancers' interests, serving as spokesperson for their right to control and profit from uses of their work in new media and otherwise. It offers members benefits and services focusing on professional development, seminars and workshops, discount services, and the opportunity to explore professional issues and concerns with their peers.

ASSOCIATION OF AUTHORS' REPRESENTATIVES

www.aaronline.org

The AAR serves more than four hundred professional literary and dramatic agents. To become a member, agents must meet the organization's minimum experience requirements and agree to adhere to its bylaws and canon of ethics. AAR offers panels, educational programs, and networking events for its members and produces an online directory of literary agents.

ASSOCIATION OF WRITERS & WRITING PROGRAMS

www.awpwriter.org

Perhaps best known for its annual conference and bookfair held in a different city each year, AWP fosters literary achievement, advances the art of writing as essential to a good education, and serves the makers, teachers, students, and readers of contemporary writing. Other programs include the *Writer's Chronicle* and a website featuring job listings and resources that support best-practice pedagogy for teaching creative writing.

AUTHORS GUILD

www.authorsguild.org

The Authors Guild works to aid and protect writers' interests in copyright, contracts, tax law, and free expression. It provides its members with free legal assistance, liability insurance, and other resources and services. It also provides information about finding literary agents, self-publishing, and navigating the writing business.

CANTOMUNDO

www.cantomundo.org

CantoMundo cultivates a community of Latinx poets through workshops, symposia, and public readings. It also hosts an annual poetry workshop for Latinx poets that provides a space for the creation, documentation, and critical analysis of Latinx poetry.

CAVE CANEM FOUNDATION

www.cavecanempoets.org

Cave Canem Foundation is dedicated to cultivating the artistic and professional growth of African American poets. Its programs include writing retreats in Greensburg and Pittsburgh, Pennsylvania; three book prizes; and community-based workshops for emerging adult poets; as well as conversations, readings, and other events.

COMMUNITY OF LITERARY MAGAZINES AND PRESSES

www.clmp.org

The Community of Literary Magazines and Presses supports and advocates for independent literary publishers by providing its members technical assistance, discounts, and funding opportunities. It also serves as a bridge between its members and other networks of literary stakeholders, including readers, writers, booksellers, librarians, and educators. CLMP hosts the annual Firecracker Awards for Independently Published Literature and LWC}NYC, an annual conference that helps writers navigate the publishing process.

KUNDIMAN

www.kundiman.org

Kundiman is dedicated to nurturing writers and readers of Asian American literature. Its programs include an annual retreat for Asian American writers at Fordham University in New York City, a youth leadership intensive, a national readings and workshops series, and a mentorship program for writers in New York City.

LAMBDA LITERARY

www.lambdaliterary.org

Lambda Literary is dedicated to nurturing and advocating for LGBTQ writers. It hosts the Lammy Awards, given to honor the best lesbian, gay, bisexual, and transgender books published each year; the annual Lambda LitFest in Los Angeles; a retreat for emerging LGBTQ writers; and a Writers in Schools program in New York City. It also maintains a website featuring events, calls for submissions, and other resources for LGBTQ writers.

NATIONAL WRITERS UNION

www.nwu.org

With regional chapters around the United States, the National Writers Union is an activist organization that promotes and protects the rights, interests, and economic advancement of its members. It also organizes writers to improve professional working conditions through collective bargaining action, provides services such as professional guidance about contracts and grievances, and offers discounted health insurance.

PEN AMERICA

www.pen.org

With offices in New York City; Washington, D.C.; and Los Angeles, PEN America stands at the intersection of literature and human rights to protect free expression in the United States and worldwide. The organization produces research and reports, advocacy efforts, and campaigns on policy issues and on behalf of writers and journalists under threat. Other programs include the annual PEN World Voices Festival in New York City, the PEN America Literary Awards, public programming across the country, and the Prison Writing Program.

THE POETRY FOUNDATION
www.poetryfoundation.org
The Poetry Foundation aims to discover and celebrate the best poetry and to place it before the largest possible audience. Publisher of *Poetry* magazine, it also awards prizes and fellowships to poets; produces a website with poems, biographies of poets, and educational resources; and administers Poetry Out Loud, the national youth recitation program.

THE RADIUS OF ARAB AMERICAN WRITERS
www.arabamericanwriters.org
Established in 1993, RAWI provides mentoring, community, and support for Arab American writers and those with roots in the Arabic-speaking world and the diaspora. The organization disseminates writing by Arab Americans and those from the Arabic-speaking world and sponsors a biennial conference with readings, panels, workshops, and conversations that emphasize inclusivity.

140 Books for Every Serious Writer's Bookshelf

Books About Writing: An Expanded List

A LITTLE BOOK ON FORM: AN EXPLORATION INTO THE FORMAL IMAGINATION OF POETRY (HarperCollins, 2017) by Robert Hass

AMERICAN AUDACITY: IN DEFENSE OF LITERARY DARING (Liveright, 2018) by William Giraldi

A POETRY HANDBOOK (Houghton Mifflin Harcourt, 1994) by Mary Oliver

A POET'S GLOSSARY (Houghton Mifflin Harcourt, 2014) by Edward Hirsch

A STRANGER'S JOURNEY: RACE, IDENTITY, AND NARRATIVE CRAFT IN WRITING (University of Georgia Press, 2018) by David Mura

BETWIXT-AND-BETWEEN: ESSAYS ON THE WRITING LIFE (Coffee House Press, 2018) by Jenny Boully

BIRD BY BIRD: SOME INSTRUCTIONS ON WRITING AND LIFE (Anchor, 1995) by Anne Lamott

BURNING DOWN THE HOUSE: ESSAYS ON FICTION (Graywolf Press, 1997) by Charles Baxter

CONSIDER THIS: MOMENTS IN MY WRITING LIFE AFTER WHICH EVERYTHING WAS DIFFERENT (Grand Central Publishing, 2020) by Chuck Palahniuk

DRAFT NO. 4: ON THE WRITING PROCESS (Farrar, Straus and Giroux, 2017) by John McPhee

DREYER'S ENGLISH: AN UTTERLY CORRECT GUIDE TO CLARITY AND STYLE (Random House, 2019) by Benjamin Dreyer

ELEMENTS OF FICTION (Grove Press, 2019) by Walter Mosley

ESSAYS ONE (Farrar, Straus and Giroux, 2019) by Lydia Davis

FIRST YOU WRITE A SENTENCE: THE ELEMENTS OF READING, WRITING . . . AND LIFE (Viking, 2018) by Joe Moran

GOOD PROSE: THE ART OF NONFICTION (Random House, 2013) by Tracy Kidder and Richard Todd

HOW FICTION WORKS (Farrar, Straus and Giroux, 2008) by James Wood

HOW TO READ A POEM: AND FALL IN LOVE WITH POETRY (Harcourt, 1999) by Edward Hirsch

HOW TO WRITE AN AUTOBIOGRAPHICAL NOVEL (Houghton Mifflin Harcourt, 2018) by Alexander Chee

HOW TO WRITE LIKE TOLSTOY: A JOURNEY INTO THE MINDS OF OUR GREATEST WRITERS (Random House, 2016) by Richard Cohen

MADNESS, RACK, AND HONEY: COLLECTED LECTURES (Wave Books, 2012) by Mary Ruefle

MEANDER, SPIRAL, EXPLODE: DESIGN AND PATTERN IN NARRATIVE (Catapult, 2019) by Jane Alison

MFA VS NYC: THE TWO CULTURES OF AMERICAN FICTION (n+1/Faber and Faber, 2014) edited by Chad Harbach

NINE GATES: ENTERING THE MIND OF POETRY (Harper, 1997) by Jane Hirshfield

ONE WRITER'S BEGINNINGS (Harvard University Press, 1984) by Eudora Welty

ON WRITING: A MEMOIR OF THE CRAFT (Scribner, 2000) by Stephen King

READING LIKE A WRITER: A GUIDE FOR PEOPLE WHO LOVE BOOKS AND FOR THOSE WHO WANT TO WRITE THEM (Harper, 2006) by Francine Prose

SCRATCH: WRITERS, MONEY, AND THE ART OF MAKING A LIVING (Simon & Schuster, 2017) edited by Manjula Martin

SISTER OUTSIDER: ESSAYS AND SPEECHES (Ten Speed Press, 1984) by Audre Lorde

STEERING THE CRAFT: A 21ST CENTURY GUIDE TO SAILING THE SEA OF STORY (Mariner Books, 2015) by Ursula K. Le Guin

STORY GENIUS: HOW TO USE BRAIN SCIENCE TO GO BEYOND OUTLINING AND WRITE A RIVETING NOVEL (BEFORE YOU WASTE THREE YEARS WRITING 327 PAGES THAT GO NOWHERE) (Ten Speed Press, 2016) by Lisa Cron

THE ART OF ATTENTION: A POET'S EYE (Graywolf Press, 2007) by Donald Revell

THE ART OF DARING: RISK, RESTLESSNESS, IMAGINATION (Graywolf Press, 2014) by Carl Phillips

THE ART OF DEATH: WRITING THE FINAL STORY (Graywolf Press, 2017) by Edwidge Danticat

THE ART OF DESCRIPTION: WORLD INTO WORD (Graywolf Press, 2010) by Mark Doty

THE ART OF FICTION: NOTES ON CRAFT FOR YOUNG WRITERS (Knopf, 1984) by John Gardner

THE ART OF HISTORY: UNLOCKING THE PAST IN FICTION AND NONFICTION (Graywolf Press, 2016) by Christopher Bram

THE ART OF INTIMACY: THE SPACE BETWEEN (Graywolf Press, 2013) by Stacey D'Erasmo

THE ART OF MEMOIR (Harper, 2015) by Mary Karr

THE ART OF MYSTERY: THE SEARCH FOR QUESTIONS (Graywolf Press, 2018) by Maud Casey

THE ART OF PERSPECTIVE: WHO TELLS THE STORY (Graywolf Press, 2016) by Christopher Castellani

THE ART OF RECKLESSNESS: POETRY AS ASSERTIVE FORCE AND CONTRADICTION (Graywolf Press, 2010) by Dean Young

THE ART OF SUBTEXT: BEYOND PLOT (Graywolf Press, 2007) by Charles Baxter

THE ART OF SYNTAX: RHYTHM OF THOUGHT, RHYTHM OF SONG (Graywolf Press, 2009) by Ellen Bryant Voigt

THE ART OF THE POETIC LINE (Graywolf Press, 2007) by James Longenbach

THE ART OF TIME IN FICTION: AS LONG AS IT TAKES (Graywolf Press, 2009) by Joan Silber

THE ART OF TIME IN MEMOIR: THEN, AGAIN (Graywolf Press, 2007) by Sven Birkerts

THE ART OF X-RAY READING: HOW THE SECRETS OF 25 GREAT WORKS OF LITERATURE WILL IMPROVE YOUR WRITING (Little, Brown, 2016) by Roy Peter Clark

THE DESTINY THIEF: ESSAYS ON WRITING, WRITERS AND LIFE (Knopf, 2018) by Richard Russo

THE ELEMENTS OF STYLE (Macmillan, 1959) by William Strunk Jr. and E. B. White

THE FOREST FOR THE TREES: AN EDITOR'S ADVICE TO WRITERS (Riverhead Books, 2000) by Betsy Lerner

THE GEEK'S GUIDE TO THE WRITING LIFE (Bloomsbury, 2017) by Stephanie Vanderslice

THE GLOBAL NOVEL: WRITING THE WORLD IN THE 21ST CENTURY (Columbia Global Reports, 2016) by Adam Kirsch

THE HIDDEN MACHINERY: ESSAYS ON WRITING (Tin House Books, 2017) by Margot Livesey

THE KITE AND THE STRING: HOW TO WRITE WITH SPONTANEITY AND CONTROL— AND LIVE TO TELL THE TALE (Viking, 2016) by Alice Mattison

THE LIFE OF POETRY (Paris Press, 1996) by Muriel Rukeyser

THE MEASURE OF OUR LIVES: A GATHERING OF WISDOM (Knopf, 2019) by Toni Morrison

THE MINDFUL WRITER: NOBLE TRUTHS OF THE WRITING LIFE (Wisdom Publications, 2012) by Dinty W. Moore

THE PROMISE OF FAILURE: ONE WRITER'S PERSPECTIVE ON NOT SUCCEEDING (University of Iowa Press, 2018) by John McNally

THE SOURCE OF SELF-REGARD: SELECTED ESSAYS, SPEECHES, AND MEDITATIONS (Knopf, 2019) by Toni Morrison

THE TRAVELING FEAST: ON THE ROAD AND AT THE TABLE WITH MY HEROES (Little, Brown, 2018) by Rick Bass

THE TRIGGERING TOWN: LECTURES AND ESSAYS ON POETRY AND WRITING (W. W. Norton, 1979) by Richard Hugo

THE TRIP TO ECHO SPRING: ON WRITERS AND DRINKING (Picador, 2013) by Olivia Laing

THE WAY OF THE WRITER: REFLECTIONS ON THE ART AND CRAFT OF STORYTELLING (Scribner, 2016) by Charles Johnson

THE WRITER'S NOTEBOOK: CRAFT ESSAYS FROM TIN HOUSE (Tin House Books, 2009)

THE WRITER'S PORTABLE MENTOR: A GUIDE TO ART, CRAFT, AND THE WRITING LIFE (University of New Mexico Press, 2010) by Priscilla Long

THE WRITER'S PRACTICE: BUILDING CONFIDENCE IN YOUR NONFICTION WRITING (Penguin Books, 2019) by John Warner

THE WRITING LIFE (HarperCollins, 1989) by Annie Dillard

THIS YEAR YOU WRITE YOUR NOVEL (Little, Brown, 2007) by Walter Mosley

THRILL ME: ESSAYS ON FICTION (Graywolf Press, 2016) by Benjamin Percy

WE BEGIN IN GLADNESS: HOW POETS PROGRESS (Graywolf Press, 2018) by Craig Morgan Teicher

WHY POETRY (Ecco, 2017) by Matthew Zapruder

WHY WRITE? A MASTER CLASS ON THE ART OF WRITING AND WHY IT MATTERS (Bloomsbury USA, 2016) by Mark Edmundson

WHY WRITING MATTERS (Yale University Press, 2020) by Nicholas Delbanco

WILD MIND: LIVING THE WRITER'S LIFE (Bantam, 1990) by Natalie Goldberg

WRITING DOWN THE BONES: FREEING THE WRITER WITHIN (Shambhala, 1986) by Natalie Goldberg

WRITING PAST DARK: ENVY, FEAR, DISTRACTION, AND OTHER DILEMMAS IN THE WRITER'S LIFE (HarperCollins, 1993) by Bonnie Friedman

WRITING THE BLOCKBUSTER NOVEL (Forge, 2016) by Albert Zuckerman

Books About Publishing

A SECRET LOCATION ON THE LOWER EAST SIDE: ADVENTURES IN WRITING, 1960–1980 (New York Public Library/Granary Books, 1998) by Steven Clay and Rodney Phillips

BEFORE AND AFTER THE BOOK DEAL: A WRITER'S GUIDE TO FINISHING, PUBLISHING, PROMOTING, AND SURVIVING YOUR FIRST BOOK (Catapult, 2020) by Courtney Maum

BEHIND THE BOOK: ELEVEN AUTHORS ON THEIR PATH TO PUBLICATION (University of Chicago Press, 2018) by Chris Mackenzie Jones

BOOK BUSINESS: PUBLISHING PAST, PRESENT, AND FUTURE (W. W. Norton, 2001) by Jason Epstein

LITERARY PUBLISHING IN THE TWENTY-FIRST CENTURY (Milkweed Editions, 2016) edited by Travis Kurowski, Wayne Miller, and Kevin Prufer

MERCHANTS OF CULTURE: THE PUBLISHING BUSINESS IN THE TWENTY-FIRST CENTURY (Plume, 2012) by John B. Thompson

SMOKING TYPEWRITERS: THE SIXTIES UNDERGROUND PRESS AND THE RISE OF ALTERNATIVE MEDIA IN AMERICA (Oxford University Press, 2011) by John McMillian

THE ART OF LITERARY PUBLISHING: EDITORS ON THEIR CRAFT (Pushcart Press, 1995) edited by Bill Henderson

THE BOOK BUSINESS: WHAT EVERYONE NEEDS TO KNOW (Oxford University Press, 2019) by Mike Shatzkin and Robert Paris Riger

THE BUSINESS OF BEING A WRITER (University of Chicago Press, 2018) by Jane Friedman

THE BUSINESS OF BOOKS: HOW INTERNATIONAL CONGLOMERATES TOOK OVER PUBLISHING AND CHANGED THE WAY WE READ (Verso, 2000) by André Schiffrin

THE ESSENTIAL GUIDE TO GETTING YOUR BOOK PUBLISHED: HOW TO WRITE IT, SELL IT, AND MARKET IT . . . SUCCESSFULLY (Workman Publishing, 2015) by Arielle Eckstut and David Henry Sterry

THE LATE AGE OF PRINT: EVERYDAY BOOK CULTURE FROM CONSUMERISM TO CONTROL (Columbia University Press, 2009) by Ted Striphas

UNDER THE COVER: THE CREATION, PRODUCTION, AND RECEPTION OF A NOVEL (Princeton University Press, 2017) by Clayton Childress

WHAT EDITORS DO: THE ART, CRAFT, AND BUSINESS OF BOOK EDITING (University of Chicago Press, 2017) edited by Peter Ginna

WHY WE WRITE: 20 ACCLAIMED AUTHORS ON HOW AND WHY THEY DO WHAT THEY DO (Plume, 2013) edited by Meredith Maran

Autobiographies And Biographies Of Editors And Publishers

ANOTHER LIFE: A MEMOIR OF OTHER PEOPLE (Random House, 1999) by Michael Korda

AN UNCOMMON READER: A LIFE OF EDWARD GARNETT, MENTOR AND EDITOR OF LITERARY GENIUS (Farrar, Straus and Giroux, 2017) by Helen Smith

AVID READER: A LIFE (Farrar, Straus and Giroux, 2016) by Robert Gottlieb

BYWAYS: A MEMOIR (New Directions, 2005) by James Laughlin

FABER & FABER: THE UNTOLD STORY (Faber & Faber, 2019) by Toby Faber

HOTHOUSE: THE ART OF SURVIVAL AND THE SURVIVAL OF ART AT AMERICA'S MOST CELEBRATED PUBLISHING HOUSE, FARRAR, STRAUS AND GIROUX (Simon & Schuster, 2013) by Boris Kachka

"LITERCHOOR IS MY BEAT": A LIFE OF JAMES LAUGHLIN, PUBLISHER OF NEW DIRECTIONS (Farrar, Straus and Giroux, 2014) by Ian S. MacNiven

LORD OF PUBLISHING: A MEMOIR (Open Road, 2013) by Sterling Lord

MAX PERKINS: EDITOR OF GENIUS (Thomas Congdon Books, 1978) by A. Scott Berg

NEAR-DEATH EXPERIENCES . . . AND OTHERS (Farrar, Straus and Giroux, 2018) by Robert Gottlieb

PUBLISHING: A WRITER'S MEMOIR (Bloomsbury, 2015) by Gail Godwin

ROGER W. STRAUS: A CELEBRATION (Farrar, Straus and Giroux, 2005)

THE ART OF THE PUBLISHER (Farrar, Straus and Giroux, 2013) by Roberto Calasso, translated by Richard Dixon

THE LADY WITH THE BORZOI: BLANCHE KNOPF, LITERARY TASTEMAKER EXTRAORDINAIRE (Farrar, Straus and Giroux, 2016) by Laura Claridge

THE TENDER HOUR OF TWILIGHT: PARIS IN THE '50S, NEW YORK IN THE '60S: A MEMOIR OF PUBLISHING'S GOLDEN AGE (Farrar, Straus and Giroux, 2012) by Richard Seaver

THE TIME OF THEIR LIVES: THE GOLDEN AGE OF GREAT AMERICAN PUBLISHERS, THEIR EDITORS AND AUTHORS (Truman Talley Books, 2008) by Al Silverman

Books About Creativity

A CRAFTSMAN'S LEGACY: WHY WORKING WITH OUR HANDS GIVES US MEANING (Algonquin Books, 2019) by Eric Gorges with Jon Sternfeld

A NATURAL HISTORY OF THE SENSES (Random House, 1990) by Diane Ackerman

BIG MAGIC: CREATIVE LIVING BEYOND FEAR (Riverhead Books, 2015) by Elizabeth Gilbert

CREATIVE QUEST (Ecco, 2018) by Questlove with Ben Greenman

CREATIVITY: THE PSYCHOLOGY OF DISCOVERY AND INNOVATION (HarperCollins, 1991) by Mihaly Csikszentmihalyi

DAILY RITUALS: HOW ARTISTS WORK (Knopf, 2013) by Mason Currey

LIGHT THE DARK: WRITERS ON CREATIVITY, INSPIRATION, AND THE ARTISTIC PROCESS (Penguin, 2017) edited by Joe Fassler

THE ARTIST'S WAY: A SPIRITUAL PATH TO HIGHER CREATIVITY (Jeremy P. Tarcher/Perigee, 1992) by Julia Cameron

THE CREATIVE HABIT: LEARN IT AND USE IT FOR LIFE (Simon & Schuster, 2003) by Twyla Tharp

THE LOST CARVING: A JOURNEY TO THE HEART OF MAKING (Viking, 2012) by David Esterly

WHERE GOOD IDEAS COME FROM: THE NATURAL HISTORY OF INNOVATION (Penguin Group, 2010) by Steven Johnson

Books About MFA Programs

A DELICATE AGGRESSION: SAVAGERY AND SURVIVAL IN THE IOWA WRITERS' WORKSHOP (Yale University Press, 2019) by David O. Dowling

AFTER THE PROGRAM ERA: THE PAST, PRESENT, AND FUTURE OF CREATIVE WRITING IN THE UNIVERSITY (University of Iowa Press, 2016) edited by Loren Glass

THE CREATIVE WRITING MFA HANDBOOK (Continuum, 2006) by Tom Kealey

THE PROGRAM ERA: POSTWAR FICTION AND THE RISE OF CREATIVE WRITING (Harvard University Press, 2009) by Mark McGurl

WORKSHOPS OF EMPIRE: STEGNER, ENGLE, AND AMERICAN CREATIVE WRITING DURING THE COLD WAR (University of Iowa Press, 2015) by Eric Bennett

Books About Books

1,000 BOOKS TO READ BEFORE YOU DIE: A LIFE-CHANGING LIST (Workman Publishing, 2018) by James Mustich

AM I ALONE HERE? NOTES ON LIVING TO READ AND READING TO LIVE (Catapult, 2016) by Peter Orner

A READER'S BOOK OF DAYS: TRUE TALES FROM THE LIVES AND WORKS OF WRITERS FOR EVERY DAY OF THE YEAR (W. W. Norton, 2013) by Tom Nissley

EX LIBRIS: CONFESSIONS OF A COMMON READER (Farrar, Straus and Giroux, 1998) by Anne Fadiman

HOWARD'S END IS ON THE LANDING: A YEAR OF READING FROM HOME (Profile Books, 2009) by Susan Hill

HOW READING CHANGED MY LIFE (Ballantine Books, 1998) by Anna Quindlen

MY BOOKSTORE: WRITERS CELEBRATE THEIR FAVORITE PLACES TO BROWSE, READ, AND SHOP (Black Dog & Leventhal, 2012) edited by Ronald Rice

PACKING MY LIBRARY: AN ELEGY AND TEN DIGRESSIONS (Yale University Press, 2018) by Alberto Manguel

THE BOOK: A COVER-TO-COVER EXPLORATION OF THE MOST POWERFUL OBJECT OF OUR TIME (W. W. Norton, 2016) by Keith Houston

THE LOST ART OF READING: WHY BOOKS MATTER IN A DISTRACTED TIME (Sasquatch Books, 2010) by David L. Ulin

THE MAN WHO LOVED BOOKS TOO MUCH: THE TRUE STORY OF A THIEF, A DETECTIVE, AND A WORLD OF LITERARY OBSESSION (Riverhead Books, 2009) by Allison Hoover Bartlett

THE YELLOW-LIGHTED BOOKSHOP: A MEMOIR, A HISTORY (Graywolf Press, 2006) by Lewis Buzbee

TIME WAS SOFT THERE: A PARIS SOJOURN AT SHAKESPEARE & CO. (St. Martin's Press, 2005) by Jeremy Mercer

WHAT TO READ AND WHY (Harper, 2018) by Francine Prose

WHAT WE TALK ABOUT WHEN WE TALK ABOUT BOOKS: THE HISTORY AND FUTURE OF READING (Basic Books, 2019) by Leah Price

20 Top Podcasts for Writers

88 Cups of Tea features authors, agents, and storytellers offering inspiration, advice, and guidance for writers who want to navigate the business of publishing. 88cupsoftea.com

Between the Covers, hosted by David Naimon in Portland, Oregon, is Tin House's series of long-form, in-depth conversations with authors. tinhouse.com/podcasts

Book Fight!, hosted by Mike Ingram and Tom McAllister, is a weekly conversation: writers talking about books they love, books they hate, books that inspire them, books that baffle them, and books that infuriate them. "These are the conversations writers have at the bar, which is to say they're both unflinchingly honest and open to tangents, misdirection, general silliness." www.bookfightpod.com

Bookworm, hosted by Michael Silverblatt, is the country's premier literary talk show. No nonsense, no frills—just a smart, careful reader talking to talented authors about their recently published books. www.kcrw.com/culture/shows/bookworm

Commonplace, hosted by Rachel Zucker, is a series of intimate and captivating interviews with poets and artists about quotidian objects, experiences, or obsessions. Zucker's conversations explore the recipes, advice, lists, anecdotes, quotes, politics, phobias, spiritual practices, and other nonliterary forms of knowledge that are vital to an artist's life and work. www.commonpodcast.com

Dan & Eric Read the New Yorker So You Don't Have To, hosted by writers Daniel Torday and Eric Rosenblum, is a weekly conversation about the contents of the latest issue of the venerable publication, plus occasional guests such as George Saunders and Keith Gessen. dananderic.podbean.com

Fiction/Non/Fiction, hosted by V. V. Ganeshananthan and Whitney Terrell, interprets current events through the lens of literature and features conversations with writers of all stripes, from novelists and poets to journalists and essayists. lithub.com/category/lithubradio/fiction-non-fiction-lithubradio

First Draft, hosted by Mitzi Rapkin, features in-depth interviews with authors discussing their work and their craft. Past episodes include conversations with Laila Lalami, Dinaw Mengestu, and Karen Russell. firstdraftwriters.libsyn.com

Hurry Slowly is a show about how you can be more productive, creative, and resilient through the simple act of slowing down. Through in-depth interviews with deep thinkers, artists, and entrepreneurs, host Jocelyn K. Glei sparks new ideas for navigating work and life at a more sustainable pace. hurryslowly.co

Literary Friction, hosted by literary agent Carrie Plitt and author Octavia Bright, is a monthly conversation about books and ideas. Each episode features an author interview, book recommendations, and lively discussion built around a related theme—anything from the novella to race to masculinity. www.nts.live/shows /literaryfriction

Longform Podcast, hosted by Aaron Lammer, Max Linsky, and Evan Ratliff, is a weekly conversation with a nonfiction writer on how they tell stories. Guests have included Michael Lewis, Gay Talese, Susan Orlean, Ta-Nehisi Coates, Evan Wright, Tavi Gevinson, and Malcolm Gladwell. longform.org/podcast

Minorities in Publishing, hosted by Jennifer Baker, features conversations with executive editors, literary agents, marketers, authors, illustrators, and others about the lack of diversity in the book publishing industry. minoritiesinpublishing.tumblr .com

Otherppl is a weekly podcast hosted by Brad Listi that features wide-ranging and irreverent interviews with today's leading authors, poets, and screenwriters. Past guests include George Saunders, Cheryl Strayed, Jonathan Franzen, Roxane Gay, Bret Easton Ellis, Ottessa Moshfegh, Jonathan Lethem, Susan Orlean, Tom Perrotta, Edwidge Danticat, Aimee Bender, and Hilton Als. otherppl.com

The Creative Shift with Dan Blank is a series of interviews with writers and artists who have doubled down on their creative vision. Blank delves into how they moved from merely dabbling with ideas to becoming a doer—someone who creates, finishes, and shares their work—and explores the aspects of managing one's career that are hidden: how we make decisions, deal with anxiety, the habits and routines that matter, and the reality of what it looks like to be a full-time creative professional. wegrowmedia.com/thepodcast

The Librarian Is In, hosted by librarians Gwen Glazer and Frank Collerius, is the New York Public Library's podcast about "books, pop culture, and the literary zeitgeist, and the world of libraries." www.nypl.org/voices/blogs/blog-channels/librarian -is-in

The Slowdown, hosted by Tracy K. Smith, brings five minutes of carefully curated poetry to subscribers each weekday. Each poem is read by the beloved author and former U.S. poet laureate. Produced by American Public Media in collaboration with the Poetry Foundation and the Library of Congress, *The Slowdown* was created "to make a daily space for poetry in an increasingly busy and chaotic world, a way of slowing things down, looking at them closely, mining each moment for all that it houses," and to explore the ways in which poetry can help us better understand one another. www.slowdownshow.org

The Stacks, hosted by Traci Thomas, features a wide array of guests from film and television stars to community leaders, publishing professionals, and best-selling authors. The conversations are presented in two parts: part one features a conversation with the guest about their reading habits, books they love, books they're embarrassed they haven't read yet, and more; in part two Thomas and her guest discuss The Stacks Book Club pick—with titles ranging from hot new releases to forgotten treasures. thestackspodcast.com

The VS Podcast, hosted by poets Danez Smith and Franny Choi, is a biweekly series where poets confront the ideas that move them, including silence, forgiveness, and solitude. www.poetryfoundation.org/podcasts/series/142241/vs-podcast

TK Podcast with James Scott features interviews with writers, editors, agents, and book lovers of all types about what goes into their writing and what they get out of their reading. tkpod.com

WMFA with host Courtney Balestier explores why and how writers write. Past episodes include interviews with Jami Attenberg, Alexander Chee, R. O. Kwon, and others. wmfapodcast.com

5 Video Playlists for Writers

Talks for People Who Love Words (TED) includes Parul Sehgal's "An Ode to Envy," Steven Pinker's "What Our Language Habits Reveal," and Anne Curzan's "What Makes a Word 'Real'?" www.ted.com/playlists/117/words_words_words

The Dodge Poetry Festival maintains an extensive archive of readings from the biennial event. www.dodgepoetry.org/archive/video/all-videos

Poets & Writers Theater features daily clips of interest to creative writers—author readings, book trailers, publishing panels, craft talks, and more. www.pw.org/theater

The Unterberg Poetry Center at the 92nd Street Y's Archive includes hundreds of readings, talks, and lectures by the biggest names in contemporary literature. www.92y .org/archives/featured-series/poetry-center-online.aspx

Twelve Talks from Authors (TED) includes Roxane Gay's "Confessions of a Bad Feminist," Lidia Yuknavitch's "The Beauty of Being a Misfit," and Elizabeth Gilbert's "Success, Failure, and the Drive to Keep Creating." www.ted.com/playlists/194/10 _talks_from_authors

Acknowledgments

"If you've made it this far, to be writing your acknowledgments page, then you owe it to all those people to take your time and think carefully about the network of folks who contributed to the life of your book." When we wrote that, back in chapter 20, we knew at some point we'd be following our own advice and naming the incredible team of individuals whose belief in and dedication to this book made the whole thing possible. And here we are. Thanks first to our editor, Jofie Ferrari-Adler, who gently urged us to take on this project multiple times over the last decade or so, and whose patience, enthusiasm, and editorial instincts have served as an education and an inspiration. Thanks to the wonderful and talented group that he has assembled at Avid Reader Press: Meredith Vilarello, Jordan Rodman, Allie Lawrence, Kayley Hoffman, Carolyn Kelly, Alison Forner, Dominick Montalto, Ruth Lee-Mui, Jessica Chin, and Brigid Black. Thanks to agent Brian DeFiore for his wisdom and guidance. Thanks to everyone at Poets & Writers whose hard work, dedication, and support of creative writers over the past fifty years is the bedrock upon which this book stands. Thanks to Elliot Figman for his steadfast leadership and for his faith in us to write this book the way it needed to be written; to Melissa Ford Gradel for her enthusiasm and support; and to the entire editorial team, past and present, including Ariel Davis, Bonnie Chau, Jessica Kashiwabara, Spencer Quong, Emma Komlos-Hrobsky, and Melissa Faliveno. Special thanks to Dana Isokawa and Emma Hine, whose editorial suggestions strengthened these pages in countless important ways. Thanks to Eric Simonoff and Amy Berkower for their advice on putting together a dynamic proposal. Thanks to Michael Bourne for his significant contributions to chapters about the business of books, and to all the editors, agents, publicists, and other publishing professionals who gave their time to talk with us about the work they clearly care so deeply about. Thanks to the many authors who provided insights into their process and whose work reminds us every day that writing can change the world. Thanks to William Giraldi for his friendship and counsel. Thanks to our family, whose love and support was vital throughout this long process, and especially to Eleanor and Luke: Thank you for helping us make space in our family for this project. Your understanding of its importance is a source of tremendous pride.

Sources

Introduction: The Freedom and the Power

Carolyn Roy-Bornstein, "Why We Write: Going Back to Where It Was," *Poets & Writers Magazine*, January/February 2015.

Kaveh Akbar, "The Whole Self: Our Thirteenth Annual Look at Debut Poets" by Dana Isokawa, *Poets & Writers Magazine*, January/February 2018.

Robin Coste Lewis, "Fractures Through Time: Our Eleventh Annual Look at Debut Poets" by Dana Isokawa, *Poets & Writers Magazine*, January/February 2016.

Jonathan Fink, "Fractures Through Time: Our Eleventh Annual Look at Debut Poets" by Dana Isokawa, *Poets & Writers Magazine*, January/February 2016.

Salman Rushdie, "Epic: An Interview with Salman Rushdie" by Porochista Khakpour, *Poets & Writers Magazine*, September/October 2017.

One: Getting Started

Lauren Cerand, "The Art of Publicity: How Indie Publicists Work with Writers" by Tess Taylor, *Poets & Writers Magazine*, March/April 2018.

Joyce Carol Oates, *Daily Rituals: How Artists Work* (Knopf, 2013), Mason Currey, editor.

Gertrude Stein, *Daily Rituals: How Artists Work*, Currey, editor.

Wallace Stevens, *Daily Rituals: How Artists Work*.

Maya Angelou, *Daily Rituals: How Artists Work*.

Grant Faulkner, "More Ideas Faster: Writing with Abandon," *Poets & Writers Magazine*, January/February 2015.

Craig Morgan Teicher, "Writing Badly: The True Source of Inspiration," *Poets & Writers Magazine*, January/February 2017.

Michael Bourne, "How to Get Paid: Freelance Writing," *Poets & Writers Magazine*, January/February 2019.

Joan Didion, "Why I Write," *New York Times Magazine*, December 5, 1976.

Zadie Smith, "Brand You: Questioning Self-Promotion" by Frank Bures, *Poets & Writers Magazine*, January/February 2016.

Two: Inspiration

Adam Gopnik, Writers Recommend, pw.org, September 7, 2017.

Hala Alyan, Writers Recommend, pw.org, July 26, 2017.

Eimear McBride, Writers Recommend, www.pw.org/content/eimear_mcbride_1, December 18, 2014.

Idra Novey, Writers Recommend, pw.org, March 3, 2016.

Vendela Vida, Writers Recommend, pw.org, July 2, 2015.

Jennifer Egan, *Why We Write: 20 Acclaimed Authors on How and Why They Do What They Do* (Plume, 2013), Meredith Maran, editor.

Morgan Parker, Writers Recommend, pw.org, May 21, 2015.

Annie Dillard, *The Writing Life* (Harper & Row, 1989).

Benjamin Percy, "Powell's Q&A," powells.com, October 14, 2016.

Frank Bures, "Inner Space: Clearing Some Room for Inspiration," *Poets & Writers Magazine*, January/February 2012.

Three: Writing Prompts

Frank O'Hara, "A Step Away from Them," *Lunch Poems* (City Lights Publishers, 1964).

Angela Duckworth, Lauren Eskreis-Winkler, and Ayelet Fishbach, "Dear Abby: Should I Give Advice or Receive It?" *Psychological Science*, October 3, 2018.

Kurt Vonnegut, *God Bless You, Mr. Rosewater, or Pearls Before Swine* (Holt, Rinehart and Winston, 1965).

Aimee Nezhukumatathil, "Penguin Valentine," *Oceanic* (Copper Canyon Press, 2018).

Emily Dickinson, "A Narrow Fellow in the Grass," *The Poems of Emily Dickinson: Variorum Edition* (Harvard University Press, 1998).

Oscar Wilde, *The Picture of Dorian Gray* (*Lippincott's Monthly Magazine*, 1890).

Paul H. Thibodeau, "A Moist Crevice for Word Aversion: In Semantics Not Sounds," *PLOS One*, April 27, 2016.

New York Public Library, *Peculiar Questions and Practical Answers: A Little Book of Whimsy and Wisdom from the Files of the New York Public Library* (St. Martin's Griffin, 2019).

Adrienne LaFrance, "The Six Main Arcs in Storytelling, as Identified by an A.I.," *Atlantic*, July 12, 2016.

Lynne Tillman, "One of Lynne Tillman's Earliest Short Stories Was a Menu," *Frieze*, September 23, 2019.

J. T. Bushnell, "This Is Your Brain on Fear: Trauma and Storytelling," *Poets & Writers Magazine*, May/June 2016.

Nicholson Baker, *The Mezzanine* (Weidenfeld & Nicolson, 1986).

Sarah M. Broom, "The New Nonfiction 2019," *Poets & Writers Magazine*, September/October 2019.

Mary Karr, *The Art of Memoir* (Harper, 2015).

Parul Sehgal, "The Romance and Heartbreak of Writing in a Language Not Your Own," *New York Times*, June 2, 2017.

Samuel Beckett, *The Letters of Samuel Beckett: Volume 1, 1929–1940* (Cambridge University Press, 2009).

Leslie Jamison, "Chris Kraus," *Interview*, July 17, 2017.

Ivan Morris, *The Pillow Book of Sei Shōnagon* (Columbia University Press, 1991).

Four: One Hundred Notes on Craft

1. Dan Beachy-Quick, "Craft Capsule: Hundreds of Eyes," pw.org, February 20, 2018.
2. Michael Schaub, "Sandra Cisneros Shares Writing Tips and Reveals What She Will Do with Her PEN Award Money," *Los Angeles Times*, February 17, 2019.
3. Kevin Larimer, "A Talk in the Woods: Barbara Kingsolver and Richard Powers," *Poets & Writers Magazine*, November/December 2018.
4. Kevin Larimer, "A Talk in the Woods: Barbara Kingsolver and Richard Powers," *Poets & Writers Magazine*, November/December 2018.
5. James Baldwin, "The Art of Fiction No. 78," interviewed by Jordan Elgrably, *Paris Review*, Issue 91, 1984.
6. Adrienne Rich, "When We Dead Awaken: Writing as Re-Vision," in *On Lies, Secrets, and Silence: Selected Prose 1966–1978* (W. W. Norton, 1995).
7. Aaron Coleman, "The History Behind the Feeling: A Conversation with Claudia Rankine," *Spectacle*, Issue 7, 2015.
8. Gregory Orr, *A Primer for Poets and Readers of Poetry* (W. W. Norton, 2018).
9. Ai, *Angles of Ascent: A Norton Anthology of Contemporary African American Poetry* (W. W. Norton, 2013), Charles Henry Rowell, editor.
10. Charles Johnson, *The Way of the Writer: Reflections on the Art and Craft of Storytelling* (Scribner, 2016).
11. Anne Lamott, *Bird by Bird: Some Instructions on Writing and Life* (Pantheon Books, 1994).
12. Elizabeth Bowen, "Notes on Writing a Novel: An Essay," *Orion II*, 1945.
13. Dani Shapiro, *Still Writing: The Perils and Pleasures of a Creative Life* (Atlantic Monthly Press, 2013).
14. Eudora Welty, from the preface to *The Collected Stories of Eudora Welty* (Mariner Books, 2019).
15. Lydia Davis, "Thirty Recommendations for Good Writing Habits," *Essays One* (Farrar, Straus and Giroux, 2019).
16. Gertrude Stein, "Poetry and Grammar" (1935).

17. Anthony Trollope, "On Novels and the Art of Writing Them," *An Autobiography* (1883).

18. Dantiel W. Moniz, Twitter, August 31, 2019.

19. Elmore Leonard, *Elmore Leonard's 10 Rules of Writing* (William Morrow, 2007).

20. Constance Hale, *Vex, Hex, Smash, Smooch: Let Verbs Power Your Writing* (W. W. Norton, 2012).

21. Veronica Chambers, "Why I Keep Coming Back to Jamaica," *Well-Read Black Girl: Finding Our Stories, Discovering Ourselves* (Ballantine Books, 2018), Glory Edim, editor.

22. Lucille Clifton, *Angles of Ascent: A Norton Anthology of Contemporary African American Poetry*, Charles Henry Rowell, editor.

23. Toni Morrison, "Write, Erase, Do It Over," interviewed by Rebecca Sutton, *NEA Arts Magazine*, Issue 4, 2014.

24. June Jordan, "Poetry Is a Political Act: An Interview with June Jordan" by Julie Quiroz-Martinez, *Colorlines*, December 15, 1998.

25. Adrienne Rich, "When We Dead Awaken: Writing as Re-Vision," *On Lies, Secrets, and Silence: Selected Prose 1966–1978*.

26. Dawn Lundy Martin, *Angles of Ascent: A Norton Anthology of Contemporary African American Poetry*, Charles Henry Rowell, editor.

27. Audre Lorde, "Poetry Is Not a Luxury," *Sister Outsider: Essays and Speeches* (Crossing Press, 1984).

28. W. H. Auden, "The Poet and the City," *The Dyer's Hand and Other Essays* (Random House, 1962).

29. Isabelle Allende, "Interview," isabelleallende.com.

30. Joan Didion, "The White Album," *The White Album* (Simon & Schuster, 1979).

31. Susan Sontag, *The Benefactor* (Farrar, Straus and Giroux, 1963).

32. Robin Hemley, *A Field Guide for Immersion Writing: Memoir, Journalism, and Travel* (University of Georgia Press, 2012).

33. Maya Angelou, "The Art of Fiction No. 119," interviewed by George Plimpton, *Paris Review*, Issue 116, 1990.

34. William Giraldi, "With His Mother Chasing Men and Money, a Boy Learns to Grow Up on His Own," *Washington Post*, June 28, 2018.

35. John McPhee, "NBCC Awards: John McPhee Accepts the Sandrof Award for Lifetime Achievement," National Book Critics Circle, bookcritics.org, March 23, 2018.

36. Bill Roorbach, *Contemporary Creative Nonfiction: The Art of Truth* (Oxford University Press, 2001).

37. Renée H. Shea, "Worth the Wait: A Profile of Arundhati Roy," *Poets & Writers Magazine*, July/August 2017.

38. Christina Baker Kline, "Craft Capsule: Tolstoy's Short Chapters," pw.org, March 28, 2017.

39. Lee Child, "A Simple Way to Create Suspense," *New York Times*, December 8, 2012.

40. Ursula K. Le Guin, *Steering the Craft: A 21st Century Guide to Sailing the Sea of Story* (Mariner Books, 2015).

41. E. M. Forster, *Aspects of the Novel* (Penguin, 1962).

42. Roy Peter Clark, *The Art of X-Ray Reading: How the Secrets of 25 Great Works of Literature Will Improve Your Writing* (Little, Brown, 2016).

43. James Salter, *The Art of Fiction* (University of Virginia Press, 2016).

44. H. G. Wells, *Experiment in Autobiography* (Victor Gollancz Ltd, 1934).

45. John Dufresne, *Flash!: Writing the Very Short Story* (W. W. Norton, 2018).

46. Aida Alami, "Laila Lalami: Whoever Tells the Story Controls the World," *Middle East Eye*, May 20, 2019.

47. Janet Burroway, *Writing Fiction: A Guide to Narrative Craft, Tenth Edition* (University of Chicago Press, 2019).

48. Walter Mosley, *Elements of Fiction* (Grove Press, 2019).

49. Janet Burroway, *Writing Fiction: A Guide to Narrative Craft*.

50. James Wood, *How Fiction Works* (Farrar, Straus and Giroux, 2008).

51. Ellen Bryant Voigt, *The Art of Syntax: Rhythm of Thought, Rhythm of Song* (Graywolf Press, 2009).

52. Edward Hirsch, "Meter," *A Poet's Glossary* (Houghton Mifflin Harcourt, 2014).

53. Natalie Diaz, "Natalie Diaz on the Physicality of Writing," from a Conversation with Brandon Stosuy, *Creative Independent*, April 14, 2017.

54. Etheridge Knight, *Angles of Ascent: A Norton Anthology of Contemporary African American Poetry*, Charles Henry Rowell, editor.

55. Laura Hillenbrand, "The Unbreakable Laura Hillenbrand" by Wil S. Hylton, *New York Times Magazine*, December 18, 2014.

56. Alexander Chee, "100 Things About Writing a Novel," in *How to Write an Autobiographical Novel* (Mariner Books, 2018).

57. Eudora Welty, "The Art of Fiction No. 47," interviewed by Linda Kuehl, *Paris Review*, Issue 55, 1972.

58. A. Van Jordan, *Angles of Ascent: A Norton Anthology of Contemporary African American Poetry*, Charles Henry Rowell, editor.

59. T. S. Eliot, "Tradition and the Individual Talent," in *The Sacred Wood: Essays on Poetry and Criticism* (Knopf, 1921).

60. William Wordsworth, from the preface to *Lyrical Ballads* by William Wordsworth and Samuel Taylor Coleridge (J. & A. Arch, 1798).

61. Marianne Moore, "The Art of Poetry No. 4," interviewed by Donald Hall, *Paris Review*, Issue 26, 1961.

62. Denise Levertov, "Some Notes on Organic Form," *New Directions in Prose and Poetry 20*, J. Laughlin, editor, 1968.

63. Gustave Flaubert, *The George Sand–Gustave Flaubert Letters* (Boni & Liveright, 1921), Aimee L. McKenzie, translator.

64. Stephen Dobyns, "Notes on Free Verse," *Best Words, Best Order: Essays on Poetry* (St. Martin's, 1996) by Stephen Dobyns.

65. Joy Harjo, "An Interview with Joy Harjo, U.S. Poet Laureate," Academy of American Poets, March 31, 2019.

66. Mark Strand and Eavan Boland, "The Stanza: The History of the Form," *The Making of a Poem: A Norton Anthology of Poetic Forms* (W. W. Norton, 2000).

67. Jack Gilbert, "The Art of Poetry No. 91," interviewed by Sarah Fay, *Paris Review*, Issue 175, 2005.

68. Joshua Beckman, *The Lives of the Poems and Three Talks* (Wave Books, 2018).

69. Mark Doty, *The Art of Description: World into Word* (Graywolf Press, 2010).

70. Muriel Rukeyser, *The Life of Poetry* (Current Books, 1949).

71. Christian Wiman, "Notes on Poetry and Religion," *Ambition and Survival: Becoming a Poet* (Copper Canyon Press, 2007).

72. Nikki Giovanni, *Conversations with Nikki Giovanni* (University Press of Mississippi, 1992), Virginia C. Fowler, editor.

73. Donald Hall, "Introduction: The Letter Farm," *Here at Eagle Pond* (Mariner Books, 1990).

74. Anthony Doerr, "'A Sort of Leaning Against': Writing With, From, and for Others" *The Writer's Notebook II: Craft Essays from Tin House* (Tin House Books, 2012).

75. Jane Alison, *Meander, Spiral, Explode: Design and Pattern in Narrative* (Catapult, 2019).

76. Karen Russell, "Orange World, Elastic Space: An Interview with Karen Russell" by Brian Gresko, pw.org, May 13, 2019.

77. Stephen King, *On Writing: A Memoir of the Craft* (Scribner, 2000).

78. Dorothy Allison, "Place," *The Writer's Notebook: Craft Essays from Tin House* (Tin House Books, 2009).

79. Anton Chekhov, *How to Write Like Chekhov: Advice and Inspiration, Straight from His Own Letters and Work* (Da Capo Press, 2008), Piero Brunello and Lena Lenček, editors, translated from the Russian and Italian by Lena Lenček.

80. James Baldwin, "The Art of Fiction No. 78," *Paris Review*, 1984.

81. Julian Randall, Twitter, August 31, 2019.

82. Max Ritvo, *Letters from Max: A Poet, a Teacher, a Friendship* (Milkweed Editions, 2018) by Sarah Ruhl and Max Ritvo.

83. Jonathan P. Eburne, "Throwing Your Voice: An Interview with Cathy Park Hong," *ASAP/Journal*, 2018.

84. John Freeman, *How to Read a Novelist* (Farrar, Straus and Giroux, 2013).

85. Tina Chang, "Mother Language: A Q&A with Tina Chang" by Jerome Ellison Murphy, pw.org, July 19, 2019.

86. Raymond Carver, "The Art of Fiction No. 76," interviewed by Mona Simpson and Lewis Buzbee, *Paris Review*, Issue 88, 1983.

87. Lynn Freed, *Reading, Writing, and Leaving Home: Life on the Page* (Harcourt, 2005).

88. George Saunders, "The Emotional Realist Talks to Ghosts" by Kevin Larimer, *Poets & Writers Magazine*, March/April 2017.

89. Colson Whitehead, "How to Write," *Black Ink: Literary Legends on the Peril, Power, and Pleasure of Reading and Writing* (37 Ink, 2018) Stephanie Stokes Oliver, editor.

90. Margot Livesey, "Nothing but Himself: Embracing Jane Austen's Second Chances," *The Hidden Machinery: Essays on Writing* (Tin House Books, 2017).

91. Stendhal, *The Charterhouse of Parma* (Modern Library, 1999), translated by Richard Howard.

92. Colum McCann, *Letters to a Young Writer* (Random House, 2017).

93. John Freeman, *How to Read a Novelist*.

94. Ernest Hemingway, *With Hemingway: A Year in Key West and Cuba* (Random House, 1984) by Arnold Samuelson.

95. Benjamin Percy, "Home Improvement," *Thrill Me: Essays on Fiction* (Graywolf Press, 2016).

96. Sarah Manguso, *300 Arguments* (Graywolf Press, 2017).

97. Mary Karr, *The Art of Memoir* (Harper, 2015).

98. John Gardner, *On Becoming a Novelist* (W. W. Norton, 1983).

99. Neil Gaiman, *Make Good Art* (William Morrow, 2013).

100. Eric Gorges, *A Craftsman's Legacy: Why Working with Our Hands Gives Us Meaning* (Algonquin Books, 2019).

Five: Finding Community

Tracy Kidder and Richard Todd, *Good Prose: The Art of Nonfiction* (Random House, 2013).

Reginald Dwayne Betts, "Where Big Books Are Born: Reginald Dwayne Betts on the Cave Canem Retreat," *Poets & Writers Magazine*, March/April 2018.

Duy Doan, "Where Big Books Are Born: Duy Doan on the Kundiman Retreat," *Poets & Writers Magazine*, March/April 2018.

Dani Shapiro, "Twenty-Two of the Most Inspiring Writers Retreats in the Country," *Poets & Writers Magazine*, March/April 2019.

Juergen Boos, www.buchmesse.de/en, October 14, 2018.

Alexander Chee, "Let Them Feed You: Practical Advice for First-Time Colonists," *Poets & Writers Magazine*, March/April 2016.

Grant Faulkner, "Applying to a Writers Residency: An Expert Breakdown of the Requirements," *Poets & Writers Magazine*, March/April 2012.

Hannah Gersen, "You Are Not Alone: Finding a Group of One's Own," *Poets & Writers Magazine*, January/February 2018.

Six: A Writer's Education

Kurt Vonnegut, "The Art of Fiction No. 64," interviewed by David Hayman, David Michaelis, George Plimpton, and Richard L. Rhodes, *Paris Review*, Issue 69, 1977.

Sarah McColl, "Ten Questions for Sarah McColl," pw.org, January 15, 2019.

Laura Sims, "Ten Questions for Laura Sims," pw.org, January 8, 2019.

Jos Charles, "Ten Questions for Jos Charles," pw.org, August 14, 2018.

Catherine Chung, "Ten Questions for Catherine Chung," pw.org, June 18, 2019.

Mona Awad, "Ten Questions for Mona Awad," pw.org, June 11, 2019.

Domenica Ruta, "Ten Questions for Domenica Ruta," pw.org, May 28, 2019.

Cameron Finch, "My MFA Experience" by Kevin Larimer, *Poets & Writers Magazine*, September/October 2019.

Raquel Gutiérrez, "My MFA Experience" by Kevin Larimer, *Poets & Writers Magazine*, September/October 2019.

Chad Harbach, editor, "MFA vs. NYC," *MFA vs NYC: The Two Cultures of American Fiction* (n+1/Faber and Faber, 2014).

Manuel Muñoz, "Manuel Muñoz Directs Arizona MFA" by Jessica Kashiwabara, *Poets & Writers Magazine*, September/October 2019.

Gionni Ponce, "My MFA Experience" by Kevin Larimer, *Poets & Writers Magazine*, September/October 2019.

Mary Pauline Lowry, "My MFA Experience" by Kevin Larimer, *Poets & Writers Magazine*, September/October 2019.

Threa Almontaser, "My MFA Experience" by Kevin Larimer, *Poets & Writers Magazine*, September/October 2019.

Faylita Hicks, "My MFA Experience" by Kevin Larimer, *Poets & Writers Magazine*, September/October 2019.

Cameron Finch, "My MFA Experience" by Kevin Larimer, *Poets & Writers Magazine*, September/October 2019.

Dantiel W. Moniz, "My MFA Experience" by Kevin Larimer, *Poets & Writers Magazine*, September/October 2019.

Julian Randall, "My MFA Experience" by Kevin Larimer, *Poets & Writers Magazine*, September/October 2019.

Rowena Alegria, "My MFA Experience" by Kevin Larimer, *Poets & Writers Magazine*, September/October 2019.

Jonathan Wlodarski, "My MFA Experience" by Kevin Larimer, *Poets & Writers Magazine*, September/October 2019.

Raquel Gutiérrez, "My MFA Experience" by Kevin Larimer, *Poets & Writers Magazine*, September/October 2019.

Seven: Writing and Time

Catherine Chung, "Ten Questions for Catherine Chung," pw.org, June 18, 2019.

Julie Orringer, "Ten Questions for Julie Orringer," pw.org, May 7, 2019.

Domenica Ruta, "Ten Questions for Domenica Ruta," pw.org, May 28, 2019.

Xuan Juliana Wang, "Ten Questions for Xuan Juliana Wang," pw.org, May 14, 2019.

Sherwin Bitsui, "Ten Questions for Sherwin Bitsui," pw.org, October 30, 2018.

Keith Gessen, "Ten Questions for Keith Gessen," pw.org, July 10, 2018.

Alison C. Rollins, "Ten Questions for Alison C. Rollins," pw.org, April 23, 2019.

Emily Skaja, "Ten Questions for Emily Skaja," pw.org, April 2, 2019.

Juliet Lapidos, "Ten Questions for Juliet Lapidos," pw.org, January 22, 2019.

A. M. Homes, "Ten Questions for A. M. Homes," pw.org, June 5, 2018.

Herman Melville, www.melville.org.

Paul Vidich, "5 Over 50," *Poets & Writers Magazine*, November/December 2016.

Anne Youngson, "5 Over 50," *Poets & Writers Magazine*, November/December 2018.

Timothy Brandoff, "5 Over 50," *Poets & Writers Magazine*, November/December 2019.

Nine: Writing and Happiness

Tara Parker-Pope, "Writing Your Way to Happiness," *New York Times*, January 9, 2015.

Chanelle Benz, "Ten Questions for Chanelle Benz," pw.org, June 25, 2019.

Lee Martin, "Ten Questions for Lee Martin," pw.org, June 12, 2018.

Maurice Carlos Ruffin, "Writers Recommend," pw.org, January 24, 2019.

Nafissa Thompson-Spires, "Writers Recommend," pw.org, June 14, 2018.

Akil Kumarasamy, "Ten Questions for Akil Kumarasamy," pw.org, June 5, 2018.

Sarah Ruhl, "Writer's Block: Variations on a Superstition," *Poets & Writers Magazine*, January/February 2020.

William Giraldi, "Author Envy: The Art of Surviving One's Own Personality," *Poets & Writers Magazine*, May/June 2019.

Ten: Writing and Family

Lauren Groff, "Severe Weather in the Sunshine State" by Bethanne Patrick, *Poets & Writers Magazine*, July/August 2018.

Julie Orringer, "Ten Questions for Julie Orringer," pw.org, May 7, 2019.

Jess Row, "Ten Questions for Jess Row," pw.org, August 6, 2019.

Domenica Ruta, "Ten Questions for Domenica Ruta," pw.org, May 28, 2019.

Helen Phillips, "Ten Questions for Helen Phillips," pw.org, July 9, 2019.

Rosellen Brown, "Ten Questions for Rosellen Brown," pw.org, October 16, 2018.

Geffrey Davis, "Ten Questions for Geffrey Davis," pw.org, April 30, 2019.

Eleven: Writing and Respect

Gene Luen Yang, reprinted by permission, copyright © 2014 Gene Luen Yang.

Susan Lardner, "Dresden," *The New Yorker*, May 9, 1969.

H. L. Mencken, "A Review of *The Great Gatsby* by F. Scott Fitzgerald," *Chicago Sunday Tribune*, May 3, 1925.

Maureen Corrigan, "Reviewers & Critics: Maureen Corrigan of NPR's *Fresh Air*" by Michael Taeckens, *Poets & Writers Magazine*, March/April 2019.

Sam Sacks, "Reviewers & Critics: Sam Sacks of the *Wall Street Journal*" by Michael Taeckens, *Poets & Writers Magazine*, September/October 2018.

Laurie Hertzel, "Reviewers & Critics: Laurie Hertzel of the *Star Tribune*" by Michael Taeckens, *Poets & Writers Magazine*, November/December 2018.

Daniel Mendelsohn, "Reviewers & Critics: Daniel Mendelsohn of the *New York Review of Books*" by Michael Taeckens, *Poets & Writers Magazine*, September/October 2019.

Leigh Haber, "Reviewers & Critics: Leigh Haber of *O, the Oprah Magazine*" by Michael Taeckens, *Poets & Writers Magazine*, January/February 2018.

Dwight Garner, "Reviewers & Critics: Dwight Garner of the *New York Times*" by Michael Taeckens, *Poets & Writers Magazine*, January/February 2015.

Twelve: Writing and the Law

Richard Curtis, *How to Be Your Own Literary Agent: An Insider's Guide to Getting Your Book Published* (Houghton Mifflin, 2003).

Julie Barer, "Anatomy of an Author Agreement: An Agent Deciphers the Most Important Clauses in a Publishing Contract," *Poets & Writers Magazine*, July/August 2010.

Thirteen: Literary Magazines

William Carlos Williams, *The Autobiography of William Carlos Williams* (Random House, 1951).

Steven Clay and Rodney Phillips, *A Secret Location on the Lower East Side: Adventures in Writing, 1960–1980* (New York Public Library/Granary Books, 1998).

Jenn Scheck-Kahn, "Telling a Different Story: How to Cultivate Inclusivity at Literary Magazines," *Poets & Writers Magazine*, November/December 2018.

Joey Franklin, "Submit That Manuscript! Why Sending Out Your Work Is So Important," *Poets & Writers Magazine*, July/August 2017.

Fourteen: Writing Contests

Ama Codjoe, "Winners on Winning: Six Authors Offer Advice for Successful Submissions," *Poets & Writers Magazine*, May/June 2019.

Emily Skaja, "Winners on Winning: Six Authors Offer Advice for Successful Submissions," *Poets & Writers Magazine*, May/June 2019.

Lillian Yvonne-Bertram, "Winners on Winning: Six Authors Offer Advice for Successful Submissions," *Poets & Writers Magazine*, May/June 2019.

Megan Giddings, "Winners on Winning: Six Authors Offer Advice for Successful Submissions," *Poets & Writers Magazine*, May/June 2019.

Sophie Klahr, "Winners on Winning: Six Authors Offer Advice for Successful Submissions," *Poets & Writers Magazine*, May/June 2019.

Mark Wagenaar, "Winners on Winning: Six Authors Offer Advice for Successful Submissions," *Poets & Writers Magazine*, May/June 2019.

Fifteen: Self-Publishing

Bowker, "Self-Publishing in the United States, 2012–2017: Print and Ebooks," 2018.

Eighteen: Independent Publishers

Fiona McCrae, "A Necessary Resilience," *Poets & Writers Magazine*, November/December 2019.

Jamia Wilson, "Truth to Power," *Poets & Writers Magazine*, November/December 2019.

Nineteen: Working with Your Editor

Marya Spence, "Four Lunches and a Breakfast: What I Learned at Lunch with Five Hungry Agents" by Kevin Larimer, *Poets & Writers Magazine*, July/August 2019.

Julie Orringer, "Ten Questions for Julie Orringer," pw.org, May 7, 2019.

Twenty-One: Publicity and Promotion

Celeste Ng, "Making Connections Through Books" by Jonathan Vatner, *Poets & Writers Magazine*, January/February 2018.

Twenty-Two: Surviving Success and Failure

Helen Phillips, "Ten Questions for Helen Phillips," pw.org, July 9, 2019.

Kevin Wilson, "The Necessity of Failure: An Examination of the Writing Life," *Poets & Writers Magazine*, March/April 2017.

Elizabeth Gilbert, "Success, Failure, and the Drive to Keep Creating," TED, March 2014, www.ted.com/talks/elizabeth_gilbert_success_failure_and_the_drive_to_keep_creating.

Shelly Oria, "Publishing Your First Book: Advice for First-Time Authors," *Poets & Writers Magazine*, March/April 2018.

Twenty-Three: Careers

"Incremental Gains," *Publishers Weekly*, November 12, 2018.

Siri Hedreen, "Work Experience or Free Labor? Learn What Makes Unpaid Internships Legal," *Business News Daily*, June 25, 2019.

"2018 Local Arts Agency Profile Report," Americans for the Arts, www.americansforthearts.org.

"Faculty Compensation Survey," American Association of University Professors, aaup.org.

"Authors Guild Survey Shows Drastic 42 Percent Decline in Authors Earnings in Last Decade," January 5, 2019, authorsguild.org.

Michael Bourne, "How to Get Paid: Book Publishing," *Poets & Writers Magazine*, July/August 2019.

Index

About the Authors

KEVIN LARIMER is the editor in chief of Poets & Writers, where he edits *Poets & Writers Magazine*; oversees editorial content on the website, pw.org; and directs the organization's program of live events, Poets & Writers Live. He received his MFA from the Iowa Writers' Workshop, where he served as the poetry editor of the *Iowa Review*, and holds a BA in journalism from the University of Wisconsin in Milwaukee. He is a member of the board of directors of the Elizabeth Kostova Foundation. He has lectured and served on publishing panels at events such as the Library of Congress National Book Festival, the Sozopol Fiction Seminars, the Anguilla Lit Fest, the Kauai Writers Conference, the Slice Literary Writer's Conference, the Iceland Writers Retreat, the Kachemak Bay Writers' Conference, Poets Forum, the Bronx Book Fair, and the Writer's Hotel.

MARY GANNON is the executive director of the Community of Literary Magazines and Presses. From 2013 to 2018, she was associate director and director of content for the Academy of American Poets, where she oversaw poets.org, the Poem-a-Day series, *American Poets* magazine, and education programming. From 2010 to 2013 she was the editorial director of Poets & Writers and led the production of pw.org and the publication of *Poets & Writers Magazine*, for which she served as editor from 2004 to 2009. She received her MFA in poetry from Arizona State University, where she was awarded a Swarthout Award in Writing, and a BA in English from Skidmore College. She is a founding member of the Brooklyn Book Festival Literary Council.